Latinx Comics Studies

Critical Graphics

Series Editor: Frederick Luis Aldama, Arts and Humanities Distinguished Professor, The Ohio State University

Volumes in the Critical Graphics series bring scholarly insight to single authors and their creator-owned graphic fiction and nonfiction works. Books in the series provide context and critical insight into a given creator's work, with an especial interest in social and political issues. Each book is organized as a series of reader-friendly scholarly chapters that precede the reprinting of short graphic fiction or nonfictional works—or excerpts of longer works. The critical insight and commentary alongside the creative works provide a gateway for lay-readers, students, and specialists to understand a given creator's work and life within larger social and political contexts as well as within comics history. Authors of these books situate the work of their subject within the creator's larger body of work and within the history of comics; and bring an engaged perspective to their analysis, drawing on a variety of disciplines, including medical humanities, environmental studies, disability studies, critical race studies, and women's, gender, and sexuality studies.

Recent titles in the Critical Graphics series:

Fernanda Díaz-Basteris and Maite Urcaregui, eds., *Latinx Comics Studies: Critical and Creative Crossings*

Andrew J. Kunka, *The Life and Comics of Howard Cruse: Taking Risks in the Service of Truth*

Jan Baetens, *Rebuilding Story Worlds: "The Obscure Cities" by Schuiten and Peeters*

Latinx Comics Studies

Critical and Creative Crossings

EDITED BY FERNANDA DÍAZ-BASTERIS AND MAITE URCAREGUI

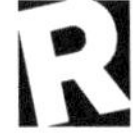

Rutgers University Press

New Brunswick, Camden, and Newark, New Jersey

London and Oxford

Rutgers University Press is a department of Rutgers, The State University of New Jersey, one of the leading public research universities in the nation. By publishing worldwide, it furthers the University's mission of dedication to excellence in teaching, scholarship, research, and clinical care.

Library of Congress Cataloging-in-Publication Data

Names: Díaz-Basteris, Fernanda, editor. | Urcaregui, Maite, editor.
Title: Latinx comics studies : critical & creative crossings / edited by Fernanda Díaz-Basteris and Maite Urcaregui.
Description: New Brunswick : Rutgers University Press, 2025. | Series: Critical graphics | Includes bibliographical references and index.
Identifiers: LCCN 2024040174 | ISBN 9781978835405 (paperback) | ISBN 9781978835412 (hardcover) | ISBN 9781978835429 (epub) | ISBN 9781978835436 (mobi) | ISBN 9781978835443 (pdf)
Subjects: LCSH: Comic books, strips, etc.—Latin America—History and criticism. | National characteristics, Latin American, in comics. | Identity (Psychology) in comics. | LCGFT: Comics criticism. | Essays.
Classification: LCC PN6790.L29 L38 2025 | DDC 741.5/698—dc23/eng/20241223
LC record available at https://lccn.loc.gov/2024040174

A British Cataloging-in-Publication record for this book is available from the British Library.

rutgersuniversitypress.org

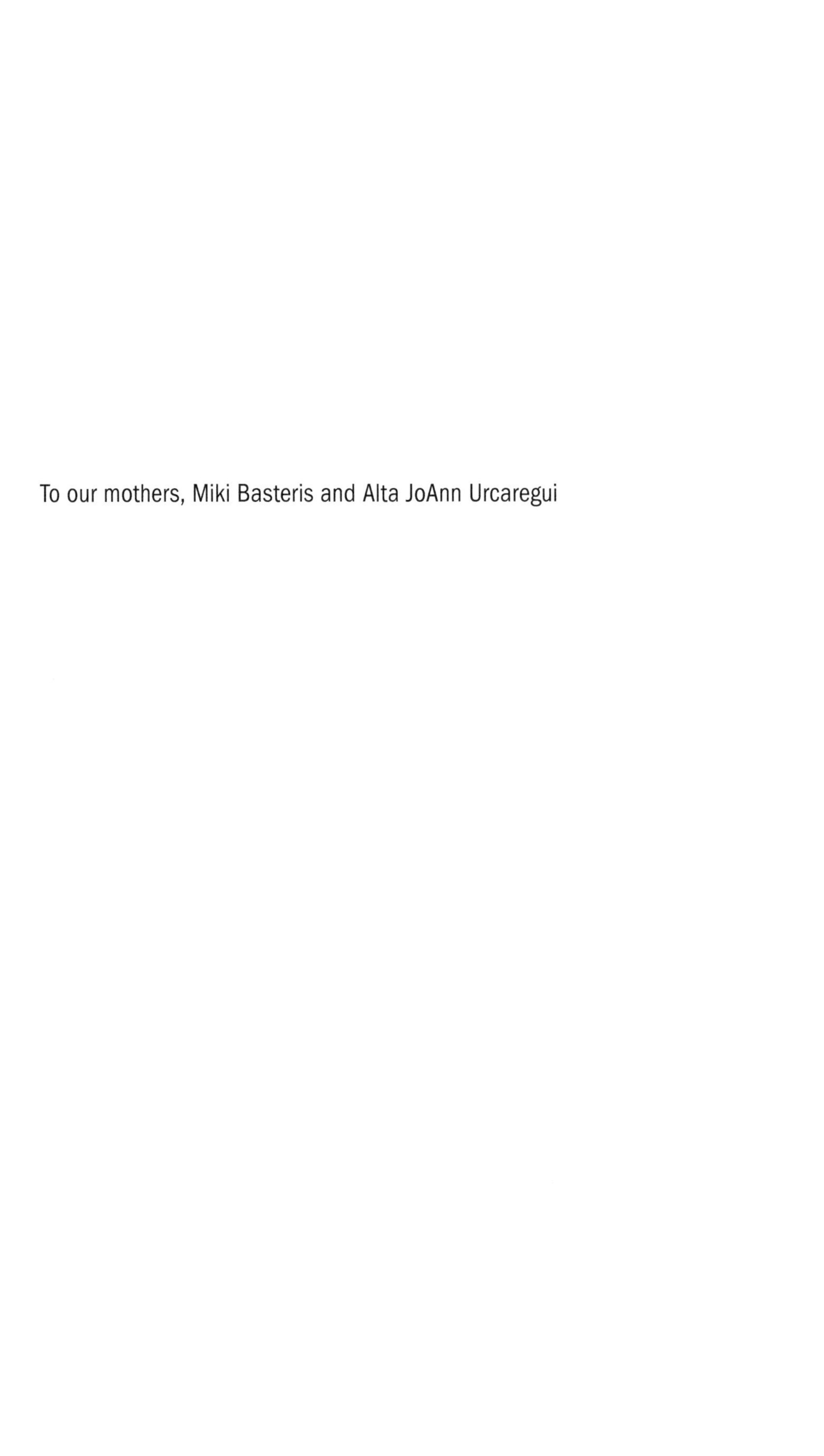

To our mothers, Miki Basteris and Alta JoAnn Urcaregui

Contents

Preface

A Comic Overview of *Latinx Comics Studies*

FRANCISCA CÁRCAMO ROJAS

LATINX COMICS STUDIES: CRITICAL & CREATIVE CROSSINGS

Rutgers University Press

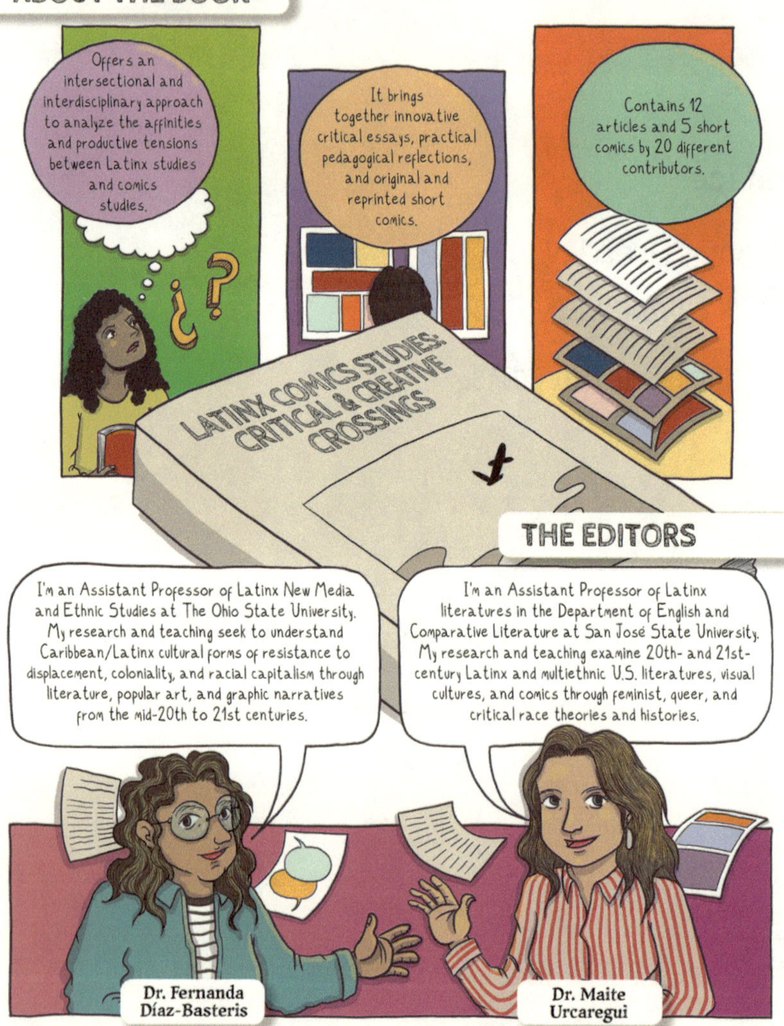

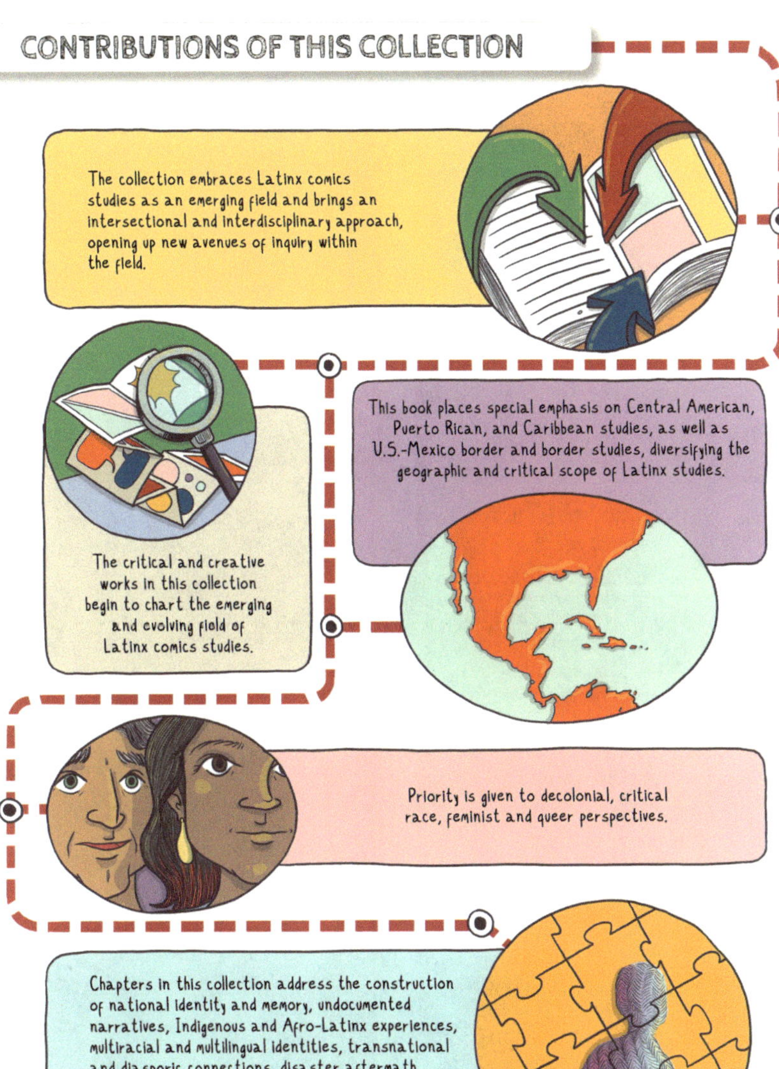
CONTRIBUTIONS OF THIS COLLECTION
The collection embraces Latinx comics studies as an emerging field and brings an intersectional and interdisciplinary approach, opening up new avenues of inquiry within the field.
This book places special emphasis on Central American, Puerto Rican, and Caribbean studies, as well as U.S.-Mexico border and border studies, diversifying the geographic and critical scope of Latinx studies.
The critical and creative works in this collection begin to chart the emerging and evolving field of Latinx comics studies.
Priority is given to decolonial, critical race, feminist and queer perspectives.
Chapters in this collection address the construction of national identity and memory, undocumented narratives, Indigenous and Afro-Latinx experiences, multiracial and multilingual identities, transnational and diasporic connections, disaster aftermath and unnatural colonial violence, feminist and queer interventions, Latinx futurities, and more!

TABLE OF CONTENTS

PEDAGOGICAL USES OF THIS PUBLICATION

INTENDED FOR READERS

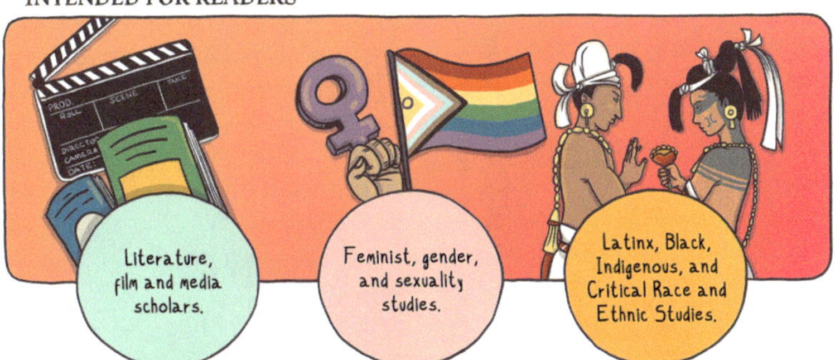

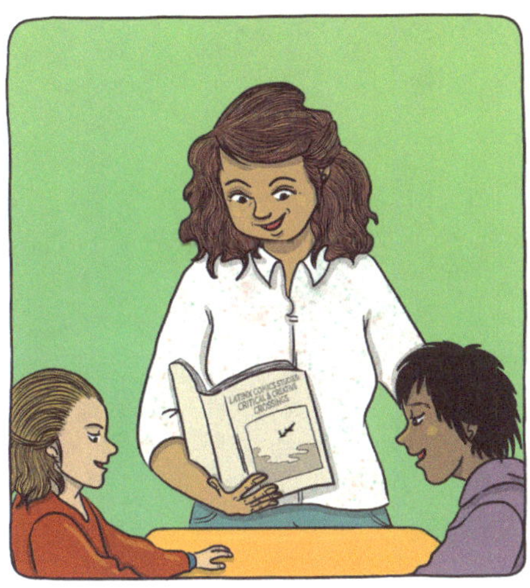

USES IN THE CLASSROOM

Because the volume incorporates practical pedagogical examples along with critical essays, it can be used by educators, including elementary, secondary, and university teachers.

Our volume provides examples of teaching history, race, citizenship, culture, and literature through comics, highlighting the effectiveness of comics not only in literature classrooms, but also in film, culture, and history classrooms.

The essays in this collection emphasize how instructors can integrate and teach comics to strengthen our students' intersectional and transnational frames of reference.

Look for Latinx Comics Studies: Critical and Creative Crossings forthcoming from Rutgers University Press in spring 2025.

Dr. Fernanda Díaz-Basteris
diaz-basteris.1@osu.edu
The Ohio State University

Dr. Maite Urcaregui
maite.urcaregui@sjsu.edu
San José State University

Comic by Panchulei — www.panchulei.com

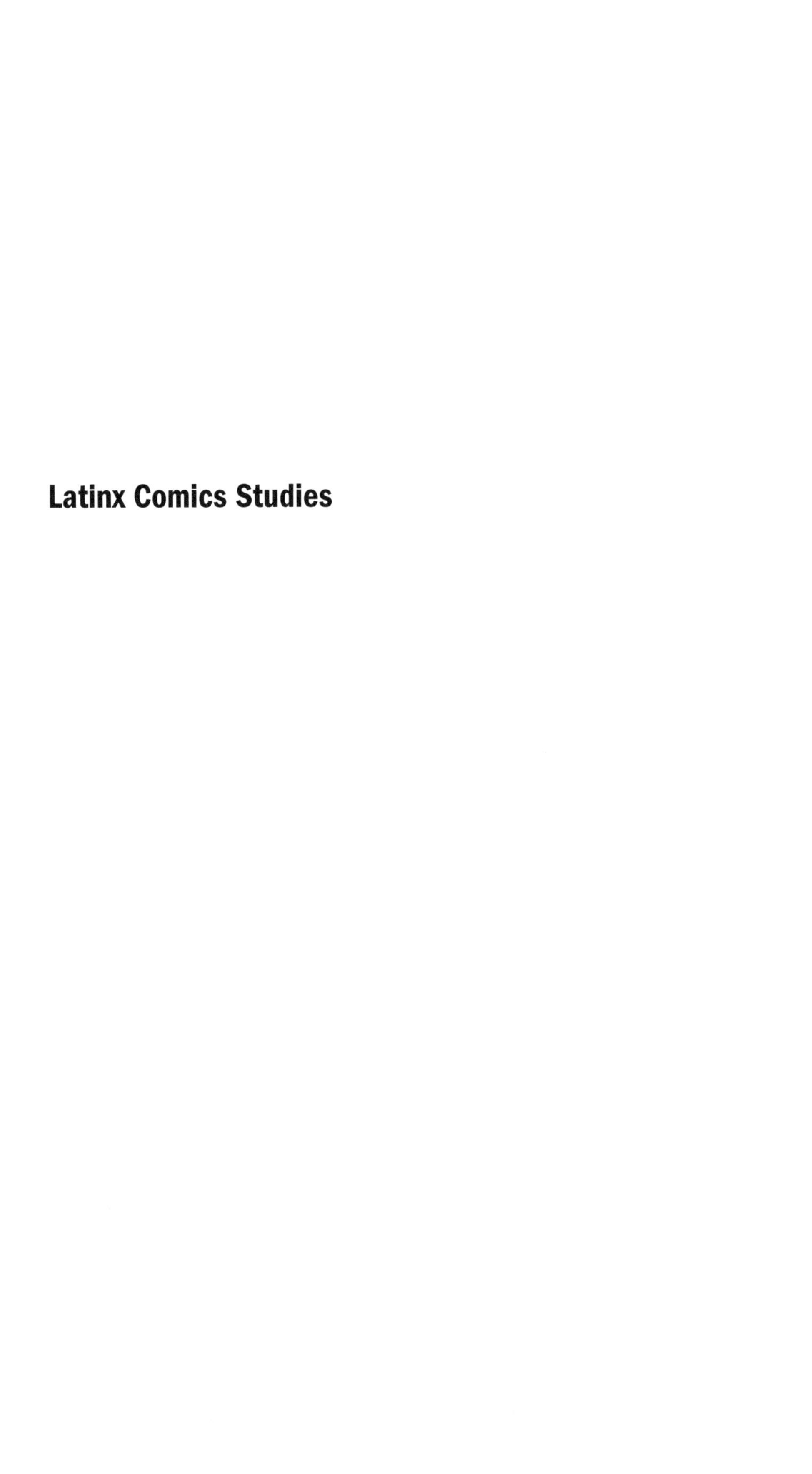

Latinx Comics Studies

Introduction

●●●●●●●●●●●●●●

Latinx Comics beyond Representation: Interdisciplinary and Intersectional Approaches

FERNANDA DÍAZ-BASTERIS
AND MAITE URCAREGUI

From the Margin to the Center: Defining Latinx Comics Studies

Our collection, *Latinx Comics Studies: Critical and Creative Crossings*, considers the role of comics and graphic narrative in picturing the rich realities of Latinx life on the page. The essays and comics it comprises explore a wide range of topics affecting Latinx people: the erasure of their histories and communities; feminist and queer forms of embodiment; Afro-Latinx and Indigenous experiences; conflicted relationships to citizenship; the duality of calling multiple places home; practices of placemaking and belonging; multilingual experiences; the ongoing devastation of settler colonialism and racial capitalism; disasters exacerbated by colonial power dynamics; and state violence and collective memory, among others. This collection, which captures just a small sliver of Latinx comic arts, includes and examines works by Chicanx, Puerto Rican, Cuban, Salvadoran, Guatemalan, Colombian, and Venezuelan American artists while also drawing out transnational connections to Spanish and Palestinian American, Mexican, Italian, and Swedish artists. It draws out the aesthetic possibilities of political cartoons, alternative and independent comics, autographics (or autobiographical comics),[1] and children's and young adult comics as well as historical fiction, noir, fantasy, and science fiction.

Latinx Comics Studies draws out the productive connections and tensions between Latinx studies and comics studies, two fundamentally interdisciplinary fields of study that have historically been marginalized within academic spaces and take up that marginalization as an object of study and critique. Latinx studies emerged through the work of student activists, predominantly Chicanx and Puerto Rican students, who demanded to see themselves and their communities represented in the university's curriculum and faculty. It uses both humanistic and social science approaches to examine the lived experiences of Latinx peoples who are marginalized on the basis of language, citizenship status, and ethnoracial and national identity.[2] Yet Latinx studies often remains on the edges of ethnic studies, as Mérida M. Rúa and Ana Y. Ramos-Zayas point out in their introduction to *Critical Dialogues in Latinx Studies*.[3] Mapping the edges of comics studies, Darieck Scott and Ramzi Fawaz argue that "the social stigma that makes the [comics] medium marginal, juvenile, and outcast from 'proper' art" is also what makes comics "a medium that thus hails counterpublics."[4] While Scott and Fawaz's work speaks to queer counterpublics in particular, we extend their claims to other underrepresented groups, such as Latinx communities. To draw on the words of Latinx comics studies scholar Frederick Luis Aldama, Latinx comics "build story worlds that imagine anew the future, and past, for Latinx subjects otherwise erased, ignored, or swept to shadowed corners."[5] Latinx comics studies offers a critical framework to shed light on the shadowed corners that still haunt our academic spaces and ways of knowing, demanding that Latinx comics, creators, and scholars be seen as vital, not marginal.

While there are many interdisciplinary affinities between Latinx studies and comics studies, there are also points of conflict. Within comics studies, for instance, Latinx comics have been even further pushed to the margins in a field that has historically tended to favor White scholars and artists and to emphasize Anglophone and European traditions.[6] The study of Japanese manga is a notable and prominent exception here, yet one that still privileges cultural production and perspectives from the Global North over the Global South. Aldama notes that, within comics, "there has been a tradition . . . of gatekeeping race- and ethnic-identified experiences and characters," and that gatekeeping, we argue, pervades comics studies as well.[7] Latinx comics studies, then, does not necessarily signal a neat marrying of these two fields but rather, by bringing them together, demands that comics scholars attend to these elisions and exclusions and the ways in which they fall along racialized, colonial, gendered, geographic, and linguistic lines of power.

Our collection's title, *Latinx Comics Studies*, names a conscious effort to establish Latinx comics as a distinct creative movement that, while not monolithic, does share certain historical contexts, political impulses, thematic and narrative tropes, and aesthetic strategies. While there is much debate over what exactly qualifies a comic as Latinx,[8] we define Latinx comics as those that are created by or in collaboration with Latinx peoples, those diasporic peoples within the United States with geographic, linguistic, ancestral, and/or cultural origins in Latin America, including Mexico, Central America, South America, and the Caribbean. We are also cognizant of the fact that many comics are created in collaboration—whether through the work of creative teams, as in many mainstream comics, or collectives, as in independent publishing spaces like Días Cómic and Laneha House (which are taken up in this collection)—where some but not all of the members may be Latinx. We include these multiracial teams in our definition of Latinx comics as well. Our definition is consciously more narrow than others, such as Isabel Millán's in *Keywords for Comics Studies*, which includes comics that either "depict Latinx characters *or* were produced by Latinx writers and artists."[9] By narrowing in this way, we hope (1) to challenge the appropriation and exoticization of Latinx aesthetics, cultures, and lived experiences by non-Latinx creators; (2) to resist the stereotypical expectations often placed on Latinx creators and characters; and (3) to center and elevate the work of Latinx writers and artists, which, as we discuss above, has long been neglected within both popular and scholarly spaces.

While our definition narrows in some ways, it also creates some capacious openings in terms of form and content. According to our definition, Latinx comics are not necessarily limited to portraying strictly realistic portraits of Latinx life (although they often do). Latinx writers and artists traverse a range of genres and styles that include but are not limited to social realism and extend into the surreal, the speculative, and the abstract. We think of Latinx comics, like the term "Latinx" itself, as naming a place of origin and creating a politicized call to action rather than a fixed or narrow notion of identity or identitarian aesthetics. Recognizing the symbolic slipperiness of Latinx, this collection also creates space for the nuanced ways Latinx readers have identified with Latinx characters and narratives created by non-Latinx authors and artists.[10] Ultimately, our definition remains open to revision, and we invite our readers to build on our work in their own ways. In defining Latinx comics, we are less interested in policing the porous boundaries of imagination and identity and more interested in moving works and creators that have been marginalized to the center of our study. We recognize, though, that when it comes to comics, "all definitions are possible yet significantly *imprecise* when approaching a medium that moves," as Jessica Quick Stark underscores.[11]

While Latinx comics are different from Latin American comics, recognizing the influence of Latin American histories, political contexts, and *historietas* is crucial for understanding the aesthetic genealogies and diasporic entanglements of Latinx comics. Latinx comics are products of many of the same sociopolitical realities and historical factors that shape Latin American comics. We recognize the unique context of Latinx comics while also underscoring these shared histories of (neo)colonialism and imperialism—which inform complicated and at times contradictory frameworks for understanding ethnoracial and national identity—as well as diasporic movements across a variety of borders (national, geographic, cultural, linguistic, formal, etc.) that Latinx and Latin American comics and communities have in common. Examining Latinx comics as part of a shared, albeit not singular, movement includes not only tracing points of connection but also grappling with difference, especially forms of social differences and inequalities that have significantly shaped Latin American and Latinx contexts.

In addition to naming a creative movement within comics, *Latinx Comics Studies* also signals a critical movement within comics studies. Our collection contributes to a growing list of works dedicated to the study of Latinx comics that have come to the fore since the early 2000s. Frederick Luis Aldama, a contributor to this collection, has been crucial for establishing the field of Latinx comics studies and recovering the creative and intellectual contributions of Latinx comics creators. Aldama's *Your Brain on Latino Comics: From Gus Arriola to Los Bros Hernandez* (2009) offers a historical overview of Latino comics history and collects interviews with predominantly Latin*o* comics creators. Aldama and Christopher González's coedited volume

Graphic Borders: Latino Comic Books Past, Present, and Future (2016) examines the physical, conceptual, and aesthetic borders that shape Latino comics, collecting critical essays on Latino comics across genre, including superhero comics, political cartoons, and alternative comics. Aldama's *Latinx Superheroes in Mainstream Comics* (2017) documents Latinx representation in mainstream comics, predominantly those published by Marvel and DC, alongside their television and film adaptations. The role of comics in the formation of national identities and histories has been taken up in Héctor Fernández L'Hoeste (another contributor to this collection) and Juan Polete's collection *Redrawing the Nation: National Identity in Latin/o American Comics* (2009) and, more recently, in Martha J. Cutter and Cathy J. Schlund-Vials's *Redrawing the Historical Past: History, Memory and Multiethnic Graphic Novels* (2018). Collections like Nhora Lucía Serrano's *Immigrants and Comics: Graphic Spaces of Remembrance, Transaction, and Mimesis* (2021) and Ralf Kauranen, Olli Löytty, Aura Nikkilä, and Anna Vuorinne's *Comics and Migration: Representation and Other Practices* (2023) examine movements across national, linguistic, and cultural borders in comics across the world, with some chapters that attend to Latin American and Latinx migrant narratives. Finally, as we emphasize above, while Latinx comics are distinct, they must be contextualized within the longer historical and aesthetic traditions of Latin American comics. Jorge Catalá, Paulo Drinot, and James Scorer's *Comics & Memory in Latin America* (2017) and Laura Cristina Fernández, Amadeo Gandolfo, and Pablo Turnes's *Burning Down the House: Latin American Comics in the 21st Century* (2023) discuss the political, economic, and cultural landscapes that have shaped Latin American comics.

The works and scholars that precede this collection have done invaluable work to document Latinx representation in comics, create historiographies of Latinx comics and creators, and examine thematic and political questions that arise from Latinx narratives. This volume builds on these earlier works through its interdisciplinary, multimodal, and intersectional approach and through its commitment to examining the ways that Latinx comics do not simply represent but actively theorize the textures, nuances, and feelings of Latinx life.

Moving Latinx Comics Studies beyond Representation

Latinx people are the "majority minority" in the United States, the second largest ethnoracial group behind White non-Latinx peoples.[12] According to the Pew Research Center, "The U.S. Hispanic population reached 62.1 million in 2020, accounting for 19% of all Americans."[13] Yet, even this statistic, which conflates "Hispanic" (a term that names the influence of the Spanish language, heritage, and, thus, colonization) with "Latinx" (a term that identifies a place of origin or descent),[14] reveals the need for more robust language, narratives, and theories to describe the variety of Latinx experiences and "the processes by which diverse Latinas/os interact with, dominate, and transculturate each other," as Frances R. Aparicio urges in her articulation of "Latinidad/es."[15]

U.S. mainstream comics have also had difficulty capturing this complexity. Aldama emphasizes this point in *Latinx Superheroes in Mainstream Comics*: "In addition to being the majority minority in the United States, Latinos are also very varied in their experiences and identities. Latinoness, or Latinidad, varies from each subgroup that makes up the Latinx whole. . . . The comic book universe is only just beginning to clue into this, and this after decades of being blind to Latinos as a whole in the United States."[16] Latinx representation has largely been absent from mainstream U.S. comics, and when Latinx characters are portrayed, they have tended to reinforce exoticizing and criminalizing caricatures, often portrayed as hypersexual spitfires, disproportionately associated with criminal enterprises, or else limited to roles of domestic and physical labor and slapstick side characters. These caricatures congeal into an image of Latinx peoples that collapses varied identities and experiences into a singular type, or stereotype, abstracted from reality and devoid of truth. The repetition of these stereotypical images creates what comics scholar Rebecca Wanzo describes as a "visual and political grammar" that "uses racialized caricature as a mechanism for constructing both ideal and undesirable types of citizens."[17] This racialized visual grammar has very real material consequences, including being excluded from educational and professional opportunities and advancement, the hypersurveillance and criminalization of Latinx spaces and communities, and, perhaps most notably, alienation from citizenship and its protective status.

While cognizant of the power of representation and its symbolic and material consequences, particularly for those who have been underserved by dominant narratives and images, our collection moves beyond representation as the primary framework for understanding Latinx comics for a couple of important and interconnected reasons. First, the emphasis on representation tends to catalog and celebrate Latinx creators and characters with little attention to aesthetic innovation or the nuances of identity. We fear that this celebratory approach risks further flattening Latinx characters into caricatures and/or turning Latinx comics into political allegories, offering unwavering critiques and transparent windows into Latinx life. Second, we are critical of the way that discussions of representation, which often fall into the binary camps of "positive" and "negative," easily become complicit in narratives of "good" and "bad" immigrants, tests of "authenticity," and the perception that Latinx represents a singular identity or monolithic community.

This collection examines the nuances that emerge when we move away from merely celebrating representation toward a more robust engagement with the narratives and images that describe, shape, and (re)imagine Latinx life. As queer of color theorists Kadji Amin, Amber Jamilla Musser, and Roy Pérez argue, marginalized artists—particularly queer artists and artists of color—are often expected to become "native informants" tasked with producing art that "testif[ies] to the sociological conditions of their own disempowerment" and "transmits information rather than pushing aesthetic boundaries."[18] These expectations can become even more pronounced in comics, where images can easily be elided as merely representational and less open to interpretation than language. Comics theorist and creator Scott McCloud reinforces this epistemological division between images and words when he declares that "pictures are **received** information" and "writing is **perceived** information," which suggests that the meaning of images is instantaneously transmitted whereas language requires more training to decode and allows more room for interpretation.[19] In addition to underestimating the interpretive power of images, McCloud's *Understanding Comics*, which has been canonized within comics studies, ultimately "seeks to understand comics through the frame of whiteness," as Johnathan Flowers powerfully argues in his critical race critique of the text.[20] The supposed neutrality of McCloud's "blank slate" avatar in *Understanding Comics* is made possible only through the assumption of Whiteness, as Flowers argues, one that extends to McCloud's implied reader and, thus, has indelibly marked the critical consciousness of comics studies.[21] Yet, rather than ignoring race and ethnicity as McCloud does, it is important that comics scholars recognize that the "power underlying the comics image becomes all the more evident when placed within the context of race and ethnicity," as Derek Parker Royal points out.[22]

Images and words come together in unexpected and unruly ways in comics, or, as comics educator, scholar, and practitioner Lynda Barry describes, drawing and writing conjure mysterious things when practiced together.[23] Take, for instance, Breena Nuñez's comic, "This Body Is Actually Unsettled," published for the first time in this collection and featured on its cover, which collages abstract lines and geometrical shapes with sparse iconic images to explore "two paths leading to de eunaited estates." In just three panels, Nuñez evokes not only the multiplicitous pathways of (im)migration but also the playfulness of multilingualism and code-switching. Their abstract black-and-white comic rejects the bright colors, stereotypical icons, cultural markers, and social realism often expected of Latinx comics. This is just one of many examples of how Latinx artists work at the limits of comics' formal possibilities to picture Latinx ways of being and knowing. It is crucial that Latinx comics studies remains open and attentive to the mysterious conjurings and aesthetic innovations of Latinx artists, as well as the "multifaceted materiality" of their work—not just for their representational or political value but for their formal, aesthetic, and stylistic contributions and their pedagogical power.[24]

Ralph E. Rodriguez argues for a similar aesthetic openness when he urges scholars to "undiscipline" Latinx literature from monolithic categories by questioning "the limits of employing the political fiction of *Latinx* to organize and analyze a corpus of literary texts."[25] Untethering Latinx literature from the burden of representation or authenticity, Rodriguez concentrates on how the formal features of literature open more playful and provisional interpretive categories "that might allow us to understand better the complexities and nuances of what we have heretofore considered Latinx literature."[26] While we do consider Latinx comics as a distinct artistic and literary tradition, we are also invested in uncovering the complexities and nuances therein. This collection thinks with Rodriguez's work by asking two questions: How do the formal devices of comics and the ways that Latinx artists experiment with them undiscipline or unravel what we think we know about Latinx narratives (both visual and verbal)? How do comics' playful blending of word and image, perspectival framing of panels, intersecting borders and boundaries, and sequential variations help us imagine more flexible, intersectional frameworks of analysis? By way of answering these questions, this volume explores how Latinx comics experiment with the definitional and narrative boundaries of Latinx, draw out the diversity within that "political fiction," and theorize its tensions, fissures, and fusions.

The *X*-Factor: Interdisciplinary and Intersectional Crossings

The insinuating *x* of the gender-neutral Latinx in this collection's title visually and linguistically signals its intersectional commitments and interdisciplinary approaches.[27] Queer and trans Latinx activists developed the term

"Latinx" in online conversations and communities as a rejection of the gender binary and the way it gets mapped onto the Spanish language (and many others). Catalina M. de Onís argues that these shifting signifiers (a/o, @, and now x and e) reveal "the evolution, fluidity, and slipperiness of language" and work to create a more inclusive lexicon.[28]

Some people in the United States with origins from Latin America also refuse the term "Latina/o/x/e" altogether, viewing it as a colonial construct that erases linguistic, geographic, cultural, and ethnoracial specificity.[29] Some prefer to be associated with their nation of origin (e.g., Colombian or Mexican) or their national intersections (e.g., Dominican American) or with a regional marker (e.g., Oaxacan) or with their Indigenous community (e.g., Quechua) or with their racial identity (e.g., Black or Afro-Latinx) and/or with a politicized identity (e.g., Chicano or Boricua). This list alone, which is by no means exhaustive, illustrates the many practices of naming with which Latinx people engage and the politics therein. Take, for instance, the protests and activism that arose in response to a leaked recording of racist anti-Black and anti-Indigenous comments made by Gil Cedillo, Kevin de León, and Nury Martinez, three prominent Latinx members of the Los Angeles City Council, and Ron Herrera, then-president of the Los Angeles County Federation of Labor, in 2022. In the signs, chants, and declarations of protests in response, many Black and Indigenous diasporic peoples with origins in Latin America and the Caribbean notably rejected identification with the term "Latinx" and the Latinx community that the city council members claimed to represent. Oaxacan Angelenos, many of whom identify as Zapotec, were some of the most vocal and visible protestors: calling attention to the colorism and racism (specifically anti-Blackness and anti-Indigeneity) that have long shaped notions of Latinidad and naming themselves as Oaxacan over and in opposition to Latinx.[30] Protests featured Oaxacan *folklórico*, and signs included messages like "Zapoteca Presente!," "Indigenous, Beautiful, and Proud," "Proud Oaxaqueña," and "With the Blacks short & tan xulos," which drew directly on the city council members' comments and reclaimed them as a point of pride and cross-racial solidarity.[31] These public protests make visible the racism, colorism, and colonialism that roil beneath the surface of mainstream identitarian and political discourse, even within Latinx communities. The uses of dance, music, and visual culture in the protests speak to the intersection of art and activism, or artivism, which we find in many Latinx comics as well.

For all of these reasons and more, it is incredibly challenging to write about these diverse and distinct experiences without reinforcing monolithic expectations. In their collection *Burning Down the House: Latin American Comics in the 21st Century*, Fernández, Gandolfo, and Turnes note a similar challenge when they describe the "particular conundrum" of writing about Latin American comics because, while they share some similar political and economic contexts, they are also filtered by the "particular characteristics, history, social qualities, and economic realities of each country."[32] Latinx comics studies indeed faces a similar conundrum of having to grapple with distinctive diasporic histories and identities without melting them into a singular stew that conforms to the United States' melting pot mythology. With these challenges in mind, we encourage our contributors and readers to embrace specificity when possible, by naming and attending to the distinct identities, national origins, and ethnoracial intersections at hand. Because our collection examines works from across Latinx diasporas and from an array of positionalities, we strategically use Latinx to name a coalitional community made up of many communities and to explore the diversity therein—not only in terms of gender and sexuality, but also in terms of geography, national identity, citizenship status, language, ethnicity, race, class, and ability, among others.[33] Our volume aims to center those who have been most marginalized within both dominant culture and Latinx communities: undocumented (im)migrants; women and queer, trans, and gender-nonconforming people; Afro-Latinx and Indigenous peoples; and working-class, poor, and unhoused communities, to name a few. Importantly, these experiences are intersecting, not isolated, and many people exist at the crossroads between and among them. Finally, we recognize that Latinx, as both a term and a hermeneutic, is not possible without the critical insights of queer, trans, and gender-nonconforming activists. Recognizing this intellectual genealogy, our volume prioritizes feminist, queer, decolonial, and antiracist perspectives and, in doing so, illuminates interdisciplinary and intersectional approaches to studying Latinx comics.

Organization and Overview

Each section of this book blends theory and practice with essays that offer critical analyses of Latinx comics from a range of (inter)disciplinary and theoretical perspectives alongside those that provide pedagogical insights and practical strategies for teaching Latinx comics. The pedagogical essays emerge from a variety of disciplinary settings, including literature, language, and education classrooms, and while they largely focus on higher education, the insights they offer are applicable to K–12 and community-based learning as well. The collection also features five comic shorts, four newly published and one reprinted, that creatively introduce the volume and portray national histories and identities, multilingual experiences, paths of migration, and Latinx speculative futures, respectively. These comics showcase the potential of the medium as a representational tool *and* a theoretical apparatus in its own right. The fluid movements, or crossings, between and among theory, pedagogy, and aesthetics throughout this collection extend from the editors' and contributors' collective desire to disentangle Latinx comics from generic expectations—including the generic conventions of academic knowledge production—and to map out multimodal avenues of inquiry for Latinx comics studies. It is our hope that these essays and comics will be taken up by scholars and teachers and will have a life of their own beyond the pages of this book.

Our collection is organized around four major sections. Part I, "Complicating National Histories and Cultural Identities," explores how graphic narratives rework dominant histories, challenge colonial expectations, and create their own counternarratives and counterarchives. Jessica Rutherford opens the collection by examining the sociospiritual traditions of the Indigenous Nahua and Maya empires (and "the bloody borderlands" between them) through Daniel Parada's comic series *Zotz: Serpent and Shield* (2011–present), which she argues reimagines Indigenous women's histories in precolonial Mesoamerica. Stephanie Contreras's chapter also takes a historical approach to examine how Iverna Lockpez and Dean Haspiel's *Cuba: My Revolution* (2010), published by DC's imprint Vertigo, "graphically challenge[s] time and space" to create a counternarrative to official histories of the Cuban Revolution from either Cuba or the United States. Also working within a Caribbean context, Jennifer Caroccio Maldonado reflects on her experience teaching the comics anthology *Puerto Rico Strong* (2018) in an undergraduate Latinx literature course as a vehicle for critically examining Puerto Rico's Indigenous histories and colonial relationship to the United States in the aftermath of 2017's Hurricane Maria. The section concludes with an original comic by Nicky Rodriguez that questions the borders of U.S. nationalism and posits the possibility of what she calls an "anticolonial nationalism" in Puerto Rico.

Part II, "Latinx Migrations: Borders and Borderlands," examines the geopolitical space of the U.S.-Mexico border, the conceptual space of the borderlands, and the formal space of comics borders or panels. The chapters in this section showcase the ways in which comics reframe material infrastructures (such as the border) and abstract categories (such as citizenship and "legality") that shape undocumented Latinx life in the United States and/or attempt to erase Latinx presence altogether. Together, Marcel Brousseau and Katherine Kelp-Stebbins explore the dynamic relationship between political borders and panel borders across a variety works, including comics by Latinx artists Jaime Hernandez, Lalo Alcaraz, and Tony Sandoval; Palestinian American artist Leila Abdelrazaq; and Italian creators Andrea Ferraris and Renato Chiocca. Through this transnational, comparative reading, they argue that comics' borders make visible processes of national exclusion through their physical and figurative arrangement on the page. Kaitlin E. Thomas and Héctor Rodriguez III discuss depictions of deportation, familial separation, and racialized and punitive border policies in Rodriguez's comic book series *El Peso Hero* (2011–present), which taps into Mexico's rich historieta tradition to lobby political critique and commentary via the comics form. The last chapter in this section moves away from the U.S.-Mexico border to the cinematic borderlands of Los Angeles, California. Héctor Fernández L'Hoeste reads Latinx presence and absence in Gilbert Hernandez's graphic novel *Maria M.* (2013, 2019) and Bryce Carlson and Vanesa R. Del Rey's comic series *HIT: 1955* (2014) and *HIT: 1957* (2016), which he argues blend comics with Hollywood's film noir aesthetics to depict local and national anxieties around shifting demographics. This section closes with a comic by Terry Blas, originally published in *Vox* and reprinted here, that depicts the threat of violence that many multilingual and Spanish-speaking Latinx people face within and beyond the borderlands while also celebrating the United States's linguistic diversity.

Part III, "Feminist and Queer Interventions," interrogates how Latinx comics creatively theorize the intersections of ethnicity, race, place, gender, sexuality, and ability and invite alternative reading and interpretive practices. Katlin Marisol Sweeney-Romero highlights the pressures of the *buena hija* ideal that many Latina daughters face within their families. Blending personal narrative with a critical analysis of Sam Humphries and Jen Bartel's Image Comics series *Blackbird* (2018–2019), Sweeney-Romero examines avenues for envisioning a self and a future outside of these gendered expectations. Building on the empowering reading practices Sweeney-Romero models, Nicole Ann Amato's chapter draws on her experience working with English language arts (ELA) teacher candidates to move beyond their initial anxieties around teaching graphic narratives that center queer protagonists of color. Amato discusses methods of teaching Gabby Rivera and Celia Moscote's graphic novel adaptation *Juliet Takes a Breath* (2020); Carmen Maria Machado, Dani, and Tamra Bonvillian's DC Comics's series *The Low, Low Woods*; and Rivera and

Royal Dunlap's BOOM! Studios comic series *b.b. free* (2020) to reconceptualize the role of comics in secondary ELA classrooms and beyond. In the final chapter of this section, Maite Urcaregui examines how independent artist Breena Nuñez uses the comics form to "translate" their nonbinary and Afro-Latinx experiences and to forge a transnational and translocal queer community of color in their autobiographical webcomics. This section is concluded by a newly published comic by Nuñez titled "This Body Is Actually Unsettled" that, as we described earlier, examines two different pathways of migration to the United States, one by car and the other by plane, and the "nomadic sensibilities" they create via bold black iconic and abstract shapes.

Part IV, "Practices of Placemaking," the final section of the collection, takes up how comics might be used to navigate space, to forge a sense of belonging, and to envision alternative futures in ways that inform our present realities. Fernanda Díaz-Basteris analyzes hyperlocal independent comics from San Juan's artistic collective Días Cómic, which she argues develops a Caribbean urban aesthetic that constitutes an artisanal and independent visual archive of the city. Frederick Luis Aldama traces movements across time, space, and mediums in his short commentary on Joakim Lindengren and Giannina Braschi's adaptation *United States of Banana: A Graphic Novel* (2021); Aldama examines how the graphic novel's paratextual elements force readers into alternative reading patterns "to see new pathways to make a better future." Lars Allen takes up this discussion of Latinx futurity in their analysis of Inés Estrada's science fiction graphic novel *Alienation* (2019), which critically comments on the environmental exploitation and racial capitalism of our present moment by envisioning a not-too-distant future in which the only escape from these twin catastrophes is through AI-generated worlds. The section ends with Conrado Parraguirre's comic "Prelude," which ironically reflects on the mundane passing of a year—a narrative that feels all the more salient in light of the COVID-19 pandemic. Like Estrada's *Alienation*, Parraguirre's "Prelude" critiques corporate and capitalistic narratives of success and happiness (albeit in a hyperrealistic setting), even as it recognizes that we all must negotiate these systems to survive.

Our collection, *Latinx Comics Studies: Critical and Creative Crossings*, brings together a variety of critical and creative approaches to reading, teaching, and making comics that explore panethnic, multiracial, and multilingual Latinx life. Our naming of Latinx comics studies is not an attempt to distill these diverse experiences and narratives into a singular canon. Rather, we aim to resignify and reevaluate how we experience, value, study, and teach Latinx comics: not as a special topic that is relegated only to identitarian questions of representation, but as a movement of cultural production made up of many varied experiences and traditions that intersect and diverge to create a dynamic network that is constantly in motion. Indeed, our hope is that this collection acts as an opportunity to take stock of this emerging and evolving field, to pay homage to what has been done and what (and who) has been ignored, to extend and at times trouble what is known, and to invite fellow scholars to envision what might be possible in and through Latinx comics.

Notes

1 Gillian Whitlock coined the term "autographics": "to draw attention to the specific conjunctions of visual and verbal text in this genre of [comics] autobiography, and also to the subject positions that narrators negotiate in and through comics." Gillian Whitlock, "Autographics: The Seeing 'I' of Comics," *Modern Fiction Studies* 52, no. 4 (2006): 965–979, 966.

2 We use the term "ethnoracial" throughout this introduction to refer to the way that ethnic, racial, and often national origin intermingle to shape "Latinx" as a panethnic and multiracial experience that is often racialized in the United States.

3 Mérida M. Rúa and Ana Y. Ramos-Zayas, "Introduction," in *Critical Dialogues in Latinx Studies*, ed. Ana Y. Ramos-Zayas and Mérida M. Rúa (New York: New York University Press, 2001), 1–10, 6.

4 Darieck Scott and Ramzi Fawaz, "Introduction: Queer about Comics," *American Literature* 90, no. 2 (2018): 197–219, 197, 200.

5 Frederick Luis Aldama, "Preface: Dreaming Latinx Realities," in *Speculative Fiction for Dreamers: A Latinx Anthology*, ed. Alex Hernandez, Matthew David Goodwin, and Sarah Rafael García (Columbus: The Ohio State University Press, 2021), ix–x, x.

6 Adrienne Resha critiques comics studies' centering of Whiteness in her review of Charles Hatfield and Bart Beaty's *Comics Studies: A Guidebook*, which as a "guidebook" is indicative of the larger field even if it offers an incomplete picture. As Resha points out, there is not a single chapter in the entire collection, which admits to favoring Anglophone traditions, devoted to "comics made by Black, Indigenous, Asian, Latinx, and/or other ethnic or racial minority creators in the US, Canada, or the United Kingdom." She goes on to argue that "*A Guidebook* identifies its 'core' subjects and research and canonizes them alongside whiteness and masculinity." Adrienne Resha, "*Comics Studies: A Guidebook* ed. by Charles Hatfield and Bart Beaty (review)," *Inks: The Journal of the Comics Studies Society* 5, no. 1 (2021): 131–132.

7 Frederick Luis Aldama, "Multicultural Comics Today: A Brief Introduction," in *Multicultural Comics: From* Zap *to Blue Beetle*, ed. Frederick Luis Aldama (Austin: University of Texas Press, 2010), 1–25, 2–3.

8 Isabel Millán asks, for instance, "What qualifies a comic as Latinx? Is it the character? The major themes within the story line? The writer? The lead artists? The target audience? Only one of these characteristics must be met to qualify or all?" Isabel Millán, "Latinx," in *Keywords for Comics Studies*, ed. Ramzi Fawaz, Shelley

Streeby, and Deborah Elizabeth Whaley (New York: New York University Press, 2021), 134–138, 135.

9 Millán, "Latinx," 135; emphasis added.

10 In her contribution to this collection, Katlin Marisol Sweeney-Romero models some of these unruly routes of identification and recognition in her analysis of Image Comics' *Blackbird* series, a story that centers a Latina protagonist but was created by non-Latinx creators Sam Humphries and Jen Bartel. Similarly, Darieck Scott and Ramzi Fawaz have discussed and modeled how queer readers of color have identified with superhero characters and comics that were not explicitly queer in unruly and unexpected ways. In their essay "Queer about Comics," Scott reads the cover of *Wonder Woman* no. 206 (1973), which features Wonder Woman and her Black twin sister Nubia, who was initially developed by White creators, in ways that allow for identification with "fantasies of black power and beauty" alongside a critique of Nubia's ahistorical portrayal and association with animality. See Scott and Fawaz, "Introduction," 205.

11 Jessica Quick Stark, "Comic Strip," in Fawaz, Streeby, and Whaley, *Keywords for Comics Studies*, 55–57, 55, emphasis original.

12 Cary Funk and Mark Hugo Lopez, "A Brief Statistical Portrait of U.S. Hispanics" (Pew Research Center, June 14, 2022), https://www.pewresearch.org/science/2022/06/14/a-brief-statistical-portrait-of-u-s-hispanics/.

13 Funk and Lopez, "Brief Statistical Portrait." Throughout this report, the authors use the terms "Hispanic" and "Latino" interchangeably and incorrectly, for instance, suggesting that "Hispanics are a diverse group with deep roots in Latin America," when Hispanic refers to Spanish speakers from Latin America, Spain, and Equatorial Guinea.

14 Terry Blas, a contributor featured in part II of this collection, explores the differences between Hispanic and Latino in his comic "You Say Latino" published by *Vox*. Both of the coeditors integrate this comic into our Latinx comics and literature courses and recommend it as a clear, concise, and accessible teaching tool. Terry Blas, "You Say Latino," *Vox*, August 12, 2016, https://www.vox.com/2015/8/19/9173457/hispanic-latino-comic.

15 Frances R. Aparicio, "Latinidad/es," in *Keywords for Latina/o Studies*, ed. Deborah R. Vargas, Nancy Raquel Mirabel, and Lawrence M. La Fountain-Stokes (New York: New York University Press, 2017), 113–117, 116.

16 Frederick Luis Aldama, *Latinx Superheroes in Mainstream Comics* (Tucson: University of Arizona Press, 2017), 3.

17 Rebecca Wanzo, *The Content of Our Caricature: African American Comic Art and Political Belonging* (New York City: New York University Press, 2020), 5.

18 Kadji Amin, Amber Jamilla Musser, and Roy Pérez, "Queer Form: Aesthetics, Race, and the Violences of the Social," *ASAP/Journal* 2, no. 2 (2017): 227–239, 227.

19 Scott McCloud, *Understanding Comics: The Invisible Art* (New York: HarperCollins, 1993), 49, emphasis original. We cite McCloud here as a point of departure and critique. As scholars and teachers, we recommend destabilizing the canonicity of McCloud within comics studies by reading and teaching it alongside critical race critiques, such as the following: Johnathan Flowers, "Misunderstanding Comics," in *With Great Power Comes Great Pedagogy: Teaching, Learning, and Comics*, ed. Susan E. Kirtley, Antero Garcia, and Peter E. Carlson (Jackson: University Press of Mississippi, 2020), 207–225; and Misha Grifka Wander, "Someone Else's Icon:

Complicating Comics and Identification," *Inks: The Journal of the Comics Studies Society* 6, no. 3 (2022): 320–328.

20 Flowers, "Misunderstanding Comics," 208.

21 McCloud refers to his avatar, the critical persona and perspective that guides readers through the book, as "practically a blank slate" whose identity is "irrelevant." McCloud, *Understanding Comics*, 37.

22 Derek Parker Royal, "Coloring America: Multi-ethnic Engagements with Graphic Narrative," *Melus* 32, no. 3 (2007): 7–22, 7.

23 Lynda Barry, *Making Comics* (Montreal: Drawn and Quarterly, 2019), 20.

24 Describing the "multifaceted materiality" of form, Amin, Musser, and Pérez suggest that "approaching the sensuous materiality of artworks expansively displaces the primacy of the visual—the regime within which queer bodies and bodies of color have been most violently subjected to the demands of cultural legibility." Amin, Musser, and Pérez, "Queer Form," 228.

25 Ralph E. Rodriguez, *Latinx Literature Unbound: Undoing Ethnic Expectation* (New York: Fordham University Press, 2018), 3.

26 Rodriguez, *Latinx Literature Unbound*, 3.

27 Claudia Milian describes the *x* of Latinx as "falling through the cracks—the spaces between the o's and the a's, the conventional understandings of what it means to be Latino or Latina." Claudia Milian, *LatinX* (Minneapolis: University of Minnesota Press, 2019), 2. Fawaz and Scott question comics' intersectional possibilities when they ask, "How might a medium made up of the literal intersection of lines, images, and bodies capture the values of intersectional analysis?" Ramzi Fawaz and Darieck Scott, "Queer," in Fawaz, Streeby, and Whaley, *Keywords for Comics Studies*, 171–175, 172.

28 Catalina M. de Onís, "What's in an 'x'? An Exchange about the Politics of 'Latinx,'" *Chiricú Journal: Latina/o Literatures, Arts, and Cultures* 1, no. 2 (2017): 78–91, 79. There is still debate over usage of Latinx. Eric César Morales argues that because Latinx does not correspond to Spanish syntax, it risks alienating recent immigrants and those who exclusively speak Spanish from their own communities. For this reason, some have begun to use "Latin*e*" as a gender-inclusive term that conforms more comfortably to Spanish. See Eric César Morales, quoted in de Onís, "What's in an 'x'?," 82.

29 One notable example is Citlalli Citlalmina Anahuac's *Don't Call Me Latina: Notes from a Decolonizing Mexicana Reclaiming Everything That Is Ours* (CreateSpace, 2022), in which the author embraces "Mexicana" over "Latina."

30 It is estimated that there are as many as 200,000 Zapotecs, the largest Indigenous group in Oaxaca, in L.A., which is home to one of the largest Oaxacan communities outside of Mexico. For more on this controversy and the protests in response, see Brittny Mejia, "Following City Council Members' Racist Remarks, Hundreds of Oaxacans March for Justice in L.A.," *Los Angeles Times*, October 15, 2022, https://www.latimes.com/california/story/2022-10-15/los-angeles-city-council-members-racist-remarks-oaxacans-march.

31 For images of this protest, see Brian Feinzimer, "Protest with Culture," *L.A. Taco*, October 17, 2022, https://lataco.com/protesting-with-culture-oaxaca.

32 Laura Cristina Fernández, Amadeo Gandolfo, and Pablo Turnes, "Burning Down the House—Introduction," in *Burning Down the House: Latin American Comics in the 21st Century*, ed. Laura Cristina Fernández, Amadeo Gandolfo, and Pablo Turnes (New York: Routledge, 2023), 1–16, 2.

33 As a politicized term of identification, "Latino" originally emerged from below, as a radical naming that was first created from within distinct communities with shared political affinities (often in opposition to terms such as "Hispanic") before it later became imposed from without as the official nomenclature of the U.S. Census Bureau in 2000. For more on the politics of naming, see Ramón A. Gutiérrez and Tomás Almaguer, "Hispanics, Latinos, Chicanos, Boricuas: What Do Names Mean?," in *The New Latino Studies Reader: A Twenty-First-Century Perspective*, ed. Ramón A. Gutiérrez and Tomás Almaguer (Berkeley: University of California Press, 2016).

Part I

Complicating National Histories and Cultural Identities

• • • • • • • • • • • • • •

Reimagining Indigenous Women's History in Precontact Mesoamerica via Daniel Parada's *Zotz: Serpent and Shield*

JESSICA RUTHERFORD

Daniel Parada's comic book series *Zotz: Serpent and Shield* (2011–present) introduces contact-era Indigenous history and culture into popular imaginaries via his depiction of the bloody borderlands that connected the Nahua and Maya empires. By representing the warrior paradigm that dominates Nahua and Mayan sociospiritual frameworks, Parada's re-creation of sixteenth-century Mesoamerica offers a decolonial twist by creating an alternate storyworld in which the Spanish conquest was unsuccessful, a powerful reimagining that helps to decenter colonial narratives. In the chronology that opens issue 1, for example, Parada orients readers outside of Western notions of time and space by listing dates according to the Maya calendar with correspondences to the Gregorian calendar in parentheses. This decolonial shift continues as Parada describes the Castilian people as having "arrived from across the sea, with the hornless deer [horses] and the weapons of thunder [guns]. These people waged war across the lands and brought great death, torture, humiliation and preached Christendom."[1] Describing horses as hornless deer and guns as weapons of thunder allows the reader to interpret these never-before-seen things according to Indigenous logic and experience. The story becomes ahistorical when Parada shifts the narrative on "5 Lord (circa1521 CE)," when "in the city of Zama [present-day Tulum], merchants saw another group of strange people from across the sea, the Turks as they are called."[2] Historically, Hernán Cortés and his army were not defeated, and the "Turks" did not arrive to the Yucatán Peninsula to colonize the region.

In the analysis of the comic series that follows, I highlight how *Zotz* opens a critical space for the in-depth study of gender and power in precolonial societies in the region. The comic is a particularly apt medium to represent sixteenth-century Mesoamerica given its unique deployment of sequential art alongside native storytelling techniques.[3] This essay contributes to the collection by unsettling dominant and/or colonial representations of conquest and colonization in Mesoamerica to highlight how the rich cultural heritage of the region contributes to the inherent diversity and heterogeneity within Latinx studies. Parada outlines his authorial intent in the introduction to issue 2 of the series, writing that he intends to "show the magnificence and sophistication of these advanced cultures that have endured Spanish invasion and subsequent oppression that followed." He goes on to explain, "Even now, despite globalization, oppressive regimes and various conflicts afflicting their respective countries, these cultures still thrive and continue playing a role in shaping our human history and experience."[4] A product of extensive archival research, Parada's comics include accurate representations of hieroglyphs and Indigenous art and culture, drawing from cultural practices and traditions that continue today. Readers see this, for example, in his precolonial depiction of sacred geographies and astronomy, such as the Sun and the Moon, who play an active role in the comic's storyworld.

Ritual engagement of humans with sacred astronomy in the series shows how animistic deity worship shaped society and culture in precolonial Mesoamerica, which informed the spiritual dimension of everyday life.[5] Moreover, a study of mythological representations of the Moon Goddess and the Primordial Grandmother in the comic highlights the centrality of women's work and knowledge in sustaining their communities. *Zotz* largely documents a mythological structure that aligns with that of the Q'eqchi', in which the Maya Hero Twins, Hunahpu and Xbalanque, and Our Lady of the Moon, Xt'actani, become Venus, the Sun, and the Moon, respectively.[6] The Sun God, Xbalanque, is represented as warrior and hunter, visualized in the comic via the jaguar spots on his skin and the blowgun that he uses to shoot a dart, while Xt'actani represents the premenopausal aspect of the waxing moon.[7] The female aspects of the waxing and the waning of the moon engender the life-death duality that is foundational to Mesoamerican cosmologies.

Broadly speaking, in comparison with Nahua cultures, Maya women operated within strict systems of gender interdependence and hierarchy, though this does not mean that there are no instances in which women occupied positions of power, despite patrilineal dominance in the political arena.[8] In her comparative study of Indigenous women's history in Latin America, Susan Kellogg finds that these gendered divisions of labor were quite diverse: "They include the gender arrangements of peoples ranging from hunting, gathering, and cultivating groups of Mesoamerica's far north to the more urban and hierarchically organized Nahuas, to the Ñudzahui people of Oaxaca (also known as Mixtec), who developed the most seemingly egalitarian gender arrangements of any Mesoamerican cultural group."[9] But while there are examples of more egalitarian gendered social conditions among Nahua cultures, this is not to say that gender hierarchy did not exist. It did.

I put the comic series in dialogue with the *Popol Vuh*,[10] a sixteenth-century text produced by K'iche' elders in the highlands of Guatemala, to begin to understand the heterogeneity of Indigenous culture in the region. The *Popol Vuh* is a well-known text written in K'iche' Maya using the Roman alphabet to preserve their history and culture in the face of Spanish conquest and colonization in what is now the highlands of Guatemala. This comparative framework shows not only how the comic series serves as an alternative archival space to educate readers on precolonial Indigenous women's history but also how comics can supplement the study of colonial documents like the *Popol Vuh*. A study of female deities across cultures in her various aspects via these texts allows readers to move beyond gender hierarchies to understand that gender operated on a spectrum, as did social agency and power for precolonial Mesoamerican women. To this end, I begin with an overview of feminist discourses on precolonial gender arrangements to set the scene for an analysis of the gendered dynamics of Mesoamerican social structures. From there, a comparative study of the visual and textual representations of the Moon Goddess and the primordial Grandmother in *Zotz* and the *Popol Vuh* highlights the gendered practices inscribed within planting, sowing, and harvest myths and rituals related to corn, providing a window into the gendered division of labor. Reading the comic alongside the *Popol Vuh* via this analytical frame highlights both the heterogeneity of Indigenous culture and the hidden histories of Indigenous women that have been too often lost in the archives. As this essay demonstrates, the reimagining of Indigenous women's history that Parada performs in *Zotz* lends significant insight into prescribed gender roles and the ways in which women operated within and beyond gender hierarchies in precolonial Mesoamerica.

Feminist Discourses on Precolonial Gender Arrangements

Beyond the limited physical documentation from this period, Indigenous women's history is clouded even further because of the patriarchal nature of the historical archive, which is true of both European accounts as well as Indigenous histories, given the male-dominated narratives that exist on both sides of the Atlantic. Precolonial mythologies vary over time and across regional cultures, creating methodological difficulty in understanding the true heterogeneity of Indigenous history and culture. In response, scholars have applied comparative approaches, as does this study, to fill in archival lacunae to gain a clearer picture of the past at present, though this strategy has its limits because the realities of lived experiences, particularly those of Indigenous women, are ephemeral and not easily preserved in archival records that inform historical reconstructions.[11] Even though the historical archive often obfuscates women's agency and power in precolonial Mesoamerica, *Zotz*, as an alternate archive, allows readers to move beyond limited representations of the past to reimagine the world in its more complex and nuanced form.

Feminist scholarship on precolonial Mesoamerica to date centers on a dominant debate in the field based on two different models that parse gendered divisions of labor as well as social, political, and economic relations: gender complementarity and gender hierarchy. While both privilege biological essentialism, which is often rejected by feminist and queer approaches to cultural studies, it is necessary to both recognize these gendered divisions and read beyond them to understand how Indigenous peoples engage with these binaries in everyday lived practices and experiences. Kellogg observes that "Mesoamerica alone can serve almost as a laboratory for examining women's lives, social patters, and statuses because the cultures of the Classic (C.E. 150–900) and Postclassic (C.E. 900–1521) offer a surprisingly broad spectrum of gendered arrangements and social variations of women."[12] Many Indigenous groups throughout Central America, Mexico, and the U.S. Southwest, including many North American First Nation peoples across the continent, view gender as a fluid spectrum in which humans negotiate cultural systems determined by constructs of gender to move through the world socially, shifting genders at different moments for different reasons. Within this cosmological frame, performing gender via ritual and other social forms of embodiment is necessary to maintain spiritual equilibrium in the physical world, a trans-Indigenous or pan-Mesoamerican phenomenon.

In his translation of the *Popol Vuh*, Allen Christenson notes that "a fundamental aspect of indigenous highland Maya religion is the belief that human beings stand as essential mediators between this world and that of their patron deities and ancestors" and goes on to explain that "sacred ritual, performed at the proper time and in a manner established by ancient precedent, is necessary to maintain this link or all creations runs the risk of collapse."[13] A direct link to precolonial social roles that embody a gender spectrum that continues to this day, for example, is evident in modern K'iche' communities in which the highest ranking and most revered patriarchs hold the title of *chuch-qajawab* (mother-fathers) and are charged with the spiritual well-being of entire family lineages or villages.[14] To maintain this equilibrium, then, many Indigenous constructs of gender allow for individuals to embody both male and female gender aspects, as is true of Mesoamerican deities.

Pete Sigal highlights the significance of the Moon Goddess for the Yucatecan Maya in relation to gender fluidity in these ritual spaces: "The preconquest Maya gendered gods in order to signify various concerns, including a division of the world into masculine and feminine. However, instead of representing the gods and goddesses as opposites, the texts present them as a duality."[15] Kellogg warns, however, that "the gendering of deities also presents a challenge to the deconstruction of their meanings, because many deities have both female and male versions or identities (with the female aspect sometimes labeled as a sister or wife), some are androgynous, and some are either solely male or female. But even those deities who are clearly male or female have complicated images and associations that are both life giving and life enhancing yet also are powerfully war-like, with negative images and associations. Sometimes these powerful and war-like female images are also demeaning."[16] As Kellogg points out here, the qualifying of gender in precolonial Mesoamerican cultures is slippery but is clearly driven by the life-death duality that defines these sociospiritual frameworks. While it is true that gender operates on a spectrum within these cosmological frames, a gendered dynamic of social organization is still evident, expressed through gendered patterns of biological, agricultural, and social reproduction.

We see this in *Zotz*, for example, in issue 2, when Kaan and Pakal are talking with a Nahua warrior before battle (see figure 1.1). The first three panels of dialogue on the page are presented to the reader via speech balloons, grounding the conversation in the physical space of the storyworld in the Nahua and Maya borderlands of Mesoamerica. This dialogue gives way to a monologue in which the balloons disappear and the warrior's speech is signaled by the text that appears in quotations overlaying images of sacred deities and domestic life, an example of how text and image advance the narrative in the comics medium. The combination of text and image in these panels allows readers to view the warrior's internal landscape. The first mental images presented to readers are those of Huitzilopochtli and Xochiquetzal, the sacred figures that preside over gendered divisions of labor in Nahua cultures for men and women, respectively. The warrior's spiritual connection to the deities is clear, as he explains that "I prayed to Huitzilopochtli and Xochiquetzal for a safe return [from battle]. I prayed so that I may see my wife and daughters back home."[17] Parada's drawings of the two deities mimic the linework and style of precolonial depictions, linking the comic to the archival sources that inform it. In the panels that follow, the warrior's narrative transports readers to a second set of mental images, these depicting a domestic space in which his wife and two daughters prepare tortillas and weave, two significant social roles assigned to women in precolonial Mesoamerica: food and textile production. As this scene depicts, the gendered division of labor within the warrior paradigm is omnipresent in Mesoamerican societies and cultures, and women were largely relegated to the domestic sphere while men went to battle.

In issue 2, depictions of Indigenous women in the comic series are complicated, however, as readers are introduced to the *ahuianime* that sometimes accompany Nahua warriors in the field, who participate by hurling insults at the opposing warriors using sexual language and gestures to emasculate them. The ahuianime,[18] often identified as "pleasure women," are associated with Ichpochtli, or Xochiquetzal, whom Parada describes as "a Goddess of

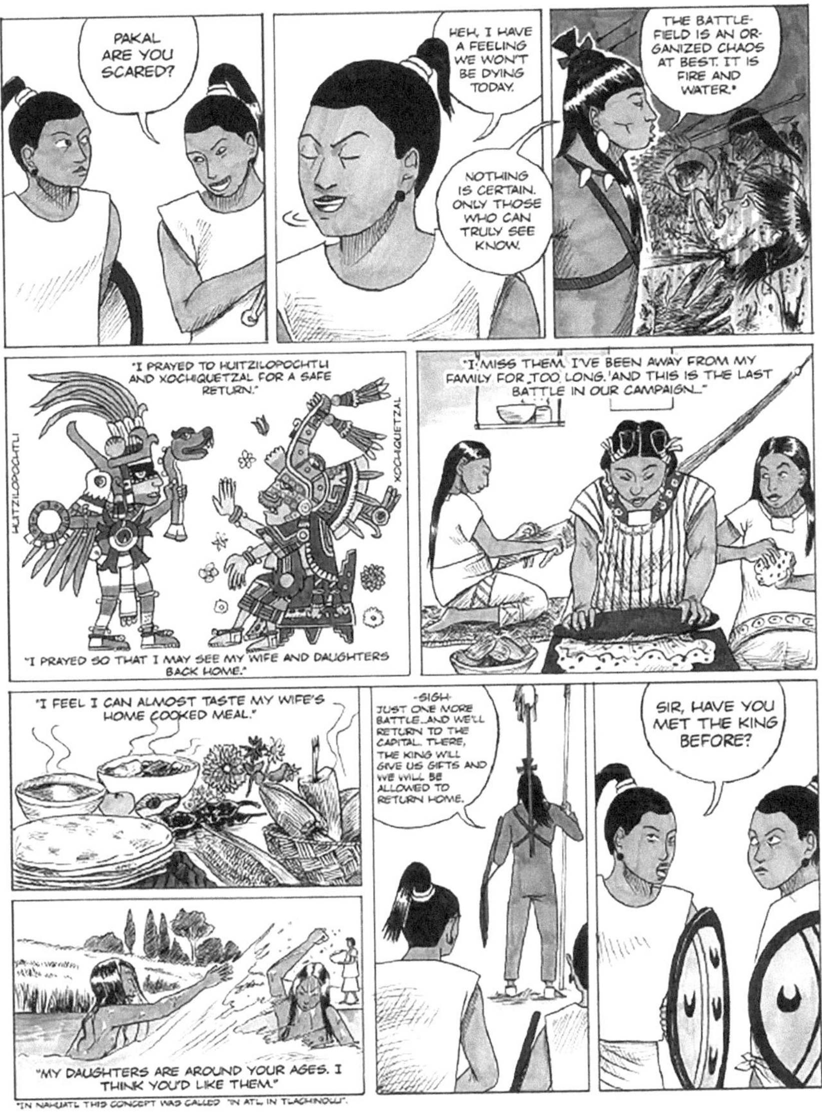

FIGURE 1.1 This page from *Zotz* no. 2 depicts the gendered division of labor within Mesoamerican warrior paradigms. Daniel Parada, *Zotz: Serpent and Shield*, no. 2 (Daniel Parada & Jorge Parada, 2011), 130.

sexuality, fertility, weaving, artisans, luxury, prostitutes and war among the Nahua people."[19] Readers are first introduced to these women in issue 2, after the battle, when Chicomecuetzpalli and Xiloxoch invite Kaan and Pakal to join them in a rite of sexual healing. It is significant to note that these acts are performed at a ritually appropriate moment postconflict, given the expectation that warriors would refrain from sex acts before battle so as to preserve their semen, their sacred life force, which they would need to fight.[20] Postbattle, and with the ceremonial guidance of the ahuianime, however, would be ritually appropriate, which Parada signals to his readers when one of the ahuianime says to "slide [Kaan's] lizard in [her] moist earth," explaining that "for tonight you are allowed to indulge."[21] While Pakal declines and has his own spiritual encounter with a "sorcerer," Kaan joins the women for a night of psychotropic trance and sex, which takes him into the depths of the Flower World.[22] As readers see in figure 1.2, the first panel shows that the drugs are working, as Kaan asks the ahuianime, "What in the . . . Am I entering the other world . . . ?" The four panels below visually represent Kaan's physiological experience of entering the psychotropic trance, as the line work around his hands indicates that his sense of his physical body movement is impaired in the first panel and that they feel like they are on fire in the second. In the final two panels of the sequence at the bottom of the page, readers become aware that Kaan has entered the Flower World, established as a separate realm in the comic via the flowers and butterflies that fill the panels. These visual symbols work to suspend the reader outside of physical time and space, transporting them from the battlefields of Mesoamerica to the Flower World.[23]

The ritual sexual encounter begins with a series of questions posed by Chicomecuetzpalli and Xiloxoch, serving in their ritual role as ahuianime, with poetic responses from Kaan typical of flower songs. Then, they ask him how he is feeling as a "young warrior"; Kaan responds, "Like a God."[24] Kaan's godlike high is an example of how humans on earth embody the characteristics of deities within rituals, which is indicative of how myth serves to prescribe social behavior in precolonial Mesoamerica—sex, in this case. The sacred embodiment of Kaan's sexual encounter is evident in several ways: First, Parada incorporates Ichpochtli (also known as Xochiquetzal) into the scene as an observer who appears in several panels throughout the sequence. The deity's presence is summoned via the ingestion of psychotropics, an example of the way in which hallucinogens served to connect humans with sacred deities. Then, as the characters engage in sexual intercourse, the ahuianime use a series of double entendres that represent sex as the agricultural reproduction of corn. The vagina, for example, is described as "fertile" or "moist" earth, while the penis is likened to a "growing corncob."[25] Although the comic is sexually explicit, precolonial society was not. Nahua and Maya cultures are generally reserved when it comes to discussing the erotic, evident in the use of agricultural euphemisms instead of direct

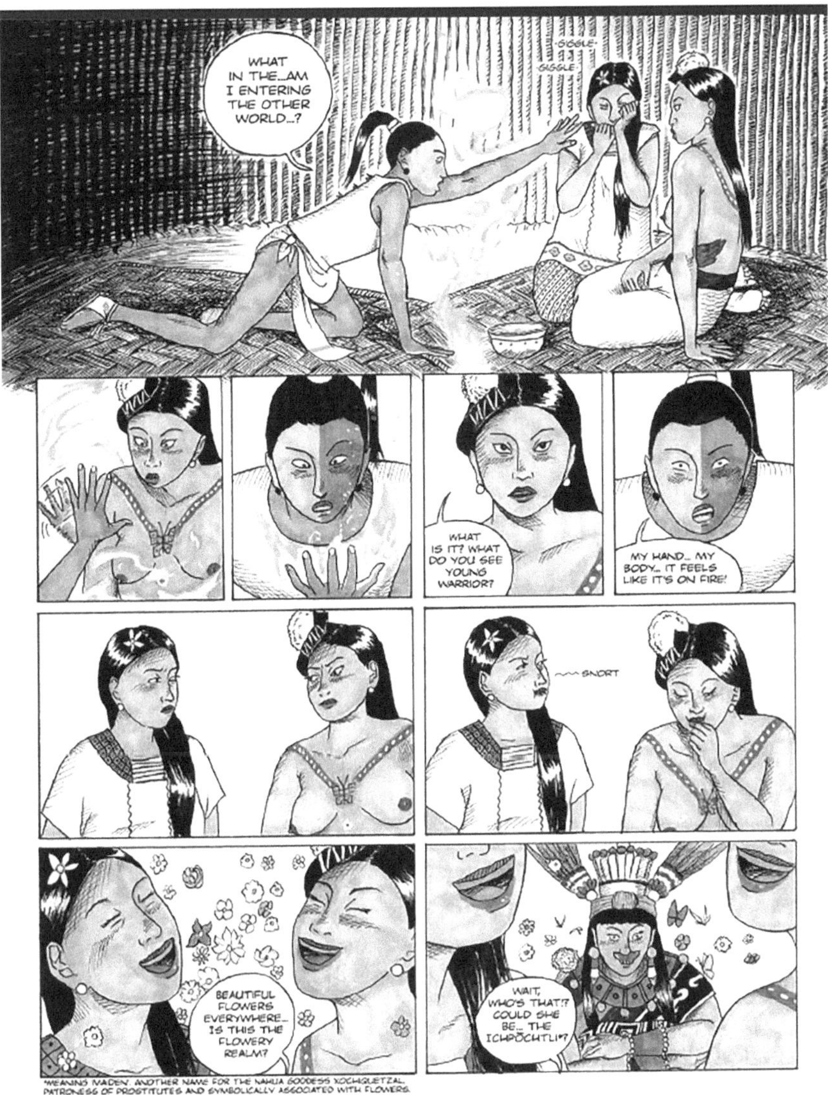

FIGURE 1.2 This page from *Zotz* no. 2 portrays Kaan's entrance into the Flower World. Parada, *Zotz* no. 2, 97.

descriptions of sex acts, as we see in the corncob metaphor with the Nahua ahuianime. This scene from the comic demonstrates how sex factors into Mesoamerican sociospiritual frameworks that use religious ritual as an everyday practice that structures life on earth, including gendered performances that sustain biological and agricultural reproduction and war. Depictions of the Flower World, and Kaan's experience in it, highlight the connections between war, sex, and agriculture that are central to precolonial Mesoamerican cosmologies.

The Sun and the Moon: Gendered Astronomy in *Zotz*

Issue 1 of *Zotz: Serpent and Shield* begins on the day 4 Lord (ca. 3114 BCE in European historical time), when "the three hearthstones were placed. Marking the beginning of the world."[26] Framing mythological narratives via this notion of primordial time is typical of Mesoamerican storytelling and sets the sacred precedent for Kaan and Pakal. The Hero Twins are a mythological duo who permeate Indigenous cosmologies throughout Central America, Mexico, and the U.S. Southwest. In the *Zotz* storyworld, Kaan and Pakal are from Chan Village, located in the highlands of present-day Guatemala. As the pair leave their village to avenge the death of their father, they find themselves at the crossroads of many different Indigenous groups that fall under the larger umbrella terms of Maya and Nahua peoples. In this geographic space, Parada incorporates a diverse set of mythologies, practices, and traditions, bringing multiple cultures into dialogue with one another. The comic series is fictionalized, but it draws upon historical accounts of Parada's version of the Maya Hero Twins' origin story that depicts Kaan's transformation into a Bat God, or Zotz, which means bat in many Mayan languages. The name Zotz derives from Kamezotz, a reference to the Death Bats that inhabit Xibalba—a cavernous underworld in Maya sacred cosmology—in the *Popol Vuh*. While the dominant storyline of the series closely follows the traditional story arc of the Hero Twins, Kaan and Pakal are guided in their journey by the Moon Goddess, whom they turn to in moments of difficulty as they come into their own as sacred warriors and community leaders in their spirit quest to avenge the death of their father. The significance of the Moon Goddess in Maya culture is clear in *Zotz*, as she makes her first appearance in issue 1's opening sequence. In this scene, Nachan, Kaan and Pakal's father, sits down with his family and community to listen to the tale of Our Lady the Moon.[27]

Prior to this moment, the *Zotz* storyworld invited readers into the sacred space of the Maya, when the narrator—whose presence is suggested on the page via an outlined form filled with black ink, a continuation of the all-black page—opens the comic by deploying the traditional invitation to begin a tale of the Maya Hero Twins, saying, "Let's drink to them."[28] As readers see throughout the series, Parada uses black ink in full-page spreads and gutters to signal to the reader that they are being transported from the present time of the storyworld to the primordial time of myths, emphasizing the way in which these dimensions operate simultaneously in precolonial Mesoamerica. In this case, the black ink symbolizes the spiritual dimension of the cave, as the narrator speaks from the shadows of a cavernous opening to invite the reader into the *Zotz* storyworld, an echo of the same invitation to begin the sacred Maya myth associated with the first two sets of primordial Hero Twins in the *Popol Vuh*. The narrator's toast to the Hero Twins, traditionally with a drink of fermented plant juice or cacao, guides the reader from the mouth of the cave into the storyworld. This is another of the many examples in which the comic represents traditional cultural practices. From there, the reader is transported to the community circle in a panel that centers on a fire made from the three hearthstones marking the sacredness of social space for the Maya, present throughout the homes and community circles in the comic series.[29] The storyteller wears a headdress made of a deer's head and feathers, possibly from that of the quetzal, one of the most sacred birds to the Maya in and around present-day Guatemala.

Next, the story cuts to a full-page spread, comprising two loosely defined panels that begin the tale of Our Lady the Moon, with the storyteller pictured on the upper half of the page and the moon glyph in the center of the page.[30] Thc moon glyph, representing the Moon Goddess, provides a transition from the top panel to the bottom that orients the reader to the story of the Moon Goddess. In the lower panel, Xbalanque—the Sun God, the Hunter, the War God—is shooting his blowgun, a consistent visual trope that follows the Hero Twins throughout oral and image-based narratives. In the lower panel, Xbalanque is surrounded by all black, a symbolic emptying of physical time in the comic that indicates to the reader that they are entering the sacred space of the myth of the Sun, the Moon, and Venus. As the myth unfolds, Parada continues to use black ink to fill the space of the gutter to suspend the reader outside of the physical time and space of the storyworld to place them in the narrative time of mythology. The story of the Sun and the Moon is one of the core mythological narratives that define a shared pan-Mesoamerican pantheon. In this myth, the sun corresponds to one or both Hero Twins, depending on the variation in question, and the moon corresponds to the Goddess in her various aspects. These aspects of the moon also relate to engendered correspondences to lightness and darkness: lightness is associated with male aspects, linked to the sun and the full moon (the moon in its brightest phase), while darkness is associated with female aspects linked to the underworld, often associated with caves within Maya and Nahua sacred geography and the sociospiritual space of birth and death. The waning phases of the moon refer to the progression in age of the female deity as she progresses through life in her role as wife, mother, and grandmother.

The *Zotz* storyworld incorporates the Q'eqchi' version of the myth, in contrast with the K'iche' variation presented in the *Popol Vuh,* in which Xbalanque, "discovered Xt'actani, daughter of the powerful mountain king . . . and her beauty was unparalleled. When her father was away, Xbalanque's passions took hold. He kidnapped Xt'actani."[31] As the legend goes, Xt'actani's father, the Mountain King, turns Xbalanque into a hummingbird as punishment, which Xt'actani "puts it in her blouse and weaves the hummingbird's image into a skirt for herself. The hummingbird in her skirt then takes human form as Xbalanque. He then sleeps with her. The father discovers hair strands and realizes what has taken place."[32] The Mountain King ultimately allows the two to marry, first requiring that Xbalanque pay the bridal price, represented here as four labors: (1) to gather firewood for the home, (2) to lay out a maize field, (3) to build a house, and (4) to bring food. The way in which the bridal price is laid out corresponds to traditional precolonial practices and lends insight into the political, economic, and cultural gendered roles for men and women in Indigenous social structures. While male aspects of society are often associated with the planter, hunter, and warrior, as we see in Xbalanque's prematrimonial tasks, Xt'actani represents the role of women as prescribed by this mythological narrative, which is linked to women's biological reproductive capacity, evident in the sexualized interaction between the two.

Once the bridal price is complete and Xbalanque and Xt'actani are married, "the hummingbird had found his nectar, his flower," a poetic insinuation for sexual intercourse (see figure 1.3). In figure 1.3, Xbalanque, the Sun, and Xt'actani, the Moon, symbolically unite as they bring their hands together, representative of their cyclical dance that links night with day and female with male, in the reproductive cycle that sustains life for humans on earth. Again, black ink appears in the gutters of the full-page spread to mark the significance of this primordial pairing and their place in mythological time. The myth of the Sun and the Moon represented by Xbalanque and Xt'actani tells the tale of two celestial objects entwined in a gendered relationship that gives rise to the first dawn, the planting and sowing of the corn, the formation of humans and animals, and the reproductive ecosystems for life on earth.

The *Popol Vuh* presents another version of the Moon Goddess typical of the K'iche' in which she is impregnated by One Hunahpu, one of the primordial Hero Twins (paired with Seven Hunahpu). In this mythological

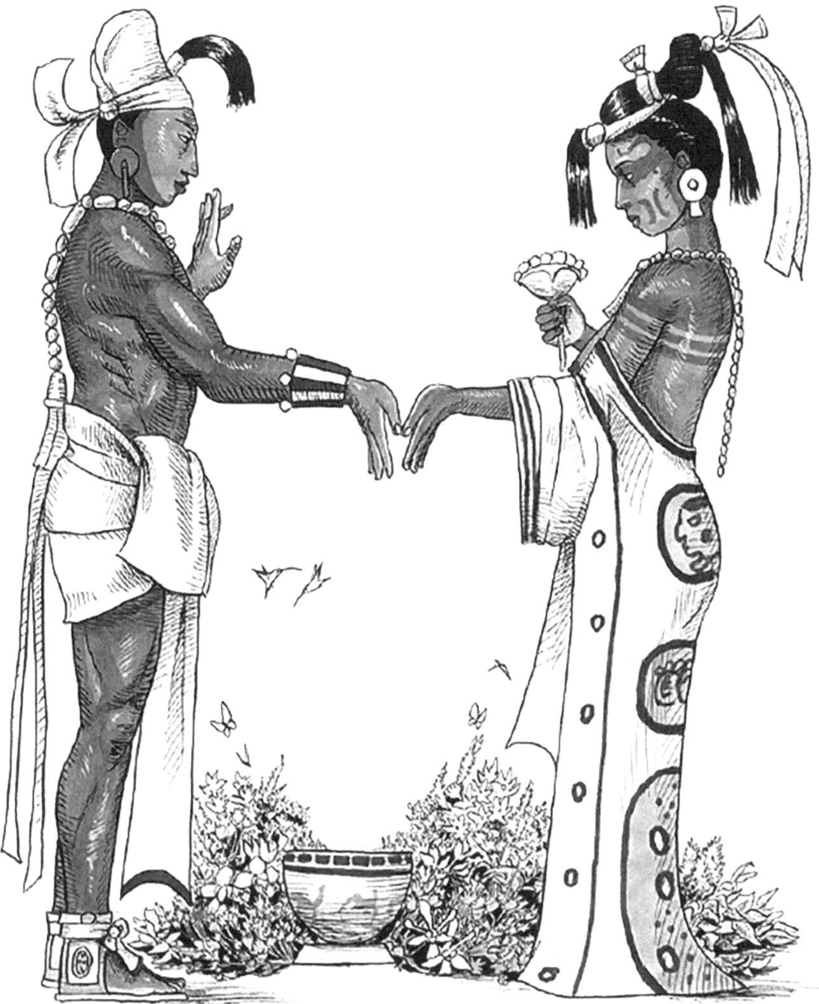

FIGURE 1.3 A panel displaying the cosmic union of Xbalanque and Xt'actani. Parada, *Zotz* no. 1, 23.

structure, Lady Blood is another aspect of the Moon Goddess, daughter of an underworld lord of Xibalba, who reaches up her right hand to receive the saliva of One Hunahpu's skull hanging from a fruit tree, which leaves her pregnant with Hunahpu and Xbalanque. When her father, Gathered Blood, discovers her secret, he, along with fellow deities One Death and Seven Death of Xibalba, sentence her to be sacrificed. Ultimately, Lady Blood tricks the lords of Xibalba into thinking they had received her heart by collecting red tree sap to congeal into a heart-like substance covered in "blood," allowing her to escape from the underworld to Earth, ultimately giving birth to Hunahpu and Xbalanque. Christenson explains that in this mythological structure, "the maiden, Lady Blood, stood as an intermediary. As the daughter of one of the principal lords of death, she belonged to the darkness of the underworld. As the consort of One Hunahpu, she had the potential to create new life from death."[33] Blood, and its lunar associations with menses, is a sacred substance across Mesoamerican culture and is a significant source of female agency and power. Paloma Martínez-Cruz, for example, makes the case for "Mexica Vulva Envy" and shows that "in a society that glorified bloodshed, these examples [of vulva envy] suggest a cultural disposition that instead of subordinating feminine fecundity, embraced women's reproductive capacity as an admirable condition of being female."[34] Women's reproductive experience in bearing children is likened to that of warriors in battle, the ultimate expression of sex and war in the life-death duality that characterizes these cosmovisions. This agency and power, of course, had limits within the male-dominated warrior paradigm in which they are inscribed.

By reading the Q'eqchi' myth presented in *Zotz* alongside the K'iche' variation documented in the *Popol Vuh*, readers begin to understand the heterogeneity of precolonial Mesoamerican cultures. Looking at the Moon Goddess provides insight into the gendered dynamics of biological and agricultural reproduction in the period. Ultimately, the sun and the moon represent the male/female reproductive pairing that is central to the creation story. Planting, sowing, and harvest rituals associated with the creation myth evoke deeply ingrained social and biological roles prescribed for men and women in precolonial Mesoamerica. Oswaldo Chinchilla Mazariegos situates the myth as "an extended explanation about the origin of the sun, the moon, and the maize—the sowing and the dawning—that brought about the onset of a new era and its inhabitants, moral people who responded to the gods' demands and provided for them."[35] Within traditional Maya cosmovisions, the sowing and the dawning are interrelated processes that allow for everyday sustenance and reproduction, and both are intimately connected to Indigenous gendered social, biological, and agricultural interactions. The complementarity of the gendered correspondences inscribed within the creation myth of the Moon Goddess and the Sun God points to the sociocultural values related to gendered roles in war, medicine, and domesticity, including food science and childbirth, for which Indigenous women played fundamental roles.

Moreover, these examples from the comic highlight the life-death duality that often characterizes female deities. In this way, the comic series not only provides readers an introduction to precolonial visual repertoires but also serves as a dynamic space to better understand Indigenous women's history and culture in the region.

The Primordial Grandmother: Cycles of Life and Death

Maya notions of gender are intimately connected with the creation myth that centers on the primordial Grandfather/Grandmother, which closely relates to the dawning of the world, the creation of humans, as well as the essential life-giving function that the sowing and planting of the corn provides. In the *Popol Vuh*, the Grandfather/Grandmother duality is central to the mythological frame of the K'iche'. The Grandmother, Xmucane, is part of the primordial pair of the Grandfather/Grandmother, Xpiyacoc and Xmucane, "defender, protector, twice a midwife, twice a matchmaker."[36] This highland version of the Maya Grandmother is likely linked to Ixchel, the lowland Mayan Goddess, whom Tedlock identifies as "an elderly goddess of medicine, childbirth, and weaving whose name is chak chel in the codices and ix chel or chakal ix chel in alphabetic documents."[37] Within this linguistic frame, the prefix "x" signifies a feminine aspect, which we see in Xmucane, Xt'actani, and Xkitza (the primordial Grandmother in the Q'eqchi' mythological structure) to different aspects of the feminine. The feminine signifier "x" is complicated further as we turn to the figures of Xpiyacoc, the Grandfather, and Xbalanque, both the Sun God linked to the warrior and the jaguar and one of the two Hero Twins in Maya cosmology. Tedlock also points out that "the male member of the pair, Xpiyacoc, has a feminine aspect that is indicated not only by the 'x,' but also by the fact that he is subsumed under the double epithet 'Grandmother of the Day, Grandmother of Light.' This recalls the fact that contemporary diviners (of either sex) are symbolically androgynous, female on the left side of the body and male on the right."[38] The Grandfather/Grandmother duality is central to the mythological frame of this religious tradition, also described as the "mother-father of life, of humankind, giver of breath, giver of heart, bearer, up bringer in the light that lasts of those born in the light, begotten in the light; worrier, knower of everything, whatever there is: sky-earth, lake-sea."[39] The Grandmother also plays a central role to the creation myth, as she grinds the corn nine times, a significant number related to the human gestation cycle, to create the human form that we know today, another example of the connection between biological and agricultural reproduction within this cosmological frame.

Xmucane appears in *Zotz* at the end of issue 3, when she is summoned by a Maya Tzotzil woman, who works to heal Kaan's wounds after a battle gone wrong. Most of the issue centers on a major battle between Tlacao Kingdom and the Teotl Empire, with Kaan and Pakal fighting with the Mictlan raiders. The warriors of Teotl are betrayed by their allies and are on the losing end of the encounter. Kaan awakens from battle to find himself in a small village, led by Bol, another Tzotzil woman, who rescued him from the battlefield. While it was not common for women to assume positions of political power and leadership, the historical record shows that there are some cases. Kellogg, for example, finds that "in addition to holding these positions, women gained both respect and access to material goods through their activities in homes, markets, neighborhoods, song houses, and temples. These material items and property rights attached to or expressed through them, by bequeathal, gifting, or investment, afforded Mexica women a degree of independence."[40] Moreover, this scene highlights the significant role that women played as healers and herbalists in their communities. As Kaan comes to, he is greeted by a young woman named Chib Chon, a physician and herbalist, who also calls on Xmucane, the primordial Grandmother, to heal Kaan. In this sequence, Parada provides readers with an opportunity to consider both the ways in which lived human experiences do not always align with prescribed gender roles via Bol's matriarchal leadership and the significant role women play as healers in their communities, requiring an extensive knowledge of local pharmacopeia. Incorporating these examples of female agency and power into the comic series opens a space in which readers can deepen their understanding of Indigenous women's history and culture in the region to highlight the relationship between gender and power, including the ways in which women both sustain their communities and exist beyond patrilineal norms and customs.

Zotz presents another variation of the primordial Grandmother, Xkitza, in issue 1, a Q'eqchi' myth in which the deity does not give life but rather operates as a cannibalistic figure.[41] Parada continues to employ the visual strategy of the black gutter to signal to readers that they have entered mythological time within the storyworld, which opens with the adoption of the primordial Hero Twins, Xbalanque and Hunhapu, by Xkitza. This variation is a cannibalistic version of a postmenopausal female deity who overfed her lover instead of feeding the Hero Twins, going so far as to attempt to eat the twins themselves. Hunahpu and Xbalanque ultimately trick Xkitza into eating her lover and then kill her after she loses at a game of riddles.[42] The erotic nature of cannibalism in this myth associates the eating of flesh (animal or human meat) with the carnality of sexual encounters, including an episode in which Xkitza eats the penis of her lover before the brothers kill and eat her. While female deities are often linked to their reproductive power to give life, this Q'eqchi' version of the Grandmother points to the opposite and complementary role of female deities to bring death. As readers study the primordial Grandmother across cultures, these variations point to the way in which female deities operated on a spectrum as complementary forces necessary to maintain the balance between life and death, understood in this sociospiritual framework as the life-death duality that maintains equilibrium between the earthly sphere and the spiritual realm.

Conclusion

Parada's visual portfolio extends beyond the comic series and includes a rich digital repertoire that further depicts precolonial Mesoamerican women, including typical clothing and hairstyles of different periods that offers more detailed information. At first glance, aesthetic representations of women in the series and the digital portfolio appear more a modern sexualization of women's bodies than a faithful representation of beautification practices in the period. Perhaps this is a product of the hypersexualization contemporary readers of comics have seen of women in the medium as a general practice. Upon further research, it appears as though Parada inks a fairly accurate portrayal in his representation of female breasts in the comic. Whether a woman would wear a top in precolonial Mesoamerican cultures varied greatly over time and across cultures, often determined by class, geography, and climate.[43] In the archaeological record, bare breasts often appear in sexualized mythological settings, such as the reproductive pairing inherent in the creation myth, or to represent the life-giving role of women as it relates to biological fertility.

Visitors find more examples of female agency and power in precolonial Mesoamerica in Parada's digital portfolio,[44] such as the Queen of Cofitachequi, "a kingdom in Routh Carolina in 1540," and Lady K'abel, a "royal woman from the snake dynasty of the Kan Kingdom (Calakmul) who married Kinich Balam II of Waka."[45] Visitors also find images of Tlahuelpuchi, "a vampiric figure in Nahua folklore in the Mexican state of Tlaxcala,"[46] and Tztitzimitl, "star 'demons' who devour the sun during eclipses in the Aztec worldview."[47] Tlahuelpuchi and Tztitzimitl further exemplify the death aspect of some female deities, necessary to balance the life-death duality that frames Mesoamerican society and culture, like that of the cannibalistic Grandmother in Q'eqchi' mythology.

The analysis presented in this essay of the myths and ritual practices centered on the Sun, the Moon, and maize allows readers to weave together a better understanding of Indigenous women in sixteenth-century Mesoamerica to reconstruct these often-fractured narratives, given the patriarchal nature of historical archives. Studying Parada's work alongside the *Popol Vuh* provides a comparative approach that begins to educate readers on the heterogeneity of precolonial Maya and Nahua cultures. These examples of the different aspects of the Moon Goddess and the primordial Grandmother show not only the import of women's work as it relates to ritual food planting and harvesting, central to community cohesion and sustenance in the Mesoamerican world, but also the way in which female deities serve to balance cycles of life and death. More specifically, Parada's work highlights how women sustain their communities via their significant roles in war, medicine, and domesticity, including food science and childbirth. Women's lived experiences, however, are not limited to these roles, and it is through a reimagining of the historical archive that we can begin to better understand the nuance and complexity of gender and power, as we see in the matriarchal Maya village where Kaan finds himself after a lost battle in issue 3. *Zotz: Serpent and Shield* offers readers a deep dive into precolonial Mesoamerica as Parada restructures dominant and/or colonial representations of conquest and colonization to preserve and reproduce a rich cultural heritage that contributes to the inherent diversity and heterogeneity of Latinx studies.

Notes

1 Daniel Parada, *Zotz: Serpent and Shield* no. 1 (Daniel Parada & Jorge Parada, 2011), 1.
2 Parada, *Zotz* no. 1, 2.
3 Jessica Rutherford, "Visualizing an Alternative Mesoamerican Archive: Daniel Parada's Comic Series *Zotz* in Historical Perspective," in *Graphic Indigeneity: Comics in the Americas and Australia*, ed. Frederick Luis Aldama (Jackson: University Press of Mississippi, 2020), 168–180, 171–172.
4 Parada, *Zotz* no. 2, 7.
5 Karen Bassie-Sweet, *Maya Sacred Geography and the Creator Deities* (Norman: University of Oklahoma Press, 2008), 53–83.

6 For an overview of the variants of these solar and lunar myths among different Mesoamerican traditions, see Oswaldo Chinchilla Mazariegos, *Art and Myth of the Ancient Maya* (New Haven, CT: Yale University Press, 2017), 159–184.

7 See Allen J. Christenson, *Popol Vuh: The Sacred Book of the Maya* (Norman: University of Oklahoma Press, 2007), 82–166.

8 On Mayan women rulers, see Erika A. Hewitt, "What's in a Name: Gender, Power, and Classic Maya Women Rulers," *Ancient Mesoamerica* 10, no. 2 (Fall 1999): 251–262.

9 Susan Kellogg, *Weaving the Past: A History of Latin American's Indigenous Women from the Prehispanic Period to the Present* (Oxford: Oxford University Press, 2005), 18.

10 This essay pulls from two annotated translations of the *Popol Vuh* from the original Maya text: Christenson, *Popol Vuh* and Dennis Tedlock, *Popol Vuh: The Definitive Edition of the Mayan Book of the Dawn of Life and the Glories of the Gods and Kings* (New York: Touchstone, 1996).

11 On the performative nature of gender within Indigenous social relations, see Rosemary A. Joyce, *Gender and Power in Prehispanic Mesoamerica* (Austin: University of Texas Press, 2000); Kellogg, *Weaving the Past*; Inga Clendinnen, *Aztecs* (Cambridge: Cambridge University Press, 1991); Miranda K. Stockett, "On the Importance of Difference: Re-Envisioning Sex and Gender in Ancient Mesoamerica," *World Archeology* 37, no. 4 (2005): 566–578; and Traci Arden, "Studies of Gender in the Prehispanic Americas," *Journal of Archaeological Research* 16, no. 1 (2007): 1–35.

12 Kellogg, *Weaving the Past*, 18–19.

13 Christenson, *Popol Vuh*, 71n66.

14 Christenson, *Popol Vuh*, 184n481.

15 Pete Sigal, *From Moon Goddesses to Virgins: The Colonization of Yucatecan Maya Sexual Desire* (Austin: University of Texas Press, 2020), 95–96.

16 Kellogg, *Weaving the Past*, 29.

17 Parada, *Zotz* no. 2, 130.

18 For a detailed description, see Clendinnen, *Aztecs*, 231–236.

19 Parada, *Zotz* no. 2, 137.

20 For Nahua metaphors related to "sex and the earth," see Pete Sigal, *The Flower and the Scorpion* (Durham, NC: Duke University Press, 2011), 38–40.

21 Parada, *Zotz* no. 2, 101.

22 The study of Mesoamerican Flower Worlds reveals a rich heterogeneity of cultural belief systems that evoke these sacred spaces, a topic explored in detail in a recent study edited by Michael D. Mathiowetz and Andrew D. Turner, *Flower Worlds: Religions, Aesthetics, and Ideology in Mesoamerica and the American Southwest* (Tucson: University of Arizona Press, 2021). For a study of Mayan Flower Worlds, see also Karl A. Taube, "Flower Mountain: Concepts of Life, Beauty, and Paradise among the Classic Maya," *Anthropology and Aesthetics* 45 (Spring 2004): 69–98.

23 Parada, *Zotz* no. 2, 91–116.

24 Parada, *Zotz* no. 2, 100.

25 Parada, *Zotz* no. 2, 101.

26 Parada, *Zotz* no. 1, 1.

27 Parada, *Zotz* no. 1, 16.

28 Parada, *Zotz* no. 1, 2.

29 Parada, *Zotz* no. 1, 17.

30 Parada, *Zotz* no. 1, 18.

31 Parada, *Zotz* no. 1, 20–21.
32 Parada, *Zotz* no. 1, 21.
33 Christenson, *Popol Vuh*, 130n278.
34 Paloma Martinez-Cruz, *Women and Knowledge in Mesoamerica: From East L.A. to Anahuac* (Tucson: University of Arizona Press, 2011), 31.
35 Mazariegos, *Art and Myth of the Ancient Maya*, 57.
36 Christenson, *Popol Vuh*, 63.
37 Tedlock, *Popol Vuh*, 216–217.
38 Tedlock, *Popol Vuh*, 217.
39 Christenson, *Popol Vuh*, 64.
40 Kellogg, *Weaving the Past*, 27.
41 Parada, *Zotz* no. 1, 22–26.
42 Parada, *Zotz* no. 1, 19–20.
43 See Andrea J. Stone, "Keeping Abreast of the Maya: A Study of the Female Body in Maya Art," *Ancient Mesoamerica* 22, no. 1 (Spring 2011): 167–183.
44 Daniel Parada, "Queen of Cofitachequi," August 1, 2023, https://daniel-parada.artstation.com/projects/VgbElX?album_id=3685861.
45 Daniel Parada, "Lady K'abel," August 1, 2023, https://daniel-parada.artstation.com/projects/KrYBNy?album_id=3685861.
46 Daniel Parada, "Tlahuelpuchi," August 1, 2023, https://daniel-parada.artstation.com/projects/xz9erX?album_id=3685861.
47 Daniel Parada, "Tztitzimitl," August 1, 2023, https://daniel-parada.artstation.com/projects/9eKlYo?album_id=3685861.

2

Filling the Holes of Cuban Memory

Remembering the Revolution and Exile in the Comics Classroom

STEPHANIE CONTRERAS

Inverna Lockpez and Dean Haspiel's *Cuba: My Revolution* (2010), published by DC's imprint Vertigo, is a literary and visual tool that mobilizes Lockpez's memories and traumas about Fidel Castro's revolutionary-era Cuba.[1] Although the revolutionary government fervently positioned itself against U.S. media culture and promoted social realism as its preferred aesthetic to render the successes of the revolution, Lockpez and Haspiel use these tools to graphically challenge time and space while engaging readers with a past that questions the official Cuban history. Lockpez's narrative recalls major historical events, such as Castro's rise to power, as well as the author's time as a loyal revolutionary, a volunteer medic at the Bay of Pigs, a prisoner of the government, and a censored visual artist. Her recollections, which are visually rendered by the colorist José Villarrubia in a gray palette and accentuated with vibrant splashes of red, black, and pink, are often noted for their "graphic" nature, a comment referring mostly to the amount of violent and visceral content that marks this period of her life rather than the medium used to portray her memories. While Lockpez's memories focus entirely on her life during the Cuban Revolution and concludes with her escape from the island, the comic facilitates the representation of multiple, simultaneous temporalities, traumas, spaces, histories, and identities.

In this essay, I show how *Cuba: My Revolution* can be incorporated in the classroom not as a historical text but as a collective and creative project that is not concerned with the legalistic definition of truth telling but rather intends to present "facts with affect" and embrace the ambivalence in between.[2] As a result, my approach is centered primarily on the following research questions: What and how are Lockpez's specific trauma experiences (re)presented throughout the text? And who and what are the collective and creative forces bringing awareness to her specific experiences and participating in memory transmission? Furthermore, I explore how the text offers a unique and permeable representation of the revolution to recast the problematics of its representation and the continued censorship of artists in Cuba from the perspective of a Cuban artist.

Cuba: My Revolution participates in a collective memory that reformulates and reclaims Cuban national identity by (re)presenting past events and questioning official representations disseminated by the revolutionary government. Throughout the text, Lockpez moves in and out of the narrative. She channels her testimony behind a fictional avatar/pseudonym, "Sonya," while also incorporating her artistic fingerprint as Inverna Lockpez through the abstract sketches that mark the three parts of her graphic novel in addition to the final photograph that closes the text. When teaching the text, I focus on the distinct approach taken to distinguish it from the typical comic book. For example, the hardcover, the greater number of pages, and the absence of advertisements in the text offer a sharp contrast to other comics, such as *Border Town*, another DC/Vertigo publication that centers on Latina/o/x immigration and identity.[3] Given the testimonial foundation and creative liberties taken within the text, Louis A. Pérez Jr. brings up a stimulating concern surrounding the Library of Congress's classification of *Cuba: My Revolution*: "It has assigned to *Cuba: My Revolution* a PN call number, placing it in the subclass 'Literature (General).' However, *Che: A Graphic Biography* was assigned an F call letter, marking it as 'History of the Americas.'"[4] This observation begs a question: At what point do cultural institutions draw the line between reality and fiction? This is not the first time that such a concern has marked the reading of a graphic novel. The Pulitzer Prize committee invented a new category for *Maus II* after being unable to categorize it as fiction or nonfiction. As a historian, Pérez cautions against the usage of comics as pedagogical tools for teaching history: "The comic medium purports to historical representation through imagined dialogue and imaginary artwork: the past as a figment of the imagination. The most tenuous claim to plausibility—'based on a true story' (or for our purposes, 'based on a true history')—seems to offer sufficient warrant to provide the comic medium with access to the classroom. This is to consign the study of a past rendered by artists unencumbered by disciplinary allegiance and narrators untethered from disciplinary canons. Not necessarily a bad thing if the purpose of purchase is principally entertainment and enjoyment."[5]

Although his hesitance is significant and should be considered when approaching any text as historical, it is also fundamental to see *Cuba: My Revolution* as a product of historical amnesia and as a reaction to it. For historians, there is a distinction between memory and history. History is seen as what happened and memory as what is remembered about what happened. Nevertheless, in the absence of records, documents, and cultural artifacts, it is imperative to remember that artistic mediums are employed by survivors to ground historical understanding. Furthermore, the purposes of purchase can be many, including a desire to understand and empathize with those who have been written out of history. Through the exploration of memory and postmemory, students can engage with cultural representations that question and shape notions of identity, trauma, and healing. Given that Pérez's critique captures the tensions relevant to this analysis, I use it to guide our reading and refer to it again as a tool for discussion in the comic classroom.

The Role of Censorship and Cubanía in *Cuba: My Revolution*

Cuba: My Revolution serves to think about Cuban experiences and brings attention to the cultural, economic, historical, political, and social issues that have affected and still affect Cubans on the island and their diaspora. As we think about undisciplining Latinx literature, we want to consider the complexities and nuances of the heterogenous communities and people that fall under the umbrella term "Latinx." For this reason, consideration and effort should be taken to contextualize relevant information regarding socioeconomic status, race, language, nationality, religion, cultural norms, and so on within the country of origin, the United States, and between immigrant populations. In the case of Cuban and Cuban American studies, generational factors also offer a great deal of insight. For instance, for some Cuban exiles, especially those from the earlier waves, a return to Cuba is out of the question if a Castro or fellow revolutionary is in power. At this point, the earlier generations have mostly died or lost hope. For newer waves of Cuban immigrants, especially more recent arrivals, maintaining ties with family and friends left behind fosters a desire and need to return to their native land. According to Pérez Firmat, for the former group, composed of exiles, expatriates, and émigrés, panethnic or hyphenated labels are typically rejected, thereby complicating their participation in Latino/a/x literature, as some authors (e.g., Herberto Padilla, Daína Chaviano, and Reinaldo Arenas) favor(ed) the designation of their nationality as Cubans.[6] Consequently, compelling connections between Cuban and Cuban American authors can be lost within the Latinx literary category and parameters. The following section contextualizes the historical experiences and specificity of the text to shed light on the aesthetic practices taken to yield its production.

Given that Lockpez lived in Cuba until the late 1960s, students can research the featured historical events, revolutionary leaders, and evolution of her revolutionary ideals. They can follow the three parts of her testimony, which are divided in chronological order: part 1 (December 1958–December 1961), part 2 (April 1961–July 1962), and part 3 (October 1962–September 1966). Her narrative begins with Fidel Castro's capture of Havana on New Year's Eve 1958. Some of the historical context offered in the first part includes Castro's victorious march into Havana; the executions of the batistianos (supporters of Batista's regime); the surveillance of the watchdog organization, such as the Committee for the Defense of the Revolution (CDR); the nationalization of all private companies; the suppression of religion in Cuba; and Operation Peter Pan. I adapt the jigsaw strategy to encourage cooperative learning and improve student motivation. This technique is also especially useful for instructors who are unfamiliar with Cuban history and are colearning with their students. Prior to discussing the text, I divide students into three-person groups and assign each group one of the historical events or others discussed later. As part of their homework, they research and prepare a five-minute presentation on their assigned segment. The following day, I form "expert groups" by assigning one student from each group and allotting twenty to twenty-five minutes to discuss the main points of their segment. For example, because Operation Peter Pan was the largest exodus of unaccompanied minors in the Western Hemisphere (fourteen thousand children) and was backed by the U.S. government and the Roman Catholic Church, students tend to have several questions and are curious to know about its aftermath. The group that assigned this topic can review the Operation Pedro Pan webpage, which has archival photos, testimonios, and a list of biographical resources;[7] listen to and react to Cuban American artist Willy Chirino's experience as a Pedro Pan in the unofficial Cuban exile anthem, "Nuestro día (ya viene llegando)";[8] and research Grupo Areíto's *Contra Viento y Marea*, which includes the testimonios of some of the children who strongly criticized the operation and felt themselves to be alienated from U.S. society.[9] After reading the first part of the comic, I ask students to connect their findings, discuss their implications for the reading, and explain their reactions.

Additionally, highlighting Lockpez's author's note offers an opportunity to contextualize Cuban migration, laws, and policies in the United States while also allowing students to identify the intention behind the book's creation and relevancy today. Furthermore, the author's short bio brings insight into not only the way she previously silenced her trauma by forgetting her memories but also the active process of reconstructing them through the testimonial process:

> There were aspects of my life I preferred to forget because they were too painful to remember. In spite of myself, flashes of past experiences appeared, and in the process of reconstructing them I learned that testimony is important to the ideals and endurance of the human spirit, as well as to my own. This book is for the people of Cuba everywhere who have not been heard, and who have endured economic hardship, who long to express themselves through art without the fear of imprisonment, and who still fight for the return of freedom once enjoyed.[10]

Unlike the autobiographical text of fellow Cuban exile Reinaldo Arenas, *Antes que anochezca*, her text is not meant to condemn Fidel Castro or to incriminate the Cuban government. Instead, she communicates a desire to serve as a beacon for oppressed Cubans. She foments awareness and solidarity with this specific group of Cubans while also highlighting the existing artistic oppression in Cuba. The usage of "still" in the final sentence breaks with the narrative past of the testimony and emphasizes a cyclical pattern of constant struggle and oppression in the present, communicating to the reader the story's sense of urgency and relevancy in the present. It is often noted that the United States has experienced a steady influx of Cubans since the triumph of Castro's revolution in 1959. Nevertheless, a relevant detail to emphasize is that the largest Cuban migration wave was documented in 2022 as a surge of Cubans attempted to cross the U.S. southern border.[11] The Cuban Research Institute of Florida International University has several resources on their website, such as "A Postrevolution Exodus Ebbs and Flows," a table that visualizes the numerous phases, relevant landmark events (e.g., historical exile, the Mariel exodus, the Balsero crisis, etc.), and number of emigrants.[12] If time permits, a jigsaw format can be assigned for students to present on these waves as well or instead of the first recommendation.

It's important to highlight that in the first part of the text, Sonya is a seventeen-year-old medical student who is enamored by the charismatic leader Fidel Castro and the values of the revolution. Her desire to become a physician is driven by her resolve as a revolutionary; after witnessing a white dove land on Fidel Castro's shoulder during his speech, she proclaims, "Oh my God, he's the chosen one! I'll serve as a physician—art can wait!"[13] Consequently, she joins the Cuban militia and later volunteers as a medic during the Bay of Pigs Invasion in 1961. This U.S.-backed invasion of Cuba was a failed preemptive strike and attempt to overthrow Castro, which was led by high officers in the CIA and executed by Brigade 2506, a CIA-sponsored group of Cuban exiles. During this first part, Sonya relates her denial of certain warnings, like witnessing her father lose his pharmaceutical company, shortages of medical personnel and equipment, and the government's increasing dependence on the Soviet Union. Reviewing this first part of the text with students and grounding them in the historical background will aid them as they make sense of Sonya's disillusionment with the revolution and its leaders. Furthermore, it highlights the transition from a time in which Lockpez felt art could wait to the moment of the text, stressing the present as a time for art.

Following the triumph of the Cuban Revolution of 1959 and the failed Bay of Pigs Invasion, Fidel Castro called for a cultural transformation in Cuba during his 1961 speech "Palabras a los intelectuales" (Words to intellectuals). The speech, delivered in the Biblioteca Nacional José Martí, intended to address the concerns of Cuban intellectuals and artists regarding censorship. In his speech, Castro stated that as a patriotic duty and moral obligation to younger generations, Cuban intellectuals and artists needed to use their works to document the revolution, by participating as eyewitnesses:

> But if a man of a future generation, a man 100 years from now is told that a writer or an intellectual of this age lived during the era of the Revolution but outside of it, and did not express the Revolution and was not part of the Revolution, that would be difficult for him to understand. This is especially so when there will be so many, many people in coming years who will want to paint the Revolution and write about the Revolution, and will want to express themselves about the Revolution, compiling data and reports in order to find out how it was, what happened, and how we lived.[14]

He recognized the historical importance of testimony and believed that to foster national unity and safeguard the principles and purpose of the revolution, Cuban intellectuals and artists needed to promote the active participation of marginalized people and marginalized people needed to provide their individual contribution to this initiative. Moreover, social realism was determined to be the preferred aesthetic of the revolution. Given that the intellectual elite previously controlled the formulations of national identity, he desired to invert this order through the cultural education and participation of the general population. Accordingly, this (re)defining of national identities would produce an archive and a defense of the revolution for and from future generations. The revolution's social reform trajectory included a strategy to revalue revolutionary historical memory and *cubanidad*.[15] As such, censorship, including strict control of artistic and ideological production in Cuba, was employed, and a staunch resistance to subversive and counterrevolutionary ideals was unleashed.

I contextualize this historical moment for students, so they see how *Cuba: My Revolution* presents the implications of the revolution's approach to "official" history and better understand Lockpez's role in it and against it. In the final part of her testimony, part 3, she is finally able to work as an artist in Cuba. We see Sonya and her artistry as fundamental to the portrayal and reproduction of the revolution. Her artistry in Cuba is determined by her ability to paint murals of the Assault of the Moncada Barracks in high schools. This failed insurrection led by Fidel Castro marked the beginning of the Cuban Revolution, and despite the numerous rebel deaths and Castro's imprisonment, it would later be immortalized in Cuban historical memory through National Revolution Day. Although Sonya is responsible for painting the revolution through social realism, Lockpez relies on her expressionistic style and abstraction throughout her life and testimony. For example, her censored abstract paintings serve as dividers between the three parts of the comic. Conversely, abstraction was not taught in art schools in Cuba during the revolution. Her art professor is depicted saying, "We won't be teaching Cubism, Abstraction and Surrealism. The people need realistic images of our country," and "the revolution needs painters who celebrate our heroes like Martí and the workers. Your art should be a vehicle to interpret the ideas of our Máximo leader [Fidel Castro]."[16]

While Sonya paints the scene of the Moncada Barracks, her art professor's words are echoed by Celia Sánchez, an important revolutionary leader and guerrilla fighter. Sonya is confronted with the reality of ideological suppression and the need to eradicate diversity when she confronts Sánchez and questions the ideals of the revolution. She says, "But Celia, it's not just about men and women. We need different opinions, not a forced ideology. Our students now are being told what to study, our artists what to paint."[17] Sánchez responds, "Diversity brings chaos" and advises Sonya to "concentrate on the work you're doing here. We chose you for your excellent designs of revolutionary murals, not for criticism of our principles." As noted by Castro's speech, the revolutionary government plays an active role in artistic production by ensuring that artists conform to the revolution's social, political, and artistic parameters. Art is seen as a weapon for the revolution and the political control of free expression as the means to regulate it.

In her narrative Lockpez highlights the hostility that her work provokes from peers and the public; specifically, the abstract painting that introduces the second part of the testimony is depicted as one of the pieces featured in the exhibit. The pieces displayed were identified as "imperialist art," and the exhibit was forced to close after three days of violent protests.[18] Lacking the permission of the National Association of Writers and Artists of Cuba (UNEAC), she identifies the organized effort to censor the exhibit. Panels depicting the protests show signs reading "arte decadente" and "bourgeois art"; a brick, a broken window, and a protester giving the middle finger depict the opposition that artists without the government's authorization faced. This level of hostility and censorship escalates, as Carlos, Sonya's boyfriend, and Oscar, her friend, are identified as "decadent capitalists" for having long hair, earrings, and a bandana. Oscar agrees to cut his hair; however Carlos is sent to the military units to aid production (UMAPs), concentration camps established to punish counterrevolutionaries, including homosexuals and Jehovah's Witnesses, through forced labor. According to Emilio Bejel, the period between the mid-1960s and the mid-1970s was Cuba's homophobic apex.[19]

Bejel indicates two monumental events that solidified Cuba's disdain for homosexuals: the UMAPs from 1965 to 1968 and the First National Congress of Education and Culture of 1971. Moral purges and neighborhood raids were used to target and persecute individuals suspected of engaging in homosexual behavior. As argued by Fidel Castro in the First National Congress on Education and Culture, homosexuality was determined to be "socially pathological," and queer individuals were to be banned from having any influence on the development of young people and from representing the Cuban Revolution abroad.[20] Although Lockpez leaves Cuba before the First National Congress, the staunch resistance to snobbism, extravagance, and homosexuality is deeply ingrained in rhetoric used by the congress and can be detected throughout her testimony. Part 3 of the text serves to outline proper and improper conduct of an artist and the institutionalization of control enforcing these measures. While hosting her own exhibit, Sonya is once again faced with the aggression of the crowd, which ultimately culminates in the confiscation of her work by the union and a ban on her artistic work, preventing her ability to exhibit again. Ultimately the oppression and violence solidify her desire to leave for exile in the United States in 1966.

In addition to the intentional usage of abstraction, the comic form of the text and the historical role of DC Comics are controversial tools in the revision of the Cuban Revolution. As is well documented by Catalá Carrasco, from 1959 to May 1960, as Cuba experienced a reorganization of its media, comics especially were categorized as imperialist ideological tools that were intended to penetrate the minds of children and youth: "Comics had been univocally—that is a product and consequence of bourgeois societies—linked to foreign (and especially American) artistic manifestations as proof of their decadent bourgeois character, which praised mass culture in, as it was perceived, a pernicious levelling effect for society."[21] In the eyes of the revolutionary government, the importation of U.S. comic books represented a precarious engagement with foreign industry and iconography. Several American comics engaged in an anti-communist and anti-Castroist campaign. For instance, American comics such as *Steve Canyon*, *Terry and the Pirates*, *Johnny Hazard*, and *Superman* were popular in Cuba, thereby propelling the production of Cuban comics to offset the U.S. influence. Jorge Vergara identified DC Comics' popular superheroes, explicitly Batman and Superman, as capitalist products and propaganda that sought to maximize profits.[22] To better serve the goals of the revolution, mass media was reorganized under the control of the Communist Party and its groups, such as the Instituto Cubano del Arte e Industria Cinematrográficas (ICAIC) and Instituto Cubano de Radio y Televisión (ICRT).

Cuba: My Revolution repositions itself within this controversy by flaunting and empowering its connection with DC Comics. For example, not only is the text published by the DC imprint Vertigo, but the cover of the text and its color palette, in part, were inspired by the cover of *Wonder Woman* no. 108, illustrated by Ross Andru and Mike Esposito.[23] Highlighting this connection for students allows them to realize the various means by which Lockpez and Haspiel (re)present her revolution and subvert the aesthetic of the revolution. Additionally, it draws attention to the aftermath of her story, specifically her inability to *be* in Cuba—as it relates to both her physical location and her existence—and to publish her testimony there. After discussing Lockpez's experience as an artist, students can research Cuban artist-activists who are imprisoned or exiled, such as Luis Manuel Otero Alcántara, Maykel Castillo Pérez ("Maykel Osorbo"), Hamlet Lavastida, and Katherine Bisquet, in addition to various artist-activists from the San Isidro and 27N movements.

Cuba: My Revolution offers students and instructors a space to reflect on the experiences and the fragmentation that mark Cuban exilic lives, feeling at home neither in exile nor in Cuba. In his analysis of Cuban coping mechanisms in exile, Alan West-Durán identifies three basic options that Cuban Americans can adopt: nostalgia, forgetting, and translation. Believing all three to yield negative outcomes, he proposes an alternative strategy to overcoming the depression of exile: the invention of an imaginary Cuba made from the remnants and pieces of what one is left with.[24] To an extent, we see this strategy in the title as it explicitly acknowledges Lockpez's sense of agency and belonging in her construction of Cuba. Thus, we see Lockpez expressing, exploring, and reclaiming her Cubanness, or, as proposed by Fernando Ortiz, her *cubanía*, that is, a Cubanness that is felt, desired, chosen, and, I would like to add, in an indefinite cycle of revolutions. According to Fernando Ortiz, and as later elaborated by Pérez Firmat, this Cuban condition is unlike the others (*cubanidad* and *cubaneo*) because it is an act of the will; it finds expression in the abstract and the ineffable—in a homeland, *una patria*.[25] She reimagines Cuba as an exile and portrays it using her tools and desired aesthetic. Her narrative guides readers through the loss of her heroes, family, friends, country, dreams, and, ultimately, herself.

Mediated Memories: Expressing Trauma and Postmemory

Despite the use of Sonya as Lockpez's avatar, there are several moments that create pause in the reader as the grip of reality finds its way into the narrative. For Lockpez as a visual artist, abstraction captures her artistic interests and influences during her life in Cuba and proves to be an essential aesthetic for *her* revolution, as such is imperative to the subversive and communicative goal of her history. As aforementioned, her censored paintings serve as dividers between the three parts of her testimony, and surrealist compositions intercalated throughout the text break with the canonic paradigm of the comic. Furthermore, the cover of the text pays homage to one of her inspirations, Dutch abstract painter Piet Mondrian. This influence can be noted in the asymmetrical arrangement of geometric shapes and black horizontal and vertical lines painted by brushstrokes.

Where language meets its limit to articulate the experiences of trauma, visual iconography is used to express these limitations. One of its key features is its graphic nature, referring to the visceral content, torture, blood, and gore that mark numerous pages. In the following sections, I analyze the articulation of two traumatic experiences: Sonya's imprisonment and sexual exploitation. When teaching this text, I focus on the ways Lockpez's traumas are represented to the reader, specifically focusing on the tools used to express her pain and suffering, which are often the moments in which the comic medium is pushed to its limits and Haspiel begins to pull from fine arts. For example, as a volunteer medic at the front lines, Sonya (Lockpez) witnesses the brigade go head-to-head with her comrades and recounts the experience in part 2 of the comic. Among the corpses and fatalities of the Cuban militia and exiles, Sonya believes to have found her high school sweetheart, Flavio. Given the scarcity of medical supplies, specifically morphine, she is instructed to reserve all use of palliative medicine for revolutionary soldiers and amputate the man's leg without morphine. This procedure inevitably leads to his death. Subsequently, she finds her actions to be a violation of her Hippocratic oath and vows never to act like that again. Unfortunately, this resolve creates suspicion among her compatriots, who suspect she is an undercover CIA agent. She is later imprisoned and tortured until her father negotiates her release.

To capture the agony of being hosed with cold and hot water, Haspiel draws on the work of Austrian Expressionist artist Oskar Kokoschka's *Pietà (Poster for Murder, Hope of Women)* to represent Sonya's flayed and blistered skin (see figure 2.1).[26] In the original painting, Kokoschka reimagines the Christian iconography of the Pietà, with a ghoulish and contorted Virgin Mary and Christ. Christ's body is deformed with bold red streaks and lighter red brush strokes communicating pain, suffering, grief, and blood loss from every inch of his body. Similar phantasmal red-and-white images of Sonya's

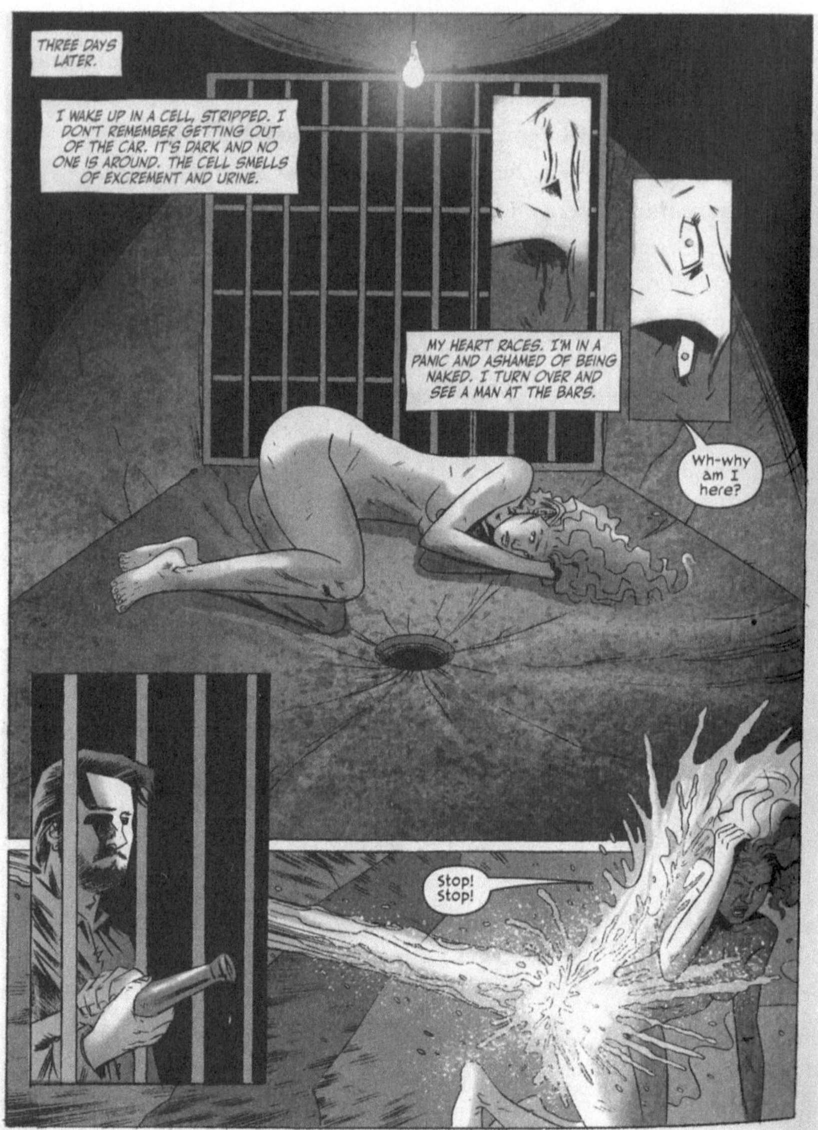

FIGURE 2.1 One of the eleven pages depicting Sonya's (Lockpez's) imprisonment. Dean Haspiel is depicted with the hose that sprays Sonya. Note that the original text does not include page numbers. The numbers depicted in the bottom corner of each page are my handwriting. Inverna Lockpez, Dean Haspiel, José Villarrubia, and Pat Brosseau, *Cuba: My Revolution* (New York: DC Comics/Vertigo, 2010), 57.

tortured self are intercalated throughout the narrative, as she experiences flashbacks to the fear and trauma experiences in the prison cell. Her sunken eyes and gaunt face and body become skeletons by part 3. Moreover, Haspiel draws inspiration from Lockpez's abstract pieces. The tools and the chair used to torture her in the interrogation room appear in the abstract piece that separates the third part of the testimony from the second. Haspiel reveals the difficulty of re-creating the torture scene: "At one point, Inverna was having a meltdown about this section and the only way to fix that was to cast myself as one of the torturers to protect her in the comics."[27]

Throughout these panels, his avatar sprays Sonya with the hose. His anachronistic presence flattens time and allows for the past to be collapsed by the present.[28] Following Eva Hoffman's research on the family and proximate groups of Holocaust survivors, she observes that in the language of family survivors do not exactly express memories through coherent narration but rather express themselves in "emanations," "flashes of imagery; in abrupt, fragmented phrases; in repetitious, broken refrains," and "a chaos of emotion."[29] I would also add that these reactions are exacerbated and compromised by the eradication of documentation, possessions, and historical records often inflicted by totalitarian regimes. The recall process is left incomplete, marked by silence, and uncontrollable. Borrowing from Hoffman's terminology, I argue that Haspiel relies on the creative liberties in the text to focus less on re-creating every detail precisely and instead supports Lockpez through the emanations, fragmentation, and chaos experienced while breaking the silence.

We are reminded that although this is Lockpez's testimony, her memories are mediated by Haspiel's representational and aesthetic choices. This detail is monumental as it reminds the reader not only of his role in the narrative and, to an extent, the consequences his project has on asking Lockpez to relive these memories, but also the way postmemory is transmitted from generation to generation. Haspiel writes, "Over the years, I kept a mental checklist of the various and mysterious anecdotes Inverna shared about her experience in Cuba and started to knit together a narrative tapestry. However, there were giant plot holes, and I didn't understand some of the things that happened to her. I needed to know how, what, and why."[30] As someone who considers Lockpez a second mother, his recognition of holes in the narrative tapestry connects with a key feature of postmemory: the task of working with fragmentary sources and foundations, which Hirsch notes are "shot with holes," evoking the existence of a past struggling to render itself fully.[31] Much like Castro anticipated, future generations are left to answer, "What happened?"

Within Hirsch's understanding of postmemory, the past is mediated not by recall but rather by "imaginative investment, projection and creation."[32] In other words, despite the project being initiated by a desire to seek understanding and context, ultimately the process of filling the holes becomes less about gaining understanding and more about the process of empathizing, healing, and learning. When confronted with vagaries and distortions of memory, loss, and deep trauma, the needs to know how, what, and why are secondary to working through the pain. Haspiel concludes, "Maybe we never come to fully understand what happened, but we can talk about it, write about it, and draw it in hopes of healing the pain, knowing that you can't change the past but you can certainly steer the future."[33] When explaining this concept to students, I use a short video by Brené Brown to clarify the difference between empathy and sympathy; this video serves as an effective tool for illustrating the meaning of "filling the hole."[34] Brown explains that empathy fuels connection by feeling *with* people. By trying to take their perspective, stay out of judgment, recognize emotions in others, and later communicate those emotions, one can feel *with* people and avoid driving disconnection. She uses the analogy of seeing someone who has fallen into a hole. An empathetic response is to get into the hole with the person and try to connect with them in that experience. A sympathetic person stays at the top of the hole, asks how they're feeling, and focuses on the silver lining of the experience by using what Brown refers to as "at least . . ." statements. Although it may seem counterintuitive, it is thought-provoking to pair this analogy with Haspiel's self-depiction as the torturer and ask students, "How does Haspiel get into the hole with Lockpez?" It would initially seem like identifying himself as the torturer would be the exact opposite of an empathic response. However, as noted by Haspiel, having Lockpez ground herself in the present and disrupt the traumatic recollection of the past, the genre of the comic facilitates her exploration of her personal identity and sense of self and agency by disqualifying the voices of those who have haunted her memories for so long.

In the literal sense, *Cuba: My Revolution* is an imaginative investment, projection, and creation specifically between Lockpez, Haspiel, and Villarrubia, yet it also adopts imaginative techniques that complicate the reader's understanding of reality, particularly the line between self-referentiality and visual and verbal modes of expression used to capture traumatic events. This imaginative approach is complicated and complemented by the sparse inclusion and strategic placement of Lockpez's photograph that closes the comic. Despite the usage of an avatar, the one wrinkled and weathered photo of a candid, young Lockpez in a black one-piece bathing suit standing in front of a building with lounge chairs in the background communicates a visual power that transports the reader into a "deathlike fixing of one moment in time."[35] Her gaze is serious and beyond the frame of the photo, unaware of the photographer and the eventual viewer of the photo. To add to its gravitas, Haspiel reveals in a later interview that this photo is one of the only candid photos remaining in Lockpez's archives.[36]

Unlike Jaime Cortez's *Sexile*, a graphic novel based on transgender artist Adela Vázquez's memories of the Cuban Revolution and her exile, Lockpez is not depicted giving her testimony. This technique creates a fluid rendering of the past until the photograph disrupts the comic representation of the narrative. It is also in this moment that the reader realizes that the backstory to this photo and her stoic gaze appear in part 3 (see figure 2.2). During the Cuban Missile Crisis, Sonya's mother obtains U.S. visas to flee Cuba; however, Sonya's visa is delayed. To help her family cover the expense of the inspection of inventory in their home, Sonya calls Eduardo, a family friend, who agrees to give her the money in exchange for sex. The next panel is a drawn mediation of the photograph of Lockpez, now Sonya, in the bathing suit; this time, the towel is a soft red, almost blush, and the setting is contrasted with shades of gray, black, and pink. Lockpez explains the significance of the color palette chosen for the book: "The majority of our life is grey, and we have splashes of pink and red and black."[37] The reproduction of these splashes serves as a signal to the reader of certain details that heighten the intensity of the memory reproduced.

In the frames that follow, Eduardo is carrying Sonya and later takes pictures of her and says, "You look like Ingrid Bergman. Come here, *mamita*. I want another picture of you. Don't move. One more now—hold it! We're going to have a great time" (see figure 2.3).[38] A close-up of the photo taken overlaps the frame, which depicts Eduardo taking the picture. The reader now realizes that the visual counterpart of the photograph, the photographer, was Eduardo. In the two panels that follow, Eduardo is shown in bed having sex with Sonya. While the first frame captures his excitement in the moment, the second demonstrates Lockpez's reoccurring survival strategy: escaping via her imagination. Haspiel depicts her legs as a mermaid tail in a blood red color; Eduardo's legs float upward above her fin, and red bubbles float around the black background. She reveals, "I am impatient for him to finish, but he takes his time and I decide to become someone else. Maybe a mermaid, this time swimming deep into the ocean, shifting, changing, always beyond the reach of men."[39] We witness Lockpez's ability to escape her reality and enter the imaginary realm that is colored in vibrant splashes of red and black, reappropriating the colors of the revolution for her own and expressing agency

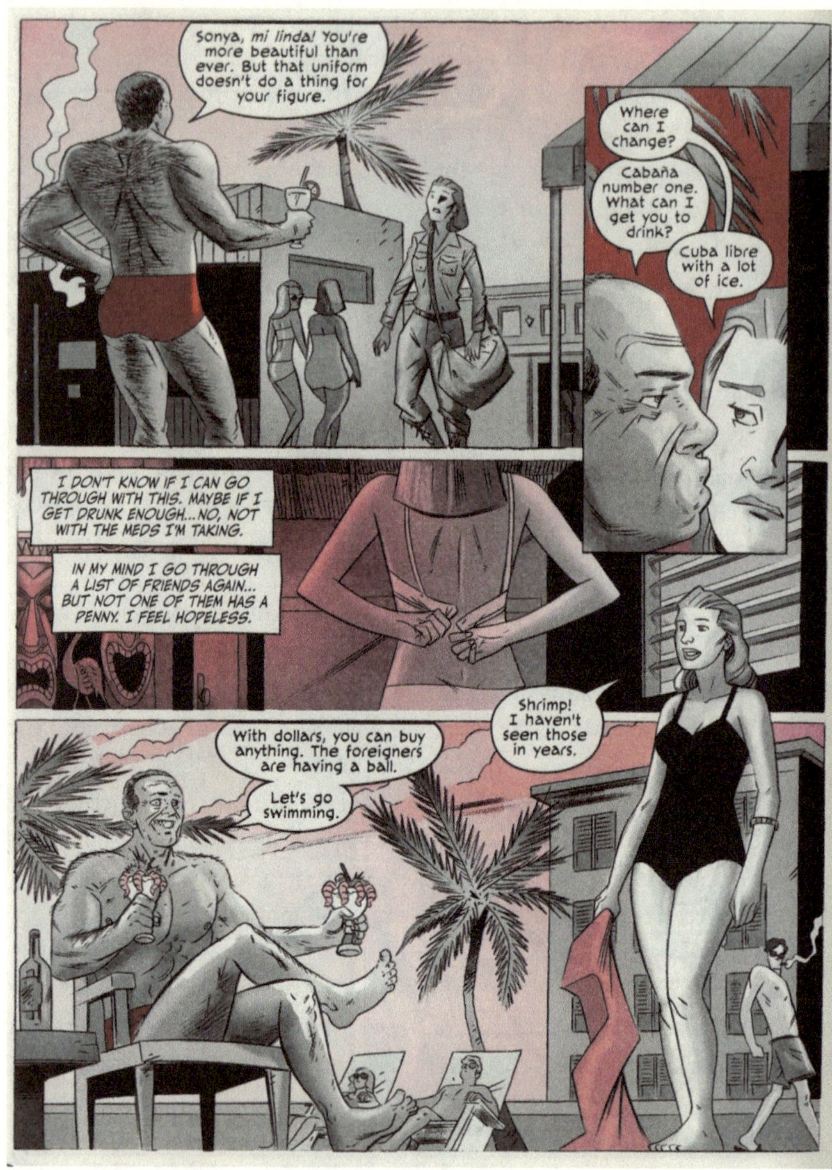

FIGURE 2.2 The final panel contextualizes and depicts a graphic representation of the archival photograph of Lockpez that concludes the comic. Lockpez et al., *Cuba: My Revolution*, 99.

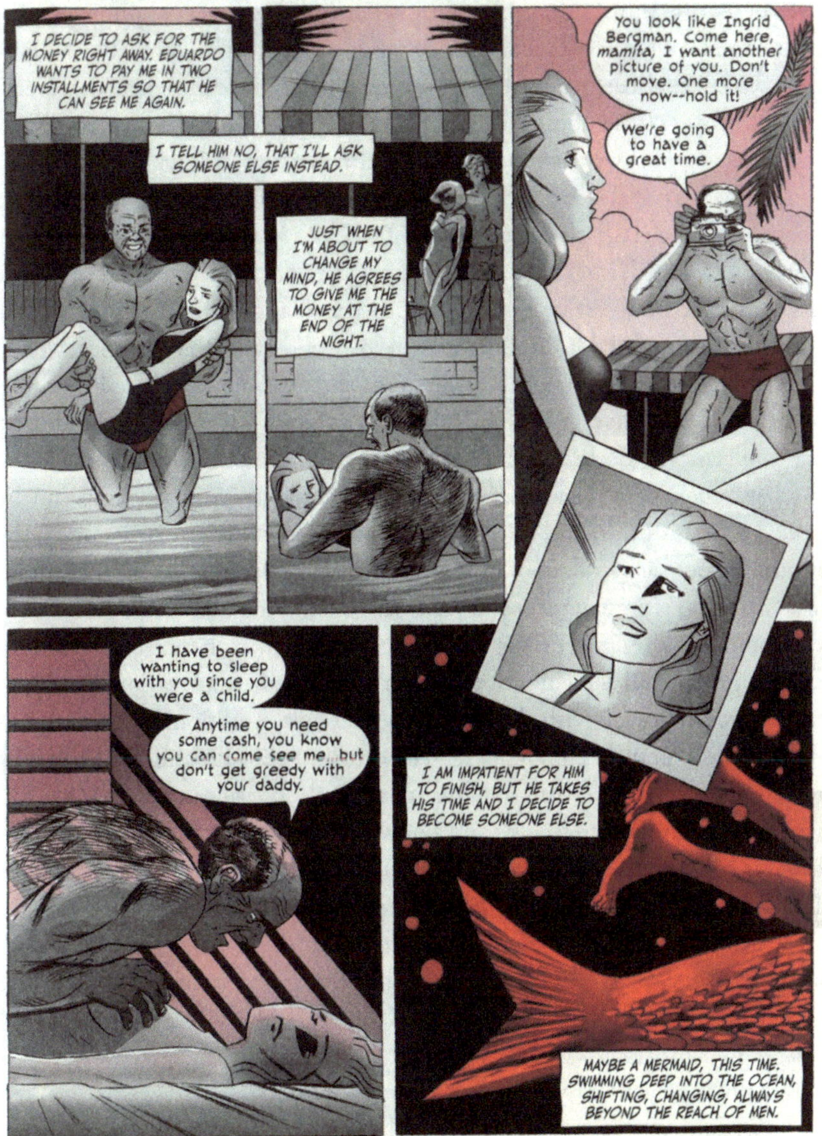

FIGURE 2.3 In need of money to help her family leave Cuba, Sonya calls Eduardo, a family friend, who agrees to give her the money in exchange for sex. The last panel depicts Sonya escaping into her imaginary realm to cope with the sexual trauma. Lockpez et al., *Cuba: My Revolution*, 100.

over her story and traumas. Bringing attention to the actual photo and its context reminds students that Lockpez's experiences represent real loss, injustice, violence, abuse, trauma, and silence. Although pain penetrates everything in this text, so does resilience and, more specifically, resistance.

Moreover, Haspiel explains that the archival photo of Lockpez was meant to serve as part of the cover. However, the decision was rejected by marketing because of "the clash of reality and fiction."[40] As highlighted by this debate, the boundaries of visual iconography through abstraction and the testimonial nature of the book created tensions with the comic book publisher as they intended to establish DC Comics within the world of autobiographical works. This is an interesting detail to bring up in the classroom because it reminds students of the interests at play. In other words, who are the stakeholders in the publication process, and how do their decisions impact the outcome of the final product? After learning of this marketing decision, students can be polled to see if they agree with the outcome. After a brief discussion of the results, I would ask students to return to Pérez's rejection of the comic medium as a historical representation and ask if this marketing decision is evidence of the comic medium purporting to historical representation but succumbing to entertainment and enjoyment. As aforementioned, there are various aspects of the comic that break with the typical comic book. Additionally, the author's note and the photo of Lockpez signal historical veracity and realism. Why would underscoring the fusion of reality and fiction result in a clash?

DC Vertigo, created in 1993 and a now discontinued imprint of DC Comics, was originally established to publish stories that did not fit the Comics Code Authority (CCA) because of their graphic nature and adult content. In the early 1990s, the label saw great success with works such as *The Sandman*, *Swamp Thing*, *Hellblazer*, and other titles that appealed to a mature reader. Simultaneously, DC Comics' publication of *Watchmen* and *The Dark Knight Returns* along with Pantheon Book's publication of *Maus I*, which was originally independently published in serial form in *Raw* magazine, sparked a renewed interest in graphic novels during the late 1980s and into the 1990s. According to Christophe Dony, Vertigo offered DC Comics the space to "offer new versions of previously existing character that are dislocated from their original contexts and re-articulated in the new ones that explore horror and the occult as well as mix self-reflexive elements that one can associate with generic subversion."[41] By understanding this history of DC's Vertigo—its purpose and intended audience—readers can better comprehend the aesthetic decisions taken to bring this text to fruition. Through the medium of the comic, Lockpez and Haspiel exhibit a willingness to play with artistic and generic traditions and boundaries, specifically by challenging high and low cultural binaries, thereby bringing into question the fusion of the fictional realm and the real.

Conclusion

Cuba: My Revolution requires from its creators and its readers the capacity to grapple with constructions of the past and present, destruction and survival, primary and secondary trauma, and memory and postmemory. As I have delineated in this essay, the inclusion of this text into our classrooms invites students to critically engage the artistic and aesthetic boundaries of comics and visual culture, while also reflecting on the interests of governments, authors, editors, colorists, illustrators, and publishers and their shared impact on a cultural artifact and its reading. By working with this text, students wrestle with questions of what it means to inherit memory and trauma and reflect on the means used to support survivors as they cope with these experiences. From denial and forgetting to abstraction and imagination, Lockpez and Haspiel's work actively resists the attempts by Cuban authorities to create and disseminate an official history and draws attention to the fate of artists who were/are targeted by forces of state. In response, Lockpez and Haspiel undertake the process of representing her unprocessed experiences from the past and working through the feelings that arise with them. Although the text does not center on the struggle of adapting to a new life in the United States and, on the contrary, intentionally ends with the beginning of a new identity as an exile living in the United States, one must not overlook its significance within Latinx literature. By so deliberately engaging with her memories and challenging their representation through the comic medium, we are reminded that part of our work as educators is making sure that our teaching practices connect students with the affective links of trauma, nostalgia, loss, belonging, devastation, and hope experienced by diasporic communities and the following generations.

Notes

1 Inverna Lockpez and Dean Haspiel, *Cuba: My Revolution* (New York: Vertigo, 2010).

2 I adopt the term "fact with affect" proposed by Catalá Carrasco in his chapter "Raising the Cuban Flag: Comics, Collective Memory, and the

Spanish-Cuban-American War (1898)," in *Comics and Memory in Latin America*, ed. Jorge L. Catalá Carrasco, Paulo Drinot, and James Scorer (Pittsburgh: University of Pittsburgh Press, 2017), 33–58, 51.

3 Some paperback editions are available of *Cuba: My Revolution*.

4 Louis A. Pérez Jr., "Spain Rodriguez. Che: A Graphic Biography; Inverna Lockpez and Dean Haspiel. Cuba: My Revolution," *American Historical Review* 123, no. 5 (2018): 1602–1603.

5 Pérez, "Spain Rodriguez," 1603.

6 Gustavo Pérez Firmat, "A Willingness of the Heart: Cubanidad, Cubaneo, Cubanía," *Cuban Studies Occasional Paper Series* 2, no. 7 (1998): 1–11, 1.

7 Operation Pedro Pan Group, "Operacion Pedro Pan: The Cuban Children's Exodus" (n.d.), https://www.pedropan.org.

8 Willy Chirino, "Nuestro día (Ya viene llegando)," track 10 on *Oxígeno* (Discos International, 1991).

9 Grupo Areíto, *Contra Viento y Marea* (Casa de las Américas, 1978).

10 Lockpez and Haspiel, *Cuba: My Revolution*, iv.

11 Camilo Montoya-Galvez, "Migrants from Cuba, Venezuela and Nicaragua Processed in Record Numbers at U.S. Border in 2022," *CBS News*, October 23, 2022.

12 Cuban Research Institute, "Cuban Migration: A Postrevolution Exodus Ebbs and Flows" (n.d.), accessed November 23, 2024, https://www.migrationpolicy.org/article/cuban-migration-postrevolution-exodus-ebbs-and-flows.

13 Lockpez and Haspiel, *Cuba: My Revolution*, 11.

14 Latin American Network Information Center (LANIC), "Castro's Speech to Intellectuals on 30 June 61" (Castro Speech Data Base, n.d.), http://lanic.utexas.edu/project/castro/db/1961/19610630.html.

15 Fernando Ortiz, "The Human Factors of Cubanidad," trans. João Felipe Gonçalves and Gregory Duff Morton, *HAU: The Journal of Ethnographic Theory* 4, no. 3 (2014): 455–480.

16 Lockpez and Haspiel, *Cuba: My Revolution*, 79.

17 Lockpez and Haspiel, *Cuba: My Revolution*, 118.

18 Lockpez and Haspiel, *Cuba: My Revolution*, 108.

19 Emilio Bejel, *Gay Cuban Nation* (Chicago: University of Chicago Press, 2001), 96.

20 Rafael Ocasio, "Gays and the Cuban Revolution: The Case of Reinaldo Arenas," *Latin American Perspectives* 29, no. 2 (2002): 78–98, 86–87.

21 Carrasco J. Catalá, "From Suspicion to Recognition? 50 Years of Comics in Cuba," *Journal of Latin American Cultural Studies* 20, no. 2 (2011): 139–160, 143.

22 Jorge Vergara, "Comics y relaciones mercantiles," *Casa de las Américas* 13, no. 77 (1973): 126–142, 130.

23 DCE Editorial, "Cuba: My Revolution Cover Process by Dean Haspiel" (DC, September 15, 2010), https://www.dc.com/blog/2010/09/15/cuba-my-revolution-cover-process-by-dean-haspiel.

24 Alan West, "My Life with Fidel Castro: A Soap Opera without Transmitter," in *Bridges to Cuba / Puentes a Cuba*, ed. Ruth Behar (Ann Arbor: University of Michigan Press, 1995), 376–388, 388.

25 Pérez Firmat, "Willingness of the Heart," 7.

26 Oskar Kokoschka, *Pietà (Poster for Murder, Hope of Women)* (1909, lithograph, 48 5/16 × 30 inches [122.7 × 78.6 cm], Museum of Modern Art, New York).

27 Rachel Aydt, "Graphic, Novel: Cuba: My Revolution Brings the Harsh Reality of Castro's Revolution to Comics," *Publishing Perspectives*, October 26, 2010,

https://publishingperspectives.com/2010/10/dean-haspiels-cuba-revolution-to-comics/.
28 Lockpez and Haspiel, *Cuba: My Revolution*, 57.
29 Eva Hoffman, *After Such Knowledge: Memory, History and the Legacy of the Holocaust* (New York: New York Public Affairs, 2004), 11.
30 DCE Editorial, "Cuba: My Revolution."
31 Marianne Hirsch, "The Generation of Postmemory," *Poetics Today* 29, no. 1 (2008): 103–128, 107.
32 Hirsch, "Generation of Postmemory," 107.
33 DCE Editorial, "Cuba: My Revolution."
34 RSA, "Brené Brown on Empathy," YouTube, December 10, 2013, https://www.youtube.com/watch?v=1Evwgu369Jw.
35 Marianne Hirsch, "Mourning and Postmemory," in *Graphic Subjects: Critical Essays on Autobiography and Graphic Novels*, ed. Michael A. Chaney (Madison: University of Wisconsin Press, 2011), 17–44, 25.
36 DCE Editorial, "Cuba: My Revolution."
37 Tania Pérez Cano, "La memoria como espacio de libertad: autobiografía y testimonio en las narrativas gráficas *Cuba: My Revolution*, de Inverna Lockpez y *Adiós mi Habana*, de Anna Veltfort," *Studia Romanistica* 20, no. 2 (2020): 57–73, 68.
38 Lockpez and Haspiel, *Cuba: My Revolution*, 100.
39 Lockpez and Haspiel, *Cuba: My Revolution*, 100.
40 DCE Editorial, "Cuba: My Revolution."
41 Christophe Dony, "The Rewriting Ethos of the Vertigo Imprint: Critical Perspectives on Memory-Making and Canon Formation in the American Comics Field," *Comicalités. Études De Culture Graphique* (2014): 4.

Pedagogical Strategies for Teaching the Comic Anthology *Puerto Rico Strong* in the Latinx Literature Classroom

JENNIFER CAROCCIO MALDONADO

Of the many responses to Hurricane Maria (monetary, volunteer, written), the comic anthology *Puerto Rico Strong* (2018), edited by Marco Lopez, Desiree Rodriguez, Hazel Newlevant, Derek Ruiz, and Neil Schwartz, is one of the most emblematic of the diaspora's desire to help those most impacted on the island.[1] The comic anthology collects stories from members of the Puerto Rican diaspora to craft a graphic response to disaster, memory, and cultural belonging. The anthology includes graphic memoirs, superhero comics, historical narratives, science fiction, and fantasy. According to the editors, "All profits from sales of *Puerto Rico Strong* will be donated to support relief and rebuilding efforts in Puerto Rico."[2] There is a desire to focus on the collective as a means of support and solidarity. I view the edited collection as a vehicle to gather shared cultural knowledge that is part of a social justice framework.

In Fall 2021, I assigned the comic anthology in an upper division undergraduate college course focused on Latinx literature at Baruch College, CUNY, a public senior college in New York City. My goal in teaching *Puerto Rico Strong* in a literature course was to draw from not only comics studies but also Latinx visual culture to find new ways that Latinx comics can continue to innovate pedagogy. The intention was to interrogate how can *Puerto Rico Strong* as a Latinx comics anthology coaxed readers to both engage with the history of Puerto Rico and its diaspora. What are some specific activities that can be implemented when assigning a Latinx comics anthology like *Puerto Rican Strong*? My essay examines how *Puerto Rico Strong* can be used in the literature classroom to open up the interdisciplinary possibilities of Latinx comics. I look at how other comic scholars have taught comics as both literature and history, coupled with an autoethnographic analysis wherein I examine my experience teaching the graphic text in the classroom. I learned from teaching *Puerto Rico Strong* the possibility of Latinx comics to address the history of sterilization on the island and the cultural amnesia of mestizaje. The comics anthology combines vibrant and varied images and text into narratives that are an entryway for students to learn about and critique U.S. and Puerto Rican official history. My pedagogical strategies show how students experience a Latinx comics anthology in a literature classroom to understand and interrogate the cultural and historical aspects of literary criticism. My task has been to help students engage with narrative, history, and memory in literature. When students engage with Latinx visual culture that has weaved historical vignettes throughout the anthology, they make connections to how history is reshaped by literature.

The first section of this chapter is concerned with how the comic anthology teaches the history of Spanish colonization, medical abuse, and the aftermath of Hurricane Maria. I chose this collection specifically because its anthology format made it accessible to read over a two-week span: short narratives that students could pick up and put down throughout the week. These comics engage with issues of cultural belonging, the state's failure to respond to disasters, and the history of colonization in the Caribbean. As María

Fernanda Díaz-Basteris argues, "We can benefit from the use of comics and graphic narratives as a groundbreaking pedagogical tool to teach and study the impact of social and natural catastrophes, including the challenges that domestically displaced communities experience across state borders."[3] *Puerto Rico Strong* is an invaluable tool for students to use literature to address the consequences of Hurricane Maria's aftermath and put it in the larger historical context of U.S. imperialism of the island. Looking to the scholarship on how teachers in secondary education use comics in their classrooms informs my reflection on how to use *Puerto Rico Strong* in college courses. Teachers in secondary education are doing great work on comics in the classroom, and their pedagogy betters my own thinking through the success and failures of my assignments. Scholarship on secondary education is important for comics pedagogy because they offer educational experiences in the high school and middle school classrooms of students who will be taking college courses in a few years.

In the chapter's second section, I set out to answer the following questions: How can I guide students' engagement with narrative, history, and memory in the literature classroom? How does Latinx visual culture transform the pedagogy of Latinx literature? I want students to explore questions of cultural memory and national identity when engaging Latinx visual culture in the literature classroom. Assigning *Puerto Rico Strong* forced me to confront assumptions of what I thought students knew. For example, there were many who didn't know what the word *Boricua* meant, which surprised me seeing as New York City has been a predominantly Puerto Rican city for decades.[4] I note that there has been an increase in Dominican, Mexican, and Central American Latinx groups in the city, which I believe reflects the limited knowledge of Puerto Rican–specific history that many students are coming into the classroom with.

Like literature, Latinx comics can be used as part of a nation-building project that reinforces ideas of nationality. And so in the chapter's third section I make a major critique of *Puerto Rico Strong*'s appropriation of Taíno culture in certain Indigenous recuperation stories included in the comic anthology. While I am weary of the mestizaje invoked by many of the creators, I find that it has a productive turn when teaching the anthology in that it provides a space for students to interrogate how the comics center and/or further marginalize/appropriate Indigenous peoples and their cultures in the Caribbean and Puerto Rico. Ultimately, my hope is that this Boricua comic anthology offers a different epistemological framework than traditional history books through its use of alternative graphic knowledge productions such as speculative history and memoir. Paul Humphrey claims that individual and collective graphic narratives depict how "colonialism persists in Puerto Rico and yet demonstrate in their content and varying forms the need for a Boricua-centered, decolonial narrative that rejects colonial ways of being and knowing to focus on collective action and stewardship of the archipelago."[5] Similarly, *Puerto Rico Strong* presents a Latinx visual culture that is both "Boricua-centered" and diasporic in nature. And so *Puerto Rico Strong* provides multiple narratives of Indigeneity in Puerto Rico that contest and reify previous colonial epistemologies.

Teaching *Puerto Rico Strong* along the Latinx Literature Canon

In this first section I map out three areas of relevant scholarship: (1) teaching with comics, (2) comics as literature and comics as history, (3) and reviews and analyses of *Puerto Rico Strong*. In my classroom, literature and history go hand in hand. It is significant that when I teach Latinx literature, which deals with the culture of marginalized groups like Puerto Ricans, I provide students with a cultural and historical context for reading that literature. *Puerto Rico Strong* enables me to do that. The breadth of coverage in this collection, specifically the comic histories that cover several centuries, is considerable but not overwhelming. In addition to offering this historical context, I underscore that *Puerto Rico Strong* is a literary text,[6] one that is rich with narratives of science fiction and fantasy, historical fiction, and memoir.

As a college instructor I find secondary educators' pedagogy to be some of the most helpful since research can often eclipse the practical pedagogical applications of comics. Secondary educators' pedagogy on how to integrate comics in the classroom is applicable to the college courses because their primary concern is to better educate students, as opposed to producing research. Comics scholars can always benefit from learning better ways of teaching comics. It is important to teach students to treat comics formally; the comics medium creates an environment that invites students to think through how the medium and form shape its message. As Marshall McLuhan argued, the medium *is the* message.[7] In comparison, Dale Jacobs presents a more formal approach to teaching comics in the classroom, emphasizing the multimodality of comics, focusing on "narrative meaning," and referring to comics as "cultural artifacts" and "discursive events."[8] Comics are then "formal considerations" that become a "medium of communication" and "sites of literacy."[9]

I focus on the visuality of the comics when discussing the narrative elements. I point out to students how the use of color denotes nostalgia in the comic title "Stories from My Father" by Adam Lance Garcia and Heidi Black.[10] I ask them to pay attention to vivid yellows and blues when the narrator talks about their childhood memories of visiting the island. The narrative in the present is black-and-white, dull compared to the joyful memories. The shift in color not only guides the reader temporally but also evokes emotions of joy and estrangement.

Communication, sociology, history, and literature are all disciplines that benefit from the integration of comics in the classroom. Comics, and by extension Latinx comics, make interdisciplinarity front and center. As many have demonstrated in their studies, comics pedagogy requires a certain amount of interdisciplinarity from the start. Jacobs asks, how can we move "towards an interdisciplinary stance that productively draws on the multiple constituents of the field"?[11] Gabriel Sealey-Morris pushes for more integration by rhetoric and composition instructors when compared to scholars of "narratology, deconstruction, and feminist and queer rhetorics."[12] As Susan E. Kirtley, Antero Garcia, and Peter E. Carlson observe, "Comics can also provide a window into other disciplines."[13] Latinx comics require students to confront historical narratives and contend with feminist and critical ethnic studies frameworks present in comics like the anthology, which requires an interdisciplinary approach. Latinx comics more broadly is a natural extension of comics scholars' calls for interdisciplinarity.

When I teach Latinx literature or cultural studies courses I always include comics to signal to students that they are not a predominately Anglo and White form.[14] While teaching *Puerto Rico Strong*, I guided students to make their own connections to history, racism, and feminism within their literary analysis. Latinx visual culture in comics prepares us as educators to tackle histories of violence in their exploration of questions of cultural memory, national identity, and belonging, as well as provide cultural products for students to study in the classroom. Memory in *Puerto Rico Strong* is used in different comic stories to both process the disaster and state policy failure of Hurricane Maria and reimagine a new Puerto Rican nationalist/diasporic identity. An example would be "Cocinar" by Vito Delsante and Yehudi Mercado.[15] Ramon is applying for a job in a Puerto Rican restaurant, and when asked why he wants to be a chef he reminisces about his childhood doing homework in his grandmother's kitchen.[16] The colors shift to pastels, and the artwork is more that of a watercolor, giving the panel the dreamy quality of memory. The art crafts how we can conceive of memory when critiquing climate change and nationhood. Daniel Arbino is concerned with how several comic anthologies reckoned with climate change and coloniality on the island in the wake of Hurricane Maria.[17] Héctor Fernández L'Hoeste argues that the stories in the anthology represent a "prosthetic nation," which is defined as "a community imagined with the memories of others—in particular, a community imagined as nation, yet a nation unlived or not experienced materially firsthand."[18] Here is where students are able to read graphic memoirs of diasporic Boricuas as they deal with memories of the island and how to help family devastated by the great storm.

Teaching Depictions of Latinx and Caribbean Diaspora

Like other CUNY schools, Baruch College—where I teach—is largely a commuter campus that serves the New York City metropolitan area. I taught this "Latinx Literature" course in my first semester at Baruch as an assistant professor. My special topics course introduced students to Latinx literature, which meant we had to tackle the question of what it is to be Latinx. For the purposes of the course (and this chapter), "Latinx" refers to any diaspora of people from Latin America, including the Francophone and Anglophone Caribbean.[19] Instead of breadth, I chose depth for my course. We read novels, memoirs, poetry, and comics in full by Latinx people in the United States. We put those texts in conversation with each other to draw larger critiques that could then be applied more broadly across the body of literature as a whole. My students read other books, like Piri Thomas's *Down These Mean Streets* (1967) and Edwidge Danticat's *Breath, Eyes, Memory* (1998), which were written within a specific cultural and historical context.

I assigned *Puerto Rico Strong* for two weeks during a fifteen-week semester. The class met synchronously online once a week, and students did asynchronous work—like discussion board posts—the other part of the week. My lesson plan for the first synchronous class meeting for this unit on *Puerto Rico Strong* began with a lecture on comics. I explained the elements of a comic page, such as panels, narration boxes, speech and thought bubbles, and the gutter. I also went over some text-image relationships and how their juxtaposition shaped the narrative: complementary (when the image and text support each other's meaning to synthesize a new message for the reader that wouldn't be understood with only the text or only the image), redundant (when the text and image offer the same information), and contrasting (when the text and image contradict each other's meaning).

Following this lecture, I had students work in groups of three or four in randomly assigned breakout rooms on Zoom. The assignment had two goals: first, students would find a commonality in the text to discuss with each other and, second, they would think through ideas of narrative and form in the comic. The class had a shared Google folder where they could find directions for the class activity and a Google doc where I had them record their classwork. The directions were to open the group number that corresponded to their breakout room number. I assigned each group a different comic in the anthology to cover. I asked them to identify the setting of the narrative, one instance of mood, and a main event in the comic that connects it to the larger theme of the anthology. Questions included, how do the color and artwork affect the mood? And what is the specific history included in this comic? Though I moved away from the trend of teaching comics that incorporate comic adaptations of classic narratives, I composed my questions based on Emira Derbel's assignment where students answer questions based on their reading of Mark Twain's *Adventures of Huckleberry Finn* and a graphic adaptation of the book.[20] Derbel outlines a fifteen-minute activity that asks students to identify setting and an instance of irony, for example, and was a helpful model for my own in-class assignment, which I go into more detail about in a later section. Derbel finds that "the act of analyzing a graphic novel includes a spontaneous alternation between the reading of the images and the narrative text," which ultimately makes comics appropriate "for reader-response theory."[21] I have found in my own teaching experience that students will often be hesitant to respond to any text, especially texts that deal with issues related to Latinx studies, for fear of "being wrong." Comics are a good starting place to garner reader response, as "comics can encourage a more deliberate reading and writing process and might also invite new kinds of expression."[22]

For the following class meeting, I wanted students' interests and questions to guide our discussion of the comics anthology. I created two corresponding discussion boards where students could openly respond to the sections they read that week. From their class discussions I observed that some students thought it was repetitive (the same stories told over and over again in different comics). I addressed the repetition during our synchronous meeting that week. Others thought it told the history in multiple ways and that visuals were more powerful than text alone. I ascertained from those comments that students thought visuals were better suited for social change. In our class meeting, I pushed them on that argument, which I believe many of us in comics/visual studies hold. Are visuals more powerful than words? I responded with an analogy, connecting to historical episodes like the proliferation of lynching postcards and contemporary police violence videos. Postcards of lynchings were part of White people's participation in violence that terrorized Black people throughout the United States. Even though they were used by abolitionists, much like the videos that are circulated on social media of police abuse in our current moment, these images are traumatizing for Black people to see, and they did not and do not always challenge anti-Black violence. It is important that we help students to interrogate how the text and images work together to craft narrative, especially with regard to juxtaposition, and understand how that is an intentional practice that has the potential for both social violence and social change.

The biggest and most surprising history lesson for my students in their reading of the anthology was that of the forced sterilization of and the experimentation with the birth control pill on Puerto Rican women. Both medical activities were performed without the informed consent of patients. Time and again, both during class meetings and on the discussion board, it was the most surprising and infuriating of stories from the anthology. In "La Operacíon" and "The Puerto Rican Birth Control Stories," Ally Shwed uses simple red, white, and blue shading to illuminate the history of medical abuse of Puerto Rican women on the island.[23] The first comic gives a quick overview of the 1898 invasion by the U.S. government—a panel depicts soldiers wielding muskets and canons as one pulls up the American flag. Though the comic is only two pages, it goes through the forced sterilization project enacted by Law 116, medical eugenics, the independence movement, and the lingering effects on Puerto Rican women's fertility and cultural history.[24]

Shwed's "La Operacíon" exemplifies how a Latinx comic incorporates history, art, and medical sciences, and it has a place within the growing field of graphic medicine.[25] One panel, which is the width of the page, depicts the hysterectomy and tubal ligation procedures, visually echoing art out of a medical textbook. In between the two drawings is a narration box that reads, "Law 116 introduced a coercive program of tubal ligation and hysterectomy without providing access to alternative forms of reversible, safe contraception."[26] Before starting my aesthetic analysis, I want to first contextualize Law 116 and "La Operacíon" in the history of U.S. colonization and the birth control movement in Puerto Rico. Iris Lopez places Law 116 within the U.S. eugenics movement, which resulted in a lack of access to safe birth control in Puerto Rico.[27] Forced sterilization stems from "Malthusian and eugenic philosophies" that certain people were not considered fit enough to reproduce because they were mentally ill, disabled, poor, and/or people of color.[28] Throughout the United States, up until the 1960s there were governmental efforts to sterilize mentally disabled people and poor Black women in South Carolina. Law 116 "was the only effective method of fertility control consistently made available to Puerto Rican women for long periods of time."[29]

"La Operacíon" shows the coercive choice forced on women on the island through the telling of one woman's willingness to pay a personal cost to control her reproductive health. Dashes that indicate cutting lines on the abdomen, showing the tubal ligation, are also used in the bookending panel at the bottom of the page, which is the width of the page. In it a woman is depicted with her arms and legs stretched out and an uneasy expression on her face; the background is a spiral, signaling confusion. A dotted line bisects the person and the panel. Puerto Rican women were seen as objects to dissect and study. The women were misinformed about the medical procedures U.S. doctors performed. The narration text tells us that even though those coercive procedures were eventually outlawed, they continued into the 1970s (see figure 3.1).[30] The forced sterilization caused a lot of emotional distress, as shown in the facial expressions. "La Operacíon" and "The Puerto Rican Birth Control Stories" present clear narratives of the history of eugenics and sterilization in Puerto Rico. Students quickly identify that history without having prior knowledge, and the comic highlights the pain and suffering caused to families in the narratives focused on individuals. Comics like these make *Puerto Rico Strong* an applicable text in any Latinx literature and studies classroom.

Comics act as cultural memory of the nation and make it so students can visually map out the process of constructing national identity. I found that even though I provided an introduction to the comic page in my opening lecture, students did not engage with the visual aspects of the anthology. I strive to conceive of new methods to teach comics in the literature classroom so that students comment on both the formal and narrative elements of comics. I believe more time spent learning about comics would be beneficial. To support students' visual analysis, I created a short exercise that allows them to practice what they've learned, wherein students identify an example of a complementary text-image relationship, for instance. I learned from teaching this class activity that I could encourage my students to engage more with the visuals. Specifically, by creating an activity focused on how reading a comic is different compared to reading a text-based narrative, in addition to the narrative/themes of cultural memory, I push students to investigate how the color, panels, and images of the comics tell multiple stories.

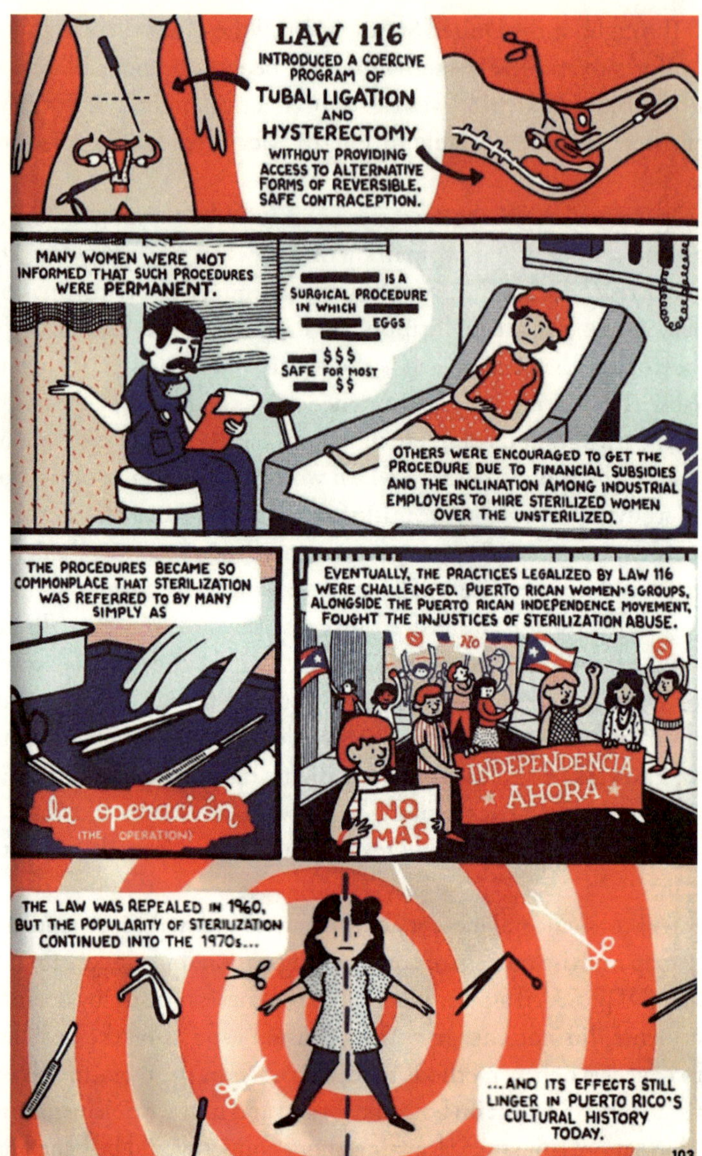

FIGURE 3.1 The dotted line in the medical drawing of the tubal ligation is used in the image of the Puerto Rican woman, showing a fractured identity. Ally Shwed, "La Operacíon" and "The Puerto Rican Birth Control Stories," in Marco Lopez, Desiree Rodriguez, Hazel Newlevant, Derek Ruiz, and Neil Schwartz, eds., *Puerto Rico Strong* (New York: Lion Forge, 2018), 103.

Because of its anthology approach, *Puerto Rico Strong* illuminates the multiple overlapping narratives of a certain historical event. While this isn't a strict comparison, however, I didn't observe shocked responses from students when I taught Piri Thomas's novel, *Down These Mean Streets* (1967) or Elizabeth Acevedo's collection of poems, *Beastgirl and Other Origin Myths* (2016). I believe students reacted differently because the comic anthology presented several different narratives around the same history in one volume, allowing students to see how an event or historical period is remembered in different ways. The novel covered drug use in New York City, and the poems focused on the Trujillo dictatorship in the Dominican Republic. While there was an appreciation for learning those histories, *Puerto Rico Strong* prompted students to think through how historical narratives are constructed. That is why Latinx comics are significant when considering how the history of Puerto Rico is integral to Latinx and Puerto Rican literature. Latinx comics provide a literary vehicle for students to pursue a critical inquiry into literature and history. Even though some students found the stories in *Puerto Rico Strong* to be repetitive, this is not necessarily an unproductive reaction. This comics anthology offers students multiple opportunities to interrogate the wide-ranging perspectives and experiences of Latinx communities, emphasizing how those communities are not monolithic. A comics anthology allows for the retelling of a specific kind of story through different visual aesthetics and narrative perspectives, a multifaceted approach to what might seem like the same tale. I would spend more time on the stories that were similar and have students ask questions like this: How does each retelling offer something new to our understanding? Having different comics on the same subject matter is an opportunity to understand Latinx visual culture in more complex and playful ways, especially when so much of the literature published is steeped in trauma and violence. The comic form allows students as readers to go back and forth between panels in a single comic and between comics throughout the anthology. I asked them to examine how the medium is the message in their investigation of repetition.

Taíno Recuperation, Indigenous Appropriation

A major critique I have of *Puerto Rico Strong* is the thread of Indigenous recuperation stories that borders on appropriation. Many of the comics center Taíno Indians, the Native Peoples of the Caribbean and Puerto Rico. Stories range from historical fiction, like "Areytos" by Jamie Hones, Vita Ayala, and Micah Myers; to accounts of mythological figures, like the Chupacabra in "Of Myths & Monsters" by Marco Lopez, Derek Ruiz, Jamie Jones, and D. C. Hopkins; to representations of the present moment, like in "Cocinar" by Vito Delsante and Yehudi Mercado. The recuperation and teaching of Taíno history are significant, and the aforementioned comics from the anthology do that work. However, as Yolanda Martínez-San Miguel points out in the beginning of her article, "Taíno Warriors?," "Indigeneity occupies a problematic place within Caribbean studies from a historical and cultural perspective."[31] Indigeneity also occupies a troublesome place in *Puerto Rico Strong* in that there is little engagement with mestizaje and White Puerto Ricans' positionality in the larger framework of empire, such as Tony Bedard and John Holmes's comic "Reality Check."[32] I examine the historical evasions in the narrative as a possibility to address the conflict with how Taíno indigeneity is represented.

One historical evasion that happens in the anthology is how some Boricuas depend on an idea of mestizaje that ignores any likely possibility of colonizer ancestry and the material benefits of being light-skinned with more Eurocentric features in a White supremacist society. "Reality Check" depicts Hispanofilia, a father telling his children a sanitized version of how Spanish conquistadors came to the island and their encounter with the native population. The father narrates, "He said Colón [Christopher Columbus] came ashore with his conquistadors to meet the Taíno Indians living here."[33] The panel presents a view from below; Columbus and his men look tall and formidable. The sun shines through. In the next panel, the father continues to tell the story: "[Columbus] was overwhelmed by the beauty of the Island. It was the most perfect place he'd seen in his travels." In a separate text box, the narration goes on, "And when he saw a beautiful Taíno child, he stroked his cheek and said. . . ." The panel is from the view of Columbus looking down at a small child; a white hand extends from out of view to gently caress the cheek of a small Brown child. Columbus says, "Truly, this is a rich port." The next two panels mirror the first two in that the third panel has one of the sons looking up at his father; the father's hand extends from out of the frame, gently touching the boy's shoulder. The pose mimics that of the small Indigenous boy from the preceding panel. In the fourth panel the father stands in a pose similar to that of Columbus in the first: benevolent, patriarchal. Again, the sun is shining down.[34] The juxtaposition is stark (see figure 3.2). While the son embodies the Taíno boy, thus visually signaling the family's Indigenous ancestry, the father becomes Columbus, benevolent patriarch. The parents are drawn as fair-skinned, the father with black straight hair and the

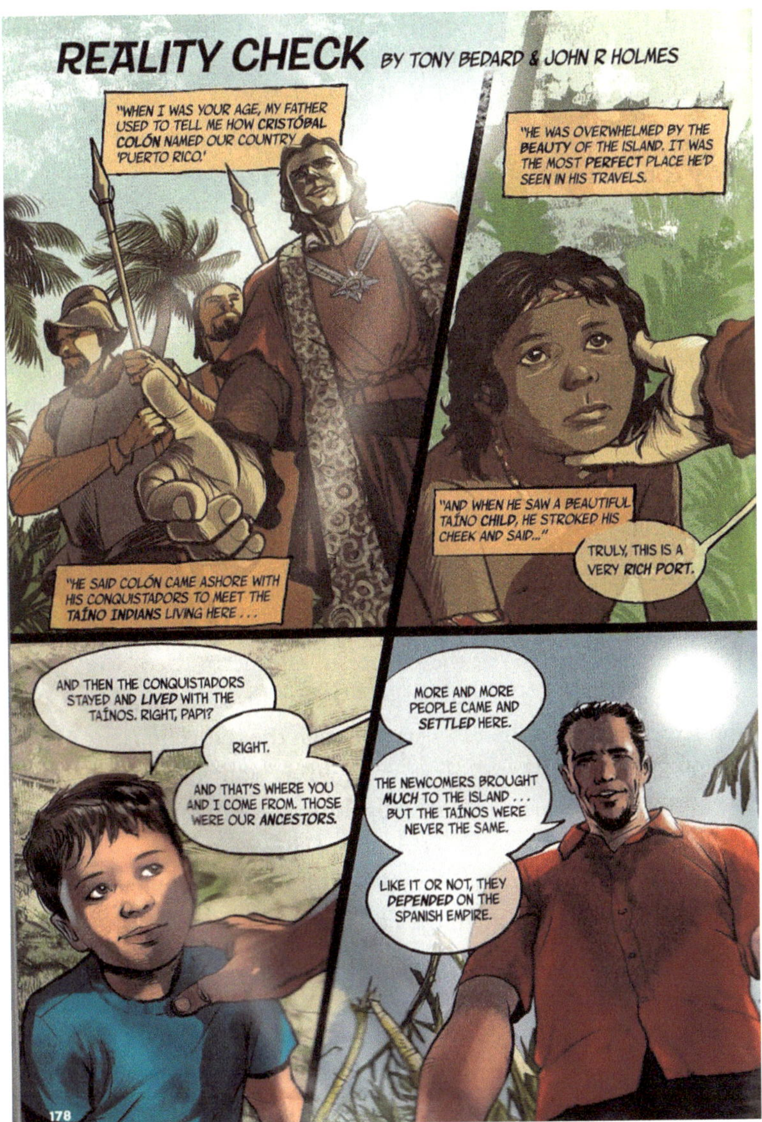

FIGURE 3.2 The juxtaposition of the panels with Christopher Columbus and the Taíno boy with the panels of the father and his son allude to the intertwined history of Spanish colonizers and the Indigenous people of the Caribbean. Tony Bedard and John Holmes, "Reality Check," in Lopez et al., *Puerto Rico Strong*, 178.

mother with light brown straight hair. Perhaps, as García argues, "the recent Taino movements [are] a way of rejecting both US and Spanish colonialisms" prevalent in Puerto Rican mestizaje.[35]

Reading the comic as a literary text that cannot be divorced from a "colonial context makes it impossible to find a narrative that is not intervened by multiple layers of translation, appropriation and assimilation of different linguistic, rhetorical and even epistemic paradigms."[36] When teaching these comics again, I would plan to have the students look more critically at "Reality Check." I would start by asking them, "Who is the family identifying with?" Then I would point out how the kids begin to playfight with wooden sticks as swords, a common occurrence in childhood. The father encourages them, shouting, "The blood of warriors runs through your veins."[37] Here is where I would contextualize that moment for students by providing a short lecture on the history of Spanish conquest in the Caribbean. The father refers to the supposed Taíno warriors, never the Spanish conquistadors. The father's depiction of Taínos as warriors exemplifies what Martínez-San Miguel points out in her first case study on the Army Reserve Officers' Training Corps (ROTC) campaign of 1996 at the University of Puerto Rico. The contradiction of their slogan was "Taíno Warriors . . . Step up to the challenge. Leadership and Excellence starts here!"—even though the Indigenous peoples of the Caribbean have been historically portrayed as nonviolent.[38] There is this mythos of the Taíno warrior invoked by Boricuas both on and off the island, despite there being little to no evidence of direct Indigenous ancestry or Taínos having an aggressive culture. After his wife questions the validity of his statements to their children, the father goes on to say, "Look, all I know for sure is that were *not* the conquistadors in this story."[39] At this point a follow-up question for students would be, "Why do you think the family never identifies with the conquistadors?" I understand the critique that the comic is trying to make: how Puerto Ricans, like the Indigenous population before them, are at the mercy of imperialists—especially considering the family in the comic is dealing with the aftermath of Hurricane Maria. However, the insistence that they are not the conquistadors in this story ignores the very real possibility that they are descendants of Spaniards, or, in other words, they are related to the conquistadors in this story.

There is also the issue of the erasure of African influence and the history of slavery and rebellion in the Caribbean. Across the stories in the anthology, whether they are historical, fantastical, or set in the present day, I saw little focus on Afro-Boricua history or African deities like the Yoruba gods. The influence of African peoples on the island did not seem to make the editorial cut. While I am not privy to the editorial decisions of the collection, I do question the absence of any strong Black experience in the collection. Ultimately, this was a missed opportunity. There are many sources that comic creators could have used to create historical graphic narrative, such as Guillermo A. Baralt's *Slave Revolts in Puerto Rico: Conspiracies and Uprisings, 1795–1873*.[40] Juan Giusti-Cordero, in his review of the book, writes, "*Slave Revolts in Puerto Rico* is an excellent, accessible introduction to the history of Puerto Rican slavery, combining general overviews with local descriptions of several plantation areas."[41] Baralt's book includes twenty accounts of rebellions by enslaved persons that could have provided material for a story about Black resistance on the island.[42] I would recommend pairing *Slave Revolts in Puerto Rico* with one of the comics in the anthology on colonial resistance to address this gap.

Conclusion

Whether it was the thoughtful responses on the discussion board or their comments during class, one thing was clear: students are eager to read Latinx comics. When I teach the comics anthology again, I would foreground class lectures and activities with concepts about the visual culture of Latinx comics, Latin American literary allusions, the history of reproductive eugenics, the Taíno revitalization movement on the island, and Afro-Boricua experiences and resistance. While I taught the comics anthology in a literature classroom, it would be valuable in a cultural studies or history course. When thinking through the history of Latinx visual culture, I would spend more time on the page layout, panels, color scheme, and narrative shifts (how panel transitions denote movement between past and present). I see the possibility to draw connections to other prominent Latinx comics, such as Gilbert and Jaime Hernandez's series *Love and Rockets* (1982–1996), which also shift between realistic and futuristic stories.[43] *Puerto Rico Strong*'s blending of memoir, medical history, and colonization is indicative of the interdisciplinary nature of Latinx comics.

I suggest anyone teaching *Puerto Rico Strong* in a literature classroom look at the allusions made in the comic "Macondo, Puerto Rico" by Javier Morillo and Dan Méndez Moore. Arbino points to the literary allusion in the comic to Gabriel García Márquez's *One Hundred Years of Solitude* (1967).[44] Specifically, the comic posits a future architecture that can withstand hurricanes and invokes the past of the fictional town of Macondo in García Márquez's novel, which is devastated by a multiyear storm.[45] For a more historical approach, Lopez's study of sterilization within the larger history of birth control in Puerto Rico would pair well with Shwed's comics "La Operacíon" and "The Puerto Rican Birth Control Stories." Lopez posits, "Migration was seen as the temporary method—the escape valve—while sterilization, or la operacíon—was considered the permanent solution."[46] "La Operacíon" must be examined within the larger framework of an empire that relied on mass migration, especially the recent wave after Hurricane Maria, which is an important part of the history of Puerto Rican reproductive rights. In addition, Shwed's comics are part of the work of graphic medicine that involves comics and public health. Graphic medicine is a field within comic studies that focuses on how comics are used to tell narratives of health care, illness, and ableism.

Those interested in critiquing the overemphasis of Taíno heritage in many of the comics would do well to read García's comparison of *Turey El Taíno* (1989) by Ricardo Álvarez-Rivón and *La Borinqueña* (2016) by Edgardo Miranda-Rodriguez, which examines how the comics craft a narrative "with this imagery and fictionalized contact with precolonial Indigenous tribes, the Taínos are absorbed as an integral part of Puerto Rican nationalism."[47] Several of the stories from *Puerto Rico Strong* that focus on a historical or speculative retelling of Taíno warriors on the island are constructive inquiries for students to examine how literature is used to develop or reimagine cultural and national belonging. In addition, we can critique mestizaje and Indigenous appropriation in Latinx literature. Whether the class to be taught is on Latinx comics or graphic narratives more generally or is a Latinx literature or cultural studies class, *Puerto Rico Strong* can be usefully studied as it is rife with the varied narratives that show the complexity of Latinx comics.

Notes

1 Marco Lopez, Desiree Rodriguez, Hazel Newlevant, Derek Ruiz, and Neil Schwartz, eds., *Puerto Rico Strong* (New York: Lion Forge, 2018).

2 Lopez et al., *Puerto Rico Strong*, back cover. Their publisher, Lion Forge, pledged to donate profits from the anthology specifically to United Way of Puerto Rico. See David Betancourt, "A New Comic Book Anthology Raises Money for Puerto Rico, Telling Stories of History and Fantasy," *Washington Post*, March 15, 2018, https://www.washingtonpost.com/news/comic-riffs/wp/2018/03/15/a-new-comic-book-anthology-raises-money-for-puerto-rico-telling-stories-of-history-and-fantasy/.

3 María Fernanda Díaz-Basteris, "Traumatic Displacement in Puerto Rican Digital Graphic Narratives," *a/b: Auto/Biography Studies* 35, no. 2 (2020): 467–474, 467.

4 "Boricua" refers to the Taíno, or Arawak, word for the original people of the island of Puerto Rico, which was called Borikén.
5 Paul Humphrey, "Framing a Decolonial Future: Hurricane María in Independent Puerto Rican Comics," *Latin American Literary Review* 48, no. 96 (2021): 61–74, 72.
6 I use text in the more general sense to refer to any piece of material that can be critically examined.
7 Marshall McLuhan, *Understanding Media: The Extensions of Man* (Boston: MIT Press, 1964).
8 Dale Jacobs, "Text, Object, Transaction: Reconciling Approaches to the Teaching of Comic Approaches to the Teaching of Comics," in *With Great Power Comes Great Pedagogy: Teaching, Learning, and Comics*, ed. Susan E. Kirtley, Antero Garcia, and Peter E. Carlson (Jackson: University Press of Mississippi, 2020), 23–37, 26.
9 Jacobs, "Text, Object, Transaction," 26.
10 Adam Lance Garcia and Heidi Black, "Stories from My Father," in Lopez et al., *Puerto Rico Strong*, 52–57.
11 Jacobs, "Text, Object, Transaction," 29.
12 Gabriel Sealey-Morris, "The Rhetoric of the Paneled Page: Comics and Composition Pedagogy," in "Comics, Multimodality, and Composition," special issue, *Composition Studies* 43, no. 1 (Spring 2015): 31–50, 32.
13 Susan E. Kirtley, Antero Garcia, and Peter E. Carlson, "Introduction: A Once and Future Pedagogy," in Kirtley, Garcia, and Carlson, *With Great Power Comes Great Pedagogy*, 3–19, 12.
14 I have taught classes on Afro-Latinx studies and Latinx memoir where I have incorporated comics from Breena Nuñez and Cristy C. Road.
15 Vito Delsante and Yehudi Mercado, "Cocinar," in Lopez et al., *Puerto Rico Strong*, 126–129.
16 Delsante and Mercado, "Cocinar," 127.
17 Daniel Arbino, "The Gifts of the Hurricane: Reimagining Post-María Puerto Rico through Comics," *eTropic: Electronic Journal of Studies in the Tropics* 2, no. 1 (2021): 156–179.
18 Héctor Fernández L'Hoeste, "The Isle Is Full of Noises: *Puerto Rico Strong*, Hurricane María, and the Role of Memory in the Reimagination of a Boricua Nation," *Camino real: estudios de las hispanidades norteamericanas* 13, no. 16 (2021): 55–84, 59.
19 I do not limit this definition to the United States because there are Latin American diasporic groups in other places, such as Dominicans in Italy.
20 Emira Derbel, "Teaching Literature through Comics: An Innovative Pedagogical Tool," *International Journal of Applied Linguistics & English Literature* 8, no. 1 (2019): 54–61, 58.
21 Derbel, "Teaching Literature through Comics," 58.
22 Kirtley, Garcia, and Carlson, "Introduction," 7.
23 Ally Shwed, "La Operacíon" and "The Puerto Rican Birth Control Stories," in Lopez et al., *Puerto Rico Strong*, 102–105.
24 Shwed, "La Operacíon," 102–103.
25 Coined by Ian Williams, "graphic medicine" refers to "the intersection between the medium of comics and the discourse of healthcare." See Ian Williams, "What Is 'Graphic Medicine'?," *Graphic Medicine*, accessed December 9, 2022, http://www.graphicmedicine.org/why-graphic-medicine.
26 Shwed, "La Operacíon," 103.

27 Iris Lopez, "The Birth Control Movement in Puerto Rico," in *Matters of Choice: Puerto Rican Women's Struggle for Reproductive Freedom* (New Brunswick, NJ: Rutgers University Press, 2008), 3–19.
28 Lopez, "Birth Control Movement in Puerto Rico," 3.
29 Lopez, "Birth Control Movement in Puerto Rico," 5.
30 Shwed, "La Operacíon," 103.
31 Yolanda Martínez-San Miguel, "Taíno Warriors? Strategies for Recovering Indigenous Voices in Colonial and Contemporary Hispanic Caribbean Discourses," *Centro, the Center for Puerto Rican Studies* 23, no. 1 (2011): 196–215, 198.
32 Tony Bedard and John Holmes, "Reality Check," in Lopez et al., *Puerto Rico Strong*, 178–180.
33 Bedard and Holmes, "Reality Check," 178.
34 Bedard and Holmes, "Reality Check," 178.
35 Enrique García, "Turey El Taíno and La Borinqueña: Puerto Rican Nationalist and Ethnic Resistance in Puerto Rican Comics Dealing with Taíno Cultural Heritage," in *Graphic Indigeneity: Comics in the Americas and Australasia*, ed. Frederick Luis Aldama (Jackson: University Press of Mississippi, 2020), 210–233, 224.
36 Martínez-San Miguel, "Taíno Warriors?," 210.
37 Martínez-San Miguel, "Taíno Warriors?," 179.
38 Martínez-San Miguel, "Taíno Warriors?," 200.
39 Bedard and Holmes, "Reality Check," 180.
40 Guillermo A. Baralt, *Slave Revolts in Puerto Rico: Conspiracies and Uprisings, 1795–1873*, trans. Christine Ayorinde (Princeton, NJ: Markus Wiener, 2007).
41 Juan Giusti-Cordero, "Review of Slave Revolts in Puerto Rico. Conspiracies and Uprisings 1795–1873 by Guillermo A. Baralt," *International Review of Social History* 54, no. 2 (August 2009): 289–291, 289.
42 Baralt, *Slave Revolts in Puerto Rico.*
43 See Enrique García, *The Hernandez Brothers: Love, Rockets, and Alternative Comics* (Pittsburgh: University of Pittsburgh Press, 2017).
44 Javier Morillo and Dan Méndez Moore, "Macondo, Puerto Rico," in Lopez et al., *Puerto Rico Strong*, 155–162.
45 Arbino, "Gifts of the Hurricane," 166.
46 Lopez, "Birth Control Movement in Puerto Rico," 9.
47 García, "Turey El Taíno and La Borinqueña," 216.

Nationalism in the Puerto Rican Context

NICKY RODRIGUEZ

THE ANTICOLONIAL NATIONALISM OF PUERTO RICO

NICKY RODRIGUEZ

NATIONALISM IS A LOADED WORD, ESPECIALLY WHEN USED IN THE CONTEXT OF THE UNITED STATES.

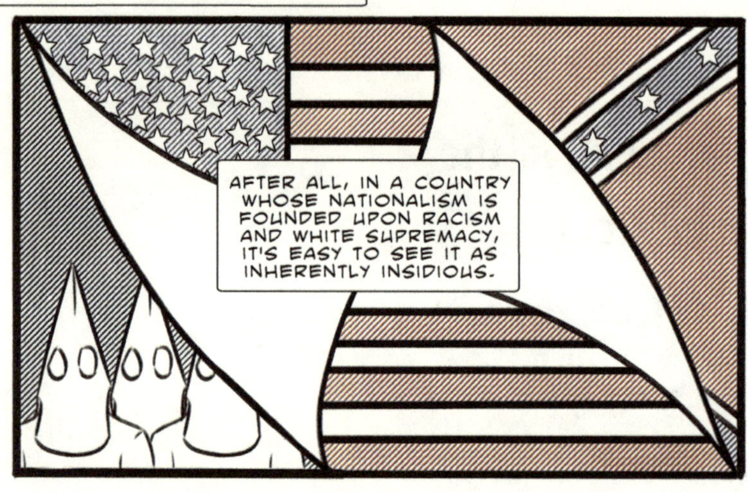

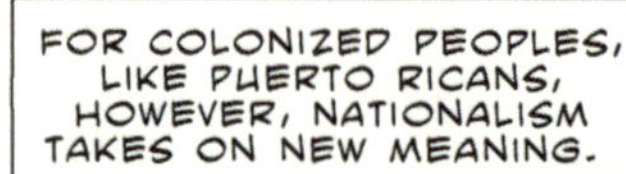

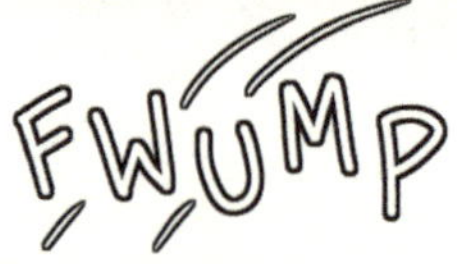

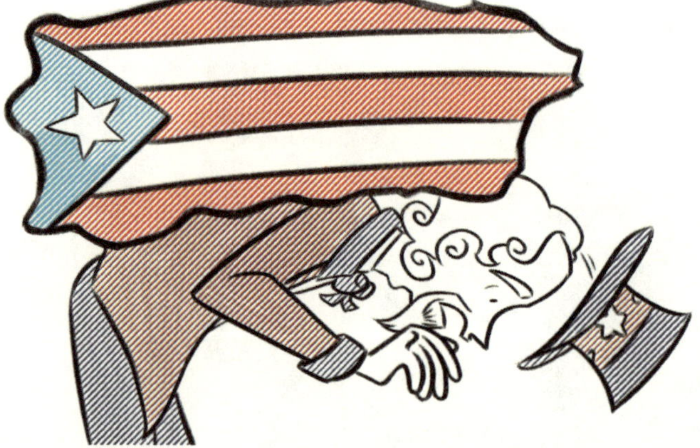

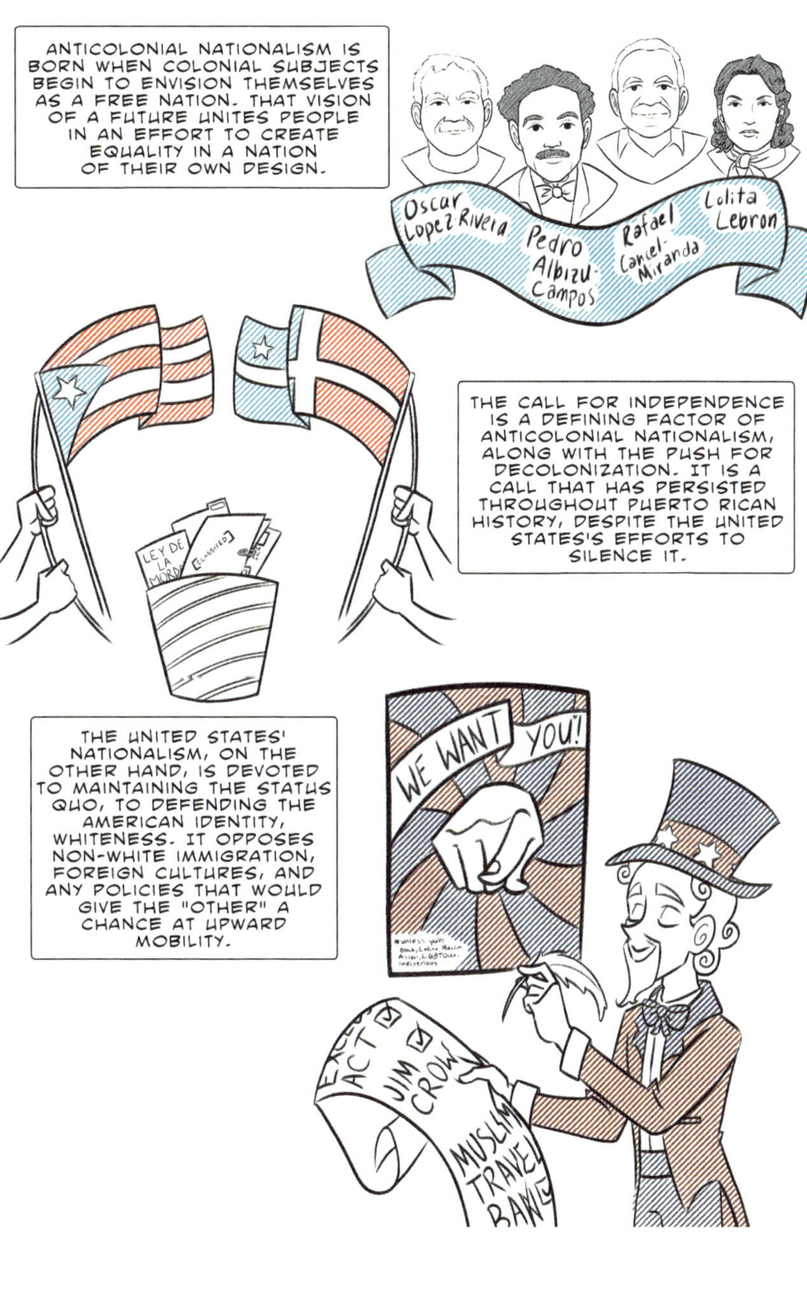
ANTICOLONIAL NATIONALISM IS BORN WHEN COLONIAL SUBJECTS BEGIN TO ENVISION THEMSELVES AS A FREE NATION. THAT VISION OF A FUTURE UNITES PEOPLE IN AN EFFORT TO CREATE EQUALITY IN A NATION OF THEIR OWN DESIGN.
Oscar Lopez Rivera
Pedro Albizu-Campos
Rafael Cancel-Miranda
Lolita Lebron
THE CALL FOR INDEPENDENCE IS A DEFINING FACTOR OF ANTICOLONIAL NATIONALISM, ALONG WITH THE PUSH FOR DECOLONIZATION. IT IS A CALL THAT HAS PERSISTED THROUGHOUT PUERTO RICAN HISTORY, DESPITE THE UNITED STATES'S EFFORTS TO SILENCE IT.
LEY DE LA MORDA
[CLASSIFIED]
THE UNITED STATES' NATIONALISM, ON THE OTHER HAND, IS DEVOTED TO MAINTAINING THE STATUS QUO, TO DEFENDING THE AMERICAN IDENTITY, WHITENESS. IT OPPOSES NON-WHITE IMMIGRATION, FOREIGN CULTURES, AND ANY POLICIES THAT WOULD GIVE THE "OTHER" A CHANCE AT UPWARD MOBILITY.
WE WANT YOU!
ACT
JIM CROW
MUSLIM TRAVEL BAN

NATIONALISM IN THE U.S. IS A CELEBRATION OF WHITE MILITANCY, WHITE CHRISTIAN VALUES, AND WHITE SUPREMATISM. THESE PERVASIVE IDEAS CONTINUE TO SHAPE AMERICAN SYMBOLS AND DEPICTIONS OF HISTORY, BE IT IMPLICIT OR EXPLICITLY.

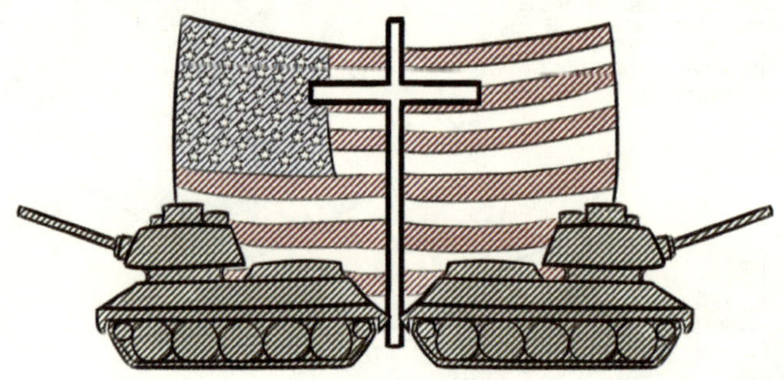

STILL, IT IS IMPORTANT TO UNDERSTAND THAT NATIONALISM ISN'T ALWAYS LIKE THIS. PUERTO RICAN NATIONALISM AND OTHER ANTICOLONIAL NATIONALISTIC MOVEMENTS EXIST TO PROMOTE DECOLONIZATION AND ARE BORN THROUGH THE RESISTANCE OF A PEOPLE AGAINST THE FORCES THAT OPPRESS THEM.

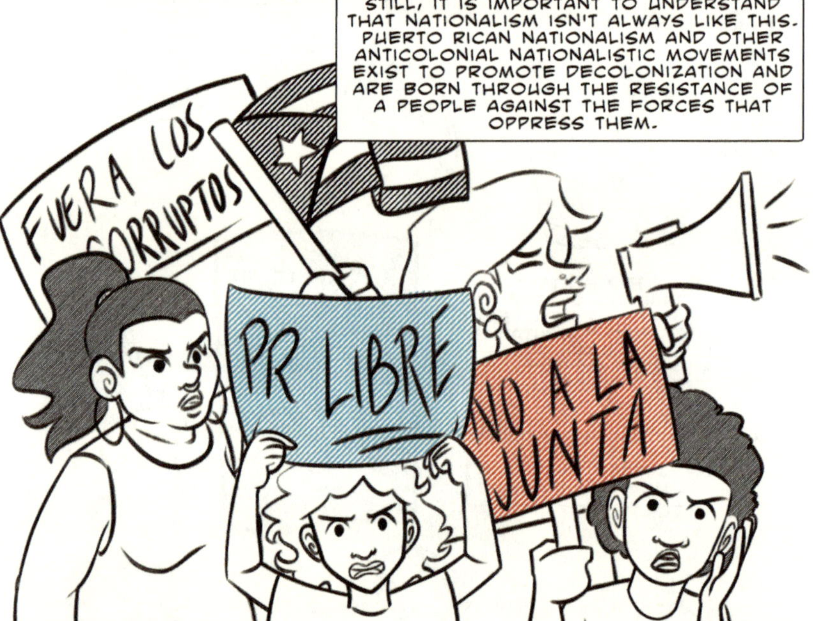

DRIVEN BY THE DESIRE FOR FREEDOM, PUERTO RICAN NATIONALISM GIVES PUERTO RICANS AGENCY TO RECLAIM THEIR HISTORY, CULTURE, AND TO SHAPE THEIR FUTURE. IT IS NOT A NATIONALISM THAT SERVES THE HEGEMONIC CLASS, BUT INSTEAD A NATIONALISM THAT FOSTERS REVOLUTION FOR A FREE AND INDEPENDENT PUERTO RICO.

DIKE, STEVEN. "LA VIDA EN LA COLONIA: OSCAR LEWIS, THE CULTURE OF POVERTY, AND THE STRUGGLE FOR THE MEANING OF THE PUERTO RICAN NATION." *CENTRO JOURNAL*, XXVI, 2014, PP. 172-191. *JSTOR*, ACCESSED 27 DEC. 2021.

GHERASIM, GABRIEL C. "AN IDEOGRAPHY OF AMERICAN NATIONALISM." *STUDIA UBB. EUROPAEA*, LXV, 2020, PP. 267-293. *JSTOR*, HTTPS://DOI.ORG/10.24193/SUBBEUROPAEA.2020.1.13. ACCESSED 27 DEC. 2021.

GO, JULIAN, AND JAKE WATSON. "ANTICOLONIAL NATIONALISM FROM IMAGINED COMMUNITIES TO COLONIAL CONFLICT." *EUROPEAN JOURNAL OF SOCIOLOGY*, 2019, PP. 31-68. *JSTOR*, HTTPS://DOI.ORG/10.1017/S000397561900002X. ACCESSED 27 DEC. 2021.

LECOURS, ANDR . "THE POLITICS OF NATIONALISM AND STATUS IN PUERTO RICO." *CANADIAN JOURNAL OF POLITICAL SCIENCE*, 2017. *JSTOR*, HTTPS://DOI.ORG/10.1017/S0008423917000488. ACCESSED 27 DEC. 2021.

LIEVEN, ANATOL. *AMERICA RIGHT OR WRONG: AN ANATOMY OF AMERICAN NATIONALISM*. OXFORD UNIVERSITY PRESS, 2012. *JSTOR*, ACCESSED 27 DEC. 2021.

MANELA, EREZ. "THE WILSONIAN MOMENT: SELF-DETERMINATION AND THE INTERNATIONAL ORIGINS OF ANTICOLONIAL NATIONALISM." *JOURNAL OF GLOBAL HISTORY*, 2011, PP. 153-155. *JSTOR*, HTTPS://DOI.ORG/10.1017/S174002281100009X. ACCESSED 27 DEC.2021.

POWER, MARGARET. "PUERTO RICAN NATIONALISM IN CHICAGO." *CENTRO JOURNAL*, XXVIII, 2016, PP. 36-66. *JSTOR*.

Part II

Latinx Migrations: Borders and Borderlands

• • • • • • • • • • • • • •

The Fence and the Grid

Reading the U.S.-Mexico Multi-Border as an Infrastructure for Comics

MARCEL BROUSSEAU AND

KATHERINE KELP-STEBBINS

Panel Borders and National Borders

Comics are a quintessential medium of border studies. The panel borders that enframe and make place on the comics page are, much like national borders, imaginary, operative, visual, and instrumental all at once. As a literal and figurative medium of border studies, comics provides an exigent method for critically analyzing the complex symbolic and material histories of the U.S.-Mexico border. Nearly two thousand miles of lines, fences, and walls defined in the nineteenth century and built piecemeal since, the border is, as Peter Andreas claims, as "expressive" as it is "instrumental," a symbol of xenophobia and also a physical mechanism for processing racialized bodies.[1] "There is no doubt that the US-Mexico border is 'the' border in Latina/o studies," Nicole Guidotti-Hernández declares, while simultaneously advocating for a "Latina/o multi-border perspective."[2] Drawing inspiration from Guidotti-Hernández, this chapter considers the ways comics reframe the U.S.-Mexico border as itself a multi-border, a real and symbolic medium characterized by historic fluctuation and transcultural referentiality.

As graphic depictions of the U.S.-Mexico multi-border intersect and merge with the panel borders of comics, the "assumed cartographies of Latina/o studies" are redrawn to encompass the subjectivity of hemispheric Americans as well as those of global artists and border crossers.[3] At stake in this graphic remapping is the meaning of Latinidad as itself a multiplicity, as what Alejandro de Acosta calls "a possibility . . . of exchanges among people of varying nationalities, subjected to different racializations, bearing the histories of many ethnicities and kinships."[4] In the comics we examine, Latinidad emerges as a transnational space of possibility for "conversations and coalitions among people marginalized in various ways" by the U.S.-Mexico multi-border.[5] This space of possibility is defined as much by a multilingual critique of biopolitical hegemony as by multiethnic origins. The comics we bring together—including works by Mexican American, or Chicano, and Mexican artists Jaime Hernandez, Lalo Alcaraz, and Tony Sandoval; Palestinian American artist Leila Abdelrazaq; and Italian creators Andrea Ferraris and Renato Chiocca—evince a transcultural resistance to the U.S.-Mexico multi-border even as they negotiate their own national positionality. The multi-border critique of these artists is not only geographically disparate but temporally diverse. Each comic engages different historical iterations of the U.S.-Mexico border, providing an anthropological timeline of border infrastructure: Hernandez and Sandoval depict the chain-link and mesh fences constructed in the 1970s and 1980s; Sandoval and Alcaraz, the landing-mat fences of the 1990s; and Abdelrazaq and Ferraris and Chiocca, the bollard walls built in the 2000s. Each work invokes the border as a thematic and formal object that examines the force of the nation-state while mediating narrative discourse. By conflating the political and artistic infrastructures of the national border and the comics grid, these multi-border comics interrogate the processes by which the "citizen" and the "foreigner," the reader and the read, are formed.

Exploring the dynamic relations between political borders and panel borders has become an emergent field of analysis as more global comics narrativize the twenty-first-century movement of refugees and migrants across transnational boundaries. As Biz Nijdam argues, in comics about the "refugee experience," panel borders thematize border structures in ways that exceed narrative, "offer[ing] an additional level of interpretation that integrates aspects of the refugee experience difficult to articulate through the comics [*sic*] verbal-visual narrative content."[6] By rethinking and rupturing the form of comics to account for political and social processes, artists "[invent] new visual strategies to communicate the [precarity of life in border zones] that mobilize the formal characteristics of the comics medium."[7] Dominic Davies likewise contends that comics' visual register confronts a reader with visions of spaces that they are not meant to see, "spaces which gather especially at [the United States'] ever-hardening borders," where migratory bodies are regulated and discarded.[8] As Davies argues, the violence of the border—enacted upon the bodies of migrants, and on women in particular, and enabled by liminal legality at the border—is a crisis of "representation and exception."[9] Those without representation—a politically visible existence, or legal rights—become subject to invisible violations and violences. Comics intervene in this social formula by not only visually representing the excluded but also depicting processes of exception through the spatial and figurative arrangements of the comics page. In Davies's analysis, comics can signify the compartmentalization of border bodies and border places and "make visible—and participate in—the array of spatial practices that challenge the violence these borders inflict."[10]

Like Davies, we center our analysis on the U.S.-Mexico border. However, as we rethink the border as a multi-border, we also focus on the particular infrastructural component of the border fence/wall, which, as multiple historically instantiated and materially distinct objects, provides material evidence of the multi-border. Focusing on the border fence/wall allows us to engage a deeper archive of graphic engagement with what Davies calls "the longer history of the border's gradually militarized hardening, as well as the endemic violence slowly brewing around it."[11] Although Davies finds only "a limited number of comics tackling the US-Mexico border [and the] the exceptional spaces and border towns scattered along the US-Mexico line,"[12] we begin our analysis in the 1980s and trace a continuous history of comics incorporating the U.S.-Mexico multi-border fence/wall in diegetic and formal ways while also crossing generic and national boundaries.

Rather than a completist history, the constellation of comics we have chosen frames the multi-border as a site in continuous revision. We offer an archive and pedagogical resource that is explicitly against the grain in its aims and methods, intended to demonstrate the border and the barriers, built, unbuilt, or imagined upon it, as "plural, hemispheric, and multi-sited."[13] As a starting node in this network of comics, Jaime Hernandez's "Queen Rena: Life at 34" (1985) is a story published in *Love and Rockets*, an alternative comic that has engaged the marketplace between underground and mainstream comics,[14] while also intersecting narratives and themes from science fiction, punk culture, and Latinx/Chicanx cultures and subcultures for the past four decades. Considering Hernandez's work from at least two critical vantages—comics studies and Latinx studies—shows that a story such as "Queen Rena: Life at 34" can be analyzed as of a piece with a 1980s "reenvisioning of comics"[15] at the same time that it can be considered as a form of Chicano "aesthetic activism" coeval with visual art by artists such as Malaquías Montoya and literature by writers such as Gloria Anzaldúa, among others.[16] Pursuing this comparison further allows one to follow the U.S.-Mexico multi-border fence as a motif connecting, for example, Montoya's 1981 silkscreen *Undocumented*, which depicts a figure labeled "undocumented" ensnared in a barbed-wire fence, with Hernandez's 1985 "Queen Rena," which shows a mesh border fence as a legal limit determining the characters' actions, with Anzaldúa's 1987 "The Homeland Aztlán: El Otro México," where barbed-wire and chain-link fencing function as poetical symbols and historical objects of violent conquest. Even a network of texts as discrete as this one reveals how Chicanx artists' aesthetic activism around the U.S.-Mexico multi-border fence extends continuously through time and across media. At the same time, each medium manifests unique modes of engagement. Hernandez's comics are, despite their political and even technical affinities, discursively different from Montoya's silkscreens and Anzaldúa's poetics. They emerge from a specific artistic genealogy and thus engage the fence in formal and narrative ways distinct from other aesthetically activist Latinx texts.

Comics frame borders differently. As Hillary Chute argues, "While all media do the work of framing, comics manifests material frames—and the absences between them."[17] Thus, Hernandez not only renders the U.S.-Mexico multi-border fence as an icon in a visual narrative but also frames the fence in borderlines of his own making, and thus analogizes the processes of national borders and comics borders. By "literaliz[ing] on the page the work of framing and making, and also what framing excludes,"[18] Hernandez and the other artists whose work we examine here use comics as a mode of analysis that deconstructs the U.S.-Mexico border and its infrastructure using the very techniques of linear allotment that ground and potentiate the border itself. Stripped to their technical substrate in the form of the comics grid, and rendered subjectively by the hand of comics artists, the border and the border fence—the verticalization of the border—are outed as inscriptions and constructions that assume the position of a necessary spatial and social order. In comics, both the fence and the grid become objects in diegetic action and means of framing that action. The tensions inherent in this multivalent aspect of comics "call for negotiation among various possible meanings" of the border.[19] If, as Charles Hatfield states, comics "beckon their readers [to] recogn[ize the] complex relationship" among their formal elements as a "prerequisite to grappling with the literary, sociohistorical and ideological aspects of the form" itself,[20] then comics depicting the border fence/wall extend the scale. They compel readers to see national borders and their infrastructures as similarly complex formalizations that order a larger narrative that may or may not include them. Likewise, the multiplicity of comics borders "concurrently delineate the drawn form's spatial proportions (via two-dimensional drawings on the page) and instantiate a flexible temporality" by making the time of each space relative to the position of the observer.[21]

As texts that locate readers relative to the U.S.-Mexico multi-border, the comics we examine span a range of genres and thus historicize the borderlands differently, even as they formalize this space using common techniques. In bringing together these disparate comics, we address what Ralph Rodriguez calls the "question of scale . . . for organizing a corpus or network of literary texts."[22] In his theoretical reconsideration of Latinx literature, Rodriguez argues for the utility of genre as a "scale that might allow us to understand better the complexities and nuances of what we have heretofore considered Latinx literature" as it also "allow[s for] regular and compelling connections to literatures that fall outside of the Latinx parameters."[23] Where Rodriguez prioritizes genre as a way to rethink and diversify ethnic canons and labels, we prioritize the multi-border as a subject that can correlate to a diverse multicanon without delimiting Latinx experiences of the U.S.-Mexico border. The comics we examine diagram multi-border fences and walls as symbolically and materially determinant technologies that make national and racial lines visible, while also marking uneasy conflations between the globalized infrastructures of national borders and the borders of the comics grid.

A Flimsy Wire to Freedom

Of all the comics we examine, Jaime Hernandez's 1985 vignette "Queen Rena: Life at 34" is the least overt in its status as a comic about the U.S.-Mexico multi-border. The story was first published in *Love and Rockets* no. 15, and you might even have to squint to catch sight of the metal mesh fence lurking in the background of four panels. Most of the identically sized sixty-four panels that compose the story (with one borderless panel providing the title) foreground the tense interpersonal exchanges between former wrestling foes Bull Marie and Rena Titañon. And yet it is the U.S.-Mexico border that both drives and constrains the circuitous narrative trajectory.

The eight pages of story, each split into eight panels, find the titular Queen Rena chasing convict Sharkey as he tries to cross the border fence. Rena delays Sharkey long enough for her nemesis Bull Marie to imprison him. Later Marie releases him, leading to yet another chase on the final page, wherein Rena stops him from crossing the fence. The circularity of the narrative suggests the border as punchline: Rena's companion, Duke, ominously warns, "If Sharkey reaches the border, no one's gonna be able to get to him!"[24] However, while Sharkey's compulsion to repeat brings him asymptotically to the fence twice, he never makes it beyond and into his imagined freedom from the women pursuing him. The joke of the story rests simultaneously on the diegetic transactions between Rena's and Bull Marie's objectives as well as on the formal structure of the story itself. Hernandez uses the comics grid to foreshadow the futility of Sharkey's quest, while Rena and Bull Marie demonstrate the ironic incompatibilities of justice and the law.

Rena is driven to avenge Sharkey's abuse of his girlfriend Rose Ramelli, while Bull Marie pursues Sharkey because "she's the law."[25] This duality is explicitly racialized by Bull Marie, who warns Duke, "I thought I told you and Titañon to butt out of my police business, Mexican!"[26] Bull Marie wields the legal power of the border as a means of discursively putting people in their place, as a tool for conflating citizenship and racial exclusion. In her utterance, "Mexican" becomes a shorthand for "non-White" that she can apply regardless of Duke's own complicated backstory or the fallaciousness of this equation.[27] Within the context of the narrative, the border sorts places, dividing the United States from Mexico, and imposes an ethics of enforcing emplacement. In the fence's first visual appearance, Bull Marie stands in the midground directly between Sharkey and his destination.[28] The next panel positions her paddy wagon likewise standing between the border and Sharkey. This panel and its paginal position in the lower right-hand corner is repeated for the final panel where the role of paddy wagon has been taken up by Rose(y), who chases Duke with a bat while he calls for the police to save him from this form of "personal" justice.[29] The role of the law is inverted from that of the antagonist, keeping Sharkey from the border, to an imagined ally against the justice he will receive.

Likewise, the symbolic status of the border is inverted from a horizon of freedom to an impassable enframing structure. The pattern on Sharkey's jacket metonymically and proleptically signals his affiliation with the border fence and establishes a theme of containment versus escape. Thus, analogized with the fence grid, Sharkey reads the border fence as a form of escape or freedom, a typical convention of the Western outlaw narrative. Once he can "cross that flimsy wire fence," Sharkey will be free from the women hunting him.[30] From a narrative standpoint, Sharkey is the central actant in that his flight toward the border furnishes the exigence for the entire sequence of events. As a "nuclear element" of the plot,[31] Sharkey's flight is characterized by the character's visual resonance with the fence and his cyclical proximity to the fence itself.

However, formally and thematically, Sharkey's interpretation is always already flagged as a misreading, since the fence is also an analogy for the regular four-by-four waffle-iron gridding structure Hernandez uses in this story. Thus, just as Sharkey's actions are delimited by the panel borders emplacing him on the page, Sharkey is metonymically situated on one side of the imagined divide the panels create. So long as we see him in the panels on the page, he has not and cannot cross over to the imagined beyond of the *planche* surface. The fence is further undermined as an escape due to the visual rhyme between the fence and the cell window of the paddy wagon into which Bull Marie throws him. The cell window's own fence-like gridded pattern is drawn as a shadow across Sharkey. The grid that contains Sharkey is written all over his face, border as *objet petit a*. Although Sharkey cannot see the border for the prison it really is, we, as readers, see in Sharkey's face the artistic relations between comics grid, border fence, prison cell, and the dead-end narrative portended by such iconic solidarity. Historically, the border fence at this point may be merely a flimsy wire, but Hernandez demonstrates its viability as a symbol, a sorting mechanism, and a stop.

Fencing the Binational Panel

While Jaime Hernandez has drawn the border fence only sparingly in his prolific career, editorial cartoonist Lalo Alcaraz has essentially documented the political history of the fence in his nearly four decades of work. The escalation of the fence in late twentieth-century border discourse is reflected by Alcaraz's 1994 revision of a comic he first drew as a student cartoonist for the *Daily Aztec* at San Diego State University in 1985.[32] In both cartoons, a U.S. border policeman wielding a baton apologizes for assaulting and battering Mr. Spock after racially misreading him as Mexican. The nearly identical scenario in the two cartoons attests to the continued state of exception determined by the multi-border, where those legally classed as "aliens"—for example, Mexicans, Central Americans, or Vulcans, in this case—can be subjected to extralegal violence. However, in Alcaraz's continuous satire, Mr. Spock's alterity as nonhuman space "alien" is not the reason for his victimization. As the police make clear, border violence is a discursive act that fundamentally equates "alien" with "Mexican."

Although his political critique remains consistent in the decade spanning the two comics, subtle changes indicate qualitative shifts in Alcaraz's perception of the multi-border. In the 1985 cartoon, the lawman is a Border Patrol agent, as indicated by block lettering on his shirt;[33] in the 1994 cartoon, it is an Immigration and Naturalization Service (INS) agent who confronts Spock.[34] The Border Patrol agent in the earlier cartoon is a blond, clean-cut man who speaks in unaccented speech, while the INS agent in the later cartoon is mustachioed and speaks with a regional dialect, as indicated by his use of the phrase "I thought you *was* a Mexican" (emphasis added). These fluctuations in the antagonist's typology indicate what Héctor D. Fernández L'Hoeste calls "the stylistic evolution of Alcaraz as he tries to figure out a more appropriate manner for a critique of the normative cultural order."[35] In his role as witness "for the predicaments and travails of Latinos,"[36] Alcaraz is daily adapting his critical gaze to hegemonic shifts in the landscape of the border. In this regard, the most telling change in the 1994 comic is the inclusion of a landing-mat border fence blocking the horizon behind Spock and the INS agent. By adding a landing-mat fence—war surplus that was used to fortify the border starting in the early 1990s—Alcaraz recontextualizes U.S. state violence in relation to what the architect of the landing-mat fence, Border Patrol chief Gustavo De la Viña, called the "delineat[ion] of the border to show the migrants and us where the U.S. began and where Mexico ended."[37] In the scenario presented by Alcaraz's second cartoon, the physical violence of policing is compounded by the environmental violence of the fence, reflecting a progressively systemized method for blocking and regulating migrant bodies that ironically results in the same viciousness and petty tyranny of earlier times.

However, Alcaraz's use of the fence to make place on the page compounds his political critique vis-à-vis the reader. By transnationally partitioning the cartoon, the fence enacts a three-dimensional border that frames the action as a geographical event on the U.S. side. This perspectival empaneling of space forces readers to position themselves proximal to the violence triangulated by the panel and border fence. This spatial constraint is matched by a temporal constraint also made possible by the fence. Alcaraz's original cartoon used a blank square to frame a moment in time; however, the insertion of the fence frames Spock's beating as a moment in history. The later cartoon is both mapped and dated by the fence, an extant artifact of U.S. violence in the borderlands. In this context, the historical subject of the cartoon is ultimately the reader who is made witness to violence done on their side of the fence.

Conceptually, Alcaraz's cartoons combat what Leo Chavez calls the "Latino threat narrative," which is defined as "a social imaginary in which [the] lives of 'Mexicans,' 'Chicanos,' 'illegal aliens,' and 'immigrants' become abstractions and [and thus] no longer flesh-and-blood people."[38] Interpellating readers into subjective relations with the multi-border remains a major technique in Alcaraz's work up to the present day. With their vision framed by the fence, Alcaraz's readers are forced to question their place in histories of violence. However, Alcaraz's prolific output also beckons the reader to understand the fence as implicated in structures of feeling extending across the borderline, where Mexican subjectivity resists militaristic hegemony through acts of mobility and deterritorialization. As depicted in Alcaraz's work, the border is also a site of "conversations and coalitions" wherein the multi-border becomes a site of play—as in a comic depicting ladder prototypes specially designed to cross border-wall prototypes—and a site of self-expression—as in comics depicting word-shaped gaps in the wall that simultaneously indicate the permeability and impermanence of the fence/wall and indict the racism it materializes. In Alcaraz's tireless oeuvre, the multiplicity of the U.S.-Mexico border is ever met by a multiplicity of imaginative critique.

Biopolitics, Necropolitics, and Nepantla

While Alcaraz's cartoons provide counterimaginaries that interpolate the reader into identificatory relations with multi-bordered lives, Tony Sandoval's graphic cronica *Rendez-vous in Phoenix* engages the reader by, in Monica

Hanna's words, "giv[ing] flesh to numbers, using narrative to humanize the stakes of migration."[39] Sandoval's narrative, which depicts his 1998 journey from Ciudad Obregon, Sonora, across the border to Phoenix, Arizona, and beyond, shows his protagonist confronting the nascent landscape of "prevention through deterrence," the U.S. government's euphemism for the fortified border zone that forces migrants to cross through dangerous desert terrain.[40]

As Tony attempts to cross, he encounters the multi-border in numerous forms, facing chain-link and landing-mat fences in Nogales, not to mention a phalanx of Border Patrol resources. Arrested for the second time near the middle of his story, Tony finds himself within the cage-like partitions of Border Patrol detention, where he and other migrants are processed for deportation.[41] In depicting this carceral contact zone, Sandoval allows the fence to fill entire panels, partitioning the depth of field—à la Alcaraz—and metaphorically capturing migrants in webs of chain-link. However, Sandoval also analogizes the posts of the fence with the gutters of the comic page, aligning a fencepost in the middle-left panel with the gutter above it and using a fencepost to nearly bisect the bottom page-wide panel (see figure 4.1). Drawing an uneasy comparison between the multicadre of the comics page and that of the multi-border jail, Sandoval wages a metacritique of his own processing, subtly indicting comics as a technology for capturing, compartmentalizing, and rendering the other. In Tony's case, both grids—carceral and comic—are biopolitical. The comics grid draws him to the United States (where he hopes to become a professional artist) and allows him to make his living, while the border grid defines and determines where and how he can move and live.

Yet Sandoval shows that the grid is not total. Off the grid, beyond the fence, Tony makes his successful crossing, following subaltern lines of flight on a tabular spread.[42] This liminal space beyond the reach of the state exceeds the biopolitical. It is open space of the nonhuman animal, yet it is also the necropolitical space between sovereignties to which Tony has been pushed, "a third zone between subjecthood and objecthood," between citizenship and incarceration.[43] The risk here is a loss of self and of life; however, as Tony discovers, his travails are also recognizable as, in Gloria Anzaldúa's terms, an entering into nepantla, the in-between space where "cultural and personal codes clash [and] different worlds coalesce" and where the "task of self-redefinition" occurs.[44] Tony's journey has required him to pare his possessions down to a knapsack of bare essentials. This necessary, practical consideration is also, in Anzaldúa's words, an occasion to "take inventory" as

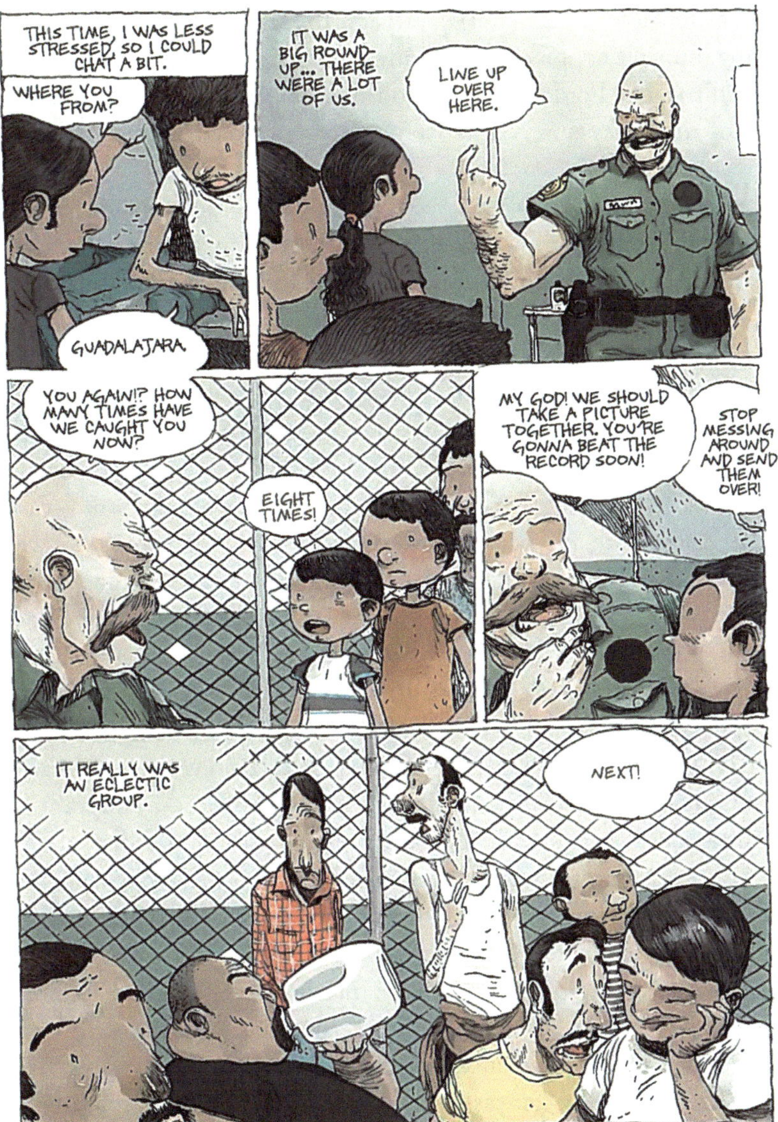

28

FIGURE 4.1 In *Rendez-vous in Phoenix*, Tony Sandoval visually analogizes the posts of migrant detention cages with the gutters of the comic page. Tony Sandoval, *Rendez-vous in Phoenix*, trans. Jeremy Melloul and Mike Kennedy (Chicago: Magnetic Press, 2016), 28.

a means to "deconstruct [and] construct" the self. After losing his knapsack during multiple apprehensions, Tony's intention to "shape new myths" for himself through border crossing is ultimately reified in a single object: a 0.3 Rotring drawing pen.[45] Neither confiscated nor stolen, the pen becomes, in Tony's words, "all I've got left."[46]

In the anxious moments between crossing the borderline and meeting the ride that will take him into Phoenix, Tony dozes off and enters a dreamscape that seems to escape both the comics grid and the border grid.[47] Finding himself in a lush desert, framed by five floating panels without borders, Tony hikes alone to the top of a butte. Conspicuously sweating, he's also visibly content and surreally buoyed by his trusty drawing pen, which has itself become almost as large as his body and has changed both color and line width. In Tony's dream world, relations have shifted at levels of content, form, and materiality: a traffic of allegorical animals—rabbits, a coyote, a reptile—casually crosses Tony's path. His pen, uncapped and oversized, traces his journey without making any lines. Tony's T-shirt, heretofore unmarked, now bears the faint artwork of *Nocturno*, a *bande dessinée* that the author Tony Sandoval will not publish until a decade later. Watercolor, used previously for the comic's backgrounds, has become the primary medium, fading into the page at the edges of the tabula's curving panels.

Tony's nighttime border crossing saw him enact a version of Anzaldúa's paradigmatic image of nepantla, wherein "the Mexican immigrant at the moment of crossing the barbed wired fence into a hostile 'paradise' of el norte, the U.S., is caught in a state of nepantla."[48] However, his watercolor dreamscape presents a more symbolic vision of how "art and la frontera intersect in a liminal space where border people, especially artists, live in a state of 'nepantla.'"[49] In his journey across the transborder tabular spread, Tony is a migrant lugging a jug of water across "uncertain terrain," traveling "into a new identity" as an undocumented immigrant in the United States.[50] In his dreamscape, however, Tony is an artist, carrying a pen with a substantial reservoir of ink, meandering "between imagination and physical existence, between ordinary and nonordinary (spirit) realities."[51] These dream wanderings not only indicate the narrative setting between the national border and the threshold of Tony's life in the United States but also index the author himself, Tony Sandoval, entering into a nepantla state brought on by his chronicling of his own narrative. As it moves through curvilinear panels, the pen Tony carries becomes nearly life-sized to the reader, bridging a gap between imagination and physical reality. Furthermore, the *Nocturno* motif on Tony's shirt places the character of Tony into a future of the author's own making and thus in between the diegetic reality of the text and the authorial present. This unordinary reality places the character of Tony into dynamic relations with the author Tony Sandoval, and shows how Tony Sandoval, the author, was able to ultimately subvert the multi-border as both a graphic and a narrative instrument. Through his graphic cronica, Sandoval rethinks how the border grid and the comics grid work to process flesh as symbol and icon. In the end, he reprocesses himself beyond national borders, as the artist he wished to be and as the artist he became, in the liminal space of a graphic cronica—a self-defining multi-border—of his own making.

Borders of No Nation

Tony, in *Rendez-vous in Phoenix*, subverts the border grid and, ultimately, reframes it by using the comics grid. However, his story is an exception to the borderland's state of exception. *Mariposa Road*, Leila Abdelrazaq's short nonfiction work from 2016, explores the U.S.-Mexico border's imbrication in a global fencescape by recounting the tribulations of Mounis (Hammouda) and Hisham (Shaban Ghalia), two Palestinian refugees detained in 2014 while attempting to enter the United States through the Mariposa Port in Nogales, Arizona. As stateless persons, the men enter Immigration and Customs Enforcement's indefinite detention. The United States will not deport them to a country that it does not recognize; concordantly, they will not be granted entrance into the United States, as there are no diplomatic visa arrangements between the United States and Palestine.

The story goes beyond even Guidotti-Hernández's description of the multi-border as "hemispheric" to implicate the U.S.-Mexico border in a *global* network of multinational commerce, carceral politics, and the management of bodies through space. Herein the axis of the hemisphere rotates to implicate assemblages of corporate and state powers invested in wall building. This global multi-border abrogates disciplinary containment as it reverberates in a local/global, historical/futuristic matrix. Material instantiations of this matrix range from low-tech salvage—such as the landing mats preserved from the Vietnam War and installed on the border in the 1990s—to high-tech surveillance architectures provided by Israeli defense contractors to the United States. As the multi-border of imperial war is imbricated with the multi-border of multinational capital, imperial borders are now transnational contracts: as Wendy

Brown attests, the United States and Israeli wall-building projects "share technology, subcontracting, and also refer to each other for legitimacy."[52]

Published on the website *Electronic Intifada* in 2016, *Mariposa Road* overlays the horizontal figuration of the border wall with a semantic network of verticality.[53] The opening pages showing Mounis and Hisham's drive to the border begin by positioning a splash panel of a horizontally oriented guardrail above another splash panel with two guard rails now projecting upward to the vanishing point in the upper quadrant of the panel and bordering the men in the car.[54] This opening instance of visual metonymy suggests the guardrail as a border (similarly evoked through the accompanying text) that is not merely the horizon of the men's transit but is, in fact, a structure of governmental control ensnaring the men in a state of exception. The following pages make this semantic network clear when vertical panels of the men producing their Palestinian passports for U.S. Customs and Border Protection visually rhyme with the American flag on the next page, hanging over them, with its stripes pointing downward like the bars of an awaiting cage.

The meaningful rotation of otherwise familiar icons and images on a vertical axis continues throughout *Mariposa Road*. In framing Mounis and Hisham's story of incarceration, Abdelrazaq stages a visual dialogue between the Israeli separation wall and the U.S. border fence. Each blockade is figured first in a horizontal trajectory, but this seeming congruence with the narrative flow is upended in a splash page where the walls are instead drawn vertically, limning our protagonists, and recalling the earlier guardrail (see figure 4.2). In what Keith P. Feldman calls the "centerpiece of the story,"[55] this image of Mounis and Hisham holding their passports outstretched between the twin concrete and bollard walls running the length of the page on either side evokes both the political symmetry of these structures as well as their ambivalent role in producing the limits of the state and states of exception. Abdelrazaq's top-down figuration of the border walls mirrors the vertically rendered stripes of the U.S. flag and echoes the prison bars that constrain Hisham and Mounis in later pages. Abdelrazaq uses a visual semantic network to correlate the U.S. border wall and Israel's partition wall as structures of control and visual containment in what Eyal Weizman calls a "politics of verticality," wherein space is annexed by the state on the vertical axis, literally subjecting noncitizens and racialized others to liminal spaces beneath the nation-state.[56] The sequence laid out by Abdelrazaq—border infrastructure, national symbolism, prison infrastructure—proposes a political calculus wherein border fences produce the nation, albeit not through citizenship, but rather through the exclusion and carceral containment of racialized "others."

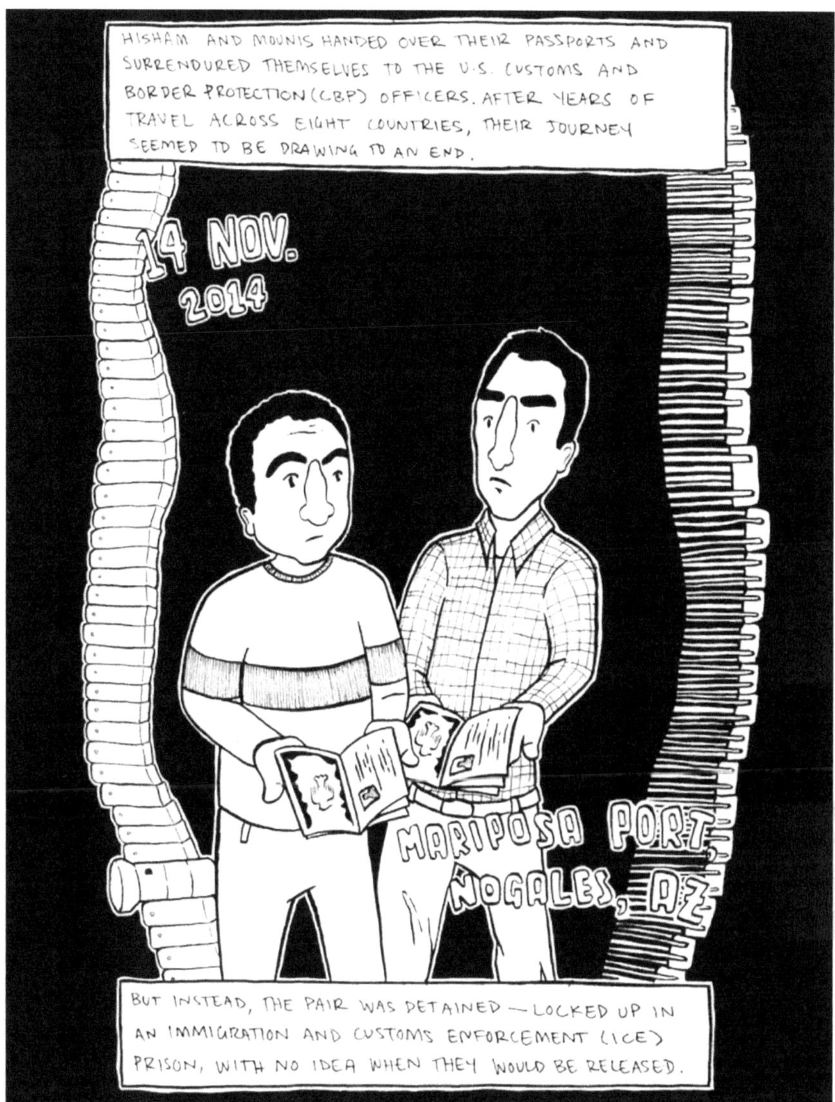

FIGURE 4.2 In *Mariposa Road*, Leila Abdelrazaq correlates the U.S. border wall and Israel's partition wall as structures of control and visual containment. Leila Abdelrazaq, *Mariposa Road* (Chicago: Bigmouth Comix, 2016), n.p.

Abdelrazaq's use of vertical orientations highlights the "conflation of separation/partition with security, violence and control" in the necropolitical aims of the state, but Abdelrazaq also uses vertical disorientation to subvert the architecture of the page and the visual logic of vertical sovereignty.[57] The rotated logic of the walls in the central page is echoed in the rotated logic of maps throughout Abdelrazaq's comic. In the first instance, the map of Central America is flipped to effect the narrative progression of Hisham and Mounis from Venezuela to Nicaragua, to Honduras, and to Mexico. Later, in a three-panel sequence, a maplike image of North America is followed by a rotated map of the Americas, which is in turn followed by an inverted image of the Atlantic, making Africa, South East Asia, South America—the so-called Global South—the primary image of the world. By rotating these maps from their White, Western, Mercator orientation, Abdelrazaq effects what Sarah Ahmed calls a "politics of disorientation," one that challenges the continued relations of the Global South to its rich, Northern neighbors.[58] Drawing them together through networked verticality, Abdelrazaq indicts the transnational corporate interests that oversee border walls, border control, and monetary flows and that relegate figures like Hisham and Mounis to "non-places."[59]

Unfolding Borders in Many Dimensions

The hyperborder of Ambos Nogales, graphically critiqued by Abdelrazaq and Sandoval, is further engaged by artist Andrea Ferraris and documentarian Renato Chiocca, in their 2017 nonfiction work *La cicatrice: sul confine tra Messico e Stati Uniti* (*The Scar: On the Border between Mexico and the United States*), which explores the Nogales border as articulating not just two nations but also the necropolitical and biopolitical aims of the nation-state. The book is itself segmented into two sections, "A Night on the Border" and "A Day on the Border." "A Night on the Border" recounts the events leading up to the murder of José Antonio Elena Rodríguez by U.S. border agent Lonnie Ray Swartz, while "A Day on the Border" contains interviews with humanitarian workers who aim to prevent migrant deaths.

Ferraris and Chiocca use the motif of the sun's passage to provide a clear division between the necropolitical and biopolitical sections of their account. This division is further amplified by the shift in Ferraris's mise-en-page between the two sections. "A Night on the Border" features framed panels throughout the section detailing the final moments of José Antonio's life, while "A Day on the Border" uses interlocking, unbordered panels to follow human rights workers. The distinct panel structures index the different goals of the professionals driving each portion. The border agents seek to maintain and control the lines separating and regulating people and places even if it means killing those who cross (or do not cross, as in the case of José

Antonio). The human rights agents seek to preserve the lives of those who cross, and their borderless panels represent the interconnectedness between people, places, plants, and animals. However, the contrast in paneling also ironically highlights the sameness of the border's effects. For those who cross, there is the threat of death; for those who stay, there is the threat of death. In the night, in the day, the border generates precarity.

Symbolically, Ferraris metaphorizes the border fence as a site of impending danger through the repeated motif of a wave.[60] A double-splash page of a rising wave precedes the narrative and recurs in the centerfold of the book, which shows the wave as it crashes on the desert and figuratively destroys those in its path like José Antonio. The final pages of the book illustrate the debris of migrants caught up in the wake. These three double-splash pages work as a sequence that interrupts and figuratively indexes the contents of *La cicatrice*. The first instance presages the devastation to come, facing the reader as a wall of water and setting the tone of imminent threat. The final pages submerge the reader under the water, imbricating the reader in the threat of border violence.

The irrevocability of the wave metaphor, which alerts the reader to the danger of the border, but leaves little room for resistance, is undercut by the format of the book itself. The jacket of *La cicatrice* folds out into its own border fence, allowing readers to put a wall between themselves and the contents of any page, including the crashing wave of the border's necropolitical impact. But they can also remove the jacket from the book entirely to erect a border wall on any surface (see figure 4.3). The very distinctive construction of *La cicatrice* (Italian) by Oblomov Edizione—as well as *La cicatrice* (French) by Éditions Rackham[61]—re-marks the border as a site of construction and deconstruction. The format of the album encourages readers to interact with the cover and to consider their own complicity and privilege in such constructions.

The U.S. translation published by Fantagraphics Underground (FU) Press, *The Scar: Graphic Reportage from the U.S.-Mexico Border*, does not preserve the format of the European albums, prompting consideration of how other borders partition and enjoin reading constituencies.[62] The smaller trim size of the U.S. version reflects the rarity of the album format in North America, but it also creates a less imposing border wall. The reader's ability to act as border architect, deconstructing and reconstructing the book jacket as a third dimension of the text, is denied by *The Scar*'s publication format whereby the book is perfect bound and the softcover has been modified from its original format to include more promotional and extradiegetic information. Thus, the

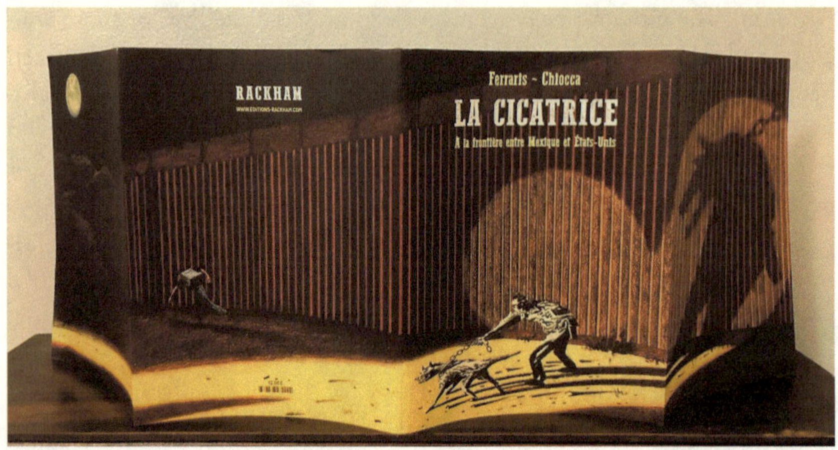

FIGURE 4.3 The jacket of Andrea Ferraris and Renato Chiocca's *La cicatrice* folds out into its own border fence. Andrea Ferraris and Renato Chiocca, *La cicatrice: sul confine tra Messico e Stati Uniti* (Quartu Sant'Elena, Italy: Oblomov Edizioni, 2017).

bollard fence of the border, which runs the height and breadth of the softcover dust jacket in the European versions, is relegated to the bottom half of the FU edition. The upper half is used for a summary and pull quote on the back cover. These seemingly minor changes in the paratext minimize the visual resonance between the cover foldout wall and the opening wave images, which in the European versions are united through mise-en-page, reflecting the enormity and eminence of the wall on those who cross it, as the reader of the album must do by opening the book itself.

Conclusion

The comics in this alternative archive allow us to visualize the U.S.-Mexico border in all its multiplicity, denying a stable object and instead offering relational perspectives and affiliations. In recognition of the multi-border's impact on the page, we must also account for its impact on these works as commodity objects, considering how their publication, translation, and circulation patterns reflect *other* borders and transnational flows within the economies of world comics. Much of our analysis in this chapter focuses on the formal aspects of these works and foregrounds the auteur as the producer. However, as Casey Brienza and Paddy Johnston remind us in *Cultures of Comics Work*, many people and collective labors are demanded by this "field of cultural production," and it is incumbent on any analysis of comics and border studies to consider "the ways in which comics work is embedded in various local and national contexts."[63] As these texts and their creators map transits among the Americas, France, Italy, and Palestine, their printing and publication trajectories suggest yet more imbricated nodes in the warp and weft of comics' globalization with printing sites in places such as Hong Kong and Canada.

Trade regulations that ensure precarity for some sides of border zones also influence the likelihood that books about Nogales will be drawn in Italy, translated in the United States, and manufactured in China. As readers, scholars, and teachers of these texts, we must acknowledge our situation vis-à-vis the unequal spheres of labor and cultural production linked together in the material histories of our comics objects. Under the hundred-mile border zone stipulation, approximately two-thirds of all U.S. residents live in a "border zone," yet it is the privilege of some to read about the border in books shipped overseas or on readily accessed web platforms that conditions the relegation of others to sites of precarity. Just as a border fence is an imaginary, symbolic, and yet grounded material construct, so are these comics imaginary and symbolic works that take place in paper, pixel, pages, and bytes. How we encounter them, how they cross into our hands, and what we do with them are the stakes of our own readerly modes of reframing the multi-border.

Notes

1 Leo R. Chavez, *The Latino Threat: Constructing Immigrants, Citizens, and the Nation*, 2nd ed. (Stanford, CA: Stanford University Press, 2013); Peter Andreas, *Border Games: Policing the U.S.-Mexico Divide*, 2nd ed. (Ithaca, NY: Cornell University Press, 2009), 11.

2 Nicole M. Guidotti-Hernández, "Borderlands," in *Keywords for Latina/o Studies*, ed. Deborah R. Vargas, Nancy Raquel Mirabal, and Lawrence La Fountain-Stokes (New York: New York University Press, 2017), 21–24, 23–24.

3 Guidotti-Hernández, "Borderlands," 24.

4 Alejandro de Acosta, "Latino/a America: A Geophilosophy for Wanderers," in *An Atlas of Radical Cartography*, ed. Lize Mogel and Alexis Bhagat (Los Angeles: Journal of Aesthetics and Protest Press, 2008), 69–76, 72.

5 Acosta, "Latino/a America," 72–73.

6 Elizabeth "Biz" Nijdam, "Tying Up Loose Ends: The Fabric of Panel Borders in Kate Evans' *Threads*," *Inks: The Journal of the Comics Studies Society* 5, no. 1 (2021): 79–99, 90.

7 Nijdam, "Tying Up Loose Ends," 96.

8 Dominic Davies, "Dreamlands, Border Zones, and Spaces of Exception: Comics and Graphic Narratives on the US-Mexico Border," *a/b: Auto/Biography Studies* 35, no. 2 (2020): 383–403, 398.

9 Davies, "Dreamlands, Border Zones, and Spaces of Exception," 392.

10 Davies, "Dreamlands, Border Zones, and Spaces of Exception," 398.
11 Davies, "Dreamlands, Border Zones, and Spaces of Exception," 388.
12 Davies, "Dreamlands, Border Zones, and Spaces of Exception," 388.
13 Guidotti-Hernández, "Borderlands," 24.
14 Enrique García, "Love and Rockets," in *Keywords for Comics Studies*, ed. Ramzi Fawaz, Shelley Streeby, and Deborah Elizabeth Whaley (New York: New York University Press, 2021), 139–143, 139.
15 Charles Hatfield cites Jaime Hernandez as one of a handful of artists responsible for a "reenvisioning of comics" as literary texts that rejected mainstream tropes, embraced new genres, and imagined comics in terms of internationalism as well as personal and political stories. Hatfield, *Alternative Comics: An Emerging Literature* (Jackson: University Press of Mississippi, 2005), x.
16 María Herrera-Sobek, "Barbed Wire Iconography and Aesthetic Activism: The Borderlands, Mexican Immigration, and Chicana/o Art," in *International Perspectives on Chicana/o Studies: "This World Is My Place,"* ed. Catherine Leen and Niamh Thornton (New York: Routledge, 2014), 150–167, 152.
17 Hillary L. Chute, *Disaster Drawn: Visual Witness, Comics, and Documentary Form* (Cambridge, MA: Belknap, 2016), 17.
18 Chute, *Disaster Drawn*, 17.
19 Hatfield, *Alternative Comics*, 65.
20 Hatfield, *Alternative Comics*, 67.
21 Cathy Schlund-Vials, "Border," in Fawaz, Streeby, and Whaley, *Keywords for Comics Studies*, 27–30, 28.
22 Ralph E. Rodriguez, *Latinx Literature Unbound: Undoing Ethnic Expectation* (New York: Fordham University Press, 2018), 3.
23 Rodriguez, *Latinx Literature Unbound*, 3.
24 Jaime Hernandez, "Queen Rena: Life at 34," in *Love and Rockets* no. 15, ed. Gary Groth (Agoura Hills, CA: Fantagraphics Books, 1985), 26.
25 Hernandez, "Queen Rena," 27.
26 Hernandez, "Queen Rena," 26.
27 See Ana Merino, "The Bros. Hernandez: A Latin Presence in Alternative U.S. Comics," in *Redrawing the Nation: National Identity in Latin/o American Comics*, ed. Héctor Fernández L'Hoeste and Juan Poblete (New York: Palgrave Macmillan, 2009), 251–269, 256; and Enrique Garcia, *The Hernandez Brothers: Love, Rockets, and Alternative Comics* (Pittsburgh: University of Pittsburgh Press, 2017), 75.
28 Hernandez, "Queen Rena," 28.
29 Hernandez, "Queen Rena," 32.
30 Hernandez, "Queen Rena," 32.
31 Roland Barthes, *Image Music Text*, ed. and trans. Stephen Heath (London: Fontana Press, 1977), 93.
32 Lalo Alcaraz, *Migra Mouse: Political Cartoons on Immigration by Lalo Alcaraz* (New York: RDV Books, 2004), 18, 67.
33 Alcaraz, *Migra Mouse*, 18.
34 Alcaraz, *Migra Mouse*, 67.
35 Héctor D. Fernández L'Hoeste, *Lalo Alcaraz: Political Cartooning in the Latino Community* (Jackson: University Press of Mississippi, 2017), 6.
36 Fernández L'Hoeste, *Lalo Alcaraz*, 6.
37 Joseph Nevins, *Operation Gatekeeper: The Rise of the "Illegal Alien" and the Making of the U.S.-Mexico Boundary* (New York: Routledge, 2002), 65.

38 Chavez, *Latino Threat*, 46–47.
39 Monica Hanna, "Chronicling Contemporary Latinidad," *American Literature* 88, no. 2 (2016): 361–389, 362.
40 Jason De León, *The Land of Open Graves: Living and Dying on the Migrant Trail* (Oakland: University of California Press, 2015), 34.
41 Tony Sandoval, *Rendez-vous in Phoenix*, trans. Jeremy Melloul and Mike Kennedy (Chicago: Magnetic Press, 2016), 28.
42 Sandoval, *Rendez-vous in Phoenix*, 46–47.
43 Achille Mbembe, *Necropolitics*, trans. Steven Corcoran (Durham, NC: Duke University Press, 2019), 79.
44 Gloria E. Anzaldúa, *Light in the Dark = Luz en lo oscuro: Rewriting Identity, Spirituality, Reality*, ed. AnaLouise Keating (Durham, NC: Duke University Press, 2015), 2; Gloria E. Anzaldúa, *The Gloria Anzaldua Reader*, ed. AnaLouise Keating (Durham, NC: Duke University Press, 2009), 310.
45 Gloria E. Anzaldúa, *Borderlands / La Frontera: The New Mestiza* (San Francisco: Aunt Lute Books, 1987), 82.
46 Sandoval, *Rendez-vous in Phoenix*, 34.
47 Sandoval, *Rendez-vous in Phoenix*, 56–57.
48 Gloria Anzaldúa, "Chicana Artists: Exploring Nepantla, El Lugar de La Frontera," *NACLA Report on the Americas* 27, no. 1 (1993).
49 Anzaldúa, "Chicana Artists."
50 Gloria Anzaldúa, "BorderArte: Nepantla, el Lugar de la Frontera," in Anzaldúa, *The Gloria Anzaldua Reader*, 180.
51 Anzaldúa, *Light in the Dark*, 2.
52 Wendy Brown, *Walled States, Waning Sovereignty* (New York: Zone Books, 2010), 8.
53 Thierry Groensteen, *The System of Comics*, trans. Bart Beaty and Nick Nguyen (Jackson: University Press of Mississippi, 2007), 158.
54 Leila Abdelrazaq, *Mariposa Road* (Chicago: Bigmouth Comix, 2016), n.p. See also Leila Abdelrazaq, "Hisham and Mounis: From Besieged Gaza to US Immigration Jail," *Electronic Intifada*, February 9, 2016, https://electronicintifada.net/blogs/leila-abdelrazaq/hisham-and-mounis-besieged-gaza-us-immigration-jail.
55 Keith P. Feldman, "Carceral Entanglement in the Work of Leila Abdelrazaq," *Qui Parle* 29, no. 1 (2020): 1–14, 6.
56 Eyal Weizman, *Hollow Land: Israel's Architecture of Occupation* (London: Verso, 2007), 12.
57 Weizman, *Hollow Land*, 11.
58 Sarah Ahmed, *Queer Phenomenology: Orientations, Objects, Others* (Durham, NC: Duke University Press, 2006), 24.
59 Abdelrazaq, *Mariposa Road*, n.p.
60 Andrea Ferraris and Renato Chiocca, *La cicatrice: sul confine tra Messico e Stati Uniti* (Quartu Sant'Elena, Italy: Oblomov Edizioni, 2017), n.p.
61 Andrea Ferraris and Renato Chiocca, *La cicatrice: À la frontière entre Mexique et États-Unis*, trans. Sylvestre Zas (Paris: Éditions Rackham, 2018).
62 Andrea Ferraris and Renato Chiocca, *The Scar: Graphic Reportage from the U.S.-Mexico Border*, trans. Jamie Richards (Seattle: Fantagraphics Underground Press, 2019).
63 Casey Brienza and Paddy Johnston, "Introduction: Understanding Comics Work," in *Cultures of Comics Work*, ed. Casey Brienza and Paddy Johnston (London: Palgrave, 2016), 7.

5

El Peso Hero

Comic Book Protagonists of the (Un)Documented Latinx Experience

KAITLIN E. THOMAS AND
HÉCTOR RODRIGUEZ III

Millennial and Gen Z Latinx comic book creatives like Héctor Rodriguez III are challenging the derogatory tokenism and tropicalization that have historically saturated U.S.-based media and framed much of how Latinx-oriented sociopolitical discussion and policymaking develops (or not).[1] Rodriguez is doing so through the creation and distribution of his series *El Peso Hero* in which real-time storylines do not shy away from the depiction and articulation of polemical topics such as deportation, familial separation, and racialized and punitive political policies. Led by a *norteño*-hailing superhero-like main character, the fictional Ignacio Rivera (aka El Peso Hero), Rodriguez leverages the comic book medium to address such topics in ways that are cathartic, normalizing, and rallying for the (un)documented Latinx reader, pushing for an empowering style of representation in which the hero is an unapologetic, border-navigating, exclusively Spanish-speaking, humanitarian champion.[2] Both Rodriguez and El Peso Hero the character have taken up the mantle as influencers willing to critically engage with twenty-first-century political and cultural landscapes by way of a visual medium with much pop culture currency to leverage. This is crucial since history has demonstrated that comic books have the "capability to reflect the harshest of matters in a package that, at first, appears harmless and . . . turns out to be wonderfully instructive in spirit."[3] This can be disarming, meaning a reader might not be aware that they are delving into as robust of a sociopolitical commentary as they are, a quirk of comic books that makes them particularly effective to shed light on and counter punitive policies and problematic narratives and representations.

With *El Peso Hero*, Rodriguez taps into the rich Mexican *historieta* tradition of pointedly engineering narratives via graphic mediums. As early as the 1920s, significant ideological clashes and propaganda campaigns spread quickly to the Mexican press. Commentary and reporting morphed into visual forums within which *lo local* could be pridefully put on exhibition in weekly *dominicales* (Sunday funnies) that became feature staples of Mexican periodicals. The main goal of such funnies was to attract an audience of readers, and attention-grabbing headlines, illustrations, and photographs were all part of their arsenal. Such visual ingenuity was vital to the emergence of a cartoon/comic-based mode of expression (and protest) that solidified the notion of an artistically informed movement taking place within the twentieth-century Mexican cultural sphere, establishing the cultural context that Rodriguez is now tapping into.

This chapter explores how the realia-laden storylines and identifiable character depiction and development in *El Peso Hero* proactively engage with cultural narratives and political landscapes of the twenty-first century.[4] Questions surrounding these notions of influence and instruction—and whether Rodriguez was aware of how well the series was accomplishing both at such crucial sociopolitical moments happening in the United States—provided an intriguing start to the authors' collaboration on this project. During one of our initial interviews, Rodriguez spoke about how nearly every issue of *El Peso Hero* includes the "very heavy themes" of immigration, human trafficking, border violence, and corruption and is "influenced by the modern-day realities of those living on both sides of the US-Mexican border."[5] It is a conscious act made by Rodriguez to deliberately author the series and portray the characters in specific ways that break with the problematic, racially charged, and culturally reductive features that have long dominated the Euro-American visual lexicon about the (un)documented Latinx community. This is a visual vocabulary rooted in well-known pre-millennium racialized and tropicalized archetypes, but also in ones that, since September 11, perpetuate even more of a "carceral governmentality" that has created a particularly effective "spectacle of enforcement" geared toward (un)documented Latinx persons.[6] Such racialized, militarized, and criminalized visual lexicon have been woven together through most media outlets and public facets of U.S. society to constantly remind "them" (the [un]documented Latinx "other") about not being White or of not having an elusive citizen-resident-visa form of documentation. *El Peso Hero* tackles such problematic messaging that dehumanizes and criminalizes by way of storylines and characters that reject visual and lexiconic narratives that "Whites [and citizens] are normal and then there is everybody else."[7]

El Peso Hero the character demands a new normal. If "visibility is associated with empowerment and invisibility with powerlessness,"[8] and "comics are about representation [which in turn] promotes inclusion,"[9] El Peso Hero carves out visibility by quite literally positioning himself at the center of situations—such as legislative sessions, employment raids, border crossing attempts that are on the cusp of disaster, families being separated—that, in the past, would have been weaponized by conservative rhetoric, ignored, or used to silence the Latinx individual or community that he defends. Through *El Peso Hero*, Rodriguez propels the comic book genre toward functioning as a type of graphic-centric socially conscious literature due to the ability of the series' plots and characters to serve as a barometer of sociopolitical attitudes. This is evident in how prolific he is with his authorship and distribution, which allows him to respond in nearly real time to events such as the 2020 issue focused on the exploitation of essential workers in the early days of the COVID-19 pandemic and the special March 2022 issue (figure 5.1), "El Peso Hero: Ucrania," in which Rodriguez addresses Mexico's refusal to criticize Russia or support Ukraine by sending El Peso Hero to the war-torn area to help.[10]

Figure 5.1 was first shared on March 8, 2022, as a standalone image via the @el_peso_hero Instagram page, an active account managed by Rodriguez that demonstrates how the rapidity and immensity of social media sharing effectively ensure that *El Peso Hero* is able to tangibly respond to (and support) causes and stances that coincide with local, national, and global events as they unfold. The post includes the accompanying text that

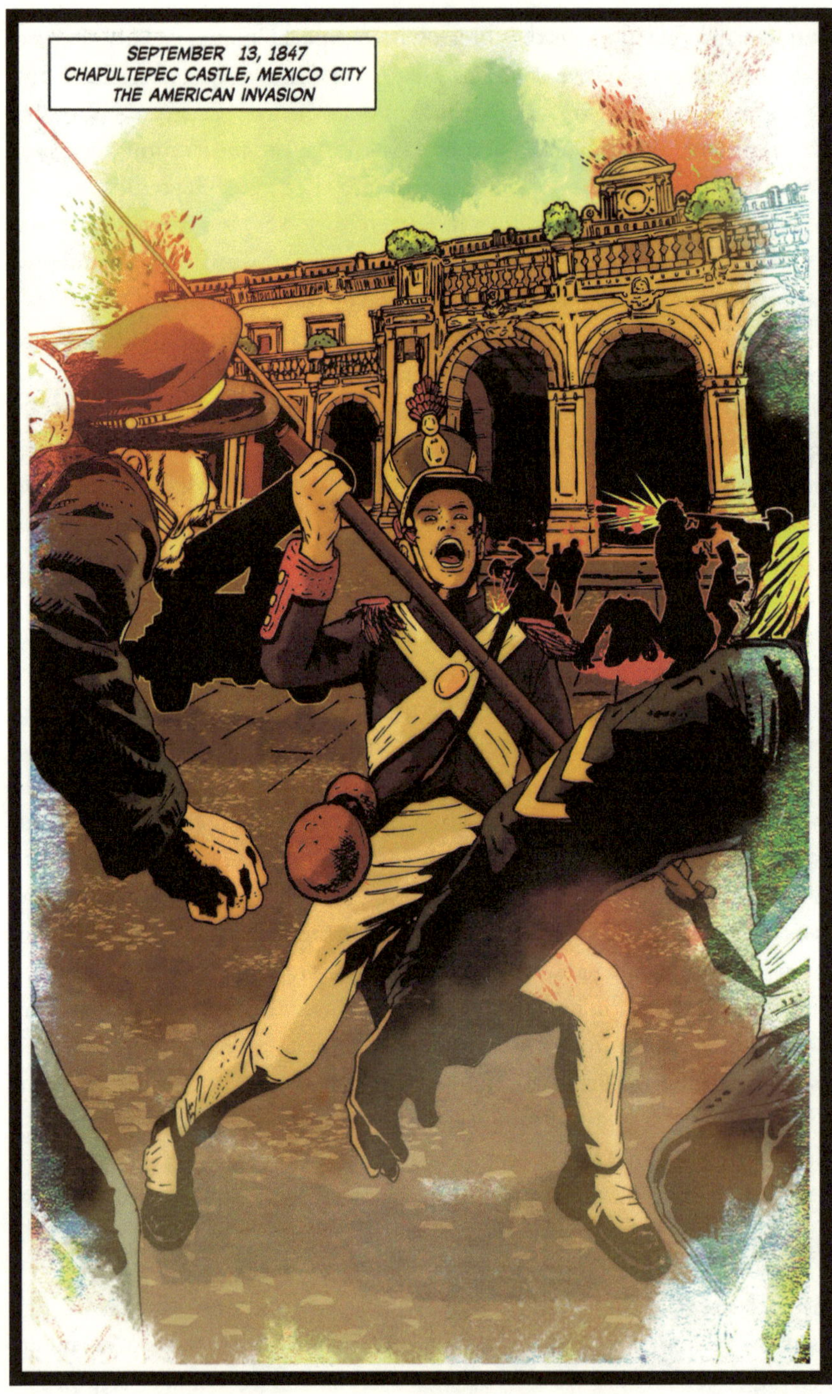

FIGURE 5.1 Mexican soldier assuming an attack stance while wielding his weapon during the 1847 U.S. invasion of Chapultepec Castle in Mexico City. Héctor Rodriguez, *El Peso Hero: La Patrona* (Dallas: Rio Bravo Comics, 2018), 1.

states, "Superheroes are about HOPE" and "@ElPesoHero protects all refugees" with a link to donate to UNICEF in support of Ukrainian children or, in subsequent posts, to the Ukraine Crisis Relief Fund.[11] This messaging was reiterated and reshared on March 31, April 5, April 9, April 13, and April 16, 2022, prior to the release of the full *El Peso Hero: Ucrania* special issue, garnering multiple likes, shares, and press spotlights.

Lan Dong proposes that "superheroes reveal some of our most basic beliefs about morality and justice, our conceptions of gender and sexuality, and our attitudes towards ethnicity and nationality."[12] When considered in relation to El Peso Hero, this suggests that creatives like Rodriguez have a responsibility in how they craft their storylines and characters, and these narrative elements are often ripe with references and allusions intended to thwart problematic Latinx archetypes and tropes while carving out new possibilities for representation and action. What is vital here is for Rodriguez and his peers to not inadvertently fall into the trap of offering more fodder to a U.S. media ecosystem that is already saturated with a prolific amount of negative visual-based messaging about (un)documented Latinx persons. Rodriguez does not. Instead, he successfully "portray[s] a world in which bias comes to light" with the intent to "bring it into the open and contest its causes."[13] He effectively melds real-time happenings, controversies, and debates with the novelty appeal of comic book page and character design. In this way, El Peso Hero the character emerges as a "cultural figurehead," one of strategic resistance to "interact with the pressing issues of the present" while injecting restrictive and narrow narratives with multipronged possibilities for what might compose social and cultural "project[s] for the future."[14]

It is with such points in mind that, in the first section of this chapter, we discuss why comic books are particularly primed, compared to other narrative forms, to offer insights into lived experiences of marginalized and politicized Latinx demographics and to spotlight alternatives to problematic archetypes and tropes. The second section turns toward a discussion of Rodriguez and *El Peso Hero* to demonstrate how and why the series unbinds narratives from a generalized Latinx ethnocultural lineage of racially refracted, stereotyped representations. Instead, the series advances toward a visual and literary space that is not limited to one narrow depiction but rather is a space that is representational, inclusive, and playful in its possibilities, illustrative of the polychromatic reality of *Latinidad*. Gender, race, language, immigration status, family separation, and national (un)belonging are themes that *El Peso Hero* tackles head-on precisely because of their prevalence for and impact on many (un)documented Latinx persons. Finally, in the third section we consider how

El Peso Hero has transformed past examples of comic-book–based outreach and activism, and why this is meaningful in the sociopolitical circumstances of the first quarter of the twenty-first century.

Comic Books: An Ideal Medium to Actualize (Un)Documented Latinx Representation

DREAMers are often referred to with this moniker to reference the 2001 Development, Relief, and Education for Alien Minors (DREAM) Act, which has failed to pass on multiple occasions. This group comprises individuals eligible for the federal government program known as Deferred Action for Childhood Arrivals (DACA), a 2012 executive order instituted under former president Barack Obama that attempted to provide temporary relief for individuals residing in the United States outside of current immigration frameworks while a more permanent reform similar to the DREAM Act was sought. Before President Trump rescinded the program in 2018, DACA eligibility consisted of not yet possessing a "legal" immigration status; being younger than thirty-one as of June 15, 2012; having arrived in the United States before turning sixteen; and residing in the United States since June 2007. As of 2021, there were roughly 800,000 to 1,000,000 eligible individuals in the United States, though a more exact number is impossible to know due to reporting challenges. The majority are between fifteen and thirty-six years old and primarily hail from Mexico, El Salvador, Honduras, and Guatemala. There are several archetypes and tropes that popular media and scholarly outlets alike attribute specifically to the undocumented Latinx segment of the DREAMer community, including not having an identity, living on the margins, having an invisible existence, and/or being pigeonholed to categories that are problematic due to their basis in racial and cultural stereotyping. William Nericcio has identified several of these categories most relevant to the visual spheres of interest here, such as "incompetent bandidos, goodhearted simpletons, easy *mujeres,* perfidious criminals, and so on, ad infinitum and ad nauseam,"[15] observations that fittingly drip with sarcasm and exasperation. While there are ill-intentioned bandit-esque characters that appear in *El Peso Hero*, the vast majority of its characters make a point to break with these long-engrained character categories. Such is the case in the COVID-19 pandemic special issue in which Rodriguez offers depictions that are not token "(im)migrants" but rather are presented to the reader as the "everyman" and "everywoman" (the "us" and the "we") that compose the tapestry of the twenty-first-century United States.

Nericcio is by no means alone in having identified such problematic racially and culturally tokenized archetypes and tropes. Aviva Chomsky has also explored how such typecasts are both closely tied to "illegality" and "undocumentedness" and calculated sociopolitical inventions generated to facilitate the exploitation and exclusion of Latinx immigrants from U.S. politics and society.[16] A cursory review of conservative, (alt)right-leaning political advertisements from the past two presidential election cycles is sufficient to see ample evidence of such rhetorical linkages in action. Chavez too has theorized about a "Latino Threat Narrative" (LTN) that, over the first two decades of the twenty-first century, has produced iterations of Latinx personification within the U.S. media that have become particularly self-serving for more conservative sociopolitical (alt)right-leaning sectors.[17] An example of this can be seen in the uproar over the ending of pandemic-era restrictions known as Title 42 in May 2023, in which threats of total border collapse, an unstoppable deluge of crossing bodies, and a total compromising of national security were invoked (all predictable and well-entrenched sound and visual bytes of the past twenty years). With the LTN in particular, the correlation between sound and seeing is important for the ways in which it reinforces what begins to feel like an inescapable truth, even when ample evidence exists to prove the opposite. Rebecca M. Schreiber would agree with this and with many of Nericcio, Chomsky, and Chavez's findings, particularly about how invested "the visual" is in the image-saturated, social-media-riddled context of the millennium regarding "relations of power."[18] Borrowing from Susan Jeffords, Schreiber explains the crucial role that visuals have in crafting "how citizens *see* themselves and how they *see* those against them." She asserts that this is vital in determining a "national self-perception" since "the very idea of a nation is itself dependent on the visual realm."[19] Comic books then are an ideal format for creatives like Rodriguez to literally visualize and narrate into existence new possibilities for self and group perception that promulgate a shifting of power relations and a recrafting of individual and collective "seeing" of oneself and one's place.

In a manner coinciding with real-time events, he addresses several of these points in *El Peso Hero: The Essentials*. This issue is a direct response to the labeling of certain sectors as essential during the COVID-19 outbreak while simultaneously excluding them from pandemic relief benefits. As COVID-19 surged in the spring and summer of 2020, El Peso Hero the character lends a helping hand in the fields and packing facilities while explaining to readers the urgent need to protect the country's farmworkers and highlighting the vital contributions made by them and other essential workers during the pandemic. The storyline makes a point to spotlight how noncitizen workers are caught between "fears of the coronavirus" and the potential for detention and deportation while moving to and from jobs deemed essential to keep society and the economy functioning.[20] The service, agriculture, and construction industries are vastly buoyed by noncitizen labor, a reality acknowledged by the March 2020 guidelines published by the Department of Homeland Security granting noncitizen (often undocumented and Latinx) farmworkers essential worker status by way of a permit to move freely to and from work despite lockdowns due to the pandemic.

While *El Peso Hero: The Essentials* takes place on a farm in the Texas Rio Grande Valley, El Peso Hero walks readers through how exclusion spans multiple employment sectors (delivery truck drivers, construction workers, postal workers, food delivery personnel, grocery store employees, educators, physicians, and other medical staff) and socioeconomic levels across several noncitizen categories (undocumented, DACA, or the H-2A temporary agriculture worker and H-1B specialized worker visa programs). He demonstrates the inconsistencies of labeling such persons as essential yet denying access to the "benefit[s] that can mean life and death as COVID-19 spreads across the country."[21] This particular issue is an example of confronting outmoded and incorrect views regarding immigration and social, structural, and economic fabrics in the United States with alternative narratives about locations, communities, and experiences that are so often manipulated by politicians and public figures seeking to benefit from the fanning of public hostility. By positioning himself side by side with (un)documented essential workers, El Peso Hero creates and holds space that "emphasizes their [Latinx] points of view and everyday lives as forms" to function as "counter-knowledge and counter-representation" of what has long been accepted as the norm.[22] The "emotive resonance" that such purposeful depictions generate is meaningful in that it can lead to cathartic politicization of a (young) reader's consciousness and offer a concrete verbalization and depiction of what Schreiber calls the "narration of migrant sorrows."[23] In other words, a publicly visible space is created and fostered, and life experiences previously relegated to the periphery are shared, made visible, and validated. When asked about this, Rodriguez observed that accessibility to such visual and narrative spaces is crucial to perpetuate excitement among his readers, particularly the youth he works with through his position in the public school system. As he noted, "Sixty percent of the student body are Latinos in Texas . . . El Peso Hero books [are] very empowering for the students because they see someone that has a last name like theirs making comic books with a superhero" that is both reinventing and holding space, one in which (un)documented Latinx readers strongly identify.[24]

Untethering Latinx-Centric Narratives, Characters, and Design to Create and Hold Space

During our interview, Rodríguez explained parts of his creative process, such as how important situational and visual realia were to character and narrative development from the very beginning and now across the entirety of the series. These are settings and objects that might appear familiar to many (un)documented Latinx readers, and foster a familiar, friendly air to stories that address traumatic experiences such as border crossings, family separation, racial profiling, community violence, and more. For example, after fully assuming the persona of El Peso Hero, Rivera uses his powers to protect the people along both sides of the U.S.-Mexico border from those who abuse their power, such as when he joins a group of refugees as they go through the registration process at a detention facility and face the dire conditions. In this scene, the borders on the page are spaced in such a way to reflect the harsh realities at the facility located in Carrizo Springs, Texas, heightening emotive engagement with the reader. Lightning punctuates the upper-right corner of the top panel, which, coupled with the slightly varying width and staggered stacking of each panel below, makes the reader feel as though each is a snippet illuminated by bursts of lightning. The deluge of rain and otherwise ominously stormy conditions might have precluded the reader from witnessing the events here and those that follow in subsequent pages, including a mother being separated from her child, fingerprints of child detainees being registered by gun-toting agents, and a mass of coughing children sitting on the floor in a jail-like cell. This experience becomes informative for the reader, showcasing the barbarity of it all as they follow along side by side, seeing everything through El Peso Hero's eyes and sensing his increasing distress at what he witnesses, communicated on the pages through color choice, the positioning of lines and paneling, the use of strategic gutters, and, of course, narration. There are multiple examples of this throughout the series. Among numerous examples of fighting cartel violence and political corruption, El Peso Hero aids children crossing rivers at the U.S.-Mexico border,[25] he breaks unaccompanied minors out from deportation centers,[26] and he frees migrants from a potentially deadly truck transportation gone wrong.[27] All these scenarios are illustrated and communicated in ways that highlight the duplicity of policies, inhumanity of conditions, and harm of punitive socioeconomic and political exclusion (all of which are based on real-life situations and policies that have come to pass).

Emotive resonance is also heightened by the inclusion of visual and verbal cultural realia. Popular regional music and food are displayed across the entire series. In *El Peso Hero* no. 4 the story's antagonist, El Catrin, enjoys the popular northern Mexican dish *migas* while he plots with his associates; and in *El Peso Hero* no. 5, renowned *ranchera* singer Vicente Fernández's song lyrics are sprinkled across dialogue and panels. Even El Peso Hero himself dresses in a way that would be immediately recognizable to the northern Mexican and southern U.S. border regions: slick cowboy boots, bold belt buckles, and fitted button-down collared shirts are staples of norteño style and serve as what could be described as El Peso Hero's superhero uniform. While all other characters in the series speak English primarily, El Peso Hero speaks only in Spanish, often peppering his speech with slang from the Mexican norteño and southern U.S. border regions (*paisa*, *vato*, *güey*, *compas*, to name a few). This narrative decision by Rodriguez emphasizes how no matter the insufferable difficulty or the impossibility of a situation that the superhero finds himself in, "it is important for him not to lose his culture, language, and self."[28] As he says, "I liked Batman, Superman, and all the Marvel superheroes but I wasn't really interested in following their exploits. Culturally they didn't connect to me. Have you ever seen Batman eat *empanadas de calabaza*?"[29] Rodriguez continues by explaining how people "get excited seeing all these things. They feel like they own El Peso Hero themselves. It's a sense of ownership that's unique to them because he may look like their *tío* dressed in blue jeans and boots."[30]

For much of the twentieth- and twenty-first-century U.S. cultural lexicon, representations of the (un)documented Latinx community have veered heavily toward debased visuals: *siesta*-seeking, tequila-drinking, sexualized bandit bad boys (and girls) hailing from elusive south-of-the-border locales, intent on bashing over "our" borders and breaking "our" laws. It is within this space that *El Peso Hero* morphs into more than mere entertainment by rejecting such representations. As Rodriguez describes in our interview,[31]

> While I was visiting my grandparents, my grandfather told me a rumor of a renegade group of Mexican commandos creating a criminal organization.

> I began to imagine a local superhero of Mexican descent fighting the group. Once I came home, I began writing the script for *El Peso Hero*. I wanted to create the name using Spanglish. Spanglish is used a lot in the border culture. I gave him a belt buckle with the initials "PH" and cowboy boots to represent the norteño culture. I wanted the hero to be unique and embody the border culture and combat its problems.

Interplay between realia, color and word(s), and lines and space, or the lack of all or any of these at selected moments, are meaningful decisions made by Rodriguez in each issue. Leveraging the uniqueness of comic-book–based storytelling means that he can be playful with such details as conscious acts of resistance or defiance and as tools to emotively connect with readers.

The strategy of manipulating color and dialogue, or in this case a lack verbal narrative, to tap into a reader's emotion is displayed particularly well throughout *El Peso Hero: Border Stories* as two unaccompanied sisters traverse through the harsh terrain in an attempt to cross the U.S.-Mexico border.[32] Yellow dominates the coloring on these pages, heightening the reader's sense of the sun's heat and uncomfortable glare as well as the desert's barren dryness. In the top image, slivers of the panels appear to be cut out, leading readers to feel that they are looking at these scenes through slowly blinking eyes or perhaps eyes that are only slightly open. This malaise is violently interrupted by the bright red pickup truck that barrels through the image in the middle, kicking up dust, debris, and noise, injecting a startling sense of alarm. The reader feels the frenetic pulse of the story increase with the series of more rigidly placed panel lines in the bottom image that depicts a sequence of frantic-feeling events that occur in quick succession. In both the panel series on the top and the bottom, only one dialogue bubble appears in either, with the rest of the narrative being conveyed by color, panel lines, the gutter, and so on. Through the vivid use of color, the reader begins the story feeling empathy for the two sisters and arrives at a place of panic and concern for their well-being. One simply must keep reading to find out what happens, at which point El Peso Hero injects narrative that is instructive and stirring for the reader to understand what is happening both in a literal sense (the scene depicted) and more broadly (the circumstances and policies that led to it).

Emotive engagement with the reader is also activated by the manipulation of space, especially the empty space between panels, a visual strategy that plays with what is, might be, or should be in that supposed blankness. It is particularly impactful when Rodriguez darkens the gutters to establish a menacing tone or to portray one's actions as disreputable (see figure 5.2). Here,

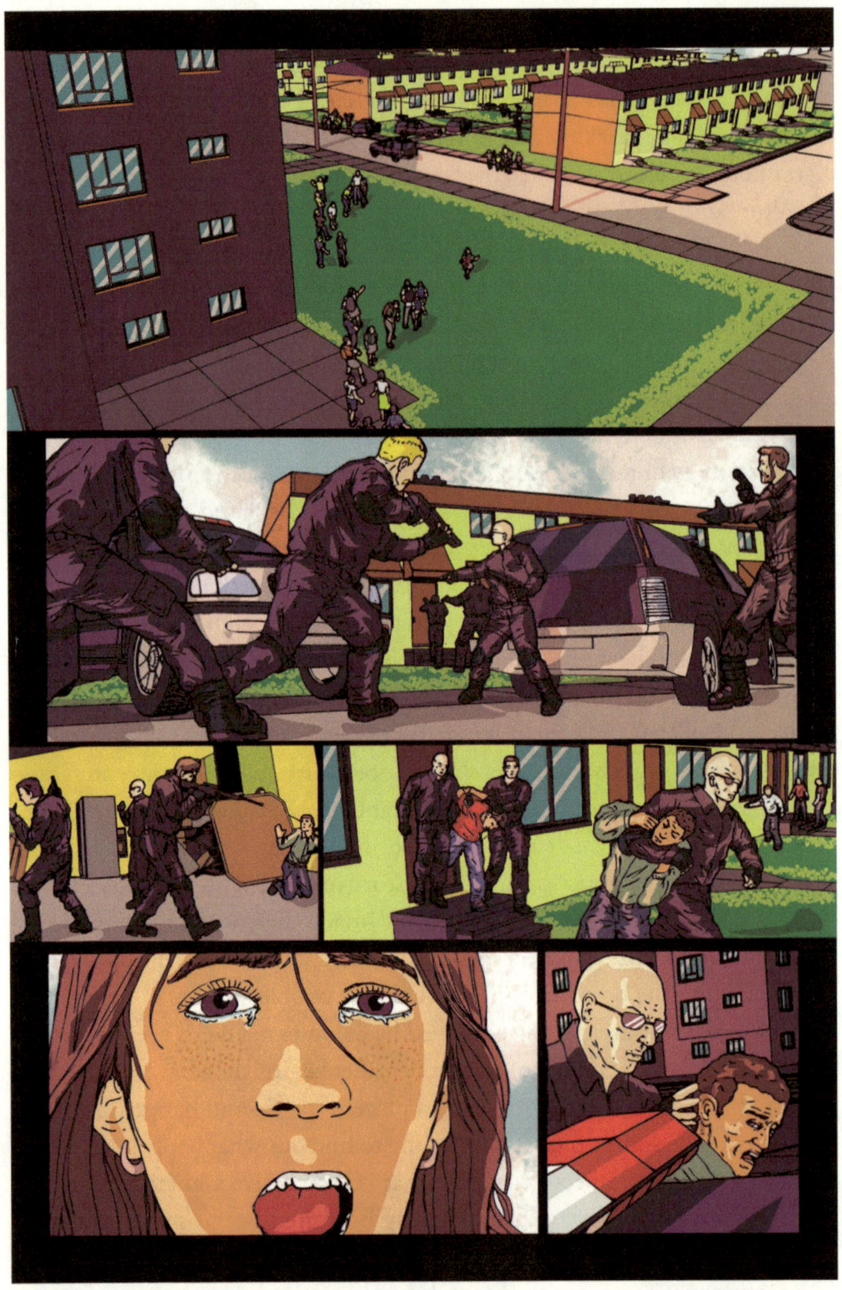

FIGURE 5.2 A child sees her father being pulled from their home and apprehended by U.S. Immigration and Customs Enforcement agents. Rodriguez, *El Peso Hero*, 13.

deportation agents from U.S. Immigration and Customs Enforcement are raiding the home of a young girl, Rosamaria, dragging her father into a police car as he tells her to run. She does but is quickly and roughly caught by a male agent and then transported along with her father to Interim Deportation Camp no. 1938 in Uvalde, Texas.[33]

Ideas of citizenry, definitions of nation, and notions of belonging can be more effectively broached and shared in the world of comic book visual narratives and storytelling since, for millennials and members of Gen Z, the "complexity and possibilities of interplay between image and words are more than obvious" due to having been "raised on a diet of audiovisual" tools.[34] It is by them and for them that *El Peso Hero* so gratifyingly fuses language and image, in turn making the series "an ideal vehicle" for the development and reinforcement of visibility and community.[35] Rodriguez explains how if "you take away all the layers, him being male, Latino, Mexican, Spanish-speaking, Norteño . . . take those away and deep down inside it's a very human story. It's a very impossible situation that he's facing. The story progresses through struggle. And sometimes it's more about the characters around him and how they respond to this unwavering character with a strong moral compass."[36] Tweaks that millennial and Gen Z Latinx cultural producers and consumers have made to existing graphic mediums like comic books speak to an "artistic" strategy gaining traction to reject the media-driven social and political status quo. They are "represent[ing] themselves in ways that push back against" tropes and politicized agendas, "expos[ing] the relations of power at work," and "providing alternative representations of themselves."[37]

El Peso Hero and Captain America: Colleagues in Comic-Book–Based Politicking

Comic books aid in the process of recasting and renegotiating narratives about (un)documented Latinx persons due to their strong connection to micro-level popular culture and dialogue. There is precedence for comic books like *El Peso Hero* to act as an "ideal medium for suggesting what cannot be said by the [mere] printed word" since comic book creatives enjoy a greater "latitude" than perhaps other genres of cultural products to "attack established ideas"; they "can say and do things . . . [that others] cannot say or do" via the medium.[38] In reflecting on instances that comic books and their creatives have succeeded in this, an intriguing parallel between the World War II era, Hitler-fighting, Nazi-featuring cover of the first issue of *Captain America* (published in 1949) and that of *El Peso Hero: Border Stories* (published in 2015) arises.

El Peso Hero punches Donald Trump in a nearly identical fashion to what was portrayed in *Captain America* no. 1, a comic whose impact in the context of World War II cannot be overstated as Captain America delivers a withering blow to Hitler amid a cadre of Nazi soldiers. For El Peso Hero, the visual details surrounding this confrontation are loaded with precisely the type of realia that would undoubtedly trigger an emotional response for readers. Much of this imagery is emblematic of the tumultuous time period leading up to the 2016 U.S. presidential election. The top of the cover begins with the bolded declaration that "LA COMUNIDAD LATINA SE UNE" (The Latinx community is united).[39] Immediately below the title "45 thrilling pages" are announced, a number that references Trump having become the forty-fifth president of the United States.

While the backdrop to Captain America's confrontation with Hitler was riddled with swastikas and Nazis, on *El Peso Hero: Border Stories* the reader sees a Macy's department store logo, alluding to the 2015 decision made by the company to sever all business dealings with Trump after the presidential candidate made incendiary comments about Mexican nationals and migrants while on the campaign trail. Immediately to the right of this is a gentleman drinking from a bottle while sitting in front of a large-screen TV on which the NBC television logo is displayed. Perhaps he is the disgraced television and radio host Billy Bush, who found himself embroiled in scandal and fired from NBC News after an audio clip of him and Trump discussing women in a derogatory and disparaging fashion went viral in 2016. Next to him stands a crown-wearing, bouquet-holding, buxom beauty queen watching on as El Peso Hero delivers his blow, a nod to Trump's long-standing connection to the "Miss Universe" beauty competitions. Written on the wall next to her is the Univision television network label. Univision had gained rights to air the pageant in partnership with NBC starting in 2015 but also cut all ties with Trump after he made racist anti-Mexican comments while campaigning for president.

It was the reality television show *The Apprentice* that arguably solidified Trump's place as a caricature in U.S. popular culture, particularly as his catchphrase "You're fired!" became a mainstream staple after the first season of shows aired in 2004. The bottom right-hand corner of the comic book cover features a man declaring, "Slimy says YOU'RE FIRED!," insinuating that El Peso Hero has "fired," or beat, Trump (and the racist rhetoric and policies promulgated by him) with his gob-smacking punch. At the bottom of

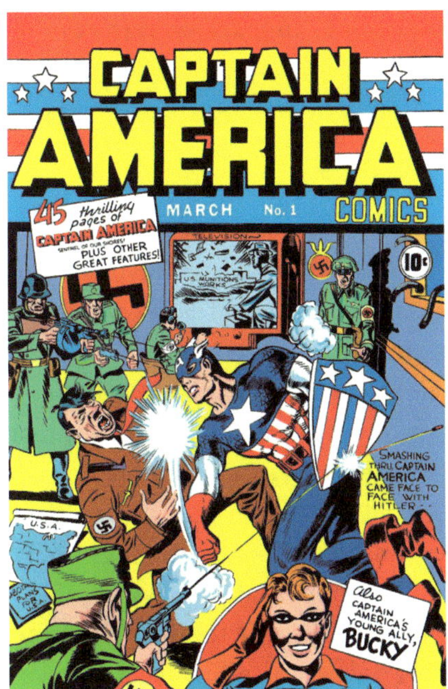

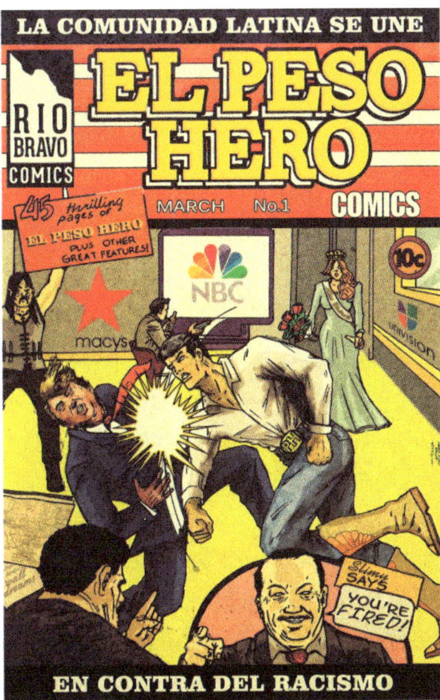

FIGURE 5.3 Rodriguez III draws on the infamous cover image of Captain America punching Hitler and gives it a contemporary twist. Jack Kirby and Joe Simon, *Captain America Comics* no. 1 (New York: Marvel Comics, 1941), cover; and Rodriguez, *El Peso Hero*, cover.

the cover, a second banner declares, "EN CONTRA DEL RACISMO" (Against racism).[40] The Latinx community is not simply uniting, as was stated at the top of the cover, but rather coming together to rally against the particularly virulent brand of racism and nationalism unleashed by Trump's alt-right-leaning rhetoric.

Figure 5.3 demonstrates how comic book visuals, characters, and narratives have the capacity to inform the debate. While the original Captain America issue that inspired Rodriguez's depiction in figure 5.3 is situated more than seventy years in the past, El Peso Hero has picked up the banner seventy years later to combat the presence of neo-Nazi jingoism that fuels an active portion of the alt-right electoral base. Rodriguez utilizes tactics throughout the entire series to pointedly speak to the immense "drawbacks of a nationalist mind-set," exposing how it "nourishes hatred and intolerance . . . allows individuals to disparage difference" while providing readers with a Latinx representation that meaningfully translates to real-world representation and emotive resonance.[41] It is no longer an Anglo all-American persona (Captain America) standing up as a voice for "them," but rather El Peso Hero, an exclusively Spanish-speaking, cartel-fighting, migrant-saving Mexican norteño, who defends "us."

Conclusion

Comic books exist within a micro-level popular culture niche and possess an ease with which they are consumed and shared. The long tradition on both sides of the U.S.-Mexico border of leveraging the comic book characters and the comic book medium itself as a sociopolitical mechanism facilitates a greater latitude for writers and illustrators to confront and mock themes that are in transition from passé to progressive. These include such noted racialized and tropicalized tropes as bungling bandidos, simpletons, hypersexualized women, and treacherous or undependable criminals, among others. *El Peso Hero* rejects the limitations and offensiveness of such portrayals by offering a world in which powerful and impactful characters include multiple tiers of diverse representation, including socioeconomic, racial, linguistic, gender, age, and sexual orientation. The series continues strategies established by Mexican *historieta* and *dominicales* traditions of leveraging the visual to grab and keep a reader's attention while also propelling the medium forward into a reimagined creative space where comic book creators can create and readers can find and immerse themselves in spaces that are more illustrative of their experiences and those of their family, peers, community members, and others.

El Peso Hero presents readers with storylines that are representative of real-time events and happenings and that do not shirk depictions and articulation of controversial topics like family separation, deportation, border crossing, and contrary punitive policymaking. Thus, comic books like *El Peso Hero* should be viewed as a type of graphic-centric literature, not as one that is hollow or lowbrow, due to their ability to recast sensitive and/or polemic situations and themes in a cathartic and enabling way. Rodriguez's own experiences with promoting the series and offering comic booking workshops around the United States provide ample anecdotal evidence that catharsis and enablement *are* by-products of reading *El Peso Hero* for the (un)documented Latinx reader (particularly among the younger audience).

Through realia-laden character and plot development that proactively seek to break from the archetypes and tropes that have long been dominated representation and depiction of (un)documented Latinx persons and communities, *El Peso Hero* storylines transform twenty-first-century cultural narratives and political landscapes into normalizing and rallying. Latinx Millennial and Gen Z comic book creatives like Rodriguez are seizing a momentum that demands the recasting and renegotiating of the long-held Euro-American-crafted identity markers related to race, gender, and intra/international relations and of those narratives that ignored or distorted lived experiences. What is different about the messages Rodriguez and his peers are proposing is that they are not becoming fossilized, stagnant, or antiquated. Twenty-plus years into the millennium, they continue to reverberate with each new sociopolitical iteration of calculated cultural production (e.g., special issues that focus on a particular event such as the COVID-19 pandemic or the Russian invasion of Ukraine) that in turn increase its visibility and ensure its relevance with audience reach and depth of meaning. Through calculated and conscious usage of page design, character visuals, realia, dialogue, and transborder storylines, millennial and Gen Z cultural producers and consumers are succeeding in reintroducing themselves and their communities in capacities that move previously marginalized, silenced, and criminalized peoples into empowering, influential roles.

Notes

1 Millennials are those born between 1981 and 1996, and Gen Z between 1996 and 2010.
2 We recognize dialogues and controversy surrounding terminology such as "documented"/"undocumented," "legal"/"illegal," "lawful"/"unlawful," "alien," etc. as related to immigrant status, presence, and rights in the United States. As such, we have made conscientious usage of such vocabulary throughout this chapter. It should be noted that "(un)documented" is the most used here as it is a moniker that some have seized to reinterpret and reuse as a point of tenacity and rallying (such as the social media slogan "Undocumented, Unafraid, Unapologetic"), including *El Peso Hero*.
3 Héctor Fernández L'Hoeste, *Lalo Alcaraz: Political Cartooning in the Latino Community* (Jackson: University Press of Mississippi, 2014), 14.
4 "Realia" are objects, or other such reference points taken from real life, used to create and heighten relatability.
5 Héctor Rodriguez III, "Interview" (interviewed by Kaitlin Thomas, October 20, 2020).
6 Rebecca M. Schreiber, *The Undocumented Everyday: Migrant Lives and the Politics of Visibility* (Minneapolis: University of Minnesota Press, 2018), 7–13.
7 Fernández L'Hoeste, *Lalo Alcaraz*, 47.
8 Schreiber, *Undocumented Everyday*, 5.
9 Fernández L'Hoeste, *Lalo Alcaraz*, 41.
10 Olivia Hampton, "Mexican American Superhero Saves Ukrainian Civilians in Comic Book Issue," *NPR*, April 6, 2022, https://www.tpr.org/2022-04-06/mexican-american-superhero-saves-ukrainian-civilians-in-comic-book-issue.
11 "Super heroes are about HOPE. In the midst of artillery bombardment, tanks and lack of help. A family is trapped. They have no options. Until there is. The last hope

that shouldn't exist but does. @ElPesoHero protects all refugees. #Ukraine. A very special free one shot story coming soon. Please share and consider donating to: UNICEF—Support Children of Ukraine: unicefusa.org."

12 Lan Dong, *Teaching Comics and Graphic Narratives* (Jefferson, NC: McFarland, 2012), 204.

13 Fernández L'Hoeste, *Lalo Alcaraz*, 131.

14 Jorge Catalá Carrasco, Paulo Drinot, and James Scorer, *Comics and Memory in Latin America* (Pittsburgh: University of Pittsburgh Press, 2017), 16.

15 William Nericcio, *Tex[t]-Mex: Seductive Hallucinations of the Mexican in America* (Austin: University of Texas Press, 2007), 20.

16 Aviva Chomsky, *How Immigration Became Illegal* (Boston: Beacon, 2014).

17 Leo R. Chavez, *The Latino Threat: Constructing Immigrants, Citizens, and the Nation* (Stanford, CA: Stanford University Press, 2013).

18 Schreiber, *Undocumented Everyday*, 8.

19 Schreiber, *Undocumented Everyday*, 8.

20 Héctor Rodriguez, *El Peso Hero: The Essentials* (Dallas: Rio Bravo Comics, 2020), 9.

21 Rodriguez, *El Peso Hero: The Essentials*, 2.

22 Schreiber, *Undocumented Everyday*, 12.

23 Schreiber, *Undocumented Everyday*, 109.

24 Rodriguez, "Interview."

25 Héctor Rodriguez, *El Peso Hero: Border Stories* (Dallas: Rio Bravo Comics, 2015), 5, 11.

26 Héctor Rodriguez, *El Peso Hero: Borderland* (Dallas: Rio Bravo Comics, 2019), 5.

27 Rodriguez, *El Peso Hero: Border Stories*, 19.

28 Rodriguez, "Interview."

29 Rodriguez, "Interview."

30 Rodriguez, "Interview."

31 Rodriguez, "Interview."

32 Rodriguez, *El Peso Hero: Border Stories*, 6–8.

33 Rodriguez, *El Peso Hero: Border Stories*, 13–15. Similarly to how El Peso Hero responded in real time on the @el-peso-hero Instagram page to the Russian invasion of Ukraine, he did so on May 25, 2022, in response to the May 24 school shooting that occurred at the Robb Elementary School in Uvalde, Texas, in which nineteen children and two adults were killed. The post is a simple black-and-white image of El Peso Hero standing to the left of the panel with his head down, balancing his face in his right hand. His posture and demeanor convey dejection, dismay, and grief for any number of reasons related to the tragedy: that yet another school shooting had occurred; at the loss of so much young life; at the failure of the Uvalde police to appropriately respond to calls for action by parents and school staff; and so on.

34 Fernández L'Hoeste, *Lalo Alcaraz*, 13.

35 Fernández L'Hoeste, *Lalo Alcaraz*, 14.

36 Rodriguez, "Interview."

37 Schreiber, *Undocumented Everyday*, 8.

38 David Keane, "Cartoon Violence and Freedom of Expression," *Human Rights Quarterly* 30, no. 4 (2008): 845–875, 847.

39 Héctor Rodríguez, *El Peso Hero: Border Stories*, variant cover art by Chema (Dallas: Rio Bravo Comics, 2015), volume 1.

40 Héctor Rodríguez, *El Peso Hero: Border Stories*, variant cover art by Chema (Dallas: Rio Bravo Comics, 2015), volume 1.

41 Fernández L'Hoeste, *Lalo Alcaraz*, 111.

6

The Missing Latinx

Updated Scenes of California Noir in the Unveiling of an American Nightmare

HÉCTOR FERNÁNDEZ L'HOESTE

In 2013, Chicano cartoonist Gilbert (Beto) Hernandez published Book 1 of *Maria M.*, his cinematographic account of the life of Maria, the mother of his renowned character Luba from the *Love and Rockets* series. In due course, the story was completed in the volume published in 2019, including the never-released Book 2. In 2014, Cuban American cartoonist Vanesa R. Del Rey illustrated Bryce Carlson's raw and gritty version of 1950s Los Angeles, *HIT: 1955*. In 2016, the full volume of the sequel, *HIT: 1957*, was released. Both graphic narratives bear the mark of Hollywood's noir tradition, a modern form renowned for its ability to evince the cracks of superficially paradigmatic societies—postwar United States, Scandinavian social democracy, China's thriving economy, and so on—while featuring aesthetic and narrative cues proper of hard-boiled accounts: a revisiting of the past by way of a narrator or the setting of events; a detective coming to the aid of a femme fatale; and precipitous episodes of violence, among other tropes. Like other books by Hernandez based on fictional pulpy B-movies—*Chance in Hell* (2007), *The Troublemakers* (2009), *Love from the Shadows* (2009), and the double feature *Hypnotwist / Scarlet by Starlight* (2021)—*Maria M.* is set as a motion picture, though on this occasion with Rosalba "Fritz" Martinez playing the role of her mother. Much of Hernandez's narrative universe also evinces the influence of Gabriel García Márquez's magical realism, interweaving stories in an underhanded manner.

Yet, in its distinct blend of noir and magical realism, a fundamental aspect marks *Maria M.*: the raw portrayal of sexuality and violence in its representation of Latinx life. The violence rises to the level of Tarantino's *Reservoir Dogs* (1992) and *Pulp Fiction* (1994), though in Hernandez's case it is not meant to be funny or ironic. In the same spirit, *HIT* revisits the stylish world of 1950s Los Angeles through an account in which Latinx presence is conspicuously absent. Its inclusion of Latinx identity is tangential at best: chiefly, in the form of Del Rey's dazzling visuals and a minor character, Eddie Fuentes, a mistreated gardener armed to the teeth, who almost sends the story's antihero, homicide detective Harvey Slater, back to square one. Both volumes of *HIT* are framed entirely as recollections, that is, as reconstructions or exercises of memory following the established model of a noir narrator. Fittingly, each text addresses the matter of Latinx presence in a particular way: *Maria M.*, by rewriting the past; *HIT*, by visually highlighting absence.

How do comics bring Latinx identity into play when it does not figure preponderantly within the story? Is there a practical, unobtrusive way to quote this absence? In this chapter, I analyze narratives that unerringly negotiate this absence, like *Maria M.*, *HIT*, and other comics narratives that, half a century later, embrace noir to rewrite Latinx presence, not as a side note in U.S. history (*Chinatown*, *LA Confidential*) or the product of traumatic excess (*American Me*, *Blood In Blood Out*), but more as an uncomfortable presence that has always been there, never acknowledged, a thorn in the side of the American Dream. While *Maria M.* embraces sexuality and violence to highlight the role of biopolitics in the Latinx experience of the 1950s and 1960s, *HIT* embraces mnemonic omission to underscore how the Anglo version of postwar California renders Latinx presence invisible in a manner analogous to previous Latinx manifestations in state history. In this sense, these narratives are noir with a twist. They do not embrace the conventions of the genre—in due course, it would imply co-optation—but rather approach them with trepidation, with the customary skepticism of the apprehensive Other.

The term "noir" emerges as the result of the work of French film critics (Nino Frank, Jean-Pierre Chartier, Raymond Borde, Étienne Chaumeton) proposing a reading of U.S. films distributed in Europe shortly after the end of World War II in the mid- to late 1940s. According to these critics, while the films were representative of what audiences initially identified as detective films, they also emphasized aspects of criminal psychology and misogyny, pointing out unsavory aspects of U.S. social reality. For the most part, though they were not the exclusive producers of films of this nature, several European expatriates linked to German expressionism—directors like Billy Wilder, Fritz Lang, Otto Preminger, and others—who migrated to Hollywood fleeing the rise of the Nazis, played a major role in the popularization of films of this kind. So, to some extent, it is possible to claim that noir primarily surfaced as a French reading of American films made by German and/or Austro-Hungarian film directors (though there were also American and/or Canadian ones, like John Huston and Edward Dmytryk).

An alluring part of this new genre that captivated European critics and audiences was its exploration of the dark underbelly of the American Dream. These films recognized that, beyond the postwar economic expansion and rise of the middle class, there was a shadier context amid a generalized landscape of never-ending suburbia, brand-new cars in every driveway, and sparkling white kitchens. Together, they attest to the fact that all could not be well in the United States and that so much economic progress could not have been attained without more questionable side effects. Thus, within the aesthetics and the social context of this late practice of noir, I argue that indeed one of the skeletons in the cupboard was/is the exclusion of Latinxs.

A case in point is the term "Mexican" standing for a demographic category which, in the case of Los Angeles County, was counted only in the 1930 census, tallying 167,024 inhabitants, not a negligible sum by any standard.[1] Subsequent figures for Los Angeles County's population in 1940 and 1950 lack information in this respect. The category disappears, rendering the growing population invisible according to census numbers. By 1980, the census introduced a nonracial category called "Spanish origin," which served as an umbrella of sorts, encompassing ethnic and national origin as well as racial background—though a large number of people under this category identified themselves as "White." All of a sudden, the numbers jumped to 1,120,014 in 1980. Without a doubt, something was amiss between 1930 and

1980. For instance, according to ethnic diversity models shared by the *Los Angeles Times*, and despite the overall diversity of the population, key sections of the Los Angeles metropolitan area—such as the East Side—were already majority Mexican by the 1960s.[2] In other words, by the 1950s and 1960s, a societal transformation was already well underway that remained remarkably absent in the cinematographic accounts of the period. It is this absence that is addressed—though through different approaches—in both *Maria M.* and *HIT.*

On Sex and Violence in the Art of *Maria M.*

As I have suggested, *Maria M.* embraces sexuality and violence to highlight the impact of biopolitics on Southern California's Latinx population. In "Right of Death and Power over Life," the final part of his first volume of *The History of Sexuality*, as well as in "Society Must Be Defended," his seminal lecture at the Collège de France, Michel Foucault offers the guiding principles for what has become one of the most thriving critical turns of the past decades. In both of these texts, Foucault explains how a series of interventions and regulatory controls play the role of supervision for the general population.[3] Chiefly, Foucault writes about how the power over death that symbolized sovereign power (the power of the sword, the French philosopher reminds us) is supplanted by the administration of bodies and the calculated management of life. In addition, he describes the deployment of sexuality as contributing generously to the technology of such biopolitical power. For Foucault, "Sexuality represents the precise point where the disciplinary and the regulatory, the body and the population, are articulated."[4] As methods of segregation and social hierarchization, the deliberate management of both life and sexuality guarantees relations of domination and the effects of hegemony.[5]

For Foucault, deployments of power are directly linked to bodies, functions, physiological processes, sensations, and pleasures, all aspects that are rendered graphically explicit in the art of Beto Hernandez and, in particular, in the story of *Maria M.* In addition, within Foucault's initial framework for biopolitics, race acts as a break into the domain of life that is under power's control: the break between who must live and who must die.[6] For Foucault, "In a normalizing society, race or racism is the precondition that makes killing acceptable."[7] Broadly speaking, Foucault claims, "racism justifies the death function in the economy of biopower by appealing to the principle that the death of others makes one biologically stronger insofar as one is a member of a race or population, insofar as one is an element in a unitary living plurality."[8] And so, while Beto's work in *Maria H.* speaks principally of ethnicity and not of race (though it also speaks of race), it is certainly feasible to extend Foucault's definition in terms of who must live and who must die. *Maria M.* makes a point of this claim, as its Latinx characters seem to supersede the conventional narrative in which characters of Latin American descent habitually play the role of victims. Thus, it is by way of their sexuality and how they embrace violence that they come to question the traditional conventions through which Anglo narratives take hold of and control Latinx bodies. By breaking the rules and conventions of the noir genre—by assigning the protagonist roles of transgressors to Latinx characters—Beto attempts to shake off some of the Anglo power of U.S. society and its state.

Gilbert Hernandez (1957) is better known as one of Los Bros Hernandez, the Chicano cartoonists who took the comics world by storm in the 1980s thanks to their alternative comic book *Love and Rockets* (1982–1996, 2001–). As part of Los Bros Hernandez, Gilbert (or Beto, as friends and fans like to call him) is responsible for the *Palomar / Heartbreak Soup* stories in the series. Typical of the Bros' style, these tales feature strong, independent women in markedly different settings within U.S. and Latin American society. Palomar, the heart of his narrative universe, is a fictional Latin American village—not unlike Gabriel García Márquez's Macondo—set somewhere close enough that, upon venturing into its seawaters, it is possible to drift with the current to California, as occurred in one story. As in the case of Maria M., some of Palomar's inhabitants eventually migrate north, giving way to new U.S.-based subplots and sagas in Beto's world.

The protagonist of Gilbert's world is Luba, Palomar's skinny-legged, full-bosomed matriarch, who begins as an entrepreneur and rises to the role of mayor. Maria Martinez, the central character and protagonist of *Maria M.*, is Luba's mother, who is forced to migrate to the United States and be apart from her children. The key thing to consider while consuming *Maria M.* is the following: the graphic novel is, in storyboard terms, an almost frame-by-frame rendition of a movie, embodying the transcription of a campy, B-grade biopic, in which Luba's younger half-sister, Fritz, plays the role of her immigrant mother. (At the end of the book, a very young Fritz informs her aging mother, Maria, about the growing interest in filming a new version of her most popular X-rated movie, given it has become a cult classic.) What we face is an intertextual, hybrid trip to the source—since it portrays how Maria migrated to the United States and had a family, including Fritz, far from

Palomar—all in the spirit of Cuban literary master Alejo Carpentier's *Viaje a la semilla* (*The Lost Steps*, 1944). The fact that the travails of Cienfuegos, Maria's life partner, hint at Cuban identity is another coincidental building block in Beto's universe. Also, the intertextuality with Carpentier, one of the first practitioners of magical realism, is not merely fortuitous, given Beto's penchant for literature of this kind. Habitual readers of *Love and Rockets* will recognize the implications.

This amusing conceit, the presentation of films as graphic novels, allows Beto to publish comics of great cinematic quality and a wild array of approaches. What we witness in *Maria M.*, though, is a story that unfolds almost surreally. After arriving in the United States in 1957, learning some English, suffering the usual rotten jobs (the food industry, modeling, waitressing), participating in countless beauty pageants, bedding a lengthy parade of suitors (including a pair of pornography producers, Ivan and Cabo, and a married cop, Valdez), moving on from one man to the next, landing a gig as Zomba de la Zonga in the porn industry, and working as a stripper—by which point, Maria is red-haired, hinting at Rita Hayworth (aka the Brooklynite Margarita Carmen Cansino) and the erasure of identity—she meets and marries Luis Cienfuegos, a Latino double dealer, who uses a lingerie business as a front. Cienfuegos's willingness to prioritize his drug business and his failure to acknowledge the role of old-country politics in the immigrant community make him the target of repeated death attempts, adding to the fear of reprisal from more reactionary elements of the Cuban American population.

Now, through it all, the expression on Maria's face is so candid—and the tone of the story is so matter-of-fact—that it is hard to mistake her for a "floozy" (a term Beto uses). Just like in Tarantino's films, these are well-attired, carefree, even well-behaved characters capable of self-control until something breaks in them—and even then, the appearance of control never fades entirely. These are not individuals prone to great dramatic outbursts, just like most noir characters. When lightning strikes, something fierce comes rushing out of them—often in the form of sex and violence—with a sort of unpredictable angst. In many instances, things appear to be incidental. Yet, what is never questioned is their capacity for action. These are not passive Latinxs, echoing the stereotypes of old. Rather, they are characters who get the job done, with an air of detachment more characteristic of other leading-role traditions. Even as they engage in sex and violence, they are not morally downgraded individuals, having embraced the latency of the hegemon. After the event, they regain composure, just like anyone mercilessly in command. They are just as well put together as Anglos who have played the part. What Beto seems to be aiming at is the notion that, if this sort of breaking down of the rules is believable for Euro-Americans, so should it be for Latinxs—without reducing them to stereotypical "thugs" and "harpies." These are people at the helm of their fate, just like imperial agents. They simply are characters who will act when the situation justifies it or buttons are pushed, very much in the manner of some of Tarantino's characters, who are all latency until something changes in them. If we are to believe that Euro-Americans can go ballistic, why not Latinxs? It is imperative that we eliminate the justification of reaction through simplistic reductions.

Through it all, it becomes clear that, though Maria's various sexual partners consistently fall short and fail to keep their promises, she embraces her sexuality as a tool of social leverage and survival. Her body is, to put it succinctly, her power and her doom. The text abounds with images of Maria having sex, including oral and anal sex, in a variety of positions. For the most part, whether she strips or is having sex, Beto illustrates her happy and smiling, as though she were enjoying the attention. In sum, the allure of sex seems to be the most efficient, expeditious way in which Maria can get others to do what she wants. The ensuing sexual tension between Maria and her stepson Gorgo is a constant reminder of this fact. Their relationship entails the sex and violence that marks the plot from beginning to end. Gorgo is a hunk of a man, and to say he serves as his father's muscle would be an understatement. The book is packed with bodies beaten, bruised, disfigured, knifed, mutilated, and simply cut to pieces by Gorgo. In addition, the fact that Maria is his stepmother spells trouble, given Gorgo's dedication to and love for his father Cienfuegos. Maria may profess affection for Cienfuegos, given his role as a protector, yet she cannot keep herself from falling for Gorgo. Though Gorgo travels south, trying to shelve his feelings, he eventually discovers Maria's past as a porn star, having watched *To Lie in Shadows*, the X-rated feature she filmed during her early days in the United States. Her photographs also resurface in men's magazines from time to time, reaching the doctor who treats her ailing husband and even a melancholic Gorgo during a stint in prison. All through this time, as a measure to ensure Gorgo's safety behind bars, Maria remains Valdez's lover. She claims to hate cops, but her physical relationship with Valdez is perhaps the steadiest association of the entire story, given the policeman's bearing on her life—initially, as a platform for her social ascent and, subsequently, as a key acquaintance of her husband. Nonetheless, Maria cannot escape the power of media, as her porn flick gains the status of a cult classic, and her fans remain loyal to her photos. The graphic novel does not suggest a continuing pecuniary connection between Maria and these productions as, for the most part, she ignores them or wishes them into oblivion. To some extent, this is an earnest reminder that, though Maria embraces her sexuality as an instrument of power, control of Latina women's bodies as a political tool oftentimes remains in the hands of the patriarchal powers that be, whether media or the state.

To make matters worse, upon Gorgo's release from prison, an aging Cienfuegos asks his son to watch over Maria. An attempted mugging by a Vietnam veteran and two other thugs staged by the Obregons, Cienfuegos's archenemies, serves as an opportunity to clarify that, despite the name calling (the assailants dub him "sp-c" and "greaser"), Gorgo validates his American condition. "I am American," he retorts. Thus, it is his American prerogative to kill the three of them in a vicious display of ferocity, stabbing one in the eye while slaughtering the two others. Next, he calmly fixes his tie. Nonetheless, Maria is drugged, kidnapped, and raped—thus conceiving "Fritz"—and Gorgo falls into depression. Maria's rape scene is represented so clinically that it may stand as an instance in which violence against women may be interpreted as a narrative trope to further the male protagonists' plot, that is, the events of the story surrounding the Cienfuegos. However, Beto embraces a clever pretense. When it happens, Maria is drugged—in fact, she is drugged by a woman—so there is no reaction on her part during the rape.[9] Hence, Beto portrays the event matter-of-factly if partially, failing to allow Maria an opportunity to express the grief associated with her trauma. By the time she recovers, she has no recollection of the event, thinking she has fallen asleep.[10] Despite Gorgo's status as a ruthless thug—he has brutalized and murdered people since the beginning of the story, a behavior Beto chronicles in great detail, as he does in response to Maria's rape (see figure 6.1)—he deems himself a failure, having been unable to protect the woman he loves. This sense of failure leads him to hide in the wild for thirteen years.

In the world of Cienfuegos, Maria becomes familiar with guns, employing them routinely for sexual pleasure, among other uses, and is accustomed to violence, proper of the settling of differences in the underworld. The degree of violence in the second part of the story is extreme. To begin with, in a manner reminiscent of a country lynching, a mobster called Baltazar is cut to pieces by the machete-wielding migrants he employs to cover his drug deals. Then, following their attempt to film a new porn movie starring Maria in which they rape her,[11] Ivan, Cabo, and Baltazar Jr. perish amid a bloody shootout. While the male characters claim the sex has been consensual to some point ("We've been f-cking you all weekend and now you're shy?" Ivan asks),

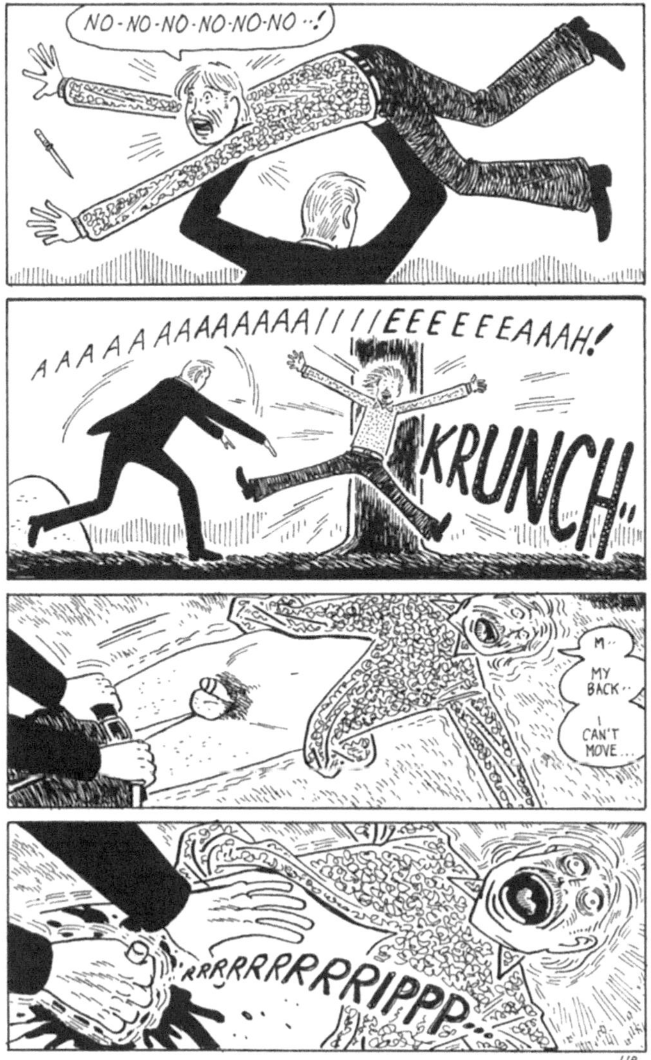

FIGURE 6.1 Gorgo's ruthless response to Maria's rapist is emphasized through visually rendered onomatopoeia. Gilbert Hernandez, *Maria M.* (Seattle: Fantagraphics Books, 2019), 118.

Maria is steadfast in her refusal to have sex in front of the cameras. When things get sadistic, Baltazar Jr. forces her to give oral sex at gunpoint, but by then Ivan and Cabo are dead. In the end, once again, Gorgo rescues her. To escape further sexual violence, Maria flees with her daughter, Fritz, and makes a living as Zonga, a stripper, a choice that allows her to survive and flourish economically while Fritz grows up and finally becomes independent. Twenty years go by before Maria returns to Cienfuegos, only to see him die as the result of the many attempts on his life. Along the way, she sticks with Valdez and also becomes the lover of Cienfuegos's other, more business-driven son Herman. Once Gorgo returns, he represents too much of a risk for his insecure brother Herman. Maria tries to protect Gorgo by delivering a gun, only to end up killing Herman herself and all his men, including Chuy, a loyal associate of Cienfuegos's, in a blood-spattering shoot-out that goes on for sixteen pages in a magnificent display of gore and mayhem.[12] And so, it is the woman who saves the man, inverting the time-honored Hollywood convention of the damsel in distress.

In truth, what Beto gives us in *Maria M.* is something contemporary Hollywood has been reticent to produce: a cinematic experience in which Latinxs figure as the dominant ethnicity and power brokers in a representation of California in the 1950s and 1960s, counted, even if demonized, in a manner analogous to Black cinema's breakthrough during the 1990s (*Boyz n the Hood*, *Menace II Society*). By way of sexuality and violence, Beto shows how the biopolitics of U.S. society attempt to get the best of Latinxs, especially Latinas, exploiting their bodies physically through the sex industry, the drug trade, and urban violence. In his version, however, things evolve differently. Much of the story chronicles Cienfuegos's tensions with his enemies—Tunga, Ruiz, Baltazar, the Obregons—who are massacred and/or dispatched in the most gruesome fashion with genital mutilation, slashed physiques, and lots of carnage, echoing Tarantino's over-the-top antics. Hence, Maria's fate is foreseeable. Kidnapped and raped by an Anglo, she runs away to hide her pregnancy from her thuggish husband, who's now impotent. She goes back to work as a stripper but ultimately reunites with her son-in-law after a bloodbath, amid which she single-handedly shoots the entire Cienfuegos criminal organization. Through all the violence and being surrounded by armed men, it is Maria who settles affairs, eliminating everyone, shooting with accuracy and aplomb, and saving Gorgo—and not the other way around. In this sense, Beto's take is completely different. Not only are Latinxs at play, but even the customary, clichéd power relations between genders also appear to be overturned. Beto's characters may seem to be victims, yet you would be hard-pressed to convince the characters themselves of this fact.

Sexuality and violence in *Maria M.* are therefore far from fortuitous. Though mostly set from the 1950s to the 1970s, the cinematic graphic novel's portrayal of women is, stylistically speaking, more evocative of late Hollywood. Women are abused and assaulted, but they also kill and scheme, revealing agency within patriarchal power. If anyone is to eliminate an entire

Latinx criminal outfit, it will be another Latinx—in this case Maria (played by Fritz)—and not for the sake of a territorial dispute, like in films that demonize Latinxs. What Beto wishes to bring out into the open is the callous way in which the entertainment industry, the Anglo culture of the past and present, has consistently benefited from and/or excluded Latinxs, even when it tries to include them. The recurring problem in Maria's life is her role in the pornographic movies that she agreed to as a desperate measure to make a living upon first migrating to the United States. Gender roles replicate the politics of the period, and sexual interactions always seem to be transactional, at best, and non-consensual, at worst. However, if the Latinx body is to be the loot—as it was in the past, only with defeatist aims—Beto's characters, both women and men, will do something about it. The B-movie quality of the cinematic graphic novel brings into the open the manufactured nature of narratives, making it apparent that it is not only that Hollywood manipulates identities for the sake of commercialism, but also that it prioritizes identities that speak of deeply internalized privilege. It was not just that Rita Hayworth was discovered, her name changed, and her hair colored to transform her into an Anglo—as it used to happen—but also that, when it comes to cinematic representation, the Latinx body needed to be erased from the face of Southern California.

Thus, Beto Latinxizes everything to heighten an absence that is not evident to those who are included. By "Latinxizing," I refer to the process of creating the depiction of a world in which Latinxs are the majority, and thus it is the Anglo who stands as an outsider. The world that Beto manufactures for *Maria M.* is a window into a California that was already there in the 1950s and 1960s—the census numbers hint at it strongly—but Hollywood refused to acknowledge or even represent beyond the control of the state. In his world, Latinxs prefer to play the part of transgressors and victimizers, of subjects of violence and sexuality, rather than objects of manipulation and exclusion. Through sex and violence, they claim ownership of their bodies and the right to take life and let live. As a result of her rape, Maria gives birth to a "new mestiza," Fritz, who incarnates the possibility of greater visibility in an Anglo culture and society without relinquishing privilege.[13] At worst, to the extent that *Maria M.* is a cinematic narrative depicting the story of Fritz's mother, Beto may be contributing to the erasure of Latinx presence. Luba may remain in Palomar, but the new U.S.-centered generation may be more conceding and its success in the north may be largely dictated by the terms of Anglo hegemony. This must change, Beto seems to warn. A case in point, it will take several decades for films like *Chinatown* (1974), Roman Polanski's reenactment of the Los Angeles of the 1940s in the 1970s, to happen and feature Lieutenant Lou Escobar (played by Perry Lopez) protecting "Jake" Gittes (played by Jack Nicholson), in a role that is, at best, patronizing, given the implications of the film's story, in which underrepresented populations are left to clean the mess made by Anglos.

On the Graphic Subversion of Historical Omission

In her work on the ways of the Dutch overseas, historian Frances Gouda explains how aspects of identity like gender and race impact how an empire imagines the colonial experience, contributing to a gendered and racialized reading of its subjects as effeminate or closer to nature, thus leading to a perception of vulnerability or weakness.[14] Gouda draws attention to the influence of selective use of memory on this process, given the ways that people tend to expand on or recall fondly positive experiences while rendering to oblivion those associated with negativity. Empire, I would suggest, is not the only political body to embrace memory selectively. Nations are just as adept at recalling meticulously that which conforms to the views of their elites and ruling classes and discarding in the dustbin of history that which may reflect badly on their political record. After all, as members of an empire, metropolitan citizens act as adeptly as colonials abroad. With time, as projects of nation evolve in response to societal shifts, national narratives strive to remain relevant and embrace mnemonic flexibility by more contemporary political sensibilities, seeking to assess past events in critical, more updated modes.

The American West, largely the result of the Mexican-American War (1846–1848) and the Treaty of Guadalupe Hidalgo (1848), has a mixed record when it comes to the consideration and inclusion of Latinx presence in its history. Both California and Texas were locations where inhabitants of Latin America, who are predominantly of Indigenous and Mexican descent, were actively discriminated against and expelled from their lands following the treaty. In California, the ordeal of Californios, the original Spanish colonists of the state, is integrated into local history as an obscure chapter, a blemish in the record of a political culture usually identified for its progressivism; otherwise, it is recollected in a romanticized and sanitized way. Overwhelmed demographically by the rapid influx of Anglo fortune seekers during the Gold Rush, which also contributed to the persecution of Indigenous peoples, many Californios were treated as foreigners in their land, eventually losing much of their property when not outright risking their lives.[15] By the late 1800s,

Euro-American hegemony was well in place in the lands of California. Thus, it is not difficult to visualize how during the postwar years, when the Latinx population was recovering demographically and making inroads into local culture and society, the entertainment industry would make the community invisible in its depictions of the period.

Latinxs are habitually absent in all of the major works of the time identified with noir, be it the pulpy fiction of Chandler, Hammett, and Spillane or movies by Lang, Wilder, Preminger, and many others. Most of these have gone into popular memory as cultural products of thoroughly Euro-American character. Aside from *Touch of Evil* (1958), the Orson Welles film in which a thinly mustachioed Charlton Heston plays the role of Mexican special prosecutor Miguel "Mike" Vargas and is bullied by captain Hank Quinlan (played by Welles), a corrupt cop from the border, there is precious little presence of Latinxs in the early annals of noir. It is no accident that, despite being celebrated by European audiences, *Touch of Evil* was shunned by the Hollywood establishment for years, given its inversion of the customary good-American / bad-Mexican duality. By the time a new version was released in 1998, incorporating Welles's instructions from a memo written to correct studio intrusions, Latinx presence in many parts of the United States was undeniable. *Border Incident* (1949), the other well-known noir of the period, starring a young Ricardo Montalbán in his first leading role as immigration investigator Pablo Rodriguez, is also set by the border. So, neither of these two films speaks of an established, societally visible Latinx presence in postwar California. Documented Latinx presence seems remarkably absent in all of the noir films exhibiting common California locations more to the north. Thus, when a comic like Vanesa Del Rey and Bryce Carlson's *HIT* comes along, it seems only sensible that most of its characters are of Euro-American descent. After all, even if it is the re-creation of a fictional recollection, it seems natural that it replicates the customary demographics of most of the films of the period, even to the point of reproducing the erasure of underrepresented groups.

If for Beto the object is to maximize the presence of Latinx characters to evince their graphic marginalization, in the case of Vanesa Del Rey, who is of Cuban origin, the approach is the opposite: the idea is to magnify the politics of omission in the reconstruction of memory. It is not only that Latinxs were erased in postwar noir, but that they can even be erased in current representations of noir set in the 1950s and 1960s by employing the same mechanisms of the past: by amplifying a homogenized racialization, forcing readers to come to terms with an exclusionary tradition through exposure to anachronistic representation. In other words, by attempting to remain faithful to the conventions of an exclusionary representation created in the past, modern-day enactments of noir maintain and preserve the omission of Latinxs from the screen and the pages of novels or, in this case, graphic novels. As people tend to say, privilege is invisible to those who hold it. Thus, the practical thing is to render it visible by emphasizing how it eclipses other groups, creating a view of Southern California that illustrates the racial politics of the 1950s with the visual aesthetics of the 2010s, fostering dissonance between the characters and the cultural/social space through the depiction of locations that we now identify with a more diverse population. In short, *HIT* poses an acute critique of homogenization by suggesting how anomalous it looks to our twenty-first-century discernments.

To remain true to the narrative concocted by Carlson while making sure readers become aware of the absence of Latinxs in the story, Del Rey focuses on form (the actual delineation of characters) as her ally.[16] The script may be by an Anglo—actually, Carlson's surname hints at Nordic descent—but the graphics prevail strongly in Del Rey's version. In the contours that she favors, Euro-American descent becomes sinister, much like in Jordan Peele's *Get Out* (2017), in which the customary dynamics of demonization are inverted, or along the lines of *Mad Men* (2007–2015), which accurately depicts the exclusion of African Americans and Latinxs from the ranks of postwar society through its attentive reenactment of racial homogeneity and privilege. At a superficial level, given that the main characters are all Euro-American—and Del Rey's options are limited by this aspect—the emphasis must be on the impact of the art upon the actions of the characters and/or the development of the plot.

Limited by the script, Del Rey illustrates an American West figuratively void of Latinxs, even if in the 1955 issue Eddie Fuentes gives the crooked cops a run for their money. In the 1957 issue, there's no such luck. Fuentes's brief participation as well as his quick following demise amid a shootout is the single Latinx appearance. Thus, if the presence of a Latinx population already in California at the time of the action is to be recalled, even though it is not explicitly visible, it must be in a way that applies to both installments of the story. Within the reigning sentiment of the postwar "melting pot," ethnic differences in *HIT* come along mostly in the stereotypical forms of Italian American mobsters (Anthony Cornero, Karlo Infantino, Carmine and Domino Marconato, Frank Costello, the Luciano crime family) and Jewish gangsters and tycoons (Mickey Cohen, Douglas Schmidt, Tommy Schwartz). After all, Euro-Americans of northern descent have routinely othered Mediterranean,

Catholic, and Semitic lineages over the past two centuries, grouping them as continental "Others." In a manner consistent with the mythology of the melting pot, other forms of Euro-American descent, proper of latitudes closer to the Equator, seem to be as far as the narrative is willing to go when it comes to picturing ethnic or racial difference. If Latinx or African American presence manages to barely creep into the visuals, surpassing literary omission while hinting at tokenism, it is only so that the mechanism works well enough to make the absence more palpable, highlighting the discomfort emanating from the dilution of tangible racial difference. While the intentionality of this aspect is a matter of personal interpretation, it is important to note that the device works unfailingly within the representation of the horrific nature of racial homogenization in the context of the western United States of the late 1950s. This is the case not only for Eddie Fuentes but also for ex-cop Terry Riggs, the African American heavy from West Las Vegas, and the allusion to a Spanish village by the sea (San Clemente, California) or to the Tropicana casino as a substitute for Havana entertainment. They slip by just to remind the reader that something ominous, a foreboding sense of demographic change, is lurking.

Within this thoroughly racialized vision, that there be scant space for Latinxs and/or African Americans is only logical, given the obsessively aestheticizing compliance of the graphics with a European ideal—never mind the frenzied, chaotic rhythm of the story. Yet, Del Rey illustrates the Euro-American men and women in ways that they appear sinister. To emphasize the role of form in her questioning of a Latinx absence, Del Rey focuses on the shapes of the bodies. Jawlines are solid and rectangular, profiles are Greek or Roman, brows are straight or hard-angled, and faces are perpetually frowned, giving most men a patently judgmental, Teutonic air—never mind the incongruity that something vaguely Mediterranean is appropriated to endorse Northern European descent, but within ethnic/racial homogenization everything is game. Most male characters are built like Burt Lancaster or Robert Mitchum, bull-necked and with broad shoulders and V-shaped torsos. All the women look like Hayworth or Veronica Lake, with wasp-like waists and infinite curves, regardless of their Hellenic facial outline. The features and physiognomies of Del Rey's characters are so angular that they appear chiseled into the page—were it not for the coloring. This visual choice underscores physical ideals based on rugged European bodily aesthetics, conflating physical power and imperial designs. Del Rey illustrates most characters in a manner reminiscent of an haute couture fashion catalog, with strong, firm strokes emphasizing length and posture. At times, *HIT*'s characters appear to be a collection of mannequins bent on posing in each frame. Yet, while the Hellenistic profiles reflect a certain omnipotence or mythological air, they also insinuate decadence. Del Rey's effort to conform to a look, to a certain type of physique, is so acutely evident that, even in the case of Fuentes and Riggs, while Latinx and African American, respectively, they are also square-jawed and built like a wall. Thus, a type of standardized anatomy is condoned in terms of class and gender that supersedes ethnicity and race (i.e., you can be Latinx or African American as long as you look like us), prompting a particular association in terms of space, one in which rectilinear configurations, to be inhabited culturally and socially by individuals with matching aesthetics, stand as normal.

Thanks to her colorists, pigments rule in Del Rey's depiction of Southern California. While the story focuses on Euro-American protagonists, the hues of blue, gray, purple, fuchsia, and ochre speak of a different tradition, more along the lines of palettes that could be described as "Mexican" (see figure 6.2). The colors appear burnt or faded, echoing red cochineal or even *añil* (indigo) blue, adding a distinct look to the locations, the lighting of the scenery, and even the attire of characters. These are the sort of shades one would expect to find in a Mexican landscape or on a structure designed by renowned architect Luis Barragán, telluric, faded tones equated with a well-defined identity, from bright magenta to cobalt blue, from warm summer yellow to sunset pink, so, while the contours of the story narrate one identity, hinting at a single way to imagine personification, the colors allude explicitly to another, blatantly visible from the plot.[17] The coloring of the Fuente de los Amantes, the Torres de Satélite, the Casa Gilardi, and the Pritzker Prize's house and studio in Mexico City, all celebrated incarnations of *mexicanidad* (Mexicanness), comes to mind. Barragán would have been at ease in the pages of *HIT*, were it not for the utter absence of Latinx people.

In all sincerity, color is an aspect with a cumulative effect. The colorist for the first volume of *HIT* (1955) is Archie Van Buren, so the blues, browns, and grays of the initial installment appear to be there as a colorful license, hoping to keep things in check while the plot grows increasingly intricate and violent. While the first volume of *HIT* toys with tints of blue, brown, yellow, purple, and red, the profusion of shades of magenta—a favorite of Barragán's—in the second volume (1957) is downright exceptional, starting with the cover. The explosion of color appears so precipitously that it is impossible to interpret it as accidental. The 1957 issue, though, is the work of Colombian-Venezuelan colorist Niko Guardia. He paints Del Rey's art with huge splashes of vivid light and darkness in his colors, inviting dramatic

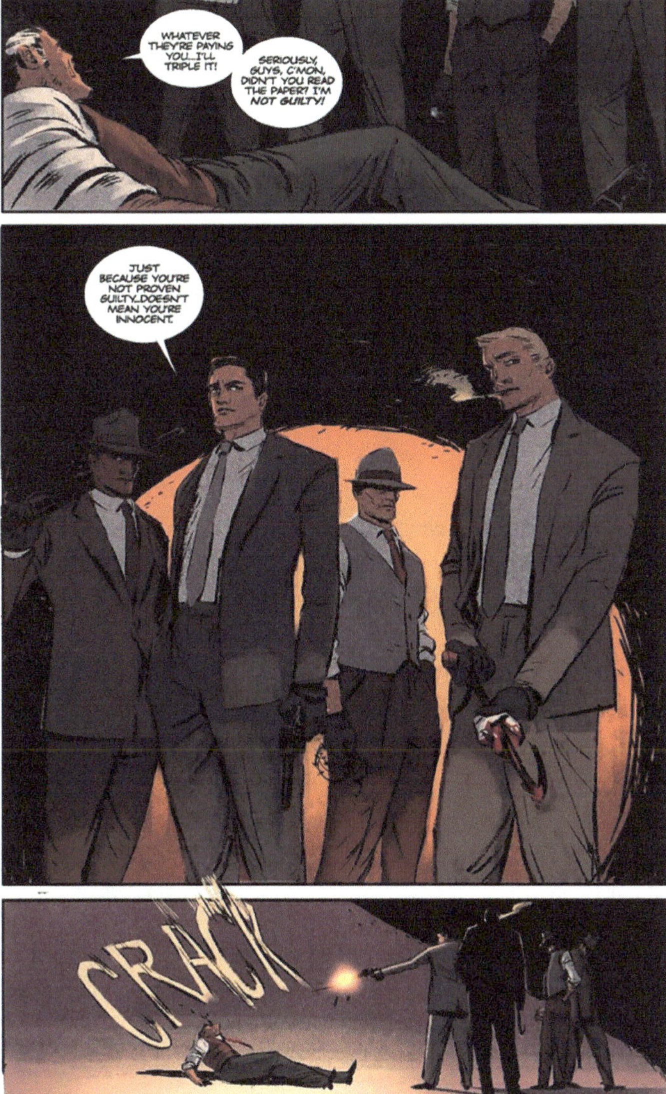

FIGURE 6.2 Archie Van Buren's colors depict Southern California through blue, gray, purple, fuchsia, and ochre hues that infuse the space with a Mexican presence. Bryce Carlson and Vanesa R. Del Rey, *HIT: 1955* (Los Angeles: BOOM! Studios, 2014), 9.

chiaroscuros—so Del Rey is not alone in her subversion of Euro-American predominance (see figure 6.3). As I have mentioned, he seems to have a thing for magenta, so the ensuing feeling is that of being surrounded by a parade of Barragán designs—or at the very least, spaces influenced by his architectural practice. Doubtlessly, these colors conform to what any well-versed art historian or architecture critic would associate with a Mexican aesthetic tradition. These are not the bright, vivacious colors proper of sunlit scenarios in Southern California or the pastels of Art Deco from the post-war era. By the time Guardia takes hold of the coloring, those appear to be remarkably absent, even if Del Rey occasionally favors an Art Deco building or two.

Color pervades space, and as we well know, space is inhabited culturally and socially. Color invites readers to think more about who inhabits which space or at least whose presence it is supposed to signify. So, when Del Rey illustrates the parade of Western settings quoted by Larson (most of them representative of American Art Deco, early American modernism, and postwar modernism), so right-angled, perspective-driven, and evocative of quintessential noir settings, she also hints at the association of space with specific populations. Thus, the body types match the locations inhabited, in sheer allusion to the exclusionary power of race and ethnicity in social space. The normative spirit of the imagery is so absolute that the more rounded, organic features of Latinxs are left to be missed. The long list of locations in the story embodies a veritable tour of the region: Hollywood (with a predominantly White population); Sunset Boulevard (White); Laurel Canyon (White); Santa Monica (White); Malibu (White); Beverly Hills (White); Brentwood (White); Manhattan Beach (White); downtown LA (nowadays Latinx as well as other groups); Broadway, Leo Carrillo State Park, and Hancock Park (White); the Ventura coast (White); Westlake (Latinx); Baldwin Hills (Latinx and African American); Boyle Heights (Latinx), Terminal Island (White), San Clemente (White); the Warehouse District and Watts (Latinx and African American); Van Nuys (Latinx); and even Las Vegas and West Las Vegas (African American)—all of which are represented in such a way that barely a trace of Latinx or African American presence is apparent, even though a great deal of the evolution of the narrative revolves around race and/or ethnicity.

In the end, what becomes clear is that Del Rey honors noir aesthetics, but from a cartoonist's perspective. That Latinxs are left out—despite tangible visual cues in terms of form and color—is certainly her intention

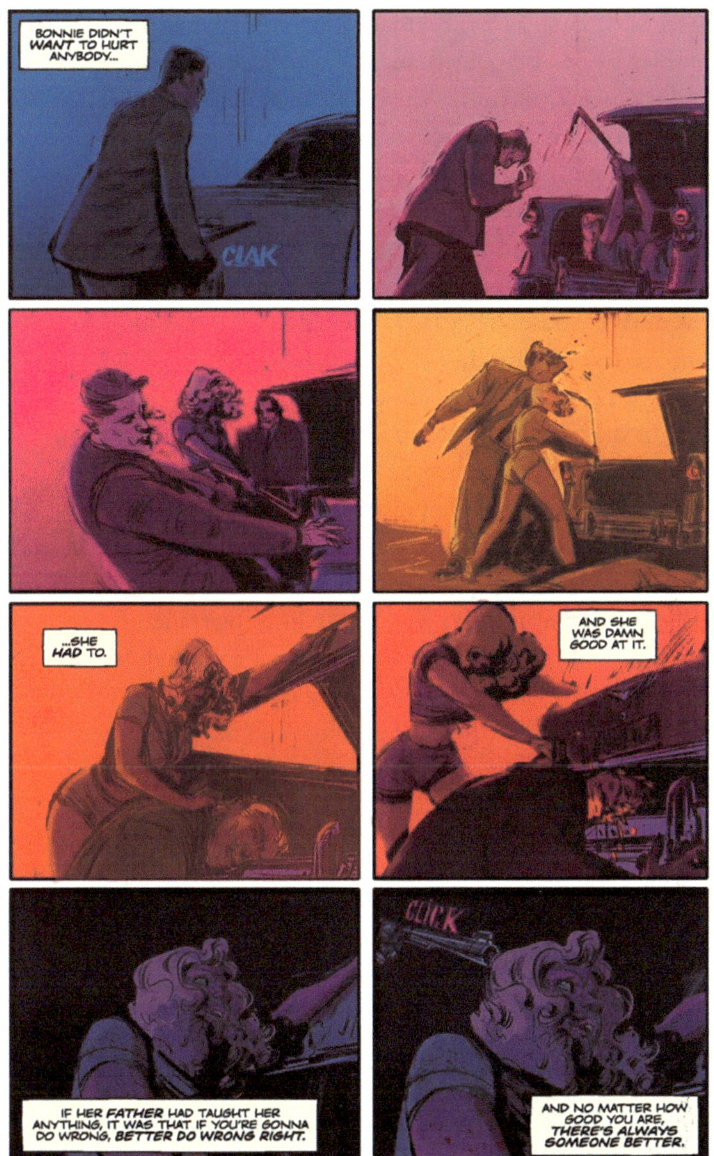

FIGURE 6.3 Niko Guardia colors the setting of *HIT: 1957* with bold blocks of bright colors that evoke light and darkness. Bryce Carlson and Vanesa R. Del Rey, *HIT: 1957* (Los Angeles: BOOM! Studios, 2016), 12.

(as well as Guardia's), as it accentuates the omissive nature of postwar society's representation. Beto Hernandez instead chooses to look at the late 1950s and 1960s and maximize the presence of Latinxs, creating previously unnarrated experiences and sometimes revisiting historic confluences. His account underlines how earlier representations of this period normalized inequality and exclusion. Nevertheless, rather than bashing the past, he turns things on their head and transforms Latinxs into the power brokers of the game. The dynamics of power in representation are similar, but the point of view, given who chooses what to show or ignore and the mechanisms implicated, intensifies the partiality of representation, forcing readers to come to terms with it. In the long run, what gains credence is that Latinx presence, as a thing of the past or the present, will reassess its role in yesteryear with the techniques of today, hoping to inform its current possibilities through the reproduction of approaches critical of past marginalization. As both works show, there are ways of addressing the exclusionary nature of historically sanctioned versions of the past without the need for reckless revisionism. In the end, it may just be a matter of educating readers, so they can gain a critical edge and recognize the artificial nature of established representation by way of offering new, more exacting narratives. Physicality and color in comics can do this.

Notes

1 See "Historical Census Racial/Ethnic Numbers in Los Angeles County 1850 to 1980," *Los Angeles Almanac*, accessed October 2, 2020, https://www.laalmanac.com/population/po20.php.

2 Emily Henry, "Map of Ethnic Diversity in Los Angeles, from 1940 to 2000," YouTube, July 19, 2009, https://www.youtube.com/watch?v=wBfrAofx8P8&t=5s.

3 Michel Foucault, "'Society Must Be Defended': Lecture at the *Collège de France*, March 17, 1976," in *Biopolitics: A Reader*, ed. Timothy Campbell and Adam Sitze (Durham, NC: Duke University Press, 2013), 61–81; Michel Foucault, "Right of Death and Power Over Life," in *The History of Sexuality*, vol. 1: *An Introduction* (New York: Pantheon Books, 1978), 135–159.

4 Foucault, "'Society Must Be Defended,'" 72.

5 Foucault, *History of Sexuality*, 139–141.

6 Foucault, "'Society Must Be Defended,'" 74.

7 Foucault, "'Society Must Be Defended,'" 75.

8 Foucault, "'Society Must Be Defended,'" 77.

9 Hernandez, *Maria M.* (Seattle: Fantagraphics Books, 2019), 116–117.

10 Hernandez, *Maria M.*, 127.

11 Hernandez, *Maria M.*, 149–155.

12 Hernandez, *Maria M.*, 224–231.

13 On the subject of mestizaje and the "new mestiza," see Edwina Barbosa, *Wealth of Selves: Multiple Identities, Mestiza Consciousness, and the Subject of Politics* (College Station: Texas A&M University Press, 2008).

14 Frances Gouda, *Dutch Culture Overseas: Colonial Practice in the Netherland Indies, 1900–1942* (Amsterdam: Amsterdam University Press, 1995).

15 For more information, see Ray Suarez, *Latino Americans* (New York: Penguin, 2013), 3–27, and Juan Gonzalez, *Harvest of Empire* (New York: Penguin, 2011), 46.

16 However, it is important to note that, though in the hands of one of her team members, coloring by Niko Guardia also plays a big role in this direction. This aspect is discussed subsequently.

17 A native of Guadalajara, Jalisco, Barragán (1902–1988) is renowned as one of Mexico's and Latin America's most important architects. His work amounts to 170 projects, though Aguilar House (1928), Cristo House (1929), the house at Avenida Parque México (1936), Barragán House (1948), Prieto López House (1948–1951), the Capuchin Convent Chapel (1954–1963), Gálvez House (1955), Torres de Satélite (1957), Lomas Verdes (1964–1967), Cobre de México (1965–1966), Cuadra San Cristóbal (19966–1968), Gilardi House (1975–1977), and Faro del Comercio (1982–1984) rank among his most renowned.

I'm American, and I'm Multilingual. Why Does It Feel So Scary to Speak in Another Language in Public?

●●●●●●●●●●●●●●

TERRY BLAS

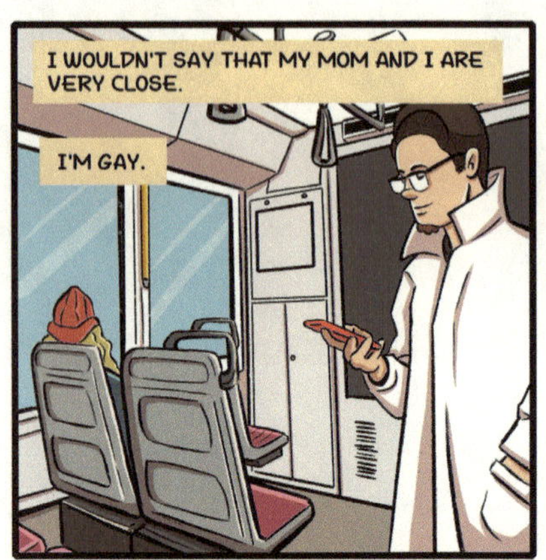
I WOULDN'T SAY THAT MY MOM AND I ARE VERY CLOSE.
I'M GAY.

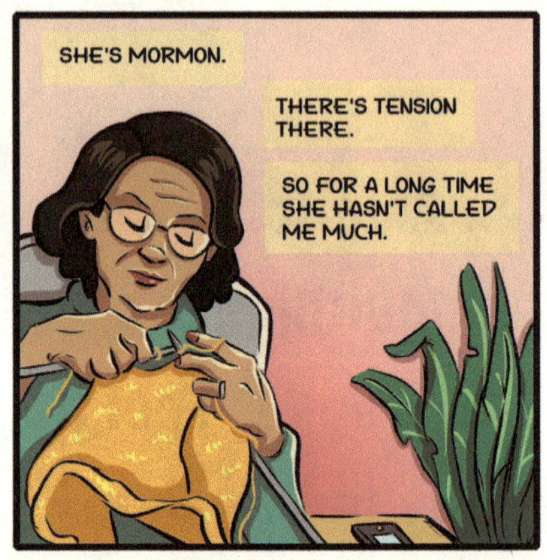
SHE'S MORMON.
THERE'S TENSION THERE.
SO FOR A LONG TIME SHE HASN'T CALLED ME MUCH.

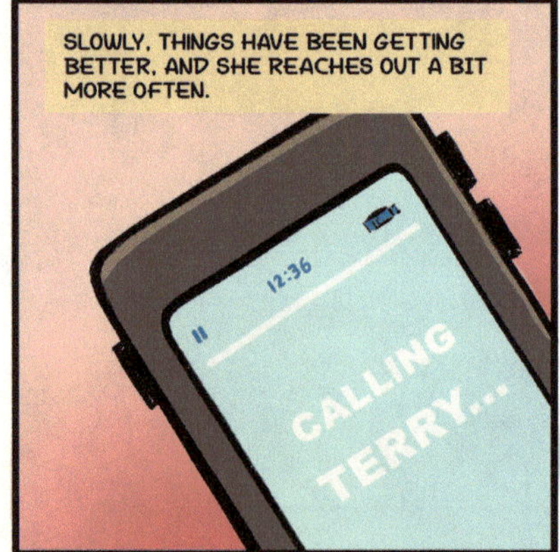
SLOWLY, THINGS HAVE BEEN GETTING BETTER, AND SHE REACHES OUT A BIT MORE OFTEN.
12:36
CALLING TERRY...

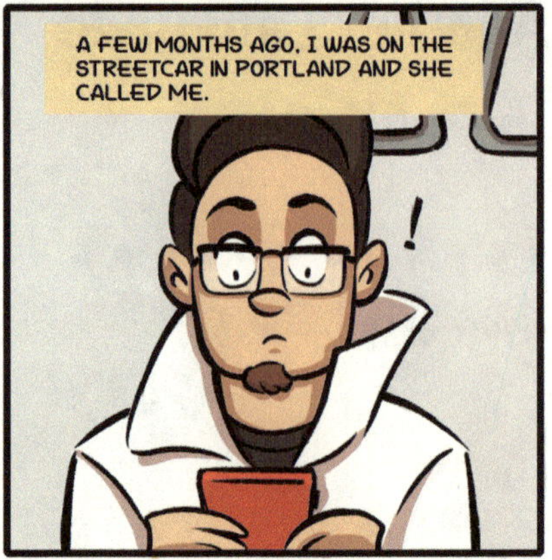
A FEW MONTHS AGO, I WAS ON THE STREETCAR IN PORTLAND AND SHE CALLED ME.
!

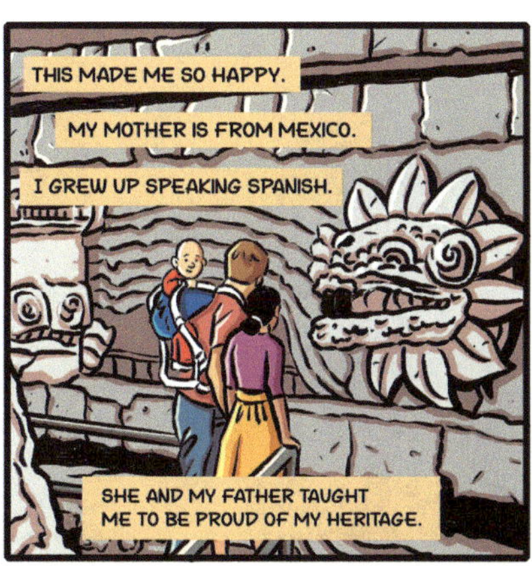
THIS MADE ME SO HAPPY.
MY MOTHER IS FROM MEXICO.
I GREW UP SPEAKING SPANISH.
SHE AND MY FATHER TAUGHT ME TO BE PROUD OF MY HERITAGE.

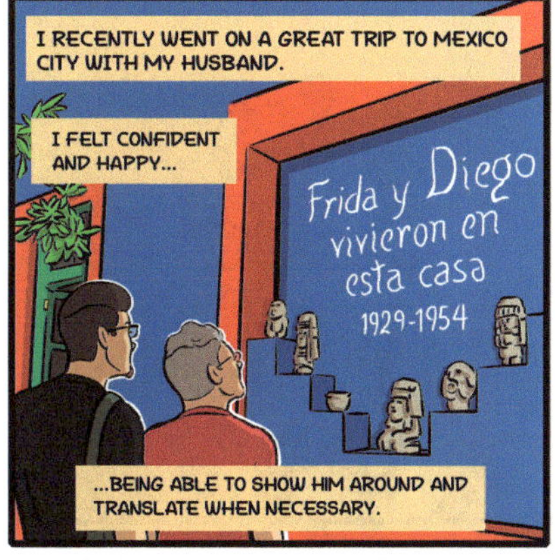
I RECENTLY WENT ON A GREAT TRIP TO MEXICO CITY WITH MY HUSBAND.
I FELT CONFIDENT AND HAPPY...
Frida y Diego vivieron en esta casa 1929-1954
...BEING ABLE TO SHOW HIM AROUND AND TRANSLATE WHEN NECESSARY.

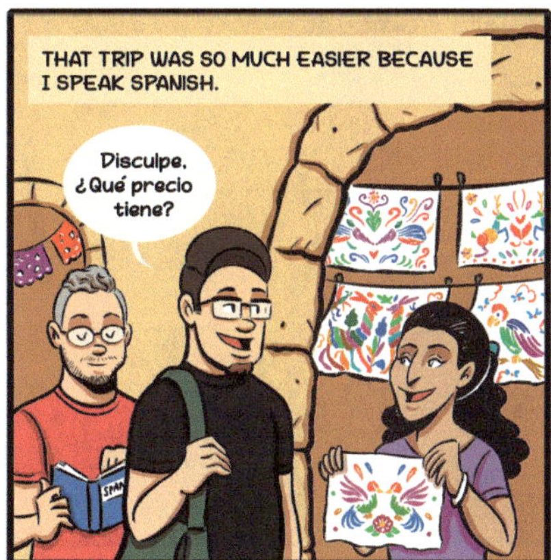
THAT TRIP WAS SO MUCH EASIER BECAUSE I SPEAK SPANISH.
Disculpe. ¿Qué precio tiene?

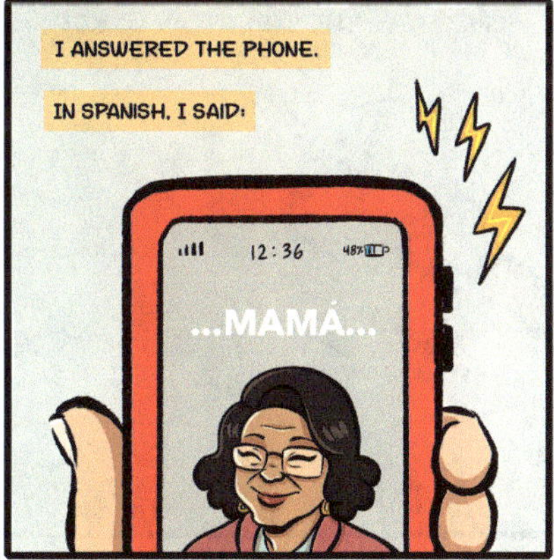
I ANSWERED THE PHONE.
IN SPANISH, I SAID:
12:36
...MAMÁ...

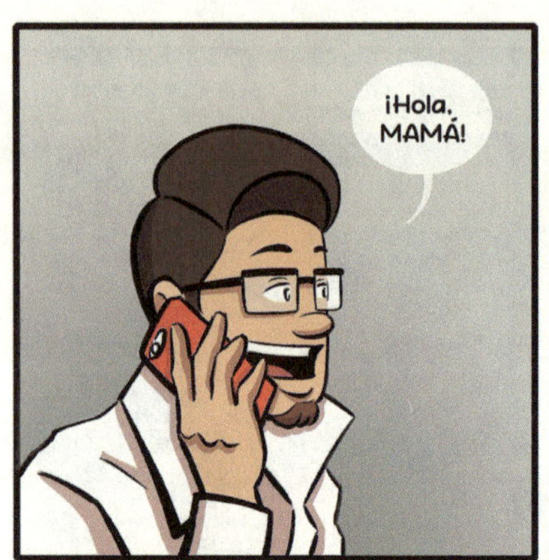
¡Hola,
MAMÁ!

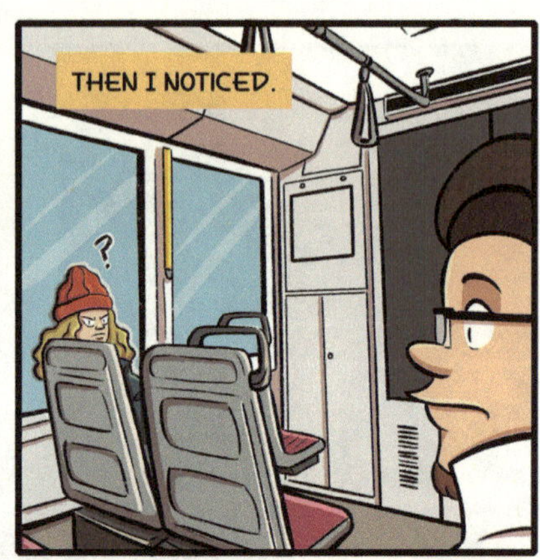
THEN I NOTICED.
?

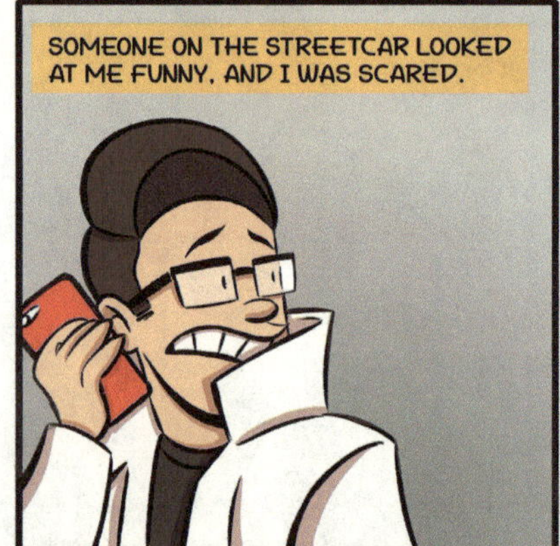
SOMEONE ON THE STREETCAR LOOKED AT ME FUNNY, AND I WAS SCARED.

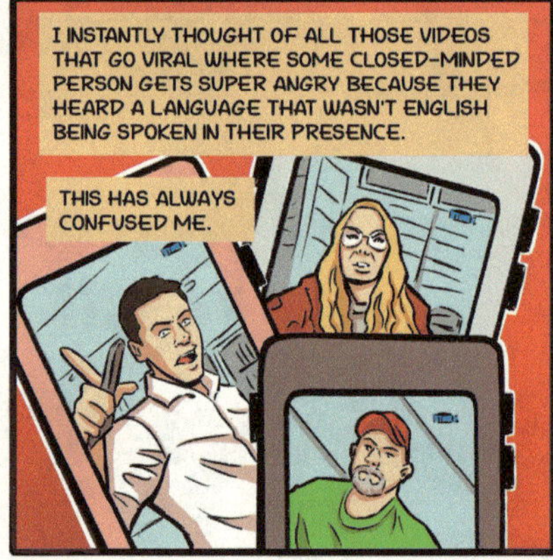
I INSTANTLY THOUGHT OF ALL THOSE VIDEOS THAT GO VIRAL WHERE SOME CLOSED-MINDED PERSON GETS SUPER ANGRY BECAUSE THEY HEARD A LANGUAGE THAT WASN'T ENGLISH BEING SPOKEN IN THEIR PRESENCE.
THIS HAS ALWAYS CONFUSED ME.

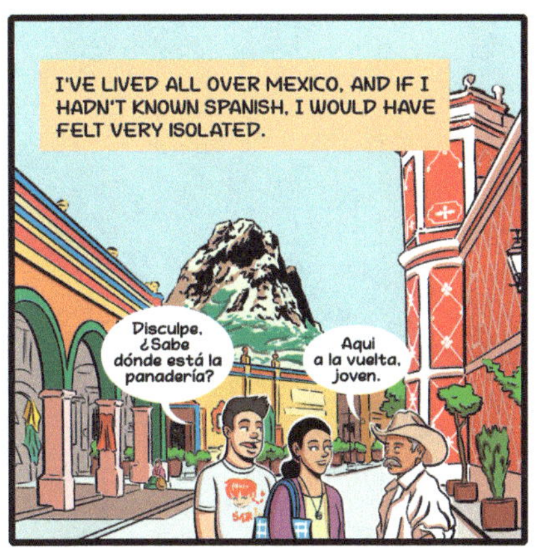
I'VE LIVED ALL OVER MEXICO, AND IF I HADN'T KNOWN SPANISH, I WOULD HAVE FELT VERY ISOLATED.
Disculpe, ¿Sabe dónde está la panadería?
Aqui a la vuelta, joven.

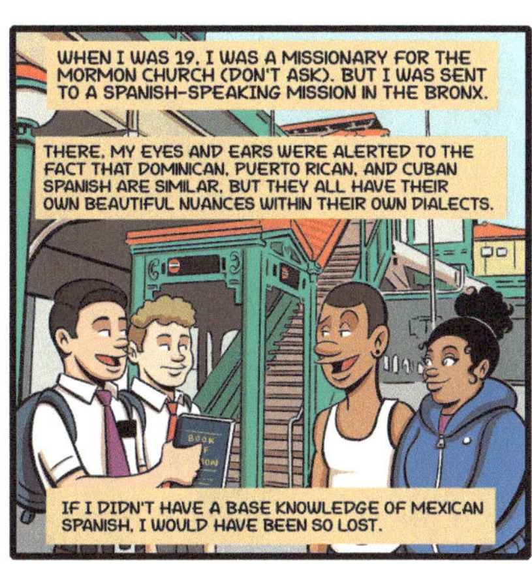
WHEN I WAS 19, I WAS A MISSIONARY FOR THE MORMON CHURCH (DON'T ASK). BUT I WAS SENT TO A SPANISH-SPEAKING MISSION IN THE BRONX.
THERE, MY EYES AND EARS WERE ALERTED TO THE FACT THAT DOMINICAN, PUERTO RICAN, AND CUBAN SPANISH ARE SIMILAR, BUT THEY ALL HAVE THEIR OWN BEAUTIFUL NUANCES WITHIN THEIR OWN DIALECTS.
IF I DIDN'T HAVE A BASE KNOWLEDGE OF MEXICAN SPANISH, I WOULD HAVE BEEN SO LOST.

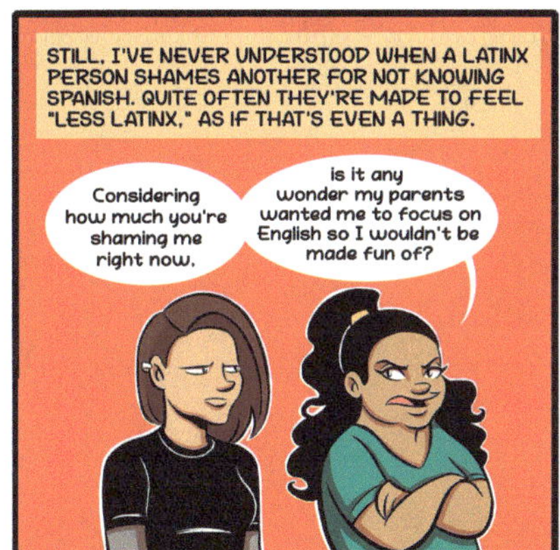
STILL, I'VE NEVER UNDERSTOOD WHEN A LATINX PERSON SHAMES ANOTHER FOR NOT KNOWING SPANISH. QUITE OFTEN THEY'RE MADE TO FEEL "LESS LATINX," AS IF THAT'S EVEN A THING.
Considering how much you're shaming me right now,
is it any wonder my parents wanted me to focus on English so I wouldn't be made fun of?

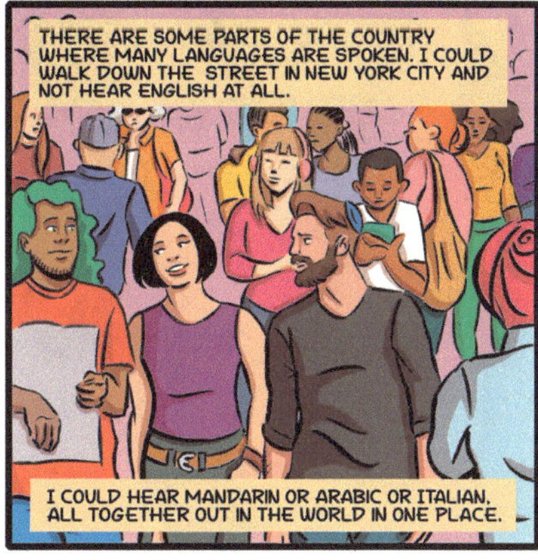
THERE ARE SOME PARTS OF THE COUNTRY WHERE MANY LANGUAGES ARE SPOKEN. I COULD WALK DOWN THE STREET IN NEW YORK CITY AND NOT HEAR ENGLISH AT ALL.
I COULD HEAR MANDARIN OR ARABIC OR ITALIAN, ALL TOGETHER OUT IN THE WORLD IN ONE PLACE.

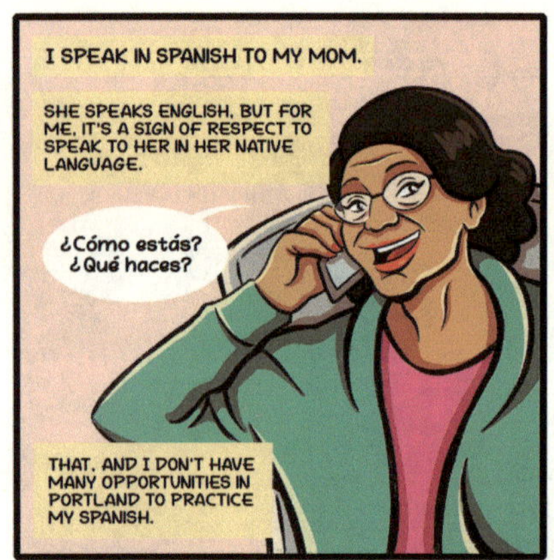
I SPEAK IN SPANISH TO MY MOM.
SHE SPEAKS ENGLISH, BUT FOR ME, IT'S A SIGN OF RESPECT TO SPEAK TO HER IN HER NATIVE LANGUAGE.
¿Cómo estás? ¿Qué haces?
THAT, AND I DON'T HAVE MANY OPPORTUNITIES IN PORTLAND TO PRACTICE MY SPANISH.

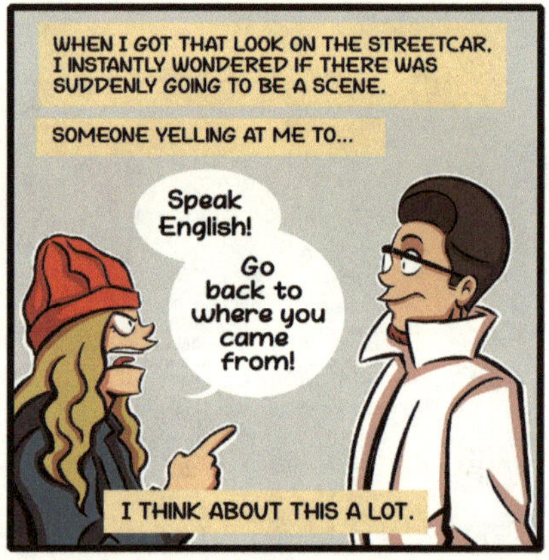
WHEN I GOT THAT LOOK ON THE STREETCAR, I INSTANTLY WONDERED IF THERE WAS SUDDENLY GOING TO BE A SCENE.
SOMEONE YELLING AT ME TO...
Speak English!
Go back to where you came from!
I THINK ABOUT THIS A LOT.

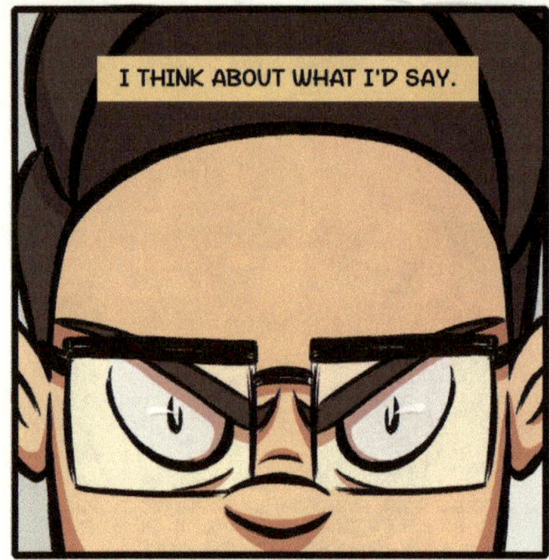
I THINK ABOUT WHAT I'D SAY.

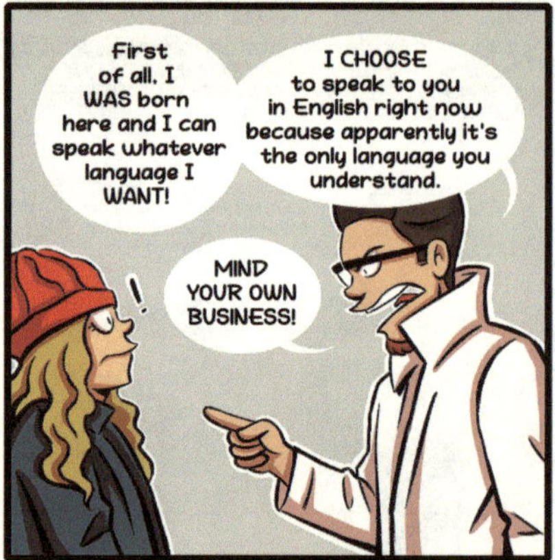
First of all, I WAS born here and I can speak whatever language I WANT!
I CHOOSE to speak to you in English right now because apparently it's the only language you understand.
MIND YOUR OWN BUSINESS!
!

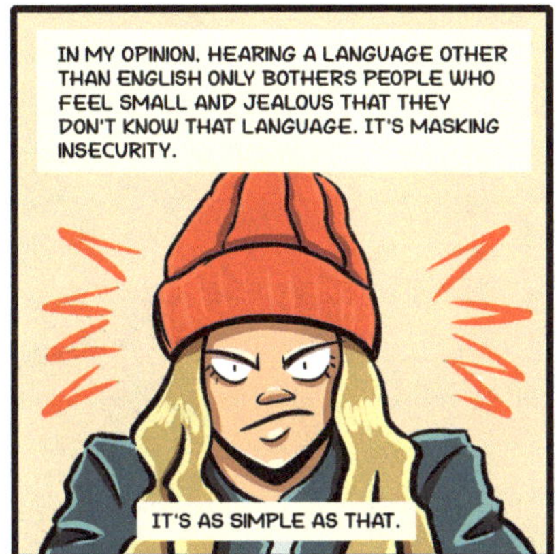
IN MY OPINION, HEARING A LANGUAGE OTHER THAN ENGLISH ONLY BOTHERS PEOPLE WHO FEEL SMALL AND JEALOUS THAT THEY DON'T KNOW THAT LANGUAGE. IT'S MASKING INSECURITY.
IT'S AS SIMPLE AS THAT.

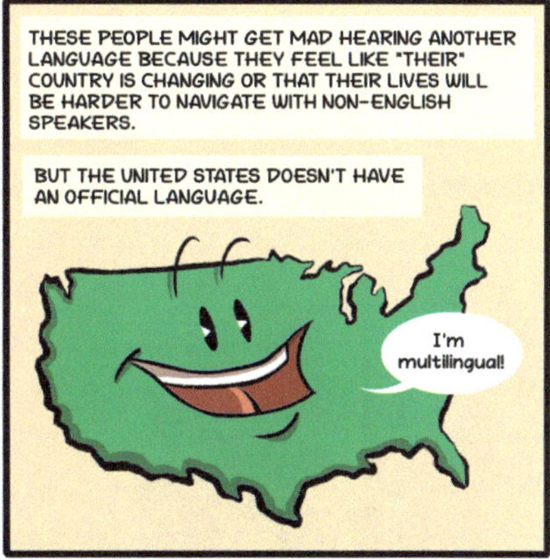
THESE PEOPLE MIGHT GET MAD HEARING ANOTHER LANGUAGE BECAUSE THEY FEEL LIKE "THEIR" COUNTRY IS CHANGING OR THAT THEIR LIVES WILL BE HARDER TO NAVIGATE WITH NON-ENGLISH SPEAKERS.
BUT THE UNITED STATES DOESN'T HAVE AN OFFICIAL LANGUAGE.
I'm multilingual!

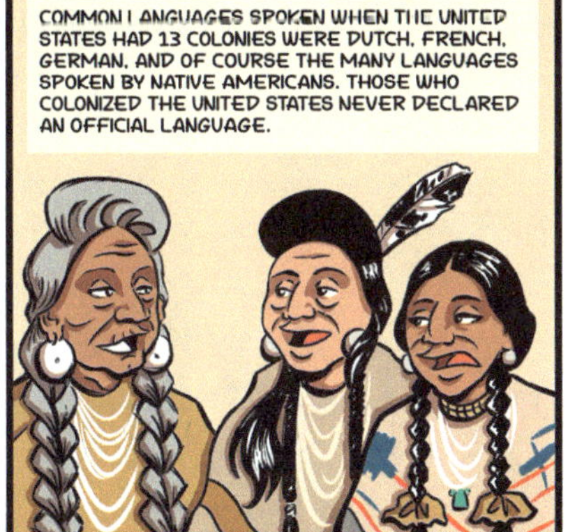
COMMON LANGUAGES SPOKEN WHEN THE UNITED STATES HAD 13 COLONIES WERE DUTCH, FRENCH, GERMAN, AND OF COURSE THE MANY LANGUAGES SPOKEN BY NATIVE AMERICANS. THOSE WHO COLONIZED THE UNITED STATES NEVER DECLARED AN OFFICIAL LANGUAGE.

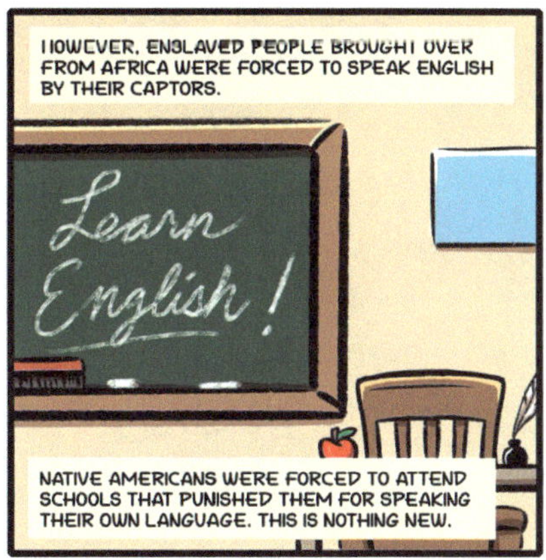
HOWEVER, ENSLAVED PEOPLE BROUGHT OVER FROM AFRICA WERE FORCED TO SPEAK ENGLISH BY THEIR CAPTORS.
Learn English!
NATIVE AMERICANS WERE FORCED TO ATTEND SCHOOLS THAT PUNISHED THEM FOR SPEAKING THEIR OWN LANGUAGE. THIS IS NOTHING NEW.

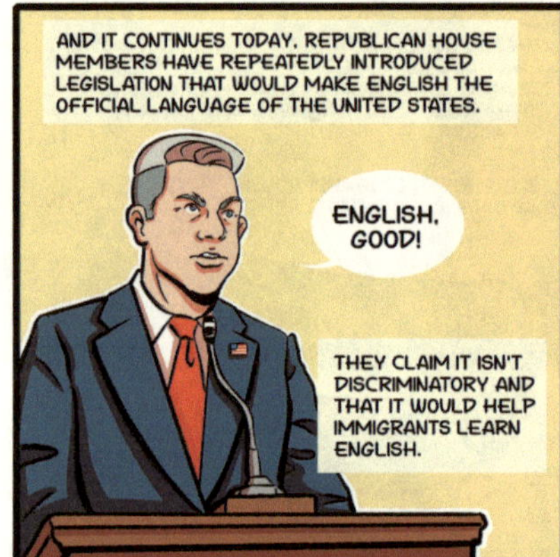
AND IT CONTINUES TODAY. REPUBLICAN HOUSE MEMBERS HAVE REPEATEDLY INTRODUCED LEGISLATION THAT WOULD MAKE ENGLISH THE OFFICIAL LANGUAGE OF THE UNITED STATES.
ENGLISH, GOOD!
THEY CLAIM IT ISN'T DISCRIMINATORY AND THAT IT WOULD HELP IMMIGRANTS LEARN ENGLISH.

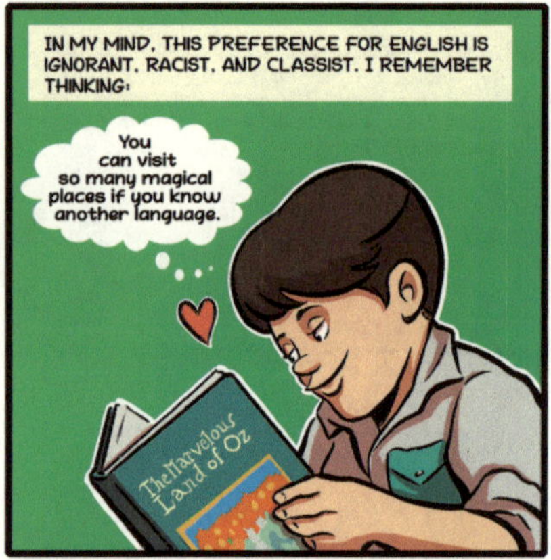
IN MY MIND, THIS PREFERENCE FOR ENGLISH IS IGNORANT, RACIST, AND CLASSIST. I REMEMBER THINKING:
You can visit so many magical places if you know another language.
The Marvelous Land of Oz

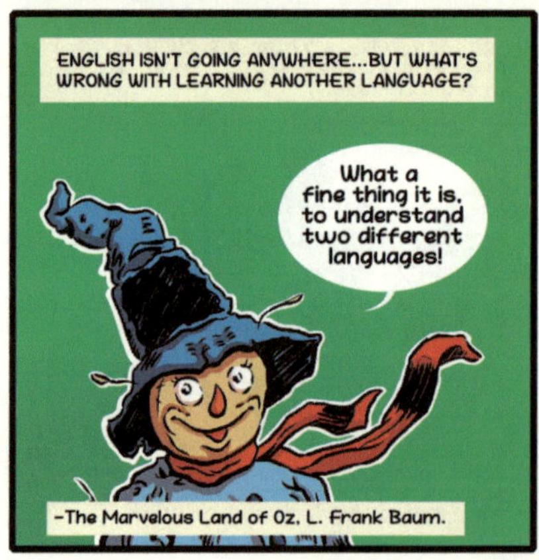
ENGLISH ISN'T GOING ANYWHERE...BUT WHAT'S WRONG WITH LEARNING ANOTHER LANGUAGE?
What a fine thing it is, to understand two different languages!
–The Marvelous Land of Oz, L. Frank Baum.

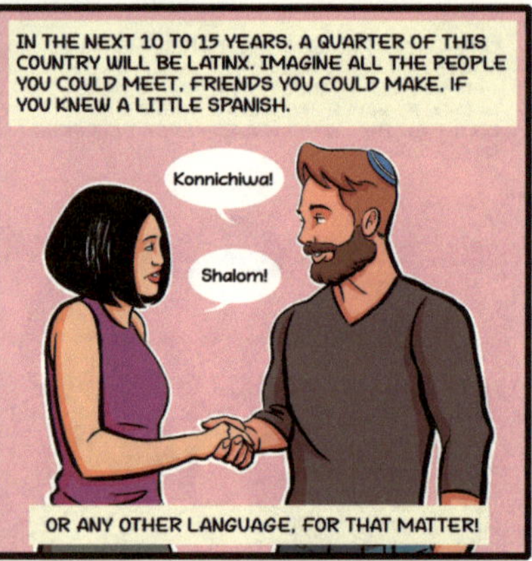
IN THE NEXT 10 TO 15 YEARS, A QUARTER OF THIS COUNTRY WILL BE LATINX. IMAGINE ALL THE PEOPLE YOU COULD MEET, FRIENDS YOU COULD MAKE, IF YOU KNEW A LITTLE SPANISH.
Konnichiwa!
Shalom!
OR ANY OTHER LANGUAGE, FOR THAT MATTER!

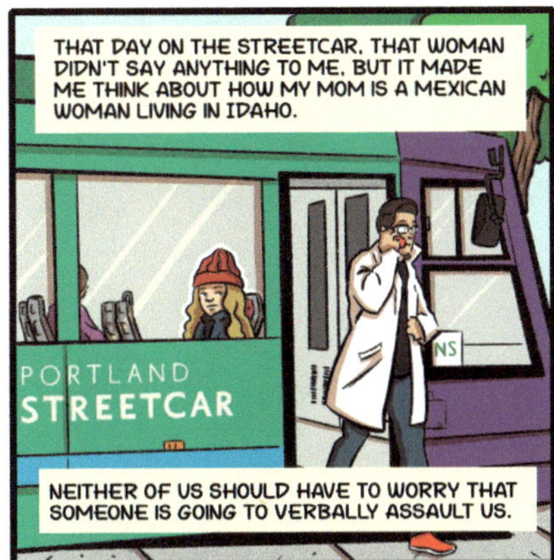
THAT DAY ON THE STREETCAR, THAT WOMAN DIDN'T SAY ANYTHING TO ME, BUT IT MADE ME THINK ABOUT HOW MY MOM IS A MEXICAN WOMAN LIVING IN IDAHO.
PORTLAND STREETCAR
NEITHER OF US SHOULD HAVE TO WORRY THAT SOMEONE IS GOING TO VERBALLY ASSAULT US.

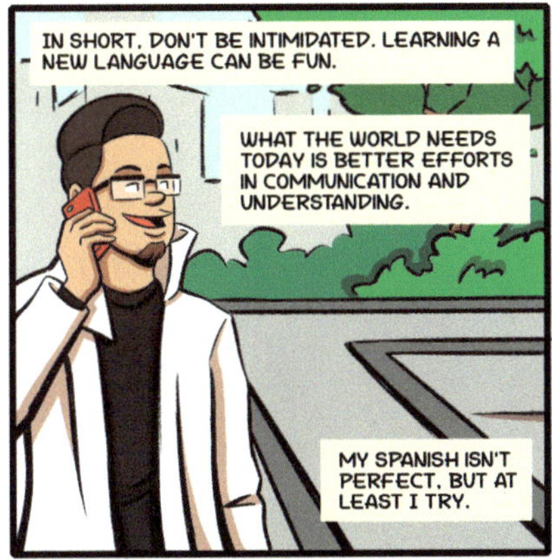
IN SHORT, DON'T BE INTIMIDATED. LEARNING A NEW LANGUAGE CAN BE FUN.
WHAT THE WORLD NEEDS TODAY IS BETTER EFFORTS IN COMMUNICATION AND UNDERSTANDING.
MY SPANISH ISN'T PERFECT, BUT AT LEAST I TRY.

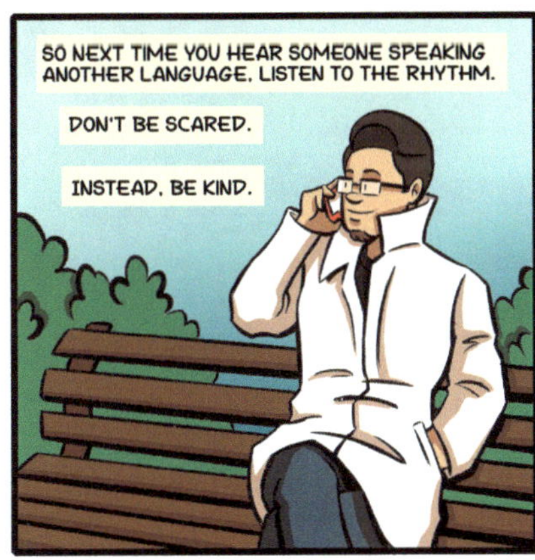
SO NEXT TIME YOU HEAR SOMEONE SPEAKING ANOTHER LANGUAGE, LISTEN TO THE RHYTHM.
DON'T BE SCARED.
INSTEAD, BE KIND.

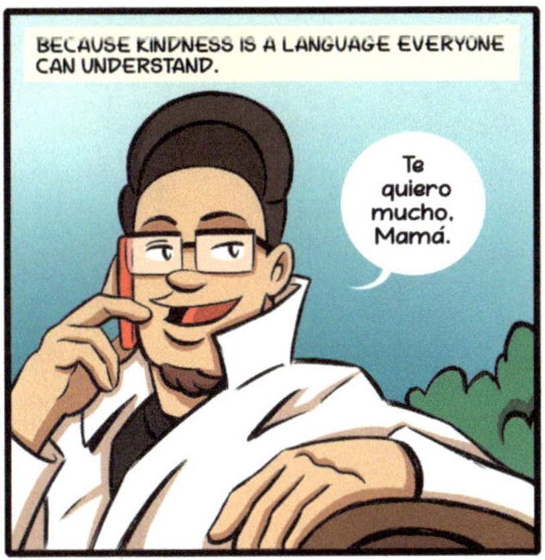
BECAUSE KINDNESS IS A LANGUAGE EVERYONE CAN UNDERSTAND.
Te quiero mucho, Mamá.

Part III

Feminist and Queer Interventions

From Conditional Belonging to Self-Definition

The Hija Loquita Breaks Free in *Blackbird*

KATLIN MARISOL SWEENEY-ROMERO

In a supernatural overlay of the Los Angeles neighborhood of North Hollywood, Nina Rodriguez seeks to remember and work through the childhood trauma repressed in her dreams so that she may heal within a transformative state of *malinalli*. Nina is the protagonist of *Blackbird*, a six-issue comic series released by Image Comics between 2018 and 2019 that was cocreated by writer Sam Humphries and artist Jen Bartel. The issues feature layout art by Paul Reinwand; coloring by Triona Farrell, Jen Bartel, and Nayoung Wilson; lettering by Jodi Wynne; design by Dylan Todd; and editing by Jim Gibbons. *Blackbird* follows Nina as she grapples with memories she believes are real, despite her family's insistence that they are not. She frequently recalls a magical earthquake—the Verdugo Earthquake—that struck her neighborhood when she was thirteen and set off a chain of traumatizing events: the disappearance of her cat, her mother Gloria's death in a car accident, her father Enrique "going crazy" and retreating into seclusion, her grandmother Leticia dying of dementia, and her older sister Marisa moving out, all of which leave Nina "cursed" and "alone."[1] Post-earthquake, Nina battles pain pill addiction, alcoholism, depression, and posttraumatic stress disorder while navigating the pain of being dismissed as a "crazy baby" by her family for believing her memories as well as the isolation brought on by the gradual dissolution of her household.

In this chapter, I recognize and foreground the tensions that arise from attempting to heal from familial wounds that you can feel and remember, even as you are told they do not exist because the events that caused them did not occur how others remember them. I weave brief personal narratives from my own life with an analysis of *Blackbird* that reads Nina as a protagonist who, like myself, is a queer, mentally ill, mixed-race Latina daughter. Across its six issues, *Blackbird* exposes the reader to Nina's vulnerable and painful process of working to embrace the parts of her identity she has been instructed to distrust while simultaneously making space for her processing to be nonlinear, complicated, and resistant. In my twenties, I also underwent a difficult journey of piecing together frayed memories and untangling my dreams from external insecurities so that I could form an identity of my own for the first time. Through our respective creative expression, Nina and I have gained an outlet where we can safely explore the parts of ourselves rejected as mala and too headstrong for the family. For Nina, it is her fixation with researching magic and paragons; for me, it is my research and collection of Latina-led comics.[2]

Both in my story and in *Blackbird*, being a Latina daughter means becoming fearfully aware of your own power before you know how to control it and even as others tell you it does not exist.[3] In this chapter, I explore the contours of being perceived of as a *loquita*: a label affixed to me and Nina in varying situations when removing the veneer of perfectionism to reveal one's vulnerable, imperfect self is met with loving teasing or threats of familial expulsion. I closely read visual and verbal aspects of Nina's narration in issue 1 that exemplify how *Blackbird* presents personal narrative as a tool that Latina daughters can use for envisioning a future self even before it fully exists. By taking a critical-creative approach that blends literary analysis with personal essay, I contemplate how the enduring image of the *hija buena*, or "good daughter," can pressure people who experience childhood as a daughter to perform a version of Latinaness that is obedient, controlled, and heteronormative—one that may lead us to suppress the parts of ourselves deemed excessive or undesirable.[4] While some Latina daughters may not be forced into the binary poles of acceptance or expulsion, others experience a belonging that is conditional. This type of belonging is predicated on a conscious performance of the *buena hija* that is oftentimes at odds with queerness, mixed identity, or mental illness and reflects the generational expectation that Latina daughters discipline ourselves into practicing selflessness, sexual modesty, domesticity, and graciousness.[5]

This chapter contends that to be a Latina daughter is to creatively cultivate healing modes of survival through which one can identify the extent to which one may reimagine one's own selfhood in affirming ways outside of and beyond the family. Both my story and Nina's story in *Blackbird* offer examples of how daughters construct identities for themselves—as an outsider, a rebel, a Blackbird, an "Hija Loquita"—by first refusing to limit themselves to the buena hija role that determines their place in the family and prescribes the terms of their visibility. Much like the "Blackbirds" in Nina's storyworld, who are most connected with their magic when trusting their own power, Latinas who deviate from the role assigned to them by *familismo* are simultaneously empowered and shamed for their rebellion. In reading Nina's narrative alongside my own, I argue that when Latina daughters work to embrace and assert the facets of our identities we have struggled to love, we create opportunities to take control of our own narrative. In doing so, we envision an alternative future composed of open endings, acknowledgment of one's own trauma, and a connection to the figurative (or, for Nina, literal) magic of being unapologetically queer, mixed, and/or mentally ill. Through these futures, we affirm the existence of wounds we have felt, yet that have remained unseen by those around us. By connecting with and embracing the parts of ourselves commonly dismissed as invalid or disruptive, we take up a conscious residence in the "in-between" as the Hija Loquita who is empowered, not ashamed, of who she is and who she can become.

Envisioning the Hija Loquita: Reading and Writing Oneself toward a Redefined Identity

For Latinas, the process by which we craft a self-identity is informed by *marianismo*, or the gendered expectation that "a Latina [will be] dedicated to one's family, be subordinate to others, and self-silencing in order to maintain harmonious relationships."[6] Coined by Evelyn P. Stevens in her foundational essay "Machismo and Marianismo," the term articulates a binary relationship between Latin American men's hypermasculine "wickedness," or *machismo*, and the sanctity of Latin American's ideal femininity. Stevens writes that in "taking its cue from the worship of Mary, marianismo pictures its subjects as morally superior and spiritually stronger than men. This constellation of attributes enables women to bear the indignities inflicted on them by men, and to forgive those who bring them pain."[7] As Gloria Anzaldúa usefully underscores, "the culture expects women to show greater acceptance of, and commitment to, the value system than men," to practice a femininity that is virginal and subservient.[8]

For U.S.-born Latinas raised by Latin American parents, they, too, experience pressure to prioritize "sacred duty, self-sacrifice, and chastity" so they may be regarded as a buena hija whose identity aligns with that of their mother and grandmother before them.[9] The generational pressure for U.S.-born Latina daughters to subscribe to the ideal *marianista* femininity projected onto their Latin American mothers is contentious and complicated. When Latina daughters break marianista expectations that they will live in the "literal and figurative shadows of men" by instead embracing a life as "an independent-minded Latina," gendered codes of respect and peaceful coexistence will likely be strained.[10] Additionally, the tenets of marianismo influence U.S.-born Latinas' mental health. The extent to which a Latina daughter shares marianista beliefs with her parents may determine the types of coping mechanisms she relies on when facing discrimination outside the home.[11] A 2017 study found that Latinas who view the "familial and spiritual pillars" of marianismo positively are more likely to turn to their relatives, friends, and religious community for support, whereas those who perceive of marianismo negatively often opt for silence instead. A 2013 study found that marianista expectations increased the likelihood of parental conflict, resulting in Latinas' heightened depressive symptoms and difficulty acculturating to life and/or college in the United States.[12]

When the Latina daughter seeks to reinvent her identity beyond the marianista ideal of the buena hija, she must locate and tap into her individuated self-energy to creatively produce forms of empowered rebellion. Gil and Vazquez refer to this process as *autonomismo* ("self-reliance"): the ability to put one's needs first in a healthy, sustainable manner that does not promote individualism or purposely enact harm on others to achieve what one desires.[13] The act of constructing a new Latina identity should not necessitate rejection of familismo or of the buena hija role altogether; however, estrangement from these ideals is likely to occur to some extent in situations when the daughter's conscious embrace of mixedness, queerness, and/or mental illness is dismissed by her loved ones as invalid or problematic. As she rebels against the patriarchal order of the family, as she becomes a "mujer mala" rather than a buena hija, the daughter takes on a new mestiza consciousness through which she crosses cultural borders, is transformed through ambiguity, and partakes in what Anzaldúa describes as "the creation of yet another culture, a new story to explain the world and our participation in it."[14] She enters an in-between—a site of remixing and formulating personal narrative—where she may connect with the self-energy of imagining a new future and story for herself.[15]

Throughout her work, Anzaldúa underscores the importance of the "in-between," the "nepantla state" for Chicanas and women of color more broadly who are queer, disabled, and/or working class and whose identity is exploring and evolving from one form to another.[16] It is through this liminal space that the Latina daughter's perspective and identity radically transform:

> In nepantla we realize that realities clash, authority figures of the various groups demand contradictory commitments, and we and others have failed living up to idealized goals. We're caught in remolinos (vortexes), each with different, often contradictory forms of cognition, perspectives, worldviews, belief systems—all occupying the transitional nepantla space. . . . Transitions are a form of crisis, an emotionally significant event or a radical change in status. During crisis the existential isolation all people experience is exacerbated. Unruly emotions and conflicts break out. In nepantla we hang out between shifts, trying to make rational sense of this crisis, seeking solace, support, appeasement, or some kind of intimate connection. En este lugar, we fall into chaos, fear of the unknown, and are forced to take up the task of self-redefinition.[17]

In entering this nepantla state and in formulating a new consciousness, the Latina daughter connects with her self-energy and develops her autonomismo, but this creative labor does not occur without tension and conflict. As Anzaldúa explains, remaking one's own identity is not a simple or straightforward process; rather, it is painful, confusing, and disorienting. It is the consistency of negotiating the in-between of the past and future self without a static starting or ending point. But even as this work is exhausting, it is vital, life-giving work to those of us who are cultural outsiders, who seek out an identity beyond the limitations of marianismo or mainstream media representation.[18] It is through transformative acts such as forming countercultures, rebelling against the familial order, acknowledging one's outsider status, and taking risks to self-identify in new, hybrid ways that Latina daughters may effectively, as Grisel Y. Acosta suggests, "disrupt the accepted norms and lead the way into the unimagined."[19]

Although Anzaldúan conceptions of queer, hybrid Chicana identity are influential to many scholars' theorizing and my own imagining of the Latina daughter's redefinition, her work has been critiqued for appropriating Aztec concepts and perpetuating anti-Blackness. In excluding Blackness from her theoretical making of the new mestiza and of the borderlands, Anzaldúa effectively mobilizes these liberatory spaces for non-Black Chicanx people in ways that shape future conceptions of Latinidad as "mutually exclusive" from Black identity.[20] Additionally, Anzaldúa's influential yet incorrect use of the Nahuatl word *nepantla* has perpetuated a widespread splintering of nepantla from its actual meaning in Aztec philosophy.[21] Marcos de R. Antuna offers a call to action that nepantla be replaced with the Aztec concept of *malinalli*, which refers to the "transformative processes at large, processes that can create novel representations from the old" that make possible a revolution or transformation of the self.[22] Antuna proposes that, by applying malinalli where nepantla was once used, scholars can both preserve Anzaldúa's vision for a revolutionary future and accurately honor the meaning of Aztec philosophy. I acknowledge Anzaldúa's nepantla theory as influential to the genesis of this project, but in my analysis of Nina's narrative, I heed Antuna's call by bridging references to nepantla with malinalli.

In drawing upon these influences, I contemplate how in *Blackbird* and in my own life, Nina and I respectively imagine alternative futures for ourselves beyond the constraints of the buena hija archetype and toward the freedom of the Hija Loquita. In working to process traumatic memories we have suppressed for others' comfort, we move toward the empowering space of first-person narration, acknowledging trauma, and refusing to believe that other people's desires for us supersede our own. Inspired by the ChicaNerds, the Latinx weirdos, the Latina Outsiders, the rebels who come before us and exist contemporaneous to us, I come to recognize myself and Nina as Hijas Loquitas. We are Latina daughters who breathe new life into the parts of ourselves ridiculed, shamed, dismissed as "a little crazy." As we reform and redefine our identity, we develop a complex space of innovative self-making and painful separation from our old selves—the power found in connecting with and trusting one's own experience, yet still consistent fear that we will never be truly understood.

Nina demonstrates the significance of the Hija Loquita by telling her own story as she works through the shame she has internalized from her family, evidenced by a multi-issue narrative shift from repeating what they have said about her to affirming in first-person narration that "I'm the only one with the power to make my life better. And I'm going to decide what's right."[23] In my own narrative, I follow Nina's lead and work through my shame by taking the first steps to tell my own story of trauma, on my own terms, without seeking permission or putting the needs of those who traumatized me above my own. This journey began when I wrote what I felt in journals that, like my voice, I kept to myself. It expanded when I started attending comics expos, meeting Latinx creators, and reading stories about other Latina girls who found meaning in their past by writing it, by telling it in their own words. My writing has transformed from scribbles stashed in a secret journal to words I put out into the world in the hopes that they will find another Latina girl who needs to hear that it is okay to leave home to find yourself. Thus, to identify as a Hija Loquita is to honor the degree to which your family's perception of your identity still influences your decision making even while rebelling against the constraints of their expectations. To be an Hija Loquita is to also refuse the idea that identifying as mixed, queer, and/or mentally ill cannot coexist with being a good Latina daughter, that it is in binary opposition to belonging in the family. To be an Hija Loquita is to be connected with one's self-energy—to achieve a state of autonomismo—through carving out space for yourself in spoken and written personal narratives to be in control of your own life.

Making Space to Remember: Sharing Personal Narrative as a Mode of Survival

As a child, I had a tremendous amount of energy. I was leaping out of my chair, enthusiastically raising my hand to answer questions in class, making jokes and putting on shows whenever I visited extended family, and laughing so hard at the dinner table that I would be sent outside to compose myself. I was loud, animated, opinionated, and, most of all, talkative. The happiness I felt was not tethered to being "good" at something, but instead glowed out of the pleasure I took in having fun. I confidently set boundaries and spoke up when I felt compelled by something. I took confidence in my ideas regardless of how others responded to them. However, these abilities became harder to tap into as I got older. For eighteen years of my life, I refrained from dreaming while

I took on the insecurities, fears of mortality, and needs of the terminally ill parent I cared for—a parent who should have sought help for the mental health crises, intense emotions, and lifelong regrets he expected his child to have the tools to handle. At the same time that I devoted my life to his care, I lived in constant fear that at any moment, I may be outed as queer by someone in my conservative town or family—a fear that has never left me as I remain closeted within a heteronormative image that comforts my loved ones from afar. These experiences have made it harder to self-advocate and feel secure in who I am. In my writing and in my life, I struggle to speak on these experiences openly or in first person out of fear that others' fondness for my loved ones will outweigh their belief in the legitimacy of my painful childhood experiences. How do you compete with other people's memories of a person who, in death, is idealized as blameless?

As I got older, my feelings of confidence were gradually replaced with shame, embarrassment, and self-doubt as I heard from the people close to me that I was too much—too enthusiastic, too talkative, too annoying, too opinionated, too inquisitive. Praise for actively participating in class was replaced with instructions to tie myself to my chair with the arms of my jacket so that I would not jump with excitement when my teacher asked questions during lessons. Eagerness to be knowledgeable about the world became withdrawing from conversations when I was derided as being stupid and incapable of articulating a sound argument if it conflicted with a family member's conservative beliefs. The freedom I found in writing my own stories was co-opted, reconstructed, and extracted as a possible source of income for the adults in my life. The protective home that was my childhood body was picked at, ridiculed, medically examined as too large, too unpredictable. The bursts of energy I had that propelled me into my daily life with excitement and creativity were derided as unintelligible and irritating to be around. When I channeled them into career goals as an adult, they were celebrated, but the limitations of this approach became quite clear when setting boundaries around my ideas, labor, and time was not received well either.

To some extent, the qualities that initially energized me through my childhood still remain within me as an adult woman in her twenties. However, to reconnect with these sources of self-energy that once came naturally as a child, I must make a routine, conscious effort to locate and make space for them in my life—to trust that they are valid, that I need not second-guess every thought I have and every choice that I have made. Doing this work is vulnerable and difficult to write about, especially when my self-energy draws from the same places in my mind, body, and spirit that have been called *loquita*, or "a little crazy," by others. Initially assigned to me as a nickname by a loved one, the term *loquita* became a sometimes explicit, other times implicit, way for others to remark when my presence in a situation needed correcting, smoothing out, adjustment. In these moments, I was laughed at, overlooked, or reprimanded for being too much. I was a disruption, a distraction, a piece that did not fit but desperately wanted to. The more that I worked to take apart and reassemble myself within the bounds of familismo, the harder it became to retain an honest relationship with mind, body, and spirit as what I should place faith in before anyone else's expectations. I could remember experiences of trauma, pain, and longing, but the more I let other voices in, the harder it became to trust that these events had in fact happened. I became disillusioned with myself as the qualities I once embraced became the focus of lighthearted teasing—before they became sites of rejection, tension, and conflict. It was not until I read a variation of this journey elsewhere that a page became a mirror, and a mirror became a pathway through which I could reconnect with these parts of myself.

When I read *Blackbird* for the first time, I was searching for narrative media that featured a Latina protagonist whose empowerment in the story did not rely on familial harmony or reconciliation. The mainstream narratives I had turned to up until then regularly endorsed marianismo as the best pathway toward being a buena hija, and I worried there was no place for me, an hija mala, in Latinx storyworlds. Having just upset my family by moving away from home to pursue an advanced degree and explore my identity for the first time, I wanted stories about Latina daughters whose own rebellion facilitated their autonomismo. To deal with my anxiety that I was doing something wrong by choosing myself, I spent hours researching, reading, and collecting comics about Latinas—both real and fictional—whose sense of self was strengthened when forming a new consciousness that reclaimed their mixedness, queerness, and/or mental illness as foundational to their identity, not something shameful to be hidden.

In *Blackbird*, I learned from and journeyed with an Hija Loquita protagonist whose reclamation of her own narrative propels her beyond the confines of the buena hija. To cope with her mental illnesses, infantilization, and family's disregard of her as an unreliable narrator of her own experiences, Nina develops an obsession with proving magic to be real. In the ten years since the Verdugo Earthquake struck, she devotes her free time to researching and talking in online chat rooms about magic figures known as paragons: "masters of magic" who belong to secret "cabals" of like-minded, magic wielders that possess wealth and power "beyond real life."[24] Her fascination with and aspiration toward paragons is especially pronounced following the death of her mother. In issues 1, 2, and 3 of *Blackbird*, Nina idealizes Gloria as the ultimate protector, role model, and influence over her life, without whom she possesses no sense of direction or coherent self.[25] However, this image is fractured when issues 4, 5, and 6 reveal Gloria to have been alive and the head paragon of the Iridium Cabal the whole time.

The surprise reunion with Gloria shatters Nina's previous worldview, as her mother had consciously berated her for believing in the existence of magic, later faking her own death so that she could conceal the paragon world from her daughters. Up until this point, Nina feels pressure to model herself after Gloria—to honor her mother's memory by performing the role of the buena hija in her family. The reveal prompts Nina to formally deviate from the civilian path of marianista ideals her mother had put her on. She ignores Gloria's declaration that she never become a paragon by joining the Iridium Cabal's tense ally, Zon Cabal. In the context of the *Blackbird* storyworld, we are led to believe in the issue 6 cliffhanger and open ending that Zon Cabal wishes to weaponize Nina against Iridium Cabal and Gloria. However, for the purposes of this chapter, I examine how her pathway toward becoming a paragon is reflective of her evolving perception of her trauma, memory, and mind as "crazy" in the ways her family has decided.[26]

In Nina's narrative, there are three plot points that propel her toward an alternative futurity as a self-directed Hija Loquita: the Verdugo Earthquake in issue 1, the reunion with Gloria in issue 3, and her initiation into the Zon Cabal in issue 6. Taken together, these events depict the trajectory of her journey from a place of conditional belonging in the family as the uncredible "crazy baby," to a multidimensional, self-energized subjecthood in which she is not only paragon but Blackbird. Each of these plot points is crucial for advancing the narrative and is central to Nina's story. But it is not only *what* happens in these moments but *how* Nina narrates them that models to other mixed-race, queer, mentally ill Latina daughters like me how we, too, can take steps to redefine ourselves as Hijas Loquitas in the in-between without needing familial approval to do so. In witnessing Nina process her story directly to the reader, narrative space is created to identify with her, to process our own memories of trauma, and to recognize the possibilities in taking control of one's own story.

The Hija Loquita Tells Her Own Story: Claiming Control through First-Person Narration

Throughout *Blackbird*, the act of sharing personal narrative is depicted as a way in which marginalized characters may honor the memories and experiences they have previously been ashamed or uncertain of. Issue 1 establishes Nina as a failed buena hija whose memories of the earthquake, obsession with magic, and struggles with mental illness disrupt the order of the Rodriguez household, which is part of the nonmagical world (referred to as "civilian" in the text). The issue opens with a splash page of Nina holding her cat, Sharpie, as she sits on the bed next to her older sister Marisa and depicts the day the Verdugo Earthquake hit (see figure 7.1). The bedroom setting suggests that the relationship between Marisa and Nina is intimate and overall stable. To the right of Nina, hand-drawn portraits of Marisa, Nina, and Sharpie are taped to the wall, with "best sister" written under Marisa's picture. Directly above these drawings, a framed family portrait positioned on the right side of a shelf depicts Gloria, Enrique, Marisa, and Nina smiling for the camera. The sole inset that appears in the bottom center of the splash page reveals the full image of the only other family picture in the room: a framed photograph on the far-left side of the same shelf that appears to be of a younger version of Marisa and Nina embracing each other in a hug. The quantity and contents of these family images suggest a stable family unit even as their tone is contrasted by that of the narration boxes and speech bubbles that appear throughout the page. In the four narration boxes placed in the upper left corner, Nina's present-day perspective as first-person narrator of the story is established. She provides a brief recap of the vision she had at thirteen that prompted her to pack a bag, get dressed, grab her cat, and be ready to leave when the earthquake struck. In the fourth narration box, she states in a matter-of-fact tone, "My whole family said I was making it up."[27] Marisa and Nina's faces are positioned in between these four narration boxes and the two speech bubbles that follow them. Nina stares straight ahead with sweat forming on her forehead and a worried expression on her face. She appears to be looking directly into the eyes of the reader, and if the reader holds her gaze, they will observe small, subtle, blue squiggle lines of emanata next to her head that visually represent her anticipation of the earthquake not being in vain. Unlike Nina, Marisa wears comfortable clothes and socks, no shoes; her eyes are closed as she rubs the sleep from them, and her shoulders are relaxed. She yawns and says, "Nina, I have to be up early tomorrow. Come on, crazy baby."[28]

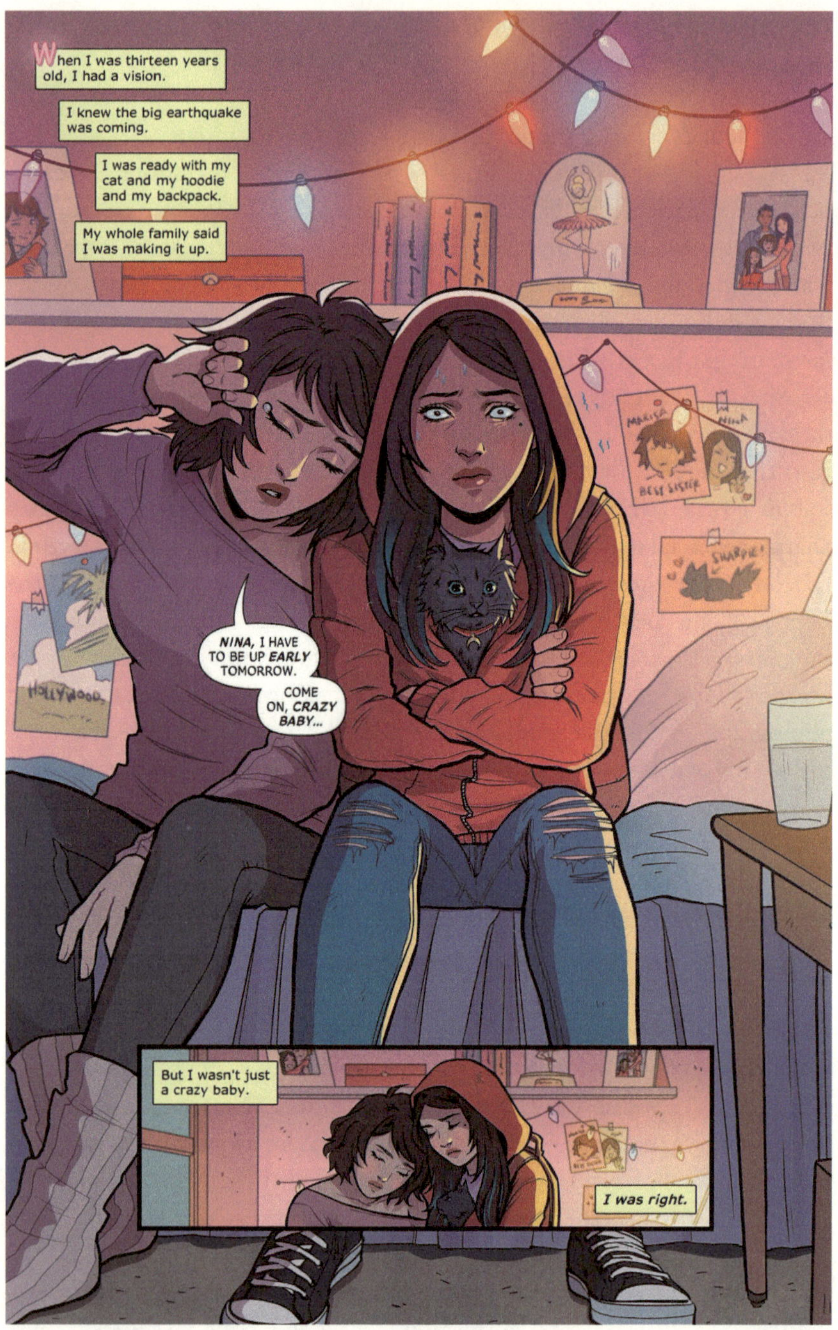

FIGURE 7.1 Marisa (left) and Nina (right) sit in a bedroom the night before the Verdugo Earthquake strikes. Sam Humphries and Jen Bartel, *Blackbird* no. 1 (Portland, OR: Image Comics, 2018), 3.

This statement marks the first usage of the term "crazy baby" by a family member responding to Nina's belief in magic, with the magic in this case being the vision predicting the earthquake. Here, Marisa is portrayed as a buena hija in her own right, as she casually refers to her sister as "crazy" and does not take the vision seriously; in this way, she stands in for the "whole family" telling Nina she is "making it up."

This term "crazy baby" being used in the first spoken lines of the series foreshadows the important role the nickname will take on in the narrative and hints at how it will haunt Nina's relationship with her trauma in subsequent years. The use of "crazy" underscores that *Blackbird*'s narrative arc situates Nina as a disruption to the normal world. By believing her vision over her family's telling of events, Nina is failing to act as a buena hija whose choices align with familismo.

However, this moment also marks the first instance in which Nina reclaims the Hija Loquita image from illegitimacy and redefines it as a form of self-energizing power she can place trust in. Following Marisa's remark, Nina is depicted in the bottom center inset as having silently turned toward her sister and closing her eyes, as if agreeing with her. However, the two narration boxes that convey her first-person perspective reveal that in her mind, she in fact disagrees with Marisa: "But I wasn't just a crazy baby. I was right."[29] Although she does not say these words out loud and it is unclear if she felt this way in real time, Nina's second reference to the "crazy baby" nickname is significant for two reasons. First, it contextualizes that its application by her family is negative even when used under the guise of teasing; it signals that she is being infantilized and dismissed. Second, it imbues the term with new, positive meaning. Nina does not negate her misfit Hija Loquita status in the family but instead reclaims it. She confirms it as "just" a part of her, not the entirety of her, when she says, "But I wasn't just a crazy baby." She further elaborates on this point by affirming her belief in magic as valid when she states, "I was right." Her use of past-tense verbs in the narration reminds the reader that the events we are seeing on the page are not occurring in real time but instead are formative, traumatic memories that Nina is recalling in the present and telling the reader as if in conversation with them. Before the devastation of the Verdugo Earthquake is depicted in the following pages, the first-person, past-tense narration challenges the reader to believe Nina—not Marisa or her family—that the events she is about to describe did in fact take place.

Over the next few pages, Nina tracks the events of the Verdugo Earthquake, which she later states "was the biggest moment of my life."[30] Instead of sheltering with her mother and grandmother in the family home, Nina recalls being inexplicably drawn toward the earthquake and unable to stop herself from "running from one disaster into the next."[31] She runs from the house and into the neighborhood, where she comes into contact with the supernatural monster that incites the earthquake. While everyone in the neighborhood reacts in horror—including Marisa, who has run after her—Nina is in awe, describing it as "the most beautiful monster. Of all time."[32] When a paragon appears and wipes the memory of all who witnessed the monster, including Marisa, Nina resists this spell and only pretends to have had her memory wiped. She is ultimately left the sole witness of the tragedy who remembers its occurrence and its magic.

It is important to note that, as Nina recounts this primary memory of the earthquake, her narration is concise but confident. She builds on the first-person, past-tense narrative structure introduced in the opening splash page by providing the reader with concrete details that support her assertion that the Verdugo Earthquake indeed happened. However, in trying to narrate memories she is less certain of to the reader, Nina takes a crucial next step in connecting with the literal and figurative power of being an Hija Loquita: she starts to unlock and believe the traumatic memories she has suppressed as real despite being told otherwise. When initially trying to explain the immediate aftermath of the earthquake, Nina wavers in confidence and admits to having a second memory of which she is less sure. Importantly, this admission occurs when she tries to present a clear conclusion to the memory—a definitive end point. The final panel associated with this primary memory depicts a "happy ending" of Nina safely reunited with Gloria, Marisa, and her grandmother Leticia (see figure 7.2). Like the photographs shown in the bedroom, the panel reads as a happy family portrait as the women smile and embrace each other in a hug. The only two speech bubbles in the panel are associated with Gloria's voice, who says in relief, "There you are! My girls! I was in the backyard. I'm so glad everyone is okay!"[33] Like a photograph that remains static behind glass, the panel's visual and verbal details represent the rest of the family's resolve that the earthquake was a nonmagical, ordinary event that Nina's unreliable memory has embellished.

It is once again through first-person, past-tense narration boxes that Nina rejects her family's conception of the crazy baby as misguided and reclaims it as an empowered Hija Loquita identity. Like in the introductory splash page, Nina turns toward her family and says nothing, as if to agree with their account of the earthquake. However, the two narration boxes featuring Nina's present-day voice in this panel challenge this account, stating, "I have another memory from that night, too. Or maybe it was a dream." In the second

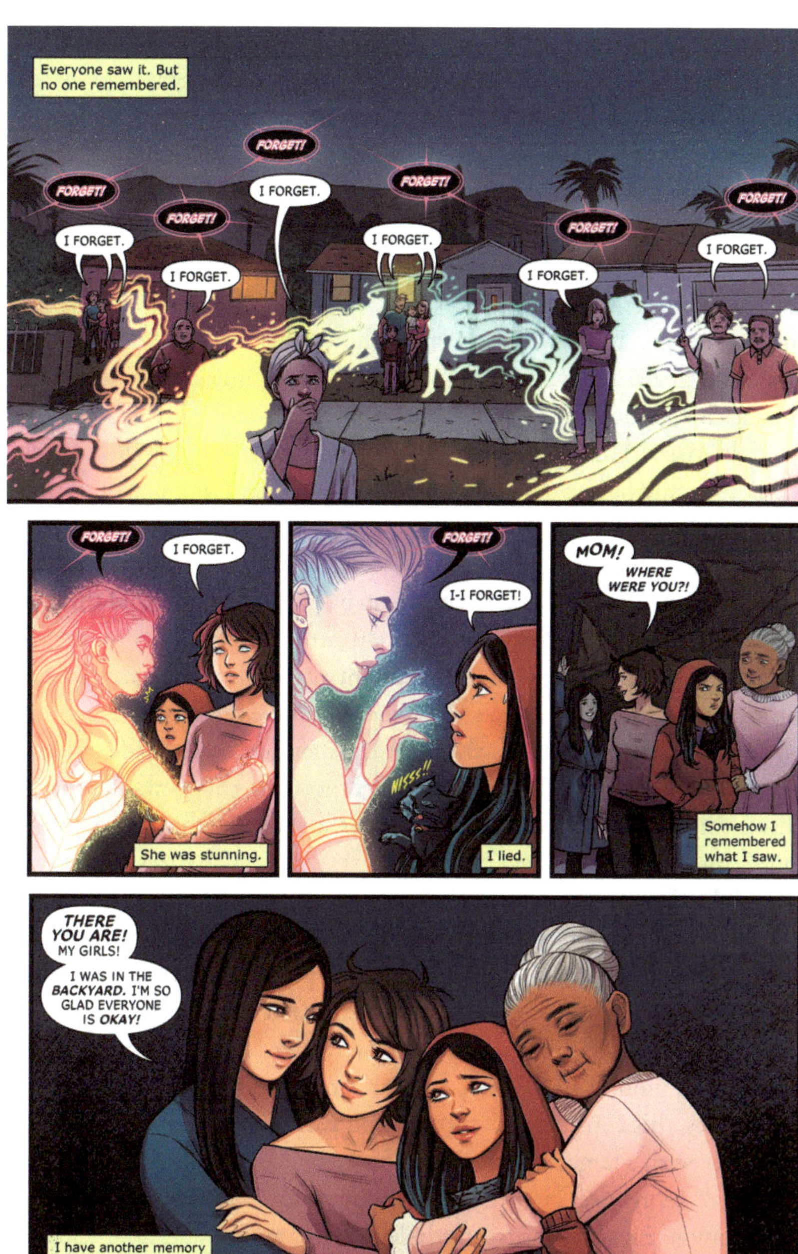

FIGURE 7.2 The Rodriguez family reunites following the Verdugo Earthquake being wiped from the neighborhood's memories. Humphries and Bartel, *Blackbird* no. 1, 7.

statement, Nina expresses doubt that her memory is correct, presumably an automatic defense that has developed from her previous attempts to share it with her family. Even so, in taking the chance to explore a repressed memory of her trauma with the reader, she effectively creates a new narrative space where she considers what it might mean to begin trusting her mind as a credible witness to and archive of her experience.

Immediately following the second narration box of "Or maybe it was a dream," a two-page spread depicts Nina's second, more suppressed memory of the earthquake. In these panels, she is shown floating in a body of water before she awakens and walks into the Grand Oasis Diner. It is revealed in a later issue that, to become a paragon, one's old self must die before one's soul is resurrected and guided through "The Grand Oasis," or "the in-between" of the civilian and paragon worlds. Upon being initiated into one of the four cabals, the paragon will form community, be largely concealed from civilian detection, and gain access to the gems needed to fully unlock their magical abilities.[34] In these pages, Nina's first-person narration that has told the story thus far is replaced with that of another narrator: a magical figure revealed in the diner to be the Beacon. This loss of control in telling the narrative mirrors the loss of control Nina feels when she is in the Grand Oasis Diner and when trying to convince the listener that the memory is not made up but is a real experience. Throughout *Blackbird*, Nina tells the reader about the doubts she has of her sanity more often than she shows us the memories that produce this insecurity. When Nina's most traumatic memories are actually made visible to the reader with a splash page or multipanel spread, the events depicted are usually supplemented with her first-person, past-tense narration boxes to explain how this moment relates to her present suffering.[35] Her fears that these memories will be rejected once more as fictitious and/or crazy are made obvious by how she never allows the reader into her mind without simultaneously guiding us to interpret the memory in exactly the way she has. In some cases, this consists of narrating each panel, and in others, she closes the memory with a larger takeaway statement.

These narration boxes give the reader insight into the extent to which Nina seeks to convince readers she is a credible narrator and to take her memories seriously. When Nina releases some control and allows herself to vulnerably process these memories, her verb tense evolves from past tense to present tense, signaling her changing perspective on the memory. In this spread, Nina momentarily allows herself to be submerged in her memories before briefly doubting herself and later developing confidence in her recollection of events. The Beacon's narration tells Nina that the locale of the Grand Oasis Diner is a liminal state between "life" and "the vortex" known as "the in-between" where it is said that "magic flows like water."[36] The magical "in-between" fully exteriorizes the state of malinalli that Nina has, up until this night, only experienced mentally in her insecurities of being the crazy baby of her family. Whereas the chaos of being unaligned with her family has previously manifested as an individuated feeling of conditional belonging, in the in-between, the anguish and chaos described by Anzaldúa engulfs Nina in a liminal space that is not normal but not entirely magical. That is, in temporarily recalling and existing in the in-between, Nina cannot suppress her emotions and instead must feel them. However, a mental block prevents her from fully processing the memory and from accepting that, in entering the nepantla state, she is forever changed. When told to trust in the Beacon, Nina panics and is depicted with her hands clawing into her face as she turns blue, her skin dissipates from her face. As she exclaims, "S-something is wrong with me. I wanna go home!" the Beacon reconfigures itself into a dark shadow and retorts, "You can't go back. Not the same as you were," before Nina screams, "Wh-what is that? What is it doing? Stop! Stay away from me!"[37] Nina's panic extends into a second vertical panel that is placed on the other side of the panel featuring the Beacon, her hands clasped to either side of her head and her mouth open in a scream—thus externalizing her fear that she cannot trust her literal or figurative point of view.

Following this spread, Nina's narration resumes control as she concisely recaps the aftermath of the earthquake—the events she is sure of. She qualifies her experience by stating, "It ***felt*** real," with "felt" emphasized in bold and italics to signal the vocal and emotional emphasis placed on legitimizing her embodied memory as valid. However, as she transitions from sharing these memories to her present-day life, Nina breaks the fourth wall once again in a splash page that shows her seemingly staring into the reader's eyes (see figure 7.3). Unlike the first splash page, Nina is singularly foregrounded and the background behind her is blurred. Five narration boxes shift her narration from first-person past tense to first-person present tense as she states confidently that, even as she is dismissed as an attention seeker for believing in her memory, "I know what I saw. There is magic in the world. I just can't find it."[38] In repeating the familiar image of Nina looking directly at the reader and enhancing it with a direct address of her reintroducing herself as "me now," issue 1 underscores the importance of Nina telling her own story, in her own words, to a reader who bears witness to it. More specifically, issue 1 of *Blackbird* depicts Nina actively starting the process of finding her autonomismo by refusing to accept her crazy baby status as a limitation but instead

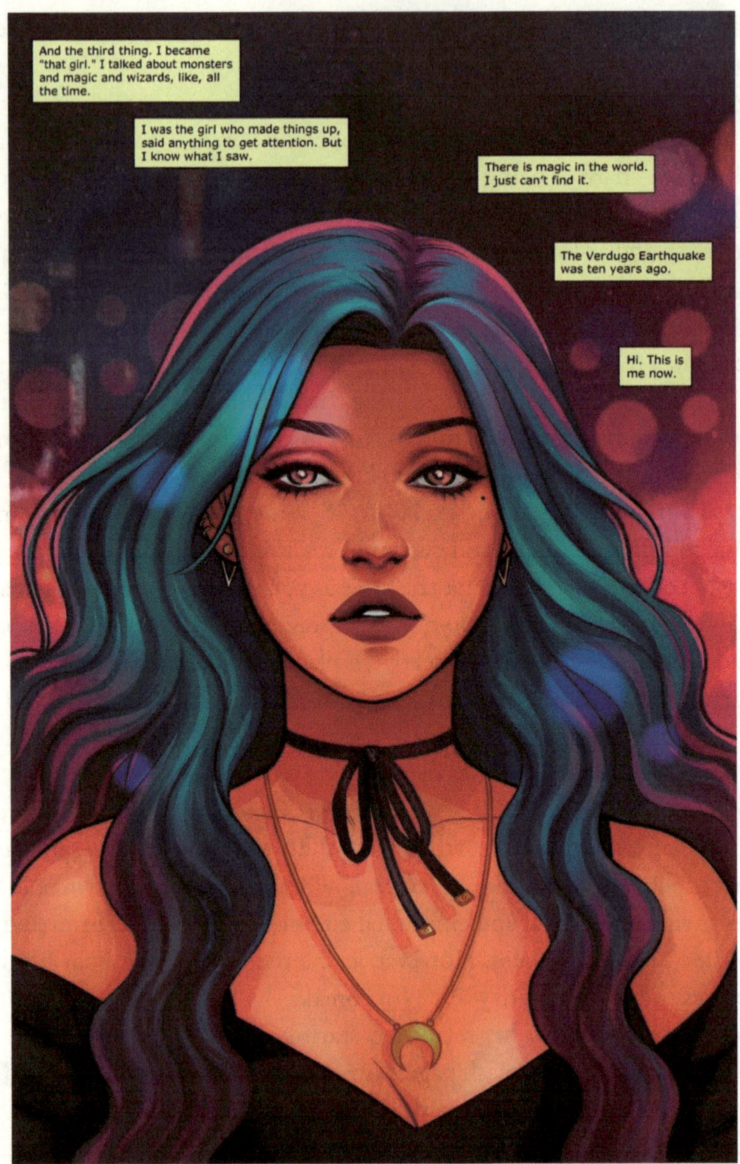

FIGURE 7.3 Nina reintroduces herself to the reader as she transitions to present-day events. Humphries and Bartel, *Blackbird* 1, 12.

viewing it as a potential new way of seeing. While the submissive, docile role of the buena hija asks Nina to disregard her memories as false, the self-energizing potential of consciously identifying as a Hija Loquita allows her to narratively explore self-definition even before she does so in the plot.

In confronting her mother and challenging the buena hija role expected of her, Nina models for fellow mixed-race, queer, mentally ill Latina daughters that they, too, may break free from the confines of marianismo. It is in her imaginative work, in her conscious connection with and acceptance of her traumatic memories, that she is able to access the autonomismo necessary for harnessing her literal and figurative self-energy. Her self-definition is not contingent on the accomplishments that make her power legible to other people, particularly her family who deride and dismiss her as a crazy baby. Instead, the freedom found in her self-definition is derived from her acceptance that to be in the in-between is not something that needs to be corrected or "solved." She is not an Hija Loquita exclusively when she is shown visually and verbally "taking control of my own life." Rather, she is an Hija Loquita from the first moment she dares to contradict the social order and imagine an alternative future as a Blackbird, as a "paragon who left the flock. One of us, but not. In between."[39] That is, Nina does not merely usurp herself into a paragon identity; rather, she initiates into it while still holding space to remake her selfhood in the in-between.

While Nina's narrative depicts her at various stages coming to terms with and accessing her self-energy, my story is still beginning to form. Like Nina, I, too, have an awareness of traumas that linger in my mind and that feel real, even as loved ones presume me to be misremembering what happened. Like Nina, I am working to take my first steps from accepting conditional belonging to declaring self-definition as a means for breaking free. When witnessing Nina's narrative for the first time, I could visualize what it might mean to honor the parts of myself that I had grown accustomed to hating, that I had accepted were wrong. When returning to Nina's narrative, I allow space for myself to contemplate what it might mean to continually say but some day finally believe for myself, "But I wasn't just a crazy baby. I was right."[40]

Notes

1 Sam Humphries and Jen Bartel, *Blackbird* no. 2 (Portland, OR: Image Comics, November 2018), 4–5.

2 Paragons are explicitly portrayed in the narrative as harnessing magical powers significant enough that they are informally "hunted and exiled" by civilians

(i.e., non-magic people) who fear that one of the four paragon cabals will break their treaty and take control of North Hollywood.

3 I wish to emphasize here that while many aspects of Nina Rodriguez's character development and narrative arc are relatable to me, I do not mean to suggest that our stories are identical or universal to every Latina who is also mixed-race, queer, and/or mentally ill. Rather, there are elements of her journey that bear resemblance to some of my own, and I find these productive to highlight when reflecting on pressures faced by Latina daughters. They represent some of the possible journeys that Latina daughters may embark on.

4 I use the phrase "people who experience childhood as a daughter" here to include folx who were assigned female at birth and were raised as cisgender girls but no longer identify with girlhood in their adulthood.

5 From this point on, I use the translation "buena hija" rather than "hija buena" as a nod to *The Maria Paradox*, in which Rosa Maria Gil and Carmen Inoa Vazquez utilize Spanglish with Americanized, "improper" grammar to linguistically emphasize how U.S.-based Latinas are caught between acculturating to U.S. society and abiding by the familial expectations of *marianismo* that their elders practiced in Latin America. See Rosa Maria Gil and Carmen Inoa Vazquez, *The Maria Paradox: How Latinas Can Merge Old World Traditions with New World Self-Esteem* (New York: Berkley, 1996).

6 Brandy Piña-Watson, Linda G. Castillo, Lizette Ojeda, and Kimberly M. Rodriguez, "Parent Conflict as a Mediator between Marianismo Beliefs and Depressive Symptoms for Mexican American College Women," *Journal of American College Health* 61, no. 8 (2013): 491–496, 491.

7 Evelyn P. Stevens, "Machismo and Marianismo," *Society* 10, no. 6 (1973): 57–63, 61.

8 Gloria Anzaldúa, *Borderlands / La Frontera: The New Mestiza* (San Francisco: Aunt Lutte Books, 2012), 39.

9 Gil and Vazquez, *Maria Paradox*, 7.

10 Gil and Vazquez, *Maria Paradox*, 4, 7.

11 See Delida Sanchez, Leann V. Smith, and Whitney Adams, "The Relationship among Perceived Discrimination, Marianismo, Gender Role Attitudes, Racial-Ethnic Socialization, Coping Styles, and Mental Health Outcomes in Latina College Students," *Journal of Latina/o Psychology* 6, no. 1 (2018): 1–15.

12 Piña-Watson et al., "Parent Conflict," 495–496.

13 Gil and Vazquez, *Maria Paradox*, 40.

14 Anzaldúa, *Borderlands / La Frontera*, 103.

15 It is important to note that self-energy is not solely composed of positive emotions. For instance, in Image's comic series *Bitch Planet*, it can also refer to the process of Black women reclaiming their anger and rage as a power source. In some ways, both Kamau Kogo of *Bitch Planet* and Nina Rodriguez of *Blackbird* achieve superhero status through their mutual confrontation of the social order and ability to envision new futures for themselves. See Kelly Sue DeConnick and Valentine De Landro, *Bitch Planet*, vol. 1 (Portland, OR: Image Comics, 2015).

16 Gloria Anzaldúa, "Chicana Artists: Exploring nepantlera, el lugar de la frontera," *NACLA Report on the Americas* 27, no. 1 (1993): 39.

17 Gloria E. Anzaldúa, *Light in the Dark / Luz en lo Oscuro: Rewriting Identity, Spirituality, Reality*, ed. Analouise Keating (Durham, NC: Duke University Press, 2015), 17.

18 See also Cristina Herrera's chapter "Band Shirts and Rebellion: Resisting the 'Buena Hija' Trope through Nerdiness in *I Am Not Your Perfect Mexican Daughter*,"

in *ChicaNerds in Chicana Young Adult Literature: Brown and Nerdy* (New York: Routledge, 2021), 88–104; Grisel Y. Acosta's introduction to *Latina Outsiders Remaking Latina Identity*, ed. Acosta (New York: Routledge, 2019), 1–10; and Trevor Boffone and Cristina Herrera, eds., *Nerds, Goths, Geeks, and Freaks: Outsiders in Chicanx and Latinx Young Adult Literature* (Jackson: University Press of Mississippi, 2020).

19 See Grisel Y. Acosta, "Punks and Hipsters: Latina Outsiders Remaking Latina Identity," in Acosta, *Latina Outsiders Remaking Latina Identity*, 26.

20 See Christopher L. Busey and Carolyn Silva, "Troubling the Essentialist Discourse of *Brown* in Education: The Anti-Black Sociopolitical and Sociohistorical Etymology of Latinxs as a *Brown* Monolith," *Educational Researcher* 50, no. 3 (2020): 176–186, and Madelaine C. Cahuas, "Interrogating Absences in Latinx Theory and Placing Blackness in Latinx Geographical Thought: A Critical Reflection," *Society & Space*, January 23, 2019, https://www.societyandspace.org/articles/interrogating-absences-in-latinx-theory-and-placing-blackness-in-latinx-geographical-thought-a-critical-reflection.

21 Marcos de R. Antuna, "What We Talk About When We Talk About Nepantla: Gloria Anzaldúa and the Queer Fruit of Aztec Philosophy," *Journal of Latinos and Education* 17, no. 2 (2018): 159–163.

22 Antuna, "What We Talk About," 161–162.

23 Humphries and Bartel, *Blackbird* no. 6, 22.

24 Humphries and Bartel, *Blackbird* no. 1, 16.

25 Humphries and Bartel *Blackbird* no. 1, 11; *Blackbird* no. 2, 9; and *Blackbird* no. 3, 5, 23.

26 Although the cliffhanger implies that the narrative arc of *Blackbird* is incomplete, it is unclear if there will be more issues or if the series has been discontinued.

27 Humphries and Bartel, *Blackbird* no. 1, 3.

28 Humphries and Bartel, *Blackbird* no. 1, 3.

29 Humphries and Bartel, *Blackbird* no. 1, 3.

30 Humphries and Bartel, *Blackbird* no. 5, 3.

31 Humphries and Bartel, *Blackbird* no. 1, 5.

32 Humphries and Bartel, *Blackbird* no. 1, 6.

33 Humphries and Bartel, *Blackbird* no. 1, 7.

34 Humphries and Bartel, *Blackbird* no. 6, 13–16.

35 Salient examples of this convention throughout *Blackbird*'s narrative arc include *Blackbird* no. 2, 5–9; *Blackbird* no. 3, 3–5; *Blackbird* no. 4, 11; and *Blackbird* no. 5, 3, 24.

36 Humphries and Bartel, *Blackbird* no. 1, 8–9.

37 Humphries and Bartel, *Blackbird* no. 1, 8–9.

38 Humphries and Bartel, *Blackbird* no. 1, 12.

39 Humphries and Bartel, *Blackbird* no. 6, 18.

40 Humphries and Bartel, *Blackbird* no. 1, 1.

8

"It's on Every Single Page"

Reading Character Development in Queer Latinx Comics for Youth

NICOLE ANN AMATO

Despite comic studies being a well-established discipline in higher education, anxiety and fear about bringing comics into K–12 classrooms is a well-documented phenomenon in teacher education scholarship within the United States.[1] Semester after semester, I witness a similar trend within my own teaching: students are hesitant to include comics within their curriculum. My research interrogates these anxieties more closely by reading comics marketed to queer youth of Color with secondary English language arts (ELA) teacher candidates in a monthly book club.[2] From July to December 2022, we met monthly to discuss comics for, by, and/or about queer youth of Color. Each session lasted for approximately 120 minutes and averaged six to ten participants per session. The book discussions were semi-structured in design. As a participant-observer *and* the facilitator, I provided flexible structures (community builders, author interviews, sticky notes, reader reflections) to guide each session.[3] Despite their expressed commitments to justice and equity, my students, teacher candidates at a predominantly White institution (PWI) in the Midwest, resisted teaching with comics and recycled negative stereotypes about comics in their discussions. For aspiring ELA teachers, who often identify as lovers of literature and the written word, reading comics demands they reconceptualize their understanding of what it means to read.[4]

Throughout the course of the book club meetings, many teacher candidates offered the criticism that the characters were not fully developed within the comics. For example, one teacher candidate expressed a longing for "slow, realistic character development." Another student claimed that Gabby Rivera and Celia Moscote's graphic adaptation of *Juliet Takes a Breath* (2020) "just worked better as a novel." While I believe there is pedagogical promise in exploring and critiquing graphic adaptations alongside their original mediums, participants' responses were reflective of long-standing attitudes about comics as inherently less complex and less literary in their form. At times, students' meaning making demonstrated a limited imagination. For example, in response to Carmen Maria Machado and Dani's comics series *The Low, Low Woods* (2019), one student argued the protagonists "have little characterization outside of the sexual assault narrative." By reducing this text to only a sexual assault narrative, this reader closed off interpretive possibilities about the characters' lives beyond the plot lines about rape and assault.

My students' responses troubled and challenged me. Where I saw rich character development and growth, they saw flat, stock characters. Where I saw pleasure, healing, and community, they saw harm. I argue that my students' responses are reflective of the ways in which Whiteness attempts to discipline readerly expectations and choices, and I want to take seriously the pedagogical implications of these moments. I am a reading teacher by trade, and my training is grounded in philosophies that assert learning is a complex social process. Learning to read is neither solitary nor standardized. Reading and sensemaking are always imbued with the prior knowledge that a reader brings to the text, and this remains true for visual mediums such as comics. As such, this chapter is guided by three inquiries. First, what constitutes slow and realistic character development in queer Latinx comics for youth? Second, how does reading for slow and realistic character development limit and constrain interpretative possibilities? And last, what narrative and aesthetic features of comics open possibilities for representations of queer Latinx life?

To answer these questions, I revisited three comics from my larger study and conducted a close reading of the central characters in tandem with my reading group participants' critiques. First, I revisited Gabby Rivera (Puerto Rican) and Celia Moscote's graphic adaptation of *Juliet Takes a Breath*, the story of young Puerto Rican woman who moves from New York City to Portland, Oregon. Second, I revisited *The Low, Low Woods*, written by Carmen Maria Machado (Cuban American), illustrated by Dani, and colored by Tamra Bonvillian. Third, I also returned to *b.b. free*, written by Gabby Rivera and drawn by Royal Dunlap, a comic I have used in literacy method courses as well as survey courses of children's and adolescent literature.[5] The writers of all three of these stories identify as queer and imbue their characters with shared identity characteristics. For example, like the author herself, many of Rivera's characters are Puerto Rican, including the protagonist of Rivera's critically acclaimed run of Marvel Comics' *America Chavez*, Marvel's first queer Latinx superhero. Together, the three comics featured within this chapter offer readers the stories of queer Brown protagonists as they come of age and explore their shifting identities in evolving contexts.

Drawing on Nick Sousanis's notion of *unflattening*, I am interested in analysis of how comics attend to "the unflat ways in which thought unfolds."[6] Sousanis defines *unflattening* as the "simultaneous engagement of multiple vantage points from which to engender new ways of seeing."[7] Similarly, scholars like Ramzi Fawaz suggest comics are a queer and disruptive medium because they "expand what we can desire from our reading experience."[8] By exploring how comics position readers and how readers position comics, educators can better understand how sensemaking is influenced when reading comics. As such, I use my students' responses to these comics as a springboard toward analysis of the visual moves the artists made to develop their protagonists: young, Brown, queer women who are coming of age. In doing so, I analyze how the authors and artists leverage the medium of comics to uniquely capture the protagonists' joy, genius, and commitment to community healing. Ultimately, readers must unlearn their expectations of character development within visual storytelling. In other words, readers, particularly those who are becoming ELA educators, must embrace ways of reading that challenge standardization and resist attempts to measure and rank readings. Before beginning the analysis portion of this chapter, I briefly offer readers a positionality statement that illuminates my politics of teaching and text selection practices. Next, I offer a close reading and analysis of the three case study texts, and I conclude with recommendations for teaching students to read comics.

Positionality: Teaching and Text Selection Are Political

Prior to seeking a career in teacher education, I worked for ten years as a high school ELA teacher in two racially, ethnically, and linguistically diverse communities in Greenville, South Carolina, and Chicago, Illinois. My students were brilliant, funny, eager, honest, and endlessly creative. Both schools were ruled by technocratic and neoliberal policies that valued narrow and standardized measures of accountability,[9] policies that storied my schools and my students with deficit language such as "at-risk" and "struggling." Scholars in Latinx studies, such as Angela Valenzuela, refer to this as *subtractive schooling*,[10] schooling that forces Latinx students to assimilate into the dominant majority by disassociating from their home languages and cultures.

It was in these schooling spaces that I began to grapple with what it meant to be a White queer woman who pursued anti-oppressive pedagogies, to be a teacher who did not just say she loved her students but who enacted an ethic of care in service of her students rather than align with a system that was narrowly defining their humanity. Now, as a teacher and researcher, I am committed to using multimodal texts to disrupt the repetition of traditionally taught novels in ELA classrooms,[11] and I teach and read from the standpoint that "text selection is a political act."[12] The comics analyzed in this study were selected with my former high school students' passions and identities in mind. They are texts I would have purchased for my classroom library and included within my curriculum had they been available when I was teaching in a high school classroom. As a White, monolingual educator, I am an outsider to the lived experiences of the protagonists within these texts, which means my meaning making with such texts will always be influenced by my own sociopolitical and cultural knowledge.[13] However, as a teacher educator of students who will go on to teach in increasingly diverse classrooms, it is my ethical responsibility to engage in pedagogical practices that resist the expansion of "canonical empires"[14] and support future educators in the pursuit of "humanizing critical sociocultural knowledge."[15]

To attend to the politics of text selection practices, I consulted a variety of reviews by scholars, teachers, librarians, and readers of Color that would help me situate these texts within broader conversations about their creation, publication, and reception so that I could avoid, as best as possible, selecting texts that catered to "whitestream consumption."[16] A play on the word mainstream, whitestream acknowledges the way narratives conform to Whiteness by reinforcing dominant narratives such as individualism, meritocracy, and color blindness. In other words, I avoided texts whose content might appeal to White readers by sanitizing or softening violent and complex historical truths. For example, in *Juliet Takes a Breath*, *The Low, Low Woods*, and *b.b. free*, all of the protagonists live with the disabling effects of climate change and environmental disasters: Juliet suffers from chronic asthma exacerbated by the air quality in New York City; the ground in El and V's world is literally on fire from over-mining in a fictional Pennsylvania coal town; and b.b. navigates life in the tropical swamplands after a plague wiped out most of the population (with the support of her amiga Chulita, who navigates the world in a badass wheelchair). Their stories underscore claims that Black and Brown communities are more severely impacted by the effects of climate change.[17] Despite the reality of their landscapes, Juliet, El, V, and b.b. are not written as victims, as young women to be pitied, or as rebellious and self-centered youth. Rather, their narratives hold space for the tensions between "joy and pain, belonging and dispossession, love and hate, power and vulnerability, life and death."[18] The young women are deeply loved, by each other, by their families, and by their larger communities. Their experiences are complex and refuse "single stories."[19] They "suspend damage centered narratives."[20] In other words, the stories featured in this chapter are not "saturated in the fantasies of outsiders."[21]

Reading Queer Aesthetics in *Juliet Takes a Breath*

Published by Boom! Box and based on the young adult novel of the same name, first published by Rivera independently in 2016 and later by Dial Books in 2019, the graphic adaptation of *Juliet Takes a Breath* is the coming-of-age story of Juliet Milagros Palante. Puerto Rican and from the Bronx, or Nuyorican, Juliet earns a summer internship with an author she deeply admires: Harlowe Brisbane, a White feminist writer who lives in Portland, Oregon. Initially, Juliet credits Harlowe with giving her the confidence to finally come out to her family. After arriving in Portland, however, Juliet's admiration for Harlowe wanes as she further develops her own feminism, one that rejects conforming to White standards and one that can hold space for all her identities at once.

My students offered two critiques of the graphic adaptation of *Juliet Takes a Breath*. First, they claimed the graphic novel lacked "slow, realistic character development," and, second, they argued that the ending "felt very rushed." One student articulated how her own reading choices may have influenced that feeling: "It did feel very quick to me . . . and maybe it was how I was moving through the book." In response to their critiques about character development and pacing, I repeatedly prompted them to read differently, and I encouraged them to pay attention to the visual work within and between the panels of the comic rather than hyperfocus on the characters' dialogue. Once students began to pay attention to these visual cues and elements, it was not long before a student offered a reflection about Juliet's evolving hairstyles: "But now I'm thinking more about the representation of her hair throughout the comic. When Juliet is with her cousin, there's a lot of curly hair that you haven't really seen. And it's on every single page. She has finally let her hair down. And it's curly, and she has it down in other moments throughout the book, but never so consistently as when she's with her cousin. And I thought that was a kind of cool move, especially leading up to when she cuts her hair at the queer party."[22] Having previously identified Juliet's haircut as a critical moment in her queer coming of age, this student returned to the pages of the comic and worked backward from this moment to look at how Juliet's hair was styled over the course of the graphic adaptation. In doing this, they were able to focus on some of the visual details overlooked in their initial reading. Additionally, this rereading for evolving hairstyles afforded readers an opportunity to consider what details are gained in graphic adaptations, rather than focusing on what is missing. While the haircut scene is critical to both the original novel and the comic adaptation, expository verbal details about Juliet's hair were less frequent than the visual depiction of her hair in the comic, which, as my student described, is "on every single page."

To extend this student's observation, I elaborate on the scene where Juliet gets her haircut to highlight how the panel structure reflects Juliet's hesitation and excitement about what a new haircut means for her sense of self as a queer Latina (see figure 8.1). Afraid that her haircut might make her look too queer, the hairstylist reminds Juliet that her queerness is more than her style and aesthetic choices. The panel structure of this page is irregular and uses uneven and inconsistent shapes and sizes. The pair of scissors cuts across the center of the page, and her clipped curls fall into the bottom half of the page to reveal a headshot of Juliet's new cut. Her hair exceeds the top boundaries of the panel. Looking at herself in a mirror, and staring directly at the reader, Juliet declares, "Oh snap, it's me."[23] Juliet's haircut marks what Jeremy Chow and Maite Urcaregui describe as "a transformative moment of queer

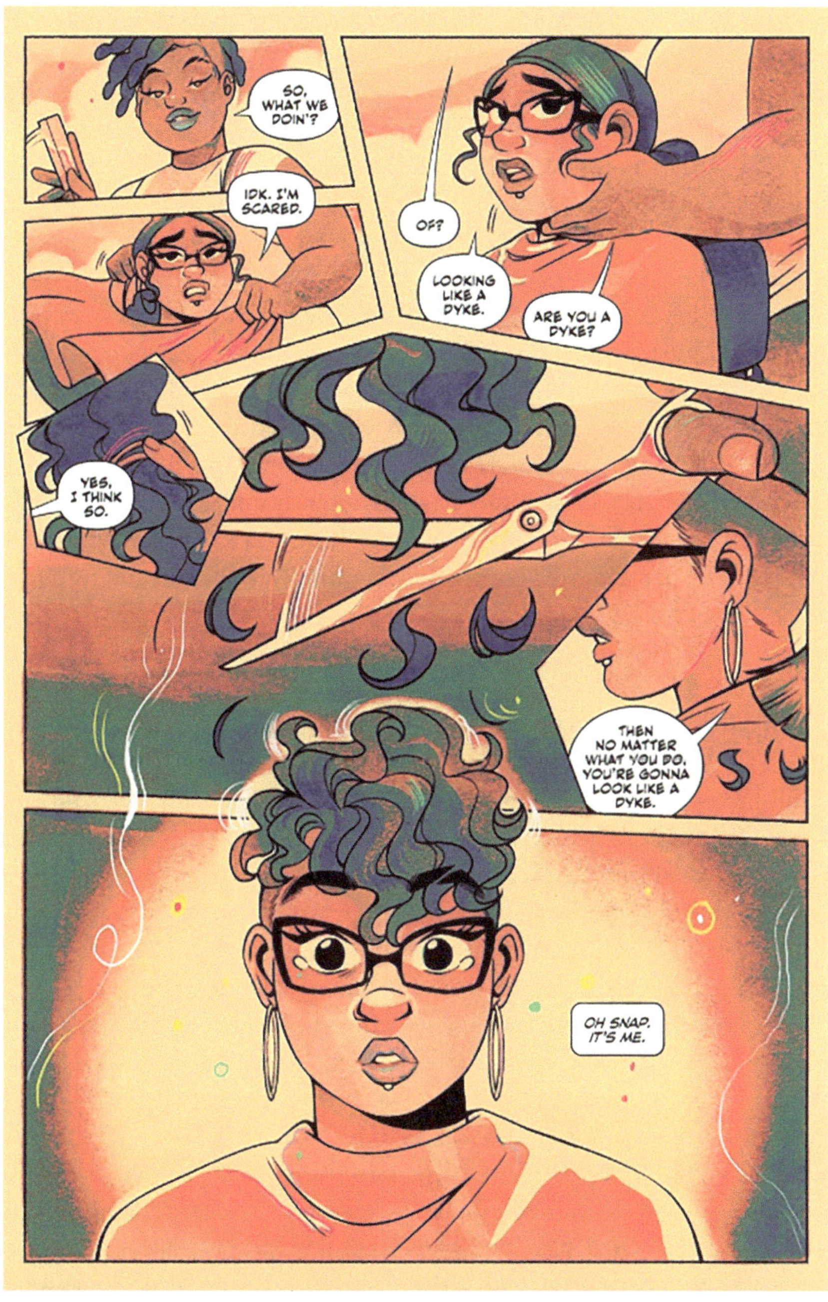

FIGURE 8.1 Image of Juliet getting her haircut in Gabby Rivera and Celia Moscote, *Juliet Takes a Breath* (Los Angeles: BOOM! Studios, 2020), n.p.

identification, self-definition, and relationality that she chooses for herself even at the risk of misunderstanding or violence."[24] Ultimately, the haircut gives Juliet permission to see herself on her own terms rather than seeing herself through the eyes of other people.

Juliet Takes a Breath is set in three primary locations: the Bronx, New York; Portland, Oregon; and Miami, Florida. As Juliet moves between these locations, she is aware of the way her race, gender, and sexuality are read differently. When readers meet Juliet in the Bronx at the start of the graphic adaptation, her hair is pulled tightly into a neat top bun. As the story progresses and Juliet begins to find community in Portland, her bun becomes looser, with curly tendrils framing her face. When Juliet first has sex with her love interest Kira, she lets her hair down, and her hair stays down and curly until she gets it cut in Miami while attending the party with her cousin. By the end of the comic, Juliet is sporting a short, curly undercut. Juliet's changing hair is one method Moscote uses to illustrate Juliet's learning about sexuality and gender, about Whiteness and feminism, and about building queer of Color families and communities.

Reading Queer Kinship in *The Low, Low Woods*

Published by Hill House Comics, an imprint of DC Comics, Machado and Dani's *The Low, Low Woods* started as a six-issue limited series in 2019 before being collected in a trade paperback in 2020. Eldora (El) and Octavia (V) are best friends and high school seniors in Shudder-to-Think, Pennsylvania, a fictional coal mining town that is perpetually on fire, causing its inhabitants to suffer from a mysterious illness that erases their memories. Together, El and V start listening to the stories of women in town to uncover what has been causing their missing memories as well as the burning ground, sinkholes, skinless men, and antlered women sighted in the surrounding forests.

The first two words of *The Low, Low Woods* are "THE END."[25] The words are in all capital letters, front and center on the page, and appear to be projected on the screen of a movie theater. In the opening sequence, the protagonists, El and V, are depicted in a single panel alone and asleep in a movie theater. As the end credits roll, El and V wake up, and El declares, "Something happened to us."[26] The girls have no memory of the movie, and El throws up in the aisle. This is the first of many moments in the text designed to disorient the reader and demand that more questions be asked than might initially be answered. El and V leave the theater, and El is determined to figure out why they, like so many other women in their town, have lost their memory.

Through flashbacks, alternating timelines, and El and V sharing the role of narrator, readers learn about their friendship, hobbies, romantic interests, career goals, and their adoring and doting parents. A source of tension in their friendship is their differing plans for college. El is determined to figure out the mysteries of the town, whereas V wants to graduate and leave for college, so she can put distance between herself and the painful town history. El's frustration with V is rooted not in jealousy or academic competition but rather in a wish for her friend to be honest and vulnerable about their experiences.

Throughout the series, when El and V are not together, they are often represented on the same page in mirrored panels. For example, when El is attacked by one of the skinless forest monsters, her lip is busted and bleeding, and she says to herself, "I miss you Vee. I miss you so much."[27] The adjacent panel is a picture of V standing in the same position, convinced she has heard someone's voice. V touches her lip and realizes it is bleeding out of nowhere. These mirrored panels offer readers moments of connection between El and V even when they are not physically together. My students frequently asked if El and V had a supernatural connection, and they expressed frustration when this connection was not explained within the narration. I, on the other hand, understood this connection as symbolic, a way for the artist to bring the reader back and forth between two different settings in the same timeline while also underscoring the depth of El and V's friendship.

This mirroring of panels happens again when V is having sex with her girlfriend Jessica, and El is pictured in the adjacent panels masturbating (see figure 8.2). Readers are taken back and forth between panels that illuminate the depth of El and V's connection. Despite their distance, the sequence of two-by-two panels leading into a single horizontal panel of the girls on opposite sides of the street concludes with the image of their embrace. Their embrace is removed from the bounds of panels and takes up a third of the page. El and V can quite literally feel each other's pain *and* pleasure. The flashbacks, dual timelines, and mirrored panels are structures of time that underscore one of the comic's central themes: "Sometimes you have to listen to someone else's story."[28] Structures of time and panel arrangements allow readers to experience a variety of community stories in a relatively small number of pages.

The students in my book club were quick to recognize that the comic is an allegory for the prevalence of sexual violence and assault against women

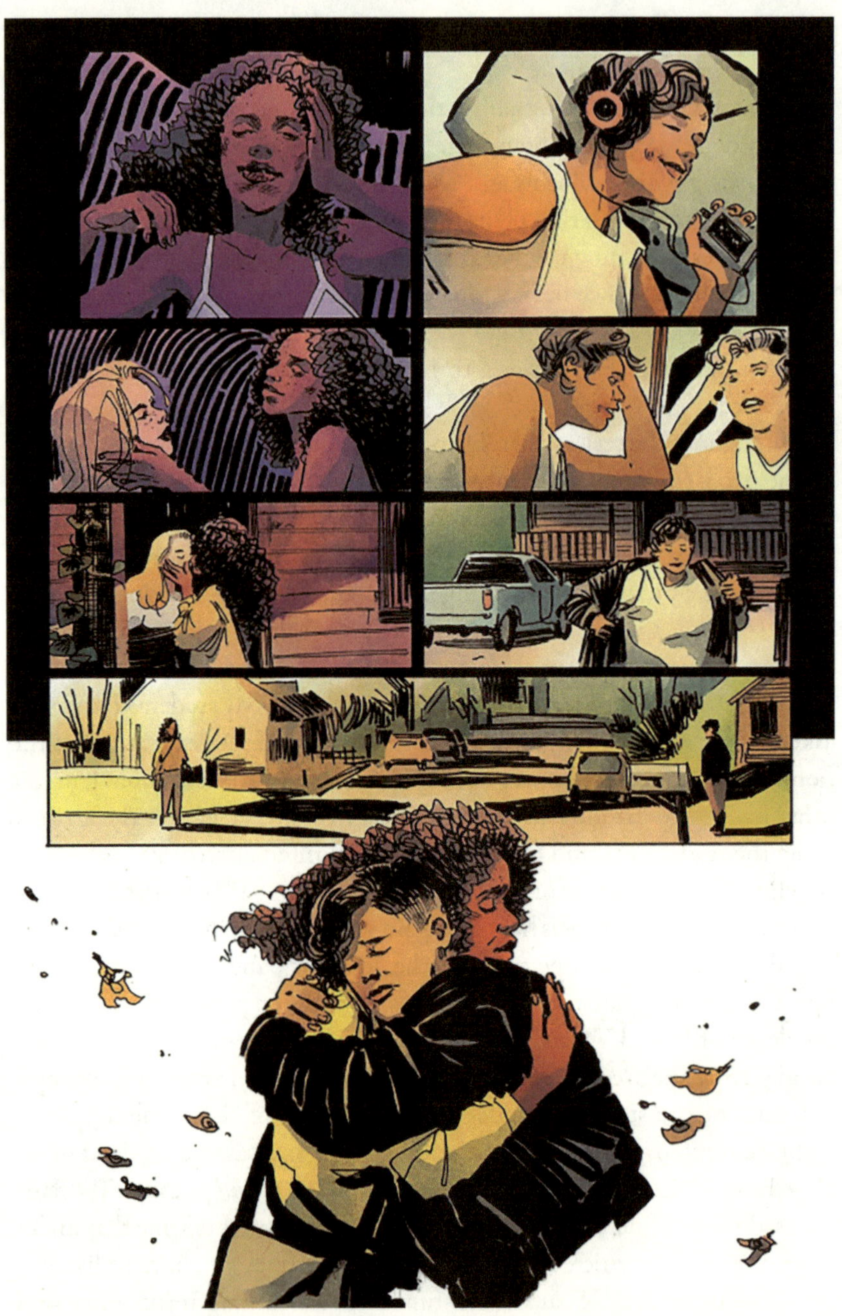

FIGURE 8.2 Octavia and Eldora embrace in Carmen Maria Machado and Dani, *The Low, Low Woods* no. 5 (Burbank, CA: DC Black Label, 2020).

and queer and trans individuals within patriarchy. Some participants referred to the comic as a #MeToo book. Overwhelmingly, students *loved* reading and discussing this comic. It was *the* text that students continued coming back to even in meetings dedicated to different comics. Their eagerness and nervousness to discuss this text underscores the need for literary studies scholarship that is responsive to the impact of #MeToo.[29] However, when we pivoted to discussions about using this text in high school classrooms, a few participants doubled down on it being both "too sexy" and "too heavy" for a high school audience. These responses positioned hypothetical students as fragile and the text as too risky. Additionally, their responses failed to recognize those students who already have firsthand experiences with sexual assault.

Participants defaulted to critiques of the medium by claiming, again, that the comic lacked an appropriate amount of character development. When pushed to elaborate, one student compared the comic to Tillie Walden's comic *Are You Listening?*[30] She argued, "We get so much time with the characters, and we get to learn about their lives outside of the sexual assault, whereas the characters of *The Low, Low Woods* have little characterization outside of the sexual assault narrative."[31] Both texts feature protagonists who have experienced sexual assault, and both comics underscore the "means, beyond language, for people to make sense of and articulate their place in the world."[32] The incidence of sexual assault in Walden's text relies on more abstract visual imagery to suggest sexual violence. For example, when the main character recalls their assault, the panels are blurred and panel lines melt into one another. Visually, it is a stunning use of panel work that effectively reflects the relationship between trauma and memory by highlighting how survivors' bodies can protect themselves from reliving and reexperiencing traumatic events. It is absolutely a comic worth studying, and I do not mean to suggest one is better suited for literature classes than the other. I was puzzled by the student's claim that El and V had "little characterization" beyond the narrative of sexual assault. By reducing *The Low, Low Woods* to a single story about rape, this student foreclosed interpretative possibilities about the dynamic and critical friendship between El and V. This kinship is what ultimately helps them survive and thrive in a world in which silences and erasures about sexual violence are ever present.

I suspect my students, at times, mistook the length of the text for an indicator of character development. Walden's *Are You Listening?* spans 320 pages, twice as long as *The Low, Low Woods*. Similarly, the graphic adaptation of *Juliet Takes a Breath* condenses a 300-page novel into 176 pages. By not considering how content and form function *differently* across prose and comics narratives, my students missed out on the visual opportunities to see El and V as complex and nuanced characters. In my reading, El and V are foils of one another, and their development throughout the story underscores the strength of their queer kinship.

Reading Queer Bodies in *b.b. free*

Published by Boom! Studios, Rivera and Dunlap's *b.b. free* was canceled after three issues, leaving b.b.'s adventures sadly unfinished for the reader. A PDF copy of these collected issues is available on Rivera's website.[33] Despite the series' limited run, the comic is a convenient and accessible option for classroom use. In a postapocalyptic version of Florida, b.b. and her father live in Buttercup Swamp, a small, self-sufficient community secluded from life beyond the swamps. The Florida Islands, now part of what is known as the Fractured States of America, are the result of a plague (i.e., climate crises caused by unchecked racial capitalism) that wiped out 60 percent of the population two hundred years prior to the start of the story.

As b.b. approaches her fifteenth birthday, she is increasingly frustrated by her father's expectations of her to be a good girl: "Sure, I see a girl. I am a girl, but sometimes . . . also, maybe a honeycomb? A manatee?"[34] Tensions between b.b. and her father are reflective of what Chicana and Latina feminist scholars understand as *marianismo*,[35] the expectation of women to emulate characteristics of the Virgin Mary: self-sacrificing, nurturing, and demonstrating femininity and sexual purity. She feels stifled by the expectations put on her by the gaze of others, stating across a three-panel sequence, "But I'm not *for* them. I'm for me. And I gotta be *free*" (see figure 8.3).[36] In the company of her crocodile friend Buttercup, b.b. makes her way through the swamp while chatting with Chulita through her headphones. Standing tall and looking up as if to make eye contact with the reader, b.b.'s exclamation "and I gotta be free" is strengthened by Dunlap's decision to draw b.b.'s body beyond the confines of the enclosed panel. Her ponytail and her toes extend beyond the top and bottom panels. Centered and taking up the bottom half of the page, b.b.'s stance is powerful and commanding. She desires a bigger world with space to learn and grow into her powers (quite literally as she appears to be developing a type of electromagnetic power). She wants to leave home and road trip across the Florida Islands with her best friend Chulita, all while hosting a collaborative radio show, *b.Chula*. Together, they want to create a show for "every fifteen-year-old making their way in these Fractured States."[37]

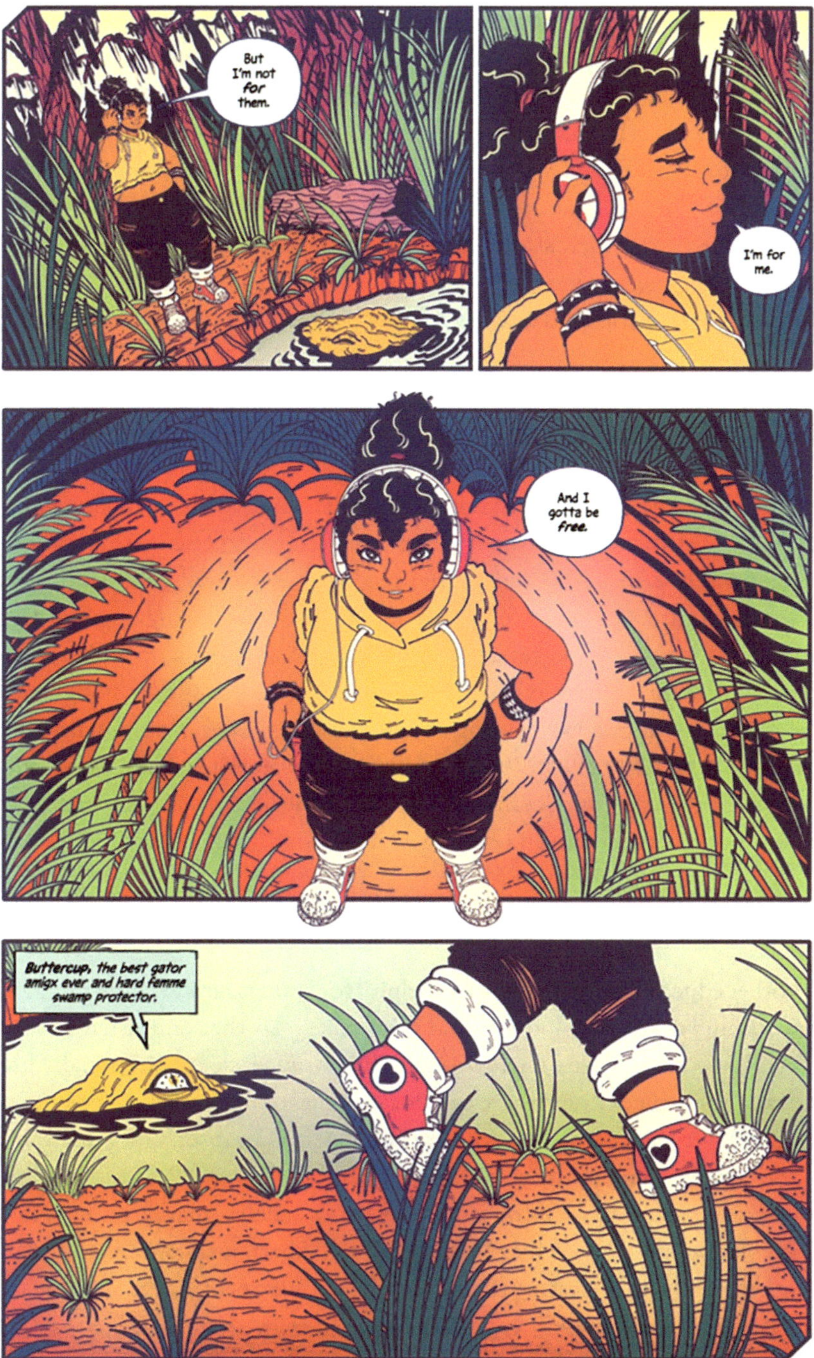

FIGURE 8.3 Image of b.b. breaking free from the panels of *b.b. free*. Gabby Rivera and Royal Dunlap, *b.b. free* (Los Angeles: BOOM! Studios, 2020), 2.

Across each of these stories, I selected images from the comics that similarly show the young women resisting being boxed into single panels: b.b. stands with her hands squarely on her hips, looking up at the reader, and declaring "I gotta be free" as her feet and bun rest in the bottom and top gutters respectively; El and V's embrace punctuates the end of a series of panels that mirrored their time apart; and Juliet's new haircut exceeds the boundaries of the panel. Their stories, and the artistic decisions made to represent them within and beyond the panels of the comic page, are reflective of their deep development as characters who prioritize community, joy, and healing.

Readerly Roles and Learning to Read Comics

Despite how these comics disrupt single stories and damage-centered narratives, it was clear to me that my students' biases and inexperience reading comics contributed to single and partial readings. Repeatedly, my work with teacher educators underscores the necessity of readers having ongoing time and access to various genres and styles of comics. Scholarship about comic readers reaffirms that expertise in traditional prose reading does not guarantee a reader will excel at reading comics.[38] Even though my students view themselves as savvy readers, non–comic readers often need additional support when engaging with comics. In the following sections, I offer three strategies to support students in rereading and responding to comics.

Building a Comics Vocabulary

As other educators have argued, it is helpful for readers new to comics to build a working vocabulary about visual grammar.[39] To that end, I have found David Low and Katrina Bartow Jacob's literature circle roles especially useful, and their cheeky names are easy for students to remember: Image Mage, Gutter Dweller, Text Maven, Synergizer, Palette Cleanser, and Superfan.[40] For example, some of the roles (i.e., Gutter Dweller and Palette Cleanser) encourage readers to focus on isolated features such as images, gutters, text, and color, while roles such as Synergizer and Superfan encourage readers to synthesize how these features come together to tell stories on and beyond the pages.

To avoid overwhelming students, I would suggest focusing on one role at a time, or on a role that lends itself to the specific comic students are engaging. For example, in each of the comics discussed within this chapter, I would want students to read as both an Image Mage and a Gutter Dweller, paying careful attention to "how images, icons, and figures are represented within a graphic text" as well as to the panels and the blank spaces between them since "gutters are used to indicate the passage of time, change of venue or perspective . . . requiring readers to make hundreds of inferences in a single text."[41] Juliet, El, V, and b.b. are developed as much in the gutters as they are in their dialogue. A careful reading of the gutters will help challenge readers who tend to rely on written text as evidence for character development.

Making Memes

This next activity is inspired by former students who were enrolled in an asynchronous section of an adolescent literature course I taught virtually during the COVID-19 pandemic. While reading and discussing Tillie Walden's webcomic *On a Sunbeam*, students began screen saving small moments or single panels that resonated with their own worldviews, passions, and quirks. They posted them to class discussion boards with captions like "Re: Relatable Content" and "Re: Seen." I did not prompt students to do this, and once it started, other students and I joined. It became a rich and revealing practice about their meaning making with the texts and helped students identify imagery, relationships, and attitudes that were important to the narrative. Additionally, it helped students practice a slow reading that pushed them to pay more attention to the visual details of the text. To re-create this activity with future students, I would suggest using this activity as a low-stakes community builder, either at the start of class or at the end of a class. Educators should invite students to first brainstorm popular catchphrases and digital lingo as inspiration for their memes. By utilizing the language students encounter on social media and in social contexts, educators are sanctioning mediums that students are often schooled out believing to be complex and literary.

One-Sentence Essays

Rather than asking students to write a traditional analytic essay, I suggest an activity I refer to as "one-sentence essays." After reading a comic (or a series of comics), I ask students to write a juicy one-sentence claim about the comic. The claim should attend to the relationship between form and content (and maybe a theoretical goal within the larger course). This exercise can be done independently or as a whole class. To justify their claim, students can only use images culled from the comics. By including this caveat in the assignment, I push students, who would otherwise focus their attention on dialogue and narration, to prioritize rereadings that highlight the visual cues within the stories.

I encourage students to photocopy or digitally capture anywhere from seven to ten panels or images that best support their claims. I then ask students to arrange the images in the order that best builds and supports their claims. Depending on the classroom space, I have students hang their one-sentence essays on the walls or digitally share them with one another via Google Jamboard. Students then spend time evaluating each other's claims, offering comments and feedback about the extent to which the claim was sufficiently supported. Alternatively, students may also consider hiding their claim from their peers, prompting each other to infer the claim based on the images. One-sentence essays are useful on their own as small-scale practice for building analysis or as a brainstorming exercise for a more traditional paper. Similar to the meme-making activity described in the previous section, one-sentence essays support students in reading and writing *differently* than they are accustomed in prose, which in turn opens up new possibilities for meaning making.

Conclusion: Reading Slowly, Teaching Queerly

The title of this chapter—"it's on every single page"—is borrowed from my student's analysis of Juliet's hair in the graphic adaptation of *Juliet Takes a Breath*. I return to this statement because I think it aptly encompasses exactly where readers can find rich and nuanced character development within comics. It is quite literally on every single page, and readers must slow their attention to the relationship between content and form. Understanding how characters are developed in visual storytelling requires *looking* for it and reading for it differently than students have been trained to do when reading prose (i.e., primarily through dialogue and interactions with other characters). For my students, their desire for "slow and realistic" character development stemmed from their experiences reading longer prose texts where the plot unfolds over many pages. The comics discussed in this chapter condensed time in unfamiliar ways for my students. As a result, students focused their reading on dialogue and paid less attention to the visual imagery until they were prompted to return to the texts. Angel Matos calls on educators in literature classrooms to teach queerly by "recognizing the dangers of monolithic and universalizing forms of reading and interpretation."[42] What must remain *slow* in comics is the reader's attention: their eyes need to roam the pages in nonlinear ways. The comics featured in this chapter demand an alternative reading practice.

For educators, text selection practices must acknowledge that our classrooms are "complex spaces that are inhabited and organized with multiple positions of privilege and oppression mingling together."[43] By exploring how readers with privileged identity markers read and make sense of queer Latinx comics such as those described within this chapter, I may have unintentionally recentered Whiteness within an anthology dedicated to untethering Latinx comics from academic pursuits within the ivory tower. But my hope is for educators to feel confident in centering texts by BIPOC creators even when they are working at PWIs. By analyzing these texts in tandem with my students' critiques, I am better able to understand the type of support some readers need to become savvy and critical consumers of visual media.

Notes

1 Spencer Clark, "'Your Credibility Could Be Shot': Preservice Teachers' Thinking about Nonfiction Graphic Novels, Curriculum Decision Making, and Professional Acceptance," *Social Studies Teacher* 104 (2013): 38–45, 42.

2 I capitalized Color for reasons similar to scholars such as Eve Ewing, who capitalize Black and White: to signal that categories of race are socially constructed and *not* naturally occurring. Ewing, "I'm a Black Scholar Who Studies Race: Here's Why I Capitalize White," *ZORA*, July 1, 2020, https://zora.medium.com/im-a-black-scholar-who-studies-race-here-s-why-i-capitalize-white-f94883aa2dd3.

3 This research was approved by the university's Institutional Review Board. All participants consented to be recorded. All names are pseudonyms.

4 Ramzi Fawaz, "A Queer Sequence: Comics as a Disruptive Medium," *PMLA* 134 (2019): 588–594, 588.

5 Since *b.b. free* was not part of the book club project, I do not have transcribed records of student responses.

6 Nick Sousanis, *Unflattening* (Cambridge, MA: Harvard University Press, 2015), 66.

7 Sousanis, *Unflattening*, 32.

8 Fawaz, "Queer Sequence," 589.

9 Pauline Lipman, *The New Political Economy of Urban Education* (New York: Routledge, 2011), 47.

10 Angela Valenzuela, *Subtractive Schooling: US-Mexican Youth and the Politics of Caring* (Albany: State University of New York Press, 1999), 6.

11 Tricia Ebarvia, Lorena Germán, Kim Parker, and Julia Torres, "#DisruptTexts," *English Journal* 110 (2020): 100–102.

12 S. R. Toliver and Heidi Lyn Hadley, "Ca(n)non Fodder No More: Disrupting Common Arguments That Support a Canonical Empire," *Journal of Language and Literacy Education* 17, no. 2 (2021): 1–28, 14.

13 Cynthia Lewis et al., *Reframing Sociocultural Research on Literacy: Identity, Agency, and Power* (Mahwah, NJ: Lawrence Erlbaum, 2007), 9.
14 Toliver and Hadley, "Ca(n)non Fodder No More," 14.
15 Keffrelyn Brown, "Trouble on My Mind: Toward a Framework of Humanizing Critical Sociocultural Knowledge for Teaching and Teacher Education," *Race, Ethnicity, and Education* 16 (2013): 316–338, 331.
16 Sandy Grande, *Red Pedagogy: Native American Social and Political Thought* (Lanham, MD: Rowman & Littlefield, 2015), 103.
17 Kay Sohini, "Breathless," *The Nib*, February 21, 2022, https://thenib.com/breathless/.
18 Deirdre Lynn Hollman, "Critical Race Comics: Centering Black Subjectivities and Teaching Racial Literacy," *Journal of Curriculum and Pedagogy* 18 (2021): 119–133, 131.
19 Chimamanda Ngozi Adichie, "The Danger of Single Story" (TED Talk, 2009), https://www.youtube.com/watch?v=D9Ihs241zeg.
20 Eve Tuck, "Suspending Damage: A Letter to Communities," *Harvard Educational Review* 79 (2009): 409–428, 409.
21 Tuck, "Suspending Damage," 409.
22 Mia (pseudonym), book club transcripts, July 2022.
23 Gabby Rivera and Celia Moscote, *Juliet Takes a Breath: The Graphic Novel* (Los Angeles: BOOM! Studios, 2020), n.p.
24 Jeremy Chow and Maite Urcaregui, "Just Keep Swimming?: Queer Pooling and Hydropoetics," *Angelaki: Journal of the Theoretical Humanities* 28, no. 1 (February 2023): 36–52, 46.
25 Carmen Maria Machado and Dani, *The Low, Low Woods* no. 1 (Burbank, CA: DC Black Label, 2019), 1.
26 Machado and Dani, *Low, Low Woods* no. 1, 1.
27 Carmen Maria Machado and Dani, *The Low, Low Woods* no. 3 (Burbank, CA: DC Black Label, 2020), 14.
28 Carmen Maria Machado and Dani, *The Low, Low Woods* no. 5 (Burbank, CA: DC Black Label, 2020), 1.
29 Heather Hewett and Mary Holland, "Introduction: Literary Studies as Activism," in *#MeToo and Literary Studies: Reading, Writing, and Teaching about Sexual Violence and Rape Culture,* ed. Mary Holland and Heather Hewett (London: Bloomsbury, 2021), 2–27, 8.
30 Tillie Walden, *Are You Listening?* (New York: First Second, 2019).
31 Jules (pseudonym), book club transcripts, August 2022.
32 Roxane Gay, "The Conditions of Our Culture," in *Drawing Power: Women's Stories of Sexual Violence, Harassment, and Survival*, ed. Diane Noomin (New York: Abrams Comicarts, 2019), vii–ix.
33 A free PDF of *b.b. free* can be found at https://gabbyrivera.com/wp-content/uploads/2019/11/bbfree-comic-by-gabby-rivera.pdf.
34 Rivera and Dunlap, *b.b. free* (Los Angeles: BOOM! Studios, 2020), n.p., Rivera and Dunlap, *b.b. free* (Los Angeles: BOOM! Studios, 2020), n.p.
35 Rebecca Rangel Campon, "Aspects of Marianismo," in *The SAGE Encyclopedia of Psychology and Gender*, ed. Kevin Nadal (Thousand Oaks, CA: SAGE, 2017), 1100–1103, 1102; Evelyn Stevens, "Machismo and Marianismo," *Society* 10 (1973): 57–63, 62.
36 Rivera and Dunlap, *b.b. free*, n.p.
37 Rivera and Dunlap, *b.b. free*,n.p.

38 Laura Jimenez and Carla Meyer, "First Impressions Matter: Navigating Graphic Novels Utilizing Linguistic, Visual, and Spatial Resources," *Journal of Literacy Research* 48, no. 4 (2016): 423–447, 424.

39 Sean Connors, "Toward a Shared Vocabulary for Visual Analysis: An Analytic Toolkit for Deconstructing the Visual Design of Graphic Novels," *Journal of Visual Literacy* 31, no. 1 (2011): 71–92, 72.

40 David Low and Katrina Bartow Jacobs, "Literature Circle Roles for Discussing Graphica in Language Arts Classrooms," *Language Arts* 95 (2011): 322–331.

41 Low and Jacobs, "Literature Circle Roles," 323–324.

42 Angel Daniel Matos, "The Politics of Teaching Queerly in Today's Literature Classroom," *Research in the Teaching of English* 54 (2019): 92.

43 Michelle Stewart, Michael Cappello, and Claire Carter, "Anti-Oppressive Education and the Trap of 'Good' Intentions: Lessons from an Interdisciplinary Workshop," *Critical Education* 5, no. 14 (October 1, 2014): 1–19, 8.

Translating Queer Afro-Latinx Experiences through Comics Aesthetics in Breena Nuñez's Autobiographical Comics

MAITE URCAREGUI

Because of the presumption of cissexism and heteronormativity—the notion that one is presumed to be cisgender and straight until suggested otherwise—queer people must continuously announce their presence through serialized speech acts, such as coming out. But what happens when queerness gets lost in translation? Analyzing queer as a "bordering concept" that fundamentally disrupts colonial logics of gender and sexuality, Héctor Domínguez

Ruvalcaba asks, "Is it then impossible to translate the silence of disruption, the resistance to the logic of reason, to the naturalized forms of oppression? Is then queerness untranslatable?"[1] How too, I might add, do intersections of racial, national, and local identity shape these queer translations, particularly within the context of Afro-Latinx experiences?

The root of the word "translation," *trans*, bespeaks multiple impulses within Latinx studies, including the "transnational, translinguistic, [and] transepistemological," as Ruvalcaba pinpoints.[2] It also evokes forms of gender-nonconforming and transgender embodiment. Trans, according to Francisco J. Galarte, "is an expansive category that might be shorthand for various forms of gendered embodiment."[3] As a prefix, trans "infers movement across, crossing, beyond, and through," and thus is an apt theoretical apparatus, in conversation with, yet distinct from, queer theory, to investigate *trans*lation's unruly movements and critical crossings.[4] Sonia E. Alvarez explores translation within feminist movements to understand "how feminist discourses and practices travel across a variety of sites and directionalities" and "to emphasize the ways these travels are politically embedded within larger questions of globalization and exchange across diverse localities, especially between and among women in Latin America and Latinas in the United States."[5] Alvarez uses translation figuratively to refer to feminisms' discursive movements across national and local borders. In *Translating Blackness: Latinx Colonialities in Global Perspective*, Lorgia García Peña explores the processes by which Afro-Latinx peoples navigate the shifting borders of ethnoracial labels. She uses "translation as a metaphor for understanding how dominant ethno-racial labels are used by multiple communities to make visible the historical processes that (re)produce their minoritized subjectivity: colonialism, global capitalism, and migration."[6] Translation becomes a means of disidentification within normative frameworks of recognition—a way of making oneself visible within them while also drawing attention to how they are shaped by overlapping systems of oppression.[7] As we can see from these diverse Latinx studies approaches, translation is more than a linguistic movement from one language to another. It offers a conceptual framework for understanding how Latinx peoples navigate multiple borders (linguistic, national, gendered, ethnoracial, and more) and fundamentally remake them in the process.

Like the scholars above, I too embrace both the material realities and conceptual possibilities of translation. Specifically, I analyze movements and moments of translation in Breena Nuñez's autobiographical comics, which explore the author's nonbinary gender alongside their Afro-Latinx diasporic identity.[8] Nuñez is an independent cartoonist who identifies themself as "a queer Afrodescendiente from the Bay Area" and uses diary comics to explore "what it means to be Central American from the US."[9] Their series *Half and Half* (2018), for instance, compiles their two zines "Being Half Guatemalan" and "Being Half Salvi" to give readers "a peek into [their] life as an Afrolatinx [*sic*] person within the Central American isthmus in the Bay Area."[10] Importantly, while Nuñez grew up in the United States and is based in California's Bay Area, many of their comics explore their visits to Guatemala and El Salvador and the way these locations inform their intersectional sense of place and self, offering both a transnational and a "translocal" Latinx perspective. Theorizing what she calls a "translocal feminist politics of translation," Alvarez advocates for a move away from the "transnational," which often affirms arbitrary national borders and tends to create a hierarchical, unidirectional flow of knowledge from North to South, toward the translocal.[11] This emphasis on the translocal "interrogate[s] and thereby destabilize[s] received meanings of race, class, sexualities, genders, and other 'locational politics'" across shifting borders and diverse localities.[12] Drawing on Alvarez's work, I too put the translocal in conversation with the transnational, when appropriate, to attend to the ways that Nuñez navigates and represents their positionality—both their geographic and social locations—across very real material borders as well as comics' creative and conceptual borders.

In this chapter, I offer an extended analysis of two of Nuñez's autobiographical comics, published both digitally and in print, "How Do You Translate Non-Binary?" (2020) and "Once Upon a Time, I Wanted to Be a Photographer" (2021).[13] "How Do You Translate Non-Binary?" directly takes up the politics and poetics of translation as it explores the artist's spiritual understanding of their gender alongside a decolonial history of gender nonconformity. "Once Upon a Time" plays with the relationship between photography and comics to reflect on and remediate Nuñez's experiences within both the United States and Central America, illustrating how place intersects with other axes of identity. These two comics draw on themes that mark much of Nuñez's work, and indeed their entire oeuvre is worthy of further study and should be widely taught, particularly within Latinx studies and comics courses. Rather than attempting to translate their intersectional, transnational, and translocal identities into a totalizing image or faithful reproduction, Nuñez uses the comics page to theorize an ongoing process of queer translation and, ultimately, embraces moments of untranslatability and incommensurability. In doing so, they reveal queer translation as "a political process," as Ruvalcaba maintains, that looks to "the margins, exclusions, abjections, and oppressions of alternative bodies" to rewrite colonial discourses of gender and race and to envision coalitional connections across national and local contexts.[14]

So, "How Do You Translate Non-Binary?": Disrupting Colonial Logics of Gender

In their comic "How Do You Translate Non-Binary?" Nuñez attempts to "translate" their experience of gender to their "cis-hetero-lady" therapist who persistently fails to understand them.[15] This short autobiographical comic was originally published online on September 28, 2020, as part of *The Nib*'s daily digital newsletter and was later republished in print in *The Nib*'s anthology *Be Gay, Do Comics!: Queer History, Memoir, and Satire* (2020). Here I analyze *Be Gay, Do Comics!*'s print version of the comic that translates the scrollable two-by-six grid of the original webcomic into three pages of a two-by-two grid. *The Nib* was a member-supported independent publisher, under the editorship of Matt Bors, that published "political cartoons and nonfiction comics about what is going down in the world" through both a daily online newsletter and a quarterly print magazine.[16] For a decade (2013–2023), *The Nib* gave independent comics artists a platform for sharing their work—work that represented the cutting edge of politically engaged satire, nonfiction, and memoir—in a way that allowed them to comment directly on contemporary issues and to speak to a community of dedicated readers and subscribers.[17] This publication context is important for understanding the social and material conditions that shape Nuñez's act of translation, both within the diegesis of "How Do You Translate Non-Binary?" and in relation to the reader's own encounter with the text. As Myriam Díaz-Diocaretz has described of her efforts to translate Adrienne Rich's poetry from English into Spanish, translation is "activated and conditioned, on the one hand, by the social organization of the individuals participating in the communicative process, and on the other hand, by the conditions in which the interaction occurs. . . . As a linguistic sign, a translation is grounded on the social interaction between its interpreter and the new horizon of virtual and actual conditions of such utterance."[18] The act of translation, rather than a linear movement from an "original" text to a faithful reproduction, is a complex process that, like all instances of literary discourse, is shaped by ongoing social and material conditions.

In "How Do You Translate Non-Binary?," Nuñez acts as the source text, author, artist, narrator, and translator of their own lived experience of gender, and the very plot of the comic is shaped by this communicative process as well as its failures and fissures. The comic opens through a retroactive framing as a narrative box informs the reader, "So I tried going to therapy for the first time last year. It was helpful until it grew to be exhausting."[19] While much of the information in the comic is relayed through speech bubbles that portray the real-time dialogue between Nuñez and their therapist, narrative boxes appear sparingly throughout the comic to offer a reflexive commentary on the conversation. In this opening narrative confession, Nuñez reflects on the emotional labor and power dynamics involved in going to therapy, particularly for queer people and people of color, who are sometimes forced to translate their identities and experiences to therapists who do not share their positionality: work that, as Nuñez points out, is "exhausting."[20] Attempting to translate nonbinary into a representational framework that their therapist might understand, Nuñez follows up, saying, "Well *for me* it's about feeling which type of energy calls to you."[21] Nuñez notes the specificity of each person's understanding of their gender, prefacing their definition with a "for me" that recognizes that gender is not universal but is instead grounded in one's lived experience. The personal nature of their description is visually reinforced as the panel zooms in on Nuñez, their facial expression, body language, and hand gestures. The twelve-panel comic centers Nuñez as the expert, narrator, and author of their own experience both narratively and visually: nine out of twelve panels portray Nuñez, and seven of those panels feature close shots of them alone as the sole visible figure.

In this initial explanation of their gender, Nuñez frames it within spiritual terms, as a "feeling" or "energy," and later they decidedly call it "a spiritual experience." By claiming gender as an affective, spiritual experience, Nuñez resists what María Lugones identifies as "the coloniality of gender," an ongoing process that distills diverse gender and sexual expressions into hierarchical binaries and positions those outside of these binaries as racialized aberrations.[22] This colonial reduction and resignification of Black and Indigenous ways of knowing and naming gender and sexuality across the Americas is an act of epistemic violence, an act of translation in which, as Ruvalcaba describes, "Native categories are silenced and subsumed to the colonizer's categories."[23] Nuñez's emphasis on the spiritual aspects of gender also bring to mind Gloria E. Anzaldúa's theory of "nepantla," a concept she draws from Nahuatl language and philosophy to describe a transformative, liminal zone between "body and psyche where image and story making takes place, where spirits surface."[24] This spiritual space of "image and story making" brings to mind the imaginative and cultural work of comics. Examining the formal flexibility of comics, Hannah Miodrag points out that, "beyond saying the form uses words and images (usually), it is not possible to declare in advance the role each element must take, for . . . the practices of comics texts themselves are extremely diverse."[25] Comics, through the fluid, ever-changing interplay of word and image, have the potential to create, even if momentarily, that imagistic space "between imagination and physical existence, between ordinary and nonordinary (spirit) realities" that Anzaldúa describes.[26]

Nuñez's translation of their nonbinary identity not only challenges colonial discourses of gender; it disidentifies with mainstream feminist and queer discourses of gender as well.[27] Taking up the notion of the gender spectrum, Nuñez says, "Some days I'll be more femme than masc, or a lil' of both."[28] A visual representation of the spectrum further explicates what they struggle to translate through a linear mapping that places nonbinary as the middle point between masculine and feminine and labels, with a "me today," where Nuñez is located in their gender expression at that given time (see figure 9.1). While Nuñez makes use of this simple spectrum as an illustrative device, they also complicate it. Despite the use of the line, their gender is not simply a point between two oppositional poles, nor is it on a progressive route to a fixed final destination. Instead, they treat the gender spectrum as a sort of sliding scale that allows them to shuttle between masculine and feminine, combining the two into "a lil' of both" in an endless array of fluid formations. Their therapist, failing to receive Nuñez's attempts at translation, or perhaps performing an antagonistic "wokeness," asks, "But I hear that *you're* supposed to reject the spectrum entirely. Isn't that the truth?"[29] Simplifying the nuance Nuñez offers into a didactic performance, the therapist forecloses what could be an opportunity for recognition and affirmation. Her probing question, "Isn't that the truth?," refuses to take her client's words as their own subjective truth by presuming there is a singular objective truth to gender identity.

This moment of miscommunication reveals the problems and pressures of "authenticity" that get placed onto Black subjects. As Jennifer Carolina Gómez Menjívar and Héctor Nicolás Ramos Flores argue, readers, here dramatized in the figure of the therapist, "assign authority to narratives to tell them about themselves, to discover the 'truth' about themselves" in ways that often "maintain a hierarchy that actively oppresses and negates Black experience to disastrous consequence."[30] The therapist does not actually bear witness to Nuñez's experience as an Afro-Latinx nonbinary person but rather

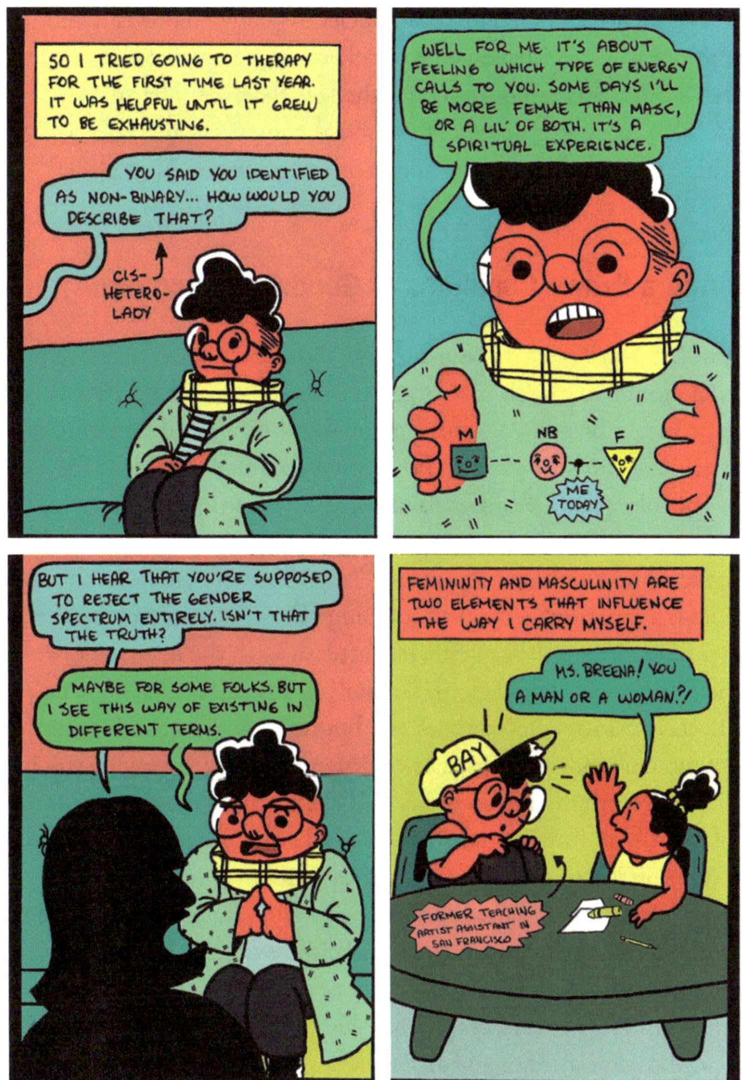

FIGURE 9.1 The first page of Breena Nuñez's "How Do You Translate Non-Binary?" Breena Nuñez, "How Do You Translate Non-Binary?," in *Be Gay, Do Comics! Queer History, Memoir, and Satire*, ed. Matt Bors (San Diego: IDW, 2020), 48.

hears an essential "truth" that reaffirms what she already knows to be true, what maintains her privilege as a "cis-hetero-lady."[31] In this moment, the visual perspective of the panel zooms out to show that the therapist has become an empty silhouette of a talking head with her mouth exaggeratedly agape. With that accusatory "you," the therapist tasks nonbinary people, here Nuñez, with the sole responsibility of disrupting the gender binary and thus alleviates herself of her own complicity in gendered power dynamics and of her responsibility to participate in collective struggles to dismantle them. In other words, this response "elides the fact that," as Johanna M. Schmidt asserts, "all expressions of gender are social constructs and effectively privileges those who conform to the norms of any given time and place."[32]

Picturing a Brown Commons of Gender Nonconformity

In "How Do You Translate Non-Binary?," Nuñez situates their specific experience of nonbinary within a larger transnational and translocal context that taps into a Brown commons of gender fluidity and nonconformity.[33] José Esteban Muñoz theorizes the "brown commons" to describe a collective of "people, places, feelings, sounds, animals, minerals, flora, and other objects" that "suffer and strive together . . . because they have been devalued by the world outside their commons."[34] The Brown commons that Muñoz describes is a capacious ecology that attempts to pry Latinidad away from the clutches of identity politics while still attending to the histories of colonialism and flows of racial (and global) capitalism that shape this sense of Brownness. Even as Muñoz destabilizes the boundaries of Latinidad, he centers those "who are rendered brown by their personal and familial participation in South-to-North migration patterns."[35] Yet, while this sense of shared vulnerability to structures of domination marks the Brown commons, it does not contain it. Muñoz emphasizes that the Brown commons "is not strictly the shared experience of harm between people and things; it is also the potential for the refusal and resistance to that often-systemic harm. Brownness is a kind of uncanny persistence in the face of distressed conditions of possibility."[36] Brownness then names not only shared vulnerabilities but also a coalitional politics of resistance and an aesthetics of survival. I see Nuñez evoking this Brown commons—one inclusive of Indigenous, Black, and Latinx experiences and solidarities—by integrating nonfictional figures of gender fluidity into "How Do You Translate Non-Binary?" and portraying them with detailed linework and coloring that creates a comics aesthetics of care and specificity (see figure 9.2).

Following their therapist's failed understanding, Nuñez attempts to translate their nonbinaryness by tracing a decolonial history of gender-fluid representation that is grounded in Indigenous ways of being and knowing across the Americas. They cite the māhū of the Kanaka Maoli, or Native Hawaiians; the muxe of the Zapotec people in Oaxaca, Mexico; and the fa'afāfine of

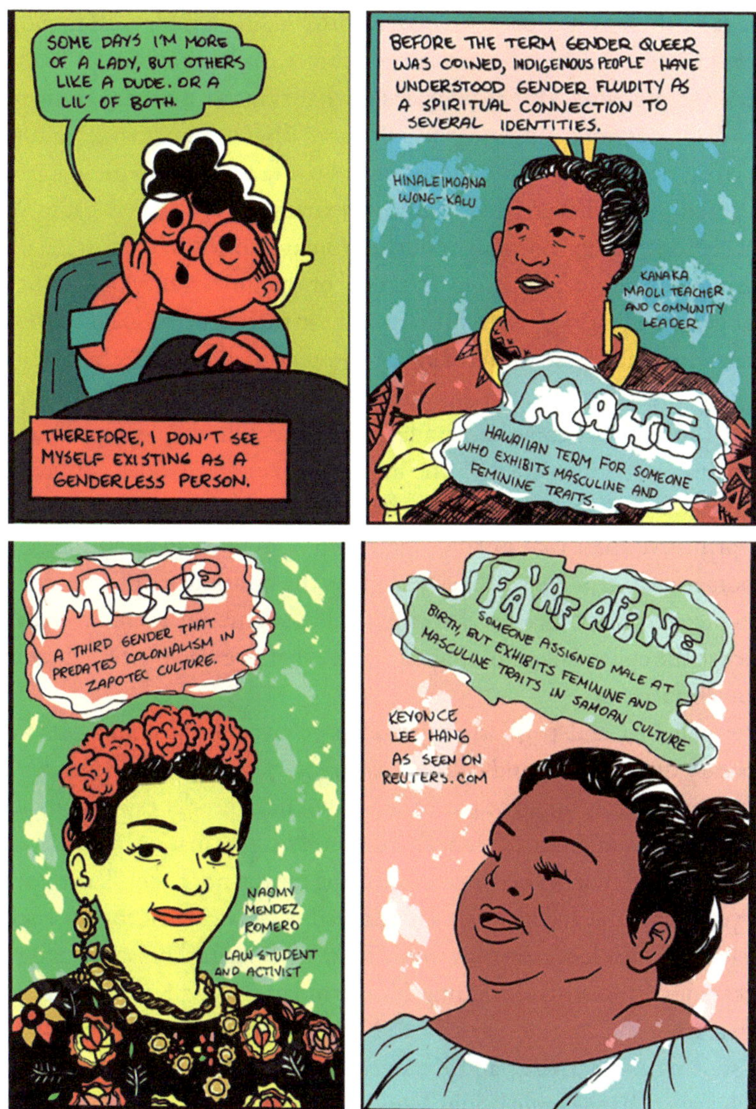

FIGURE 9.2 Nuñez portrays themself next to portraits of Indigenous activists and models of gender nonconformity. Nuñez, "How Do You Translate Non-Binary?," 49.

Native Samoans. Each of these terms name a culturally specific third gender that exists outside of the binary of male/female and does not neatly translate into Western notions of "transgender," although they are sometimes described as such in contemporary discourse. Traditionally, these figures have taken on important spiritual and educational roles within their respective communities, often preserving and transmitting cultural knowledge and traditions.

More recently, however, these terms have also taken on trans- and homophobic connotations imposed from outside forces. In her analysis of fa'afāfine experience, Johanna M. Schmidt warns that translating these Indigenous forms of gender nonconformity into Western discourses of gender and sexuality risks "positioning populations such as the fa'afāfine as representative of a supposedly more natural and primitive sexuality that has been lost to Western societies," which "not only results in romanticization but also . . . allows these populations to be utilized as 'proof' of the universality of specific sexual or gender identities" with little regard for their specific local contexts.[37] Nuñez notes that these forms of gender fluidity predate Western discourses of gender without romanticizing them: "Before the term gender queer was coined, Indigenous people have understood gender fluidity as a spiritual connection to several identities."[38] The history Nuñez traces does not present a linear teleology that positions these forms of gender nonconformity as part of a "primitive" past that justifies their own nonbinary identity in the contemporary moment. Rather, they recognize the multiplicity of forms of gender nonconformity, briefly defining and recognizing each, in order to challenge the epistemological singularity or superiority of Western discourses of gender queerness.

The paneling and page structure on page two of the comic place contemporary māhū, muxe, and fa'afāfine activists in relation to one another and to Nuñez (see figure 9.2). The page offers a mosaic of gender expressions across the Americas that inform Nuñez's own evolving formation of their Afro-Latinx and nonbinary experience while being careful not to conflate these distinct yet interconnected histories. Nuñez further situates these forms of gender expression in their local and geographic context by paying homage to and naming present-day activists, including Hinaleimoana Wong-Kalu, the "Kanaka Maoli teacher and community leader"; Naomy Méndez Romero, the Oaxacan "law student and activist"; and Keyonce Lee Hang, the Samoan singer and church leader.[39] The comic brings Nuñez into both a spatial and a visual relationship with these three activists, as all four of them are shown in portrait in four nearly symmetrical two-by-two panels. Nuñez draws the three activists in a more realistic style, moving away from the round cartoony lines that they use to portray themself. Whereas Nuñez draws their own eyes as two wide black circles that match their "o" of a mouth in the first panel, they draw Hinaleimoana, Naomy, and Keyonce with a finer line that reveals the textures of eyelids, lashes, and hair. The coloring also becomes more textured: their clothing includes prints and pleats, and the backdrop of the panels takes on a splotched watercolor effect. Additionally, they are adorned with jewelry, tattoos, makeup, and accessories. Nuñez's use of realism is an act of reverence that breaks with the cartoony style of the rest of the comic to portray a Brown commons or coalition that inhabits and envisions queer forms of gender fluidity in all of their local particularity. It enacts what Maylei Blackwell calls *translenguaje*, or "a committed practice of transnational translation" that is "a key step in cross-border coalition building."[40]

On the final page, Nuñez further models these cross-border coalitions by connecting these Indigenous histories of gender nonconformity to Black diasporic epistemologies. Thinking through the way their nonbinaryness intersects with their Afro-Latinidad, Nuñez states that "seeing and reading the ways other Black queer folk relate to their gender reaffirms my approach to my non-binaryness."[41] They cite Shanna Collins's *Medium* article "The Splendor of Gender Non-Conformity in Africa," which also describes gender identity as a spiritual frequency, something that is "purely energetic" and vibrates between and across male and female, similar to Nuñez's earlier description.[42] Now, by the comic's conclusion, the reader can appreciate that when Nuñez notes that they are "influenced by these energies," they are not spouting some New Age nonsense but are situating their nonbinaryness within a Black diasporic lineage, one that is in conversation with Indigenous epistemologies and forms of embodiment.[43] These Black and Indigenous genealogies are drawn together, in part, through colonialism. They note that "due to colonialism, LGBTQ rights and gender nonconformity have been criminalized in many nations across the globe," a recognition of the global reach of trans- and homophobia that also subtly points to how shared experiences of colonialism create the very conditions that give rise to a Black and Brown commons.[44] In the top-left panel of the final page of the comic, Nuñez sits at their computer—doing their homework to unlearn the colonial myth of the gender binary and, in doing so, uncovering the decolonial histories of Black and Indigenous peoples that model alternative ways of being and being together. Yet even as Nuñez points the reader to various texts throughout the comic to deepen their understanding of gender nonconformity, Nuñez themself acts as the primary text, placing the autobiographical comic within a tradition of Latina and Black feminist writings that position lived experience as the stuff of theory, such as Cherríe Moraga and Gloria Anzaldúa's *This Bridge Called My Back* (1981), Anzaldúa's *Borderlands / La Frontera* (1987), Audre Lorde's biomythography *Zami: A New Spelling of My Name* (1982), and Conceição Evaristo's escrevivências.[45]

Nuñez's "How Do You Translate Non-Binary?" ends with a cringeworthy moment that reveals both the limitations and possibilities of queer translation. As García Peña says of translation, it "presents us with the possibility of *seeing* the Other" in "an act of recognition that can contra*dict* hegemonic knowledge."[46] In the final moments of the comic, however, this possibility of recognition is denied as the "cis-hetero-lady" therapist crowds out Nuñez's understanding of their nonbinaryness with her own, an anxious speech act (or balloon) that imposes itself on Nuñez who turns their face toward the reader in an exaggerated cringe. Sadly, while Nuñez—as author, artist, narrator, translator, and subject—has an intimate understanding of their own fluid and fluctuating gender expression, their effort to translate this experience to their therapist ends in a failure of understanding. Nuñez's nonbinaryness is ultimately untranslatable. This conclusion is sharp with the very real pain of misrecognition, tinged with the therapist's willful ignorance and failed allyship. At the same time, this moment of misrecognition speaks to the way that queerness refuses to translate itself into traditional discursive and representational forms. Nuñez's exaggerated cringe refuses a celebratory conclusion; instead, it makes visible what Leticia Alvarado describes as the ambivalent belonging of "Latinidad's abject otherness."[47] By mapping a collective of Black, Indigenous, and queer ways of being within Latinidad, Nuñez embraces this abject otherness to draw together (quite literally on the page) "a collectivity with and through the incommensurable."[48]

Picturing the Intersections of Race and Place in "Once Upon a Time, I Wanted to Be a Photographer"

Nuñez's webcomic "Once Upon a Time, I Wanted to Be a Photographer" (2021) dramatizes the ways in which comics give creative form to the author's queer translations, translocal experiences, and intersectional identities. On their website, Nuñez introduces the work as "a short experimental memoir comic about understanding why I imagined myself being a photographer, but found myself being in love with memoir and diary comics."[49] The comic was commissioned by Visibles, a Guatemala-based organization that works to create queer community, support queer storytelling, and fight for LGBTQIA+ rights within public discourse and policy throughout Central America and its diasporas.[50] In an effort to connect with multilingual readers across the United States and Central America, the comic was published in both Spanish and English. Like with "How Do You Translate Non-Binary?," which was published with *The Nib*, "Once Upon a Time" was published as part of a collective that uses comic art as a political tool and works to highlight marginalized stories.

"Once Upon a Time" is a neon-colored meta-memoir that examines how visual culture, specifically photography and comic art, helps Nuñez construct their identity and grounds them in a sense of place, or rather places. Drawing themself with a nostalgic polaroid camera for a head, Nuñez connects the technology of the camera to the form of comics. After opening with the titular invocation, "Once upon a time, I wanted to be a photographer," they describe the camera as "acting as a conduit between my eyes and these places I found myself returning," their multiple homes of Antigua, Guatemala; the El Sereno neighborhood in Los Angeles, California; and Santa Ana, El Salvador.[51] Nuñez's photographic metaphor blends machine and body to viscerally visualize the artist's own personal archive within the longer colonial histories of their homes as they move between and among them. Against a backdrop of palm trees, Nuñez confesses, "Home is a tricky word for me sometimes. I never stayed in one place. And I kind of come from many places."[52] The skyline of palm trees is evocative of the trickiness of home for those who have been impacted by the flows of colonialism and capitalism. In the U.S. West, there is only one species of native palm, the California palm or *Washingtonia filifera*.[53] Other palm species, including the most iconic, the coconut palm, are not native to the Americas but were introduced through a process of ecological imperialism intended to modify the landscape to conform to the colonial (and neocolonial) gaze.[54] Considering the iconic value of palm trees, Juan Martin Dabezies points out, "Although palms are natural elements, their current special distribution, their ornamental use and their iconography are acts of enunciation of space and the collective imaginary."[55] Nuñez leans into this collective imaginary, using the visual iconicity of the palm trees—which punctuate the landscapes of California and Central America—to signal the "many places" they come from and to theorize the transnational and translocal ties (both personal and political) that connect them.

While the camera allows Nuñez to capture these places, it is through comics, not photography, that they feel they are best able to translate their experiences within them. On the next page, they pull from their backpack a handful of Polaroid pictures, the source material for the comic. As they sit down in front of their sketchbook, they inform the reader, "I realized that I needed comics to investigate who I am, without feeling forced to believe in false narratives that were imposed on my identity."[56] While the use of the camera evokes the aesthetics of documentary comics, "Once Upon a Time" is more firmly housed within the tradition of confessional diary comics. Through Nuñez's camera lens eye, the reader follows them not from the objective distance of documentary but through their own intimate account, a first-person perspective. The visual motif of the camera as head, which is sustained until the final panel of the comic, suggests that the camera is a conduit not simply for seeing but also for thinking. Similar to how Nuñez's own embodied experience was the source text for "How Do You Translate Non-Binary?," in "Once Upon a Time" Nuñez blends diary and documentary forms through their own body: their head transformed into a camera with a cyclops lens that captures images and spits them out of a mechanical mouth. This motif is illustrative of what Zeb Tortorici, theorizing archiving as a metaphorical form of digestion, describes as "the visceral archives of the body."[57] This visceral approach to archival processes "explore[s] the fraught (and anachronistic) relations between past and present, archive and document, historian and witness, writer and written of, consumer and consumed."[58] The image of the camera as head suggests that the photographs Nuñez represents in the comic were spit from their own mouth, a regurgitation that reverses the fraught relations that Tortorici describes. Nuñez is artist, archivist, and archive all in one, using comics to explore their identity across time and space without the imposition of "false narratives."[59]

The comics form re-mediates the photographs of the multiple geographies that inform Nuñez's identity as the white frame of the Polaroid becomes the frame of the panel (see figure 9.3). While the photographs portray these different geographic locations in their separateness, captured by the shutter and enclosed by a spacious white gutter, the comic brings them together in the same time and place, in the spatiotemporality of the page. The way that Nuñez's social locations, or the various axes of their identity, intersect and diverge is further illustrated through their use of the paneling in the final page of the comic, as they disrupt the neat grid of the previous pages. As Nuñez reflects on "colonialism's effort to disconnect [them] from holding onto Blackness, Central Americanness, and queerness,"[60] a thin black gutter demarcates three distinct yet interconnected triangular panels. The gutter enacts what Ariella Aïsha Azoulay, tracing the camera's ways of seeing not to its invention in 1816 but to 1492 (the date of Christopher Columbus's first colonial expedition), describes as the dividing lines of the imperial shutter—in time, in space, and in the body politic.[61]

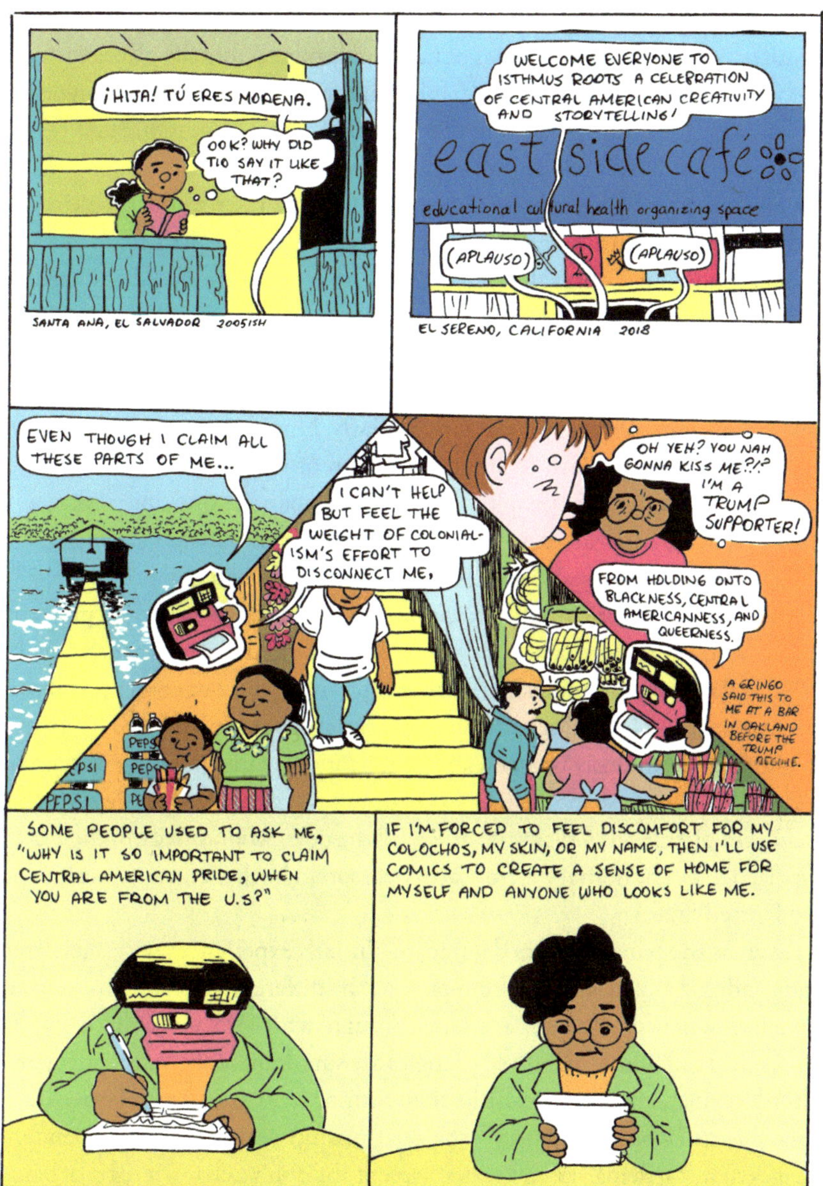

FIGURE 9.3 Nuñez illustrates the intersections of place and identity through the interconnected yet independent triangular panels. Breena Nuñez, "Once Upon a Time, I Wanted to Be a Photographer" (2021), accessed August 7, 2023, https://www.breenache.com/#/new-gallery/.

Nuñez illustrates the ways in which these colonial divisions continue to manifest, particularly along lines of race and gender across the places they call home. Nuñez animates a "photograph" that pictures themself in Santa Ana, El Salvador, in 2005, by adding speech balloons and thought bubbles (see figure 9.3). As they sit reading on a balcony, someone yells up to them, "¡Hija! Tú eres morena," a racialized term often used to refer to darker-skinned, Indigenous, and Afro-descended Latin American and Latinx people that caries ambiguous and ambivalent meanings.[62] It is sometimes used as a term of endearment, as suggested with its proximity to "¡Hija!," yet is still tinged with anti-Blackness. Nuñez's portrayal of this quotidian encounter with anti-Blackness reveals how notions of mestizaje and Latinidad are shaped by coloniality and White supremacy.[63] Similarly, Nuñez represents what Moya Bailey terms misogynoir, or the intersection of racism and sexism against Black women and queer people,[64] that runs rampant in the United States in a panel that recounts an experience in which a drunk "Gringo" "Trump supporter" sexually harasses them, asking, "Oh yeh? You nah gonna kiss me?!?"[65] By naming the political affiliations and racial identity of the perpetrator, Nuñez notes how experiences of gendered and sexual violence are shaped by racialized power dynamics and political discourse. (It is not coincidental that the man supports a politician who made racist comments about Latinx im/migrants and famously bragged about nonconsensually grabbing women by the genitals.) In these moments, Nuñez draws on and from their own visceral archive to picture the violent ruptures and the open wounds within their lived experience as a nonbinary Afro-Latinx person in both Central America and the United States.

Even as the panel borders demarcate Nuñez's experiences with racialized and gendered violence, they also represent the different axes of their intersectional experience, creating a prism through which to view the different places they call home. The three triangles are simultaneously independent and interdependent in a relationship that comics scholar Thierry Groensteen describes as "iconic solidarity": the relationship between "interdependent images that, participating in a series, present the double characteristic of being separated . . . and which are plastically and semantically over-determined by the fact of their coexistence *in praesentia*."[66] While all of the triangular panels work independently, enclosing distinct scenes from different times and places, they also coexist, coming together to create a kaleidoscopic rectangular panel. The three triangular panels are connected by Nuñez's camera head, which interrupts and disrupts the divisions of the gutter as it snaps and spits out photographs, presumably of the scenes represented within the comic. The speech balloons that emanate from Nuñez's camera mouth create a textual link between the panels, as Nuñez critically reflects on their relationship to these different parts of themself. Just as the comic moves between and across different geographic locations, it also moves readers in and out of different visual perspectives, picturing Nuñez's first-person visual perspective in some panels and viewing them from a distance in others; these shifts in perspective mimic the situatedness of positionality. The iconic solidarity between the panels speaks to the sense of solidarity that Nuñez forges between their geographic locations—Guatemala, El Salvador, and California—and their social locations—their "Blackness, Central Americanness, and queerness."[67] While anti-Blackness, coloniality, cissexism, and heteronormativity attempt to divide the different aspects of Nuñez's identity by turning them into oppositional categories, Nuñez braids them together—each element indivisible from the whole.

In their movements across multiple geographies, their strategic use of perspective and positionality, and their resistance to colonial paradigms, Nuñez enacts an intersectional comics aesthetics. Positioning comics as "a distinctly queer mode of cultural production," Ramzi Fawaz and Darieck Scott see the potential for intersectional analysis built into the comics form itself, through "the literal intersection of lines, images, and bodies on the page."[68] In "Once Upon a Time," the comics form is both the subject of the comic, which traces Nuñez's move away from photography toward cartooning, and its methodology. Through comics, Nuñez comes into a deeper understanding of their intersectional experiences and manifests, or rather "tranifests,"[69] what Chela Sandoval describes as a differential consciousness, a mode of coalitional politics that interweaves varying oppositional ideologies to find "new modes of resistance."[70] In the comic's final panel, Nuñez extends this consciousness into community. As their head returns to its human form, they look down at their sketchbook, stating, "If I'm forced to feel discomfort for my colochos, my skin, or my name, then I'll use comics to create a sense of home for myself and anyone who looks like me."[71] In "Once Upon a Time, I Wanted to Be a Photographer," comics do not necessarily help Nuñez translate their identity but, rather, facilitate the forging of community—a Brown commons that attends to social differences and violences while glimpsing moments of connection and solidarity. Nuñez, as the camera, archive, and artist, looks to comics to construct "a sense of home"—a place of belonging where the different aspects of their identity do not necessarily cohere into a monolithic whole but are housed together, in all their complexity and conflict, under the same roof.

Conclusion: Speaking "Africanismos" to Voice Queer Afro-Latinx Experiences

In their zine *Speak Africanismos* (2021), self-published with Laneha House, a small press that Nuñez runs with their partner and fellow cartoonist Lawrence Lindell, Nuñez explores Spanish words with West African origins through single-panel cartoons. The single-panel cartoons rely primarily on images with sparse verbal text (mostly labeling, speech balloons, and thought bubbles) to create humor, instruct readers, and offer a critical commentary that draws on the traditions of both editorial cartoons and children's picture books. In the cartoon for "Banana," for instance, a pile of chocolate-covered bananas states that it is "here to make y'all feel closer to the motherland" in the foreground of a sign for "Mitchell's Ice Cream," a San Francisco landmark.[72] To what homeland the bananas refer exactly is unclear if not impossible to identify. Because the name banana has West African origins, it could refer to Africa, but as Latin America is a major producer of bananas (behind Asia and followed by Africa), it could also refer to it.[73] Historically, bananas link Nuñez's two motherlands, as Portuguese colonizers brought bananas from Africa to the Americas. While the bananas evoke these multiple motherlands simultaneously, they are also associated with another place—San Francisco's Mitchell's Ice Cream, a visual calling card in which Nuñez proudly identifies themself as a Bay Area cartoonist. Just as they do in their original comic in this collection, Nuñez explores multiple homelands or motherlands and brings Black and Latinx diasporic routes of migration into relief in the span of a single panel.[74]

In *Speak Africanismos*, Nuñez does not teach readers how to speak, or translate, Africanismos. Instead, they draw out the cross-continental, diasporic entanglements of language as a way of reflecting on Afro-Latinx histories. As the panel for "Chamba" (work) makes clear, the way in which Nuñez chooses to translate these experiences is through comics. In their autobiographical comics, Nuñez explores gender on and beyond the spectrum, disrupting dominant discourses of gender to embrace the spiritual experience of their nonbinaryness. Yet, even as their exploration of gender is grounded in their own lived experience, they also situate it within a longer genealogy of gender nonconformity that centers and celebrates contemporary māhū, muxe, and fa'afāfine activists, creating a translocal and transnational Black and Brown commons. Ultimately, the visual language of comics provides Nuñez with a representational framework for moving between and across the multiple places they call home and for understanding various intersections that shape their experience as a queer Afro-Latinx person within those locales. These creative and conceptual movements ask us to queer our understandings of Latinidad and to attend to the spiritual, the local, and, indeed, the untranslatable experiences that have been marginalized therein.

Notes

1 Héctor Domínguez Ruvalcaba, *Translating the Queer: Body Politics and Transnational Conversations* (London: Zed Books, 2016), 5.
2 Ruvalcaba, *Translating the Queer*, 4.
3 Francisco J. Galarte, *Brown Trans Figurations: Rethinking Race, Gender, and Sexuality in Chicanx/Latinx Studies* (Austin: University of Texas Press, 2021), 12.
4 Galarte, *Brown Trans Figurations*, 12.
5 Sonia E. Alvarez, "Introduction to the Project and the Volume: Enacting a Translocal Feminist Politics of Translation," in *Translocalities/Translocalidades: Feminist Politics of Translation in the Latin/a Américas*," ed. Sonia E. Alvarez, Claudia De Lima Costa, Verónica Feliu, Rebecca J. Hester, and Millie Thayer (Durham, NC: Duke University Press, 2014), 1–18, 1.
6 Lorgia García Peña, *Translating Blackness: Latinx Colonialities in Global Perspective* (Durham, NC: Duke University Press, 2022), 7.
7 José Esteban Muñoz describes "disidentification" as a strategy of survival developed by queer people of color that opts for neither assimilation nor strict opposition but instead works within and against dominant power structures. José Esteban Muñoz, *Disidentifications: Queers of Color and the Performance of Politics* (Minneapolis: University of Minnesota Press, 1999), 11.
8 At this time, Nuñez uses both "she" and "they" pronouns. For the sake of clarity, I use the singular "they" to refer to Nuñez throughout this chapter.
9 Breena Nuñez, "About," accessed August 7, 2023, https://www.breenache.com/about.
10 Breena Nuñez, *Half and Half: One*, accessed August 7, 2023, https://www.breenache.com/#/half-n-half/.
11 Alvarez, "Introduction," 8.
12 Alvarez, "Introduction," 8.
13 I abbreviate the title to "Once Upon a Time" from here on.
14 Ruvalcaba, *Translating the Queer*, 5.
15 Breena Nuñez, "How Do You Translate Non-Binary?," in *Be Gay, Do Comics! Queer History, Memoir, and Satire*, ed. Matt Bors (San Diego: IDW, 2020), 48–50, 48.
16 "About *The Nib*," *The Nib*, July 24, 2019, https://thenib.com/about/.
17 Sadly, in August 2023 *The Nib* shut down, citing "the rising cost of paper and postage, the changing landscape of social media, subscription exhaustion, inflation, and the simple difficulty of keeping a small independent publishing project alive with relatively few resources." "The Future of the Nib," *The Nib*, May 22, 2023, https://thenib.com/the-future-of-the-nib/.
18 Myriam Díaz-Diocaretz, *Translating Poetic Discourse: Questions of Feminist Strategies in Adrienne Rich* (Amsterdam: John Benjamins, 1985), 8.
19 Nuñez, "How Do You Translate Non-Binary?," 48.

20 While I do not explore the comic as a work of graphic medicine in the scope of this chapter, it is an important representation of barriers to access and potentials for harm within mental health care for queer people of color, particularly given its publication during the COVID-19 pandemic, which disproportionately affected Black and Latinx communities.

21 Nuñez, "How Do You Translate Non-Binary?," 48, emphasis added.

22 María Lugones, "Toward a Decolonial Feminism," *Hypatia* 25, no. 4 (2010): 743–744.

23 Ruvalcaba, *Translating the Queer*, 24. In his discussion of colonial translations of Indigenous ways of knowing and naming sexuality, Ruvalcaba turns to the following example: "the word *xochihua*, which in Nahuatl would mean literally 'the flower bearer,' in the *Florentine Codex* was translated as *puto* (f-ggot)" (Ruvalcaba, *Translating the Queer*, 24). This turn to the Nahuatl language to theorize queer Latinx ways of being connects Ruvalcaba to Anzaldúa and her conceptualization of "nepantla."

24 Gloria E. Anzaldúa, Simon J. Ortiz, Inéz Hernández-Avila, and Domino Perez, "Speaking across the Divide," *Studies in American Indian Literatures* 15, no. 3/4 (2003): 7–22, 17. As contributor Katlin Marisol Sweeney-Romero points out, some Latinx and Indigenous studies scholars have critiqued Anzaldúa's use of "nepantla" for separating the term from its historical and epistemological origins in Nahuatl language and philosophy. See Sweeney-Romero's chapter in this collection; and Marcos de R. Antuna, "What We Talk About When We Talk About Nepantla: Glora Anzaldúa and the Queer Fruit of Aztec Philosophy," *Journal of Latinos and Education* 17, no. 2 (2018): 159–163.

25 Hannah Miodrag, *Comics and Language: Reimagining Critical Discourse on the Form* (Jackson: University Press of Mississippi, 2013), 88.

26 Gloria E. Anzaldúa, "Preface: Gestures of the Body—Escribiendo para idear," in *Light in the Dark / Luz en lo Oscuro: Rewriting Identity, Spirituality, Reality*, ed. Analouise Keating (Durham, NC: Duke University Press, 2015), 1–8, 2.

27 For more on the mainstreaming and narrowing of the queer movement's intersectional origins, see Roderick A. Ferguson, *One-Dimensional Queer* (Medford, MA: Polity, 2018).

28 Nuñez, "How Do You Translate Non-Binary?," 48.

29 Nuñez, "How Do You Translate Non-Binary?," 48, emphasis added.

30 Jennifer Carolina Gómez Menjívar and Héctor Nicolás Ramos Flores, "Introduction: A Black Transcontinental Movement for the Future," in *Hemispheric Blackness and the Exigencies of Accountability*, ed. Gómez Menjívar and Ramos Flores (Pittsburgh: University of Pittsburgh Press, 2023), 3–21, 6–7.

31 Nuñez, "How Do You Translate Non-Binary?," 48. Interestingly, it is unlikely that Nuñez's therapist would have disclosed her gender and sexuality to her client, so the identification of "cis-hetero lady" suggests the therapist is an archetypal stand-in rather than identifies their gender and sexuality with certainty.

32 Johanna M. Schmidt, "Translating Transgender: Using Western Discourses to Understand Samoan fa'afāfine," *Sociology Compass* 11 (2017): 1–17, 2.

33 While Muñoz does not capitalize the "brown commons," I do in order to emphasize Brown as a racialized and politicized term that names a collective of various races and ethnicities while recognizing its potential to elide differences. See Kristen Mack and John Palfrey, "Capitalizing Black and White: Grammatical Justice and Equity"

(MacArthur Foundation, August 26, 2020), https://www.macfound.org/press/perspectives/capitalizing-black-and-white-grammatical-justice-and-equity.
34 José Esteban Muñoz, *The Sense of Brown*, ed. Joshua Chambers-Letson and Tavia Nyong'o (Durham, NC: Duke University Press, 2020), 2.
35 Muñoz, *Sense of Brown*, 3.
36 Muñoz, *Sense of Brown*, 4.
37 Schmidt, "Translating Transgender," 6.
38 Nuñez, "How Do You Translate Non-Binary?," 49.
39 Nuñez, "How Do You Translate Non-Binary?," 49.
40 Maylei Blackwell, "*Translenguas*: Mapping the Possibilities and Challenges of Transnational Women's Organizing across Geographies of Difference," in Alvarez et al., *Translocalities/Translocalidades*, 299–320, 301.
41 Nuñez, "How Do You Translate Non-Binary?," 50.
42 Shanna Collins, "The Splendor of Gender Non-Conformity In Africa," *Medium*, October 9, 2017, https://medium.com/@janelane_62637/the-splendor-of-gender-non-conformity-in-africa-f894ff5706e1.
43 These intersections of Blackness and Indigeneity within and across the Americas should bring to mind the influence of Garifuna peoples. While, to my knowledge, Nuñez has never identified themself as Garifuna, they explore Garifuna histories within Central America and in relation to their experience as an Afro-Salvadoran-Guatemalan in their comic "I Exist!" Breena Nuñez, "I Exist!," *The Nib*, February 19, 2020, https://thenib.com/afro-salvadoran-identity/.
44 Nuñez, "How Do You Translate Non-Binary?," 50.
45 *Escrevivências*, a term coined by Evaristo, is a portmanteau of *escrita* (writing) and *vivência* (lived experience). In their introduction titled "*Cuir*/Queer Américas: Translation, Decoloniality, and the Incommensurable" to their special issue of *GLQ: A Journal of Lesbian and Gay Studies*, Joseph M. Pierce, María Amelia Viteri, Diego Falconí Trávez, Slavador Vidal-Ortiz, and Lourdes Martínez-Echazábal name women of color escrevivências as "one of the most important lines of thought" in a what they call "the *contrapunteo cuir*," or contrapuntal queer, within the Americas. See Pierce et al., "Introduction: *Cuir*/Queer Américas: Translation, Decoloniality, and the Incommensurable," *GLQ* 27, no. 3 (2021): 321–327, 323, 324.
46 García Peña, *Translating Blackness*, 6, emphasis original.
47 Leticia Alvarado, *Abject Performances: Aesthetic Strategies in Latino Cultural Production* (Durham, NC: Duke University Press, 2018), 23.
48 Muñoz, *Sense of Brown*, 7.
49 Breena Nuñez, "Once Upon a Time, I Wanted to Be a Photographer" (2021), accessed August 7, 2023, https://www.breenache.com/#/new-gallery/.
50 See "Nuestra organización," *Visibles*, accessed August 7, 2023, https://visibles.gt/acercade/.
51 Nuñez, "Once Upon a Time."
52 Nuñez, "Once Upon a Time."
53 See Miriam L. Bomhard, *Palm Trees in the United States* (Washington, DC: U.S. Department of Agriculture, Forest Service, 1963), https://archive.org/details/CAT87210867.
54 Analyzing palm trees within contemporary Uruguay, Juan Martin Dabezies examines the role they play not only within the neocolonial tourism industry but also within the visual systems and cultural imaginary of the nation. See Dabezies,

"Visuality, Palm Trees and Tourism in Uruguay: Between Tropical and Traditional Representations," *Annals of Tourism Research* 81 (2020): 1–12.
55 Dabezies, "Visuality, Palm Trees and Tourism in Uruguay," 2.
56 Nuñez, "Once Upon a Time."
57 Zeb Tortorici, "Visceral Archives of the Body: Consuming the Dead, Digesting the Divine," *GLQ: A Journal of Lesbian and Gay Studies* 20, no. 4 (2014): 407–437, 407.
58 Tortorici, "Visceral Archives of the Body," 409.
59 Nuñez also acts as archivist by making this webcomic, along with several others, freely available on their website.
60 Nuñez, "Once Upon a Time."
61 Ariella Aïsha Azoulay, *Potential History: Unlearning Imperialism* (New York: Verso Books, 2019), 5.
62 Nuñez also explores this language in their comic "They Call Me Morena . . . For a Reason" in which they question, "Can I even claim AfroLatinx as part of my identity even though the anti-Blackness runs deep in our history? Was queerness always there too? Who are you foo?" Breena Nuñez, "They Call Me Morena . . . For a Reason," in *Tales from La Vida: A Latinx Comics Anthology*, ed. Frederick Luis Aldama (Columbus, OH: Mad Creek Books, 2018), 20–21.
63 Tanya Katerí Hernández, for instance, notes that "many Latina/o scholars have been content to focus on *mestizaje*-pride without thoroughly interrogating its subtext of white supremacy." Hernández, "Afro-Latinas/os," in *Keywords for Latina/o Studies*, ed. Debora R. Bargas, Nancy Raquel Mirabel, and Lawrence La Fountain-Stokes (New York: New York University Press, 2017), 7–9, 8. Tatiana Flores offers a comprehensive review of how the term "Latinidad" and its cognates, including "Latina/o/x," have come under attack as an anti-Black construct by Afro-Latinx activists and artists. Flores, "'Latinidad Is Cancelled': Confronting an Anti-Black Construct," *Latin American and Latinx Visual Culture* 3, no. 3 (2021): 58–79. Jennifer A. Jones similarly critiques the way that Latinidad excludes Blackness and upholds White supremacy while also asking, "What would it mean to think of *Latinidad* as proximate to and/or inclusive of Blackness?" Jones, "Blackness, Latinidad, and Minority Linked Fate," in *Critical Dialogues in Latinx Studies: A Reader*, ed. Ana Y. Ramos-Zayas and Mérida M. Rúa (New York: New York University Press, 2021), 425–437, 425.
64 "Misogynoir" was initially coined and theorized by Moya Bailey. The term participates in a long genealogy of Black feminist thought that critiques how racism, sexism and cissexism, and heteronormativity collude. See Bailey and Trudy, "On Misogynoir: Citation, Erasure, and Plagiarism," *Feminist Media Studies* 18, no. 4 (2018): 762–768.
65 Nuñez, "Once Upon a Time."
66 Thierry Groensteen, *The System of Comics*, trans. Bart Beaty and Nick Nguyen (Jackson: University Press of Mississippi, 2007), 18.
67 Nuñez, "Once Upon a Time."
68 Ramzi Fawaz and Darieck Scott, "Queer," in *Keywords for Comics Studies*, ed. Ramzi Fawaz Shelley Streeby, and Deborah Elizabeth Whaley (New York: New York University Press, 2021), 172.
69 Drawing on the experimental lexicon of "black radical warriors/healers," Kai M. Green and Treva Ellison theorize "tranifest" as an action verb that means "to mobilize across the contradictions, division, and containment strategies produced by the state and other such large-scale organizations of power that work to limit our

capacity to align ourselves across difference in ways that are necessary for social transformation." Green and Ellison, "Tranifest," *TSQ: Transgender Studies Quarterly* 1, no. 1–2 (2014): 222–225, 222.

70 Chela Sandoval, *Methodology of the Oppressed* (Minneapolis: University of Minnesota Press, 2000), 153.

71 Nuñez, "Once Upon a Time."

72 Breena Nuñez, *Speak Africanismos* (Oakland, CA: Laneha House, 2021), n.p.

73 "All About Bananas and Why Bananas Matter," *Banana Link*, accessed August 7, 2023, https://www.bananalink.org.uk/all-about-bananas/.

74 See Breena Nuñez's contribution to this collection, "This Body Is Actually Unsettled."

This Body Is Actually Unsettled

• • • • • • • • • • • • • •

BREENA NUÑEZ

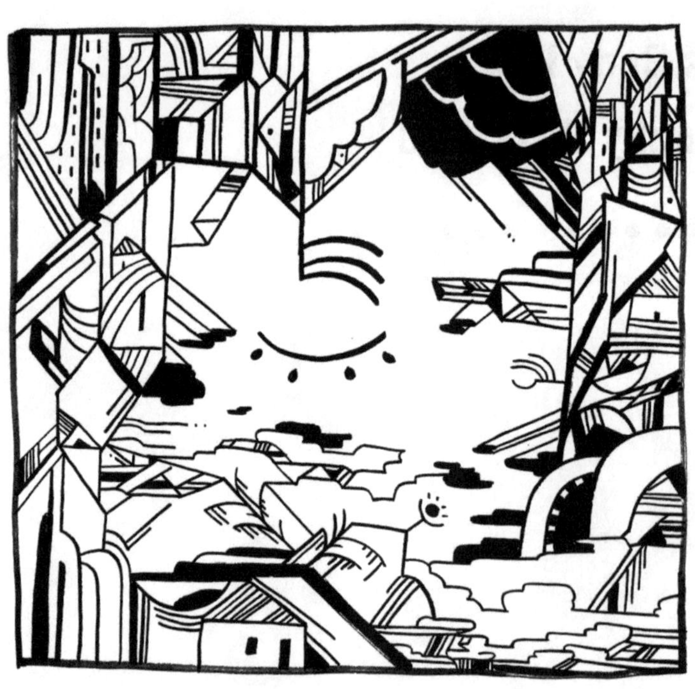

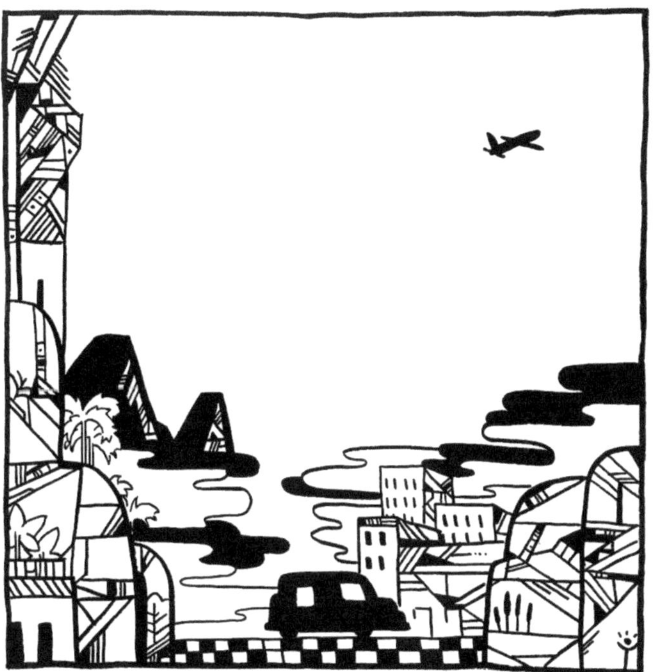

two paths leading to de eunaited estates

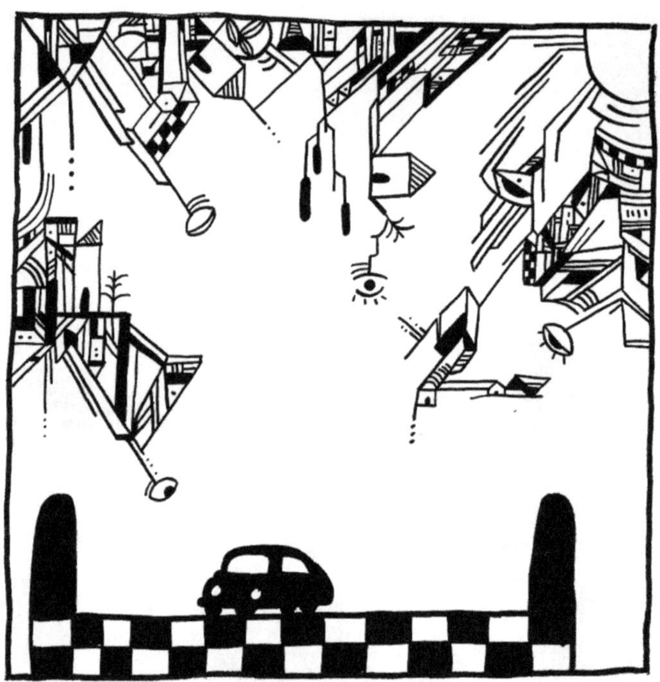

lead me to my privilege of having nomadic sensibilities

Part IV

Practices of Placemaking

10

Caribbean Urban Belonging

• • • • • • • • • • • • • •

Thinking Paradoxes of Citizenship with Independent Puerto Rican Comics

FERNANDA DÍAZ-BASTERIS

Rosaura Rodríguez and Omar Banuchi—two Boricuas born and raised in the island and formally trained in literature, visual arts, and teaching education—created the independent comic art collective Días Cómic in 2011. I argue that their local, independent graphic narratives shape a wide variety of meanings in relation to citizenship. Through comics, zines, magazines, and anthologies, they materialize belonging within the urban Caribbean landscape. Días Cómic creates a discursive platform of affects that recognizes Puerto Rico's problematic relationship to the United States and the nuances of an imposed American citizenship. With this chapter I propose Banuchi and Rodríguez's comics as a Caribbean urban aesthetic that constitutes a testimonial, popular, artisanal, and independent graphic archive of the metropolitan area of San Juan. By visualizing and documenting areas of the tropical city through its materialized affects, these independent comics are reacting against the dehumanizing U.S. colonial agenda. Archiving the urban landscape with this medium prevents erasure in the collective Puerto Rican memory; it is an active work of memorizing and memorializing what will be displaced and forgotten in the increasingly gentrified tropical, whitewashed future. Días Cómic embodies the tropical colonial city from within, from its fragile ruins to its gentrified zones, unwrapping the spontaneity of urban life in the Global South, making connections with the diasporic Latinx gaze in the United States and with multiple urban-centered experiences portrayed in Latin American comics of the twentieth and twenty-first centuries.

When reading and teaching Caribbean comics, I ask, which narratives remain inside the island? How are comics funded to stay independent? How do these visual products circulate within multilingual, multiethnic Caribbean communities? Why is it important to teach representation of affects, citizenship, and belonging through visual storytelling? This chapter started in 2017, after my last long stay in San Juan. Over the years I developed several sections. I start explaining my relationality to comics and *caribeñidad*, as well as my positionality regarding my Mexican citizenship and my Caribbean belonging to the Latinx diaspora. Using the concept of "fragile city" and looking at interactive digital maps, I tell how coastal urban communities experience an accelerated, disorganized, violent, and disserving development that leaves residents with few options but to alienate, fight back, or migrate.[1] I complement my observations with some examples of my pedagogical praxis when using Días Cómic's comics as a narrative tool to discuss urban autobiographical stories from artists that are fighting to stay in their fragile cities and hold public institutions accountable for their lack of care. By incorporating multimodal narratives, diverse testimonies, and digital techniques, Caribbean independent comics have positioned themselves as strong popular products in the visual market and international media as well as for academic research. The collaborative autobiographical medium shared by Rodríguez and Banuchi depicts a nonfictional narrative of the city within an "external reality that can be verified."[2] I'm hoping with this chapter to present scholars in the United States with a growing independent Puerto Rican graphic narrative archive,[3] with the intention of documenting mediated personal stories of tropical urban spaces as part of twenty-first-century Caribbean/ Latinx cultural visual works of resistance.

My Caribbean Urban Belonging: Thinking Paradoxes of Citizenship

The comics I analyze in this chapter center the city of San Juan as a narrative space for its inhabitants to reflect about urban collective participation within the colony. Instead of creating a discourse of a coastal touristic paradise, the fictionalized Taino past, or the predicted fantastic Westernized future, Días Cómic's products decolonize the American-created Caribbean imaginary through the depiction of precarious urban spaces and their affects. In *Visible Cities, Global Comics* Benjamin Fraser proposes what I would like to extend in this essay: "The key question is whether the city is imagined as a space for urbanites to use and enjoy, or whether it is a mere tool in cycles of capitalist reproduction and profit."[4] The Spanish-speaking Caribbean cities such as San Juan in Puerto Rico, Santo Domingo in the Dominican Republic, Mérida and Cancún in the Yucatán Peninsula, Belmopan in Belize, Cartagena and Barranquilla in Colombia, and many others are enclaves of fighting forces, where local resilience is built against climate change, touristic speculation, and government corruption.

As a Mexican citizen belonging to the multilingual multiethnic Caribbean community and currently living in the Latinx diaspora, I'm drawn to the ways that nonfictional Puerto Rican comics help me discuss and articulate the cultural meanings and challenges of my constrained citizenship, the affects and relations of my Caribbean urban belonging, and my academic positionality as a Latinx/Ethnic studies professor. Before identifying as Mexican, I consider myself Caribbean.[5] Different racial ethnicities were part of my upbringing in the Yucatán. I grew up inside the coastal city surrounded by Lebanese, Chinese, Maya, Anglo-White American, and European communities; therefore, I am critical of a single-nation Mexican state citizenship based on White proximity and idyllic mestizaje even as I must participate in it.[6] This regional sense of belonging is not only mine but also part of the historical idiosyncrasy of the Yucatán Peninsula. Scholars at the Universidad Autónoma de Yucatán (UADY) explain the paradox between Mexican citizenship and Caribbean belonging as part of the premature cartography that positioned the Yucatán as separate from the rest of the nation; the peninsula was imagined as an island in 1532.[7] Later, during the nineteenth century, local governments founded (twice!) the Hermana República de Yucatán, which existed until 1848. Once the Centralist Republic of Mexico became the Estados Unidos Mexicanos and the White European settlers in the Yucatán required federal military assistance to end la Guerra de Castas, the Maya led revolts against the *hacendados*, criollos, or the so-called children of Spaniards.[8] While researching at the UADY, I explored these Yucatecan cultural claim contradictions within Mexican citizenship as well as Puerto Rican cultural identity within American citizenship: both coexisting alongside Maya and Taino heritage and imposed colonial languages, social classism, and racial structures. I developed my academic positionality through constant exposure to Caribbean scholarship, literature, and music in Spanish, French, and English. Throughout my academic journey I have done several research trips to different cities in México, the United States, the Dominican Republic, Cuba, and Puerto Rico in search of independent comics.

According to Evelyn Nakano Glenn, citizenship is continually constituted and challenged through political struggle, thus citizenship and belonging are not interchangeable but connected. Citizenship is "a matter of belonging,"[9] and communities decide the boundaries of their citizenship. The internationally known Mexican state symbolic icons do not represent me.[10] When I must self-identify, I do it with the memory of my nervous system collapsing in the humid lowland rainforest of the Yucatán or of the skin-burning heat while riding public transportation through chaotic local traffic with nonexistent urban planning. My Caribbean belonging is connected to cumbias and the joy of watching pitaya plants grow on downtown roofs made of concrete in 120°F temperatures. I know I'm Caribbean when I feel sad about forgetting the facade of an abandoned vacant building where a new boutique hotel has suddenly emerged. My caribeñidad refers to local, affordable Lebanese street food during a baseball game night; layers of paint stripping off from the colonial Mérida city walls resembling La Habana, Santo Domingo, or San Juan historic/colonial downtown; and always talking about family struggles to pay irrational bills for Coca-Cola-owned potable water and privatized electricity while getting weekly power outages in return. As most coastal Caribbeans, I sustain endless contact and complex, even ancestral interactions with North American and European visitors, investors, and neocolonizers: the White undocumented immigrants, so-called "ex-pats."

Puerto Rican urban comics created in both Spanish and English allow me to materialize my sense of Caribbean belonging and activate the limits of my Mexican citizenship. Through engaging with the nonfiction graphic narratives of Días Cómic, I understand overlapping connections among the island and the Yucatán Peninsula; I experience nostalgia, hope, and joy in conscious political participation through the ins and outs of my caribeñidad.

Caribbean Urban Autobiographical Belonging: A Decade Amplifying Everyday Life

Caribbean and Latinx ontologies can be understood as parallel frameworks whose meanings overlap citizenship, diaspora, and belonging. In her book *LatinX*, Claudia Milian explains in what way "LatinX" echoes a sociocultural and political experience of belonging to a colonized Global South; each Latinx community "navigates and handles the ontological category differently."[11] Consecutively, established Caribbean scholars in the United States have registered how local, diasporic, and transnational Caribbean experiences can merge broad ethnicities and cultural practices embodied in literary works and photographic/visual archives.[12] Therefore, multiple forces, attachments, or what are called affects occur when materializing Caribbean and Latinx belonging. Telling personal stories through comics can both complicate and interrogate the category of citizenship and create meanings of belonging with others who may be grappling with similar collective issues. During my investigations in Puerto Rico in 2015, 2017, and 2019, I found, for the first time, a comparable fragile city like Mérida (Yucatán) depicted in Rodríguez and Banuchi's comics. The Puerto Rican local independent comic's circulation and mobile boundaries allowed me to relate nonfictional local images and representations with mental snapshots and emotional descriptions of my hometown. I acquired a single-issue bundle, a set of three booklets titled *Días* volume 2, numbers 1, 2, and 3 at Mondo Bizarro, a local independent bookstore in Paseo De Diego in Río Piedras. In the now-shuttered independent café and bookstore, Libros AC in Santurce, I met the owner Samuel Medina and bought the book *Días*, which compilates volume 1, numbers I to XIII. In the following parts of this essay, I briefly document the trajectory, production, and circulation of a decade of Días Cómic's visual products from 2011 to 2021.

Banuchi and Rodríguez are well-known local artists who constantly collaborate with their local peers to put on independent art shows, comic workshops, festivals, and crafting experiences across the island. Their social interactions among the independent art circuit have situated them as comic educators and community innovators, providing them with enough real-life content to build a particular autobiographical local archive. Días Cómic started in 2011 when Rodríguez and Banuchi resided in the same neighborhood and worked in San Juan. Rosaura Rodríguez was working at a glass store before she became an art schoolteacher and began working at the Museo de Arte Contemporáneo de Puerto Rico. From 2011 to 2016, her storytelling illustrated the Puerto Rican urban experiences and real-life local characters of metro San Juan. Rodríguez's main art is handmade illustrations and organically made watercolors. She is interested in natural pigments and contemporary art experimentation. After moving out of the city in 2017, Rodríguez now focuses on the flora, wildlife, and countryside landscapes of the mountains of Jayuya and other countryside towns. In 2011, Omar Banuchi worked for the Auto Express Service Center, the Puerto Rican private highway network office in San Juan. His daily job consisted of scheduling and receiving calls concerning toll grievances and petitions from Puerto Ricans within the island. Banuchi developed the habit of digitally illustrating himself and stories of his daily life in the city and the office space. Banuchi now focuses on independent erotic art and digital illustration projects. Alongside Rosa Colón Guerra, an independent Puerto Rican comics creator who runs Soda Pop Comics, Banuchi has curated several erotic comics shows in local independent art galleries. In 2020, Rodríguez and Banuchi evolved into Días Cómic, an editorial publishing house that is dedicated to producing local graphic narratives.

Since the start, Días Cómic has existed as a homegrown endeavor outside the mainstream commercial circuit: no superheroes are depicted, and no fictional characters were created in the entire first volume (nos. I–XIII). Días Cómic's autobiographical work from 2011 to the present is an archival effort to directly engage affects with places, time, and space in Puerto Rico. The initial project, "Días," was a zine: a homemade self-publication as a black-and-white photocopy on 8.5 by 11 paper, folded in half and stapled in the middle. Each comic/zine was sold for approximately two dollars, an affordable price in a portable format. The digital newspaper *Diálogo* of the University of Puerto Rico Río Piedras also published panels from the comic on their website. The first single issues were distributed in student-oriented independent venues in Río Piedras. With this artistic technique, Rodríguez and Banuchi positioned independent comics in relation to urban space politics in San Juan. The autobiographical medium through which "a regular person emphasizes their personality and builds an intimate graphic narrative without implying any fiction" was what first attracted me to their collection in 2015.[13] Andrew

Kunka explains how autobiographical comics are central to small press comic production and not necessarily a single manufactured process: "Comics is also often a collaborative medium, much more than prose, where various duties in the creation of a text can be shared by multiple people."[14] Accordingly in Días Cómic, the writers, the narrators, the main characters, the publishers, and the distributors are all the same people: Rosaura Rodríguez and Omar Banuchi, the placemakers.

In Días Cómic's products the city is presented as a space that reflects belonging. Colonial dynamics and their affects are situated in relation to multiple impermanent urban spaces, such as work offices, bars and music venues, school classrooms, public transportation sites, streets, and sidewalks. I'm interested in how Rodríguez and Banuchi connect human passions among city dwellers. In the first page of the book *Días* (2013) the collective explains, "You have in your hands a comic that is not fundamentally intended to be funny. These are simple real-life daily stories of two individuals that sometimes turn out to be funny. We are sorry for the inconvenience."[15] The ins and outs of Caribbean urban life are investigated as the verbal narrative progresses in each volume, while the story continues chronologically in real life, from numbers I–XIII, Omar and Rosaura change jobs, outgrow relationships, travel across the United States, sustain social interactions with strangers, and progress in personal maturity. Días Cómic's verbal narrative is hyperlocal and minimal: they use language variations of Puerto Rican slang, Spanglish, and Puertoriqueño to complete the artists' personal experience reflecting on Puerto Rican collective belonging and communities' affects. Such narrative fosters knowledgeable interchange with local readers, students, University of Puerto Rico educators, comic collectors, and local commercial vendors. Banuchi and Rodríguez equally distributed their individual artistic contributions to each volume by alternating each paneled page. This way, the reader experiences two different creative styles with each turning page. In volume 1, number 1, published in 2011, Banuchi has a series of self-portraits on the even pages, and Rodríguez drew scenes of her local interactions along the walk to the train station for her daily commute on the odd pages. When teaching number 1, I emphasize how both contributions work together to bring a multifaceted visual reproduction of affects and aesthetics of the city, and I name this an "urban Caribbean belonging." I ask students to examine the formal aspects of each panel from Banuchi's self-portraits through the following close reading exercise: First, I request that students describe how panels and gutters work to shape the character's narrative in a sequence. Second, I invite students to imagine a possible Banuchi diegetic universe, focusing on space and temporality: Where is he?

When is he talking? Third, I ask the class to work in groups and discuss a couple of icons embodying ethnicity and citizenship in a tropical city space. When we study Rodríguez's panels, I ask students to focus on representations of the local community: Who are these characters? Why does their representation matter in graphic narratives from/about the city? We focus on the well-known human-size TV puppet La Comay, the local clown Remi, the feral and free-range chickens, and the dead animals on the Seventeenth Street's sidewalk. I suggest students analyze how Rodríguez and Banuchi's production speaks to their experiences with specific, significant contemporary historical events in Puerto Rico.[16] Readers can gain a multimodal experience from elsewhere than the island—the international audience in California, México, or Iowa—or else they can relate to Banuchi's life experience as a young queer Latinx, anticolonial artist, documenting their daily activities from a critical point of view inside a colony.

When I taught the book *Días* in a Latin American studies course as part of the Spanish major at the University of California, Davis, I asked students to spend time in groups identifying Rodríguez and Banuchi's different creative styles as well as the written emotions of the city depending on each story. An interesting example of combining urban belonging and autobiographical narrative is juxtaposed in figure 10.1. As the initial storytelling started in 2011, the reader finds volume 1, number 1 opening with Rodríguez's match-cutting sequence. Three small panels in horizontal order maintain transitions to each of the three scenes displaying framed panels like wood-built gutters

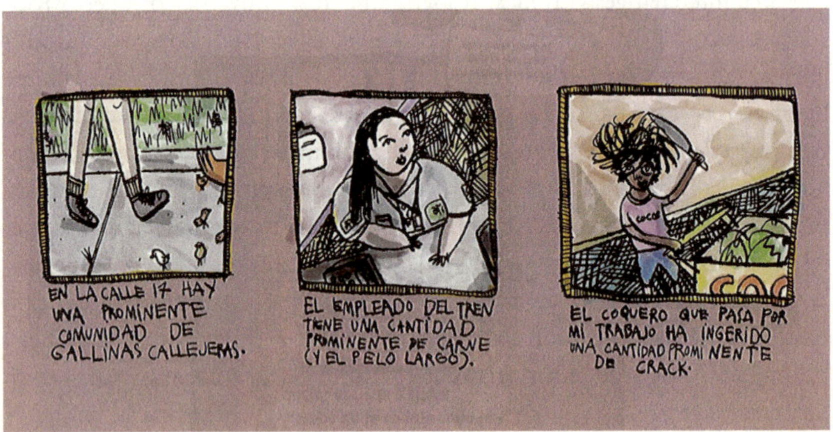

FIGURE 10.1 This opening three-panel sequence shows snapshots of scenes from San Juan's Seventeenth Street. Omar Banuchi and Rosaura Rodríguez, *Días*, vol. 1, no. 1 (2011; 2nd ed. published in color, 2016), 2.

(see figure 10.1). The brief verbal narrative below the panel's gutter is only one sentence for each snapshot. The first panel shows a close-up angle of a passerby's legs and shoes on the sidewalk of Seventeenth Street, followed by five small chickens and a hen's tail. The verbal narration reveals that "on Seventeenth Street there is a prominent community of chickens."[17] The second panel to the right features an urban train employee inside of the stall; the employee has long hair and is looking at the ceiling. The narration notes, "The train employee has a prominent amount of beef and long hair." The third and final panel of the sequence features a disturbed coconut street vendor; he is holding up a big machete with his left hand and pushing his coconut cart with his right hand. The verbal narrative keeps repeating the word "prominent": "The coconut-man passing by my work has ingested a prominent amount of crack."

The panel with the high-functioning drug addict selling coconuts depicts the iconic visual edible fruit advertised in the marketing touristic agenda as a "b side" story that is juxtaposed with airline billboards. The chickens are local icons closing the gap between the urban landscape and the small-town countryside lifestyle in Latin American and the Caribbean. The reader is invited to deconstruct stereotypes of hardworking U.S. citizens living in the San Juan metropolitan area, those who shape Caribbean urban landscapes outside the spaces curated for tourists and agendas.

Much work has been published by Latinx geographers and sociologists about the Latinx and Caribbean diaspora and urban placemaking in major U.S. cities,[18] but few comics and media studies scholars have approached independent Caribbean comics written in Spanish inside the islands that explore its complicated nomenclature and function in constructing visual belonging. According to Lok Siu, belonging is shaped not only by the relations one has with their homeland but also by the relations that developing countries in the Global South have with the United States as well as all the difficulties diasporic and immigrant communities navigate beyond formal citizenship.[19] Geographer Nicholas De Genova traces the unique historical practices of modern-state political struggles of Mexican and American citizenship. Neither citizenship was intended for non-White individuals in North America. As a parallel case to the Mexican citizenship formation, De Genova documents how the U.S. political authorities "considered Puerto Ricans to be an 'alien race'" right after the 1898 war, but it was not until 1917 when the United States "conferred citizenship upon Puerto Ricans collectively and legally abolish their prior quasi status as citizens of Puerto Rico."[20] From this perspective, fueled by my nonresident alien status in my challenged diasporic

Caribbean life in the United States, I approach Puerto Rican independent comics as a medium to express, embody, and communicate Caribbean urban belongings and their affects in the context of Latinx graphic narratives and Latin American visual storytelling. According to Kirtley, Garcia, and Carlson, "Researchers are often approaching comics instruction from different ontological perspectives."[21] I teach and write about Puerto Rican independent comics because they have fundamentally shaped my Caribbean sense of belonging, my ways of seeing and reading urban landscapes, and my belief in the cultural work and the political possibilities of grassroots art movements and collective archives of memory.

San Juan: An Illustrated Liminal Fragile City

A student once asked where to place comics from San Juan in the Latin/X American comic production, and a prolific academic discussion came out of this question. I explained the canonical comic traditions across the continent, which includes traditional twentieth-century Latin American *historietas* written and published in Spanish expected to signify nationalisms and its consumptions in developing countries of the Global South. Some examples of urban *vecindades*, equal rights criticism, and popular icons I grew up with are *La Familia Burrón*, by Mexican Gabriel Vargas; *Condorito*, created in Chile by René Pepo Ríos; and *Mafalda*, by Argentinian creator Quino. But when Días Cómic's products feature abandoned buildings, public squares, public transportation, and its social interactions, what they represent is the liminal space of a colonial coastal city and its belonging to Latin America, to the Caribbean, and to the Global South without removing their overlooked American citizenship. Días Cómic's city depictions are far from what emerging Latinx comics—published by Image Comics, Vertigo, Marvel Comics, and DC Comics—illustrate as continental cities in California, Florida, New York, Maryland, Texas, and Illinois. Instead, Días Cómic's creations reveal connections with twenty-first-century art collectives and independent artists across the Global South,[22] especially by depicting nostalgia, joy, and hope where urban landscapes, buildings, and public transportation intersect. A crucial sequential art project illustrating citizens' experiencing their cities in Colombia, Brazil, Argentina, Mexico, and Uruguay is the "Premio de Novela Gáfica Ciudades Iberoamericanas," a transatlantic graphic novel project that promotes visual expressions of affects, citizenship, and belonging beyond the nation-state master narrative. Young, independent Latin American comic artists are drawing cities across the continent and visualizing its affects to specific neighborhoods, local business, and national products. When teaching and writing about Días Cómic, I position their storytelling as part of this hemispheric tradition of urban comics.[23] These narratives amplify the collective meanings of urban landscapes across Spanish-speaking places with shared histories of colonialism. Días Cómic builds an intricate puzzle portraying San Juan from the ground, from literally the bricks of the streets in Old San Juan, the sidewalks of Río Piedras, the cats, dogs, and chickens strolling around Santurce's backstreets, and the nonfiction passersby in abandoned dusty streets. The fragile tropical city of San Juan depicted in the comics contrasts and complements urban comics from Latin American capitals such as São Paulo, Santiago de Chile, México, and Bogotá, where the urban life meets the marvelous real literary affections that accentuate its complexities.[24] Días Cómic's aesthetic constitutes a countervisual imaginary diverging from the American skyline, the Latin American *vecindad*, and the busy traffic avenues of the metropolitan superheroes' cities.

A Comic Map of San Juan: From Photocopies to Independent Comic Publishers

As I explained before, the book *Días* collects most of the printed single-issue comics between 2011 and 2013, organized from numbers I to XIII. The book reads in chronological order, like instant photographs; the series centers its attention on human expressions, public bus and train compartments, iron bars protecting houses' front doors and windows, cracked sidewalks across metropolitan areas, concrete walls and murals, hanging cables, gray office spaces, street signs, and pedestrians' shoes. The first thirteen numbers lack illustrations of coastline scenarios, which is indicative of the complexity of local Caribbean interactions; in this case, the city is the discursive space of a hybrid Latinx / Caribbean / Latin American form of belonging bordered by water.

After the book, Rodríguez and Banuchi published three short projects in magazine format. Between 2013 and 2015, they invited local artists to collaborate in creating stories about life in the city and its daily challenges. Each booklet is around twenty pages printed in full color. The same title, *Días*, is displayed on the front cover with a different design. The art collective brought these pieces together in *Días* volume 2. During those years, the collective again published a zine, number XIV, as a continuation of volume 1 that contained more autobiographical stories about their neighborhood. In a short lecture I explain to students how the expressed affect of belonging can be represented in the in-betweenness of accumulative besideness.[25] By *affect*, I understand different media practices that reveal the "felts" of everyday life, social interactions, and power structures, "how things feel, for whom, and what potential." I ask students to consider how Rodríguez and Banuchi use panels and gutters to express their bodies' capacities and sensibilities that belong in urban spaces, and I show students how these affects contradict the imposed American citizenship. Días Cómic has developed what I call a graphic map of belonging. It is fascinating how each artist's display of affects is different, yet they complement each other's storytelling.

Illustrated Hope in Puerta de Tierra's Neighborhood

For Rosaura Rodríguez, hope is an important affect through which she materializes her belonging in the urban landscape. In her autobiographical comics, she emphasizes this affect throughout narratives of community care, abandonment, and resistance. With students at UC Davis, I examined page 53 of *Días*, volume 1, number III, where Rodríguez depicts the moment, she left her job at a stained-glass store in Puerta de Tierra, a popular neighborhood in the north of the city (see figure 10.2). The verbal narrative is composed of three different paragraphs interlayered horizontally within two panels; the longest paragraph, second from the top, states that hope is a relational characteristic of such locality: "I will miss Puerta de Tierra. It is a magical place where the bums are your friends, where the beach is in front of the park, where they serve you two pesos of rice and beans if that's all you have."[26] Rodríguez is rewriting Puerta de Tierra as a space where hope actualizes the city narrative and the human practices in such place. By depicting small rituals, such as sharing affordable comfort food walking distance from the ocean, Rodríguez aims to humanize the marginalized community and to protect what is left before the "criollo block," the capitalist local class, takes over and gentrifies Puerta de Tierra.[27]

In figure 10.2, with a master overview layout, Rodríguez rewrites the public space into a hopeful space, naming the positive relations in the community with a small four panels in the first grid.[28] The verbal narrative has no speech bubbles in the sequence depicting a person riding inside a train. The unhoused friendly individuals, the proximity of the water, and the low-priced accessible traditional foods named in the layered paragraphs are absent in the

SÍ, SE ACERCAN MUCHOS CAMBIOS, AUNQUE ESTARÉ TOMANDO LA MISMA RUTA QUE HACÍA ANTES, SOLO QUE ME BAJARÉ UN POCO ANTES.

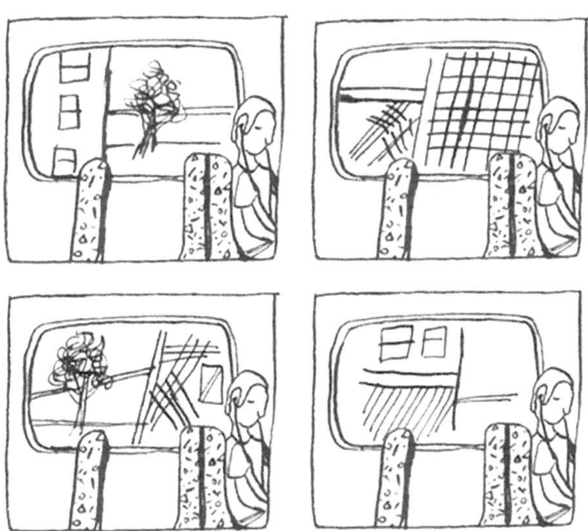

VOY A EXTRAÑAR PUERTA DE TIERRA. ES UN LUGAR MÁGICO DONDE LOS BUMS SON TUS AMIGOS, DONDE LA PLAYA ESTÁ FRENTE AL PARQUE, DONDE TE SIRVEN DOS PESOS DE ARROZ CON HABICHUELAS SI ESO ES LO ÚNICO QUE TIENES.

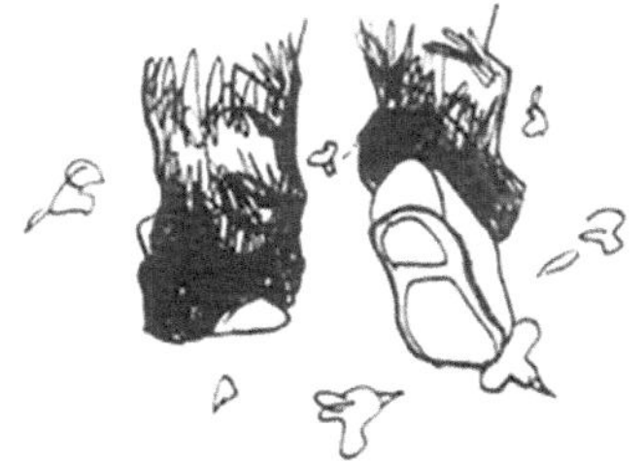

QUIZÁ CUANDO PASEN LAS SEMANAS SE DEN CUENTA QUE YA NO VOLVÍ.

FIGURE 10.2 This page portrays the popular Puerta de Tierra neighborhood in the north of San Juan. Banuchi and Rodríguez, *Días*, vol. 1, no. 3 (2013), 53.

panels. In their place, readers experience a body with the capacity to affect and be affected by its urban surroundings. To complete the hopeful narrative, readers get a ground-level view of feet walking away. Puerta de Tierra is portrayed from the bottom, the ground, the urban concrete roots. Rodríguez's sympathetic experiences in Puerta de Tierra are part of a history of resistance in the neighborhood, in which local residents have been fighting against predatory housing practices of the criollo block, the U.S. government, and foreign investors. Puerta de Tierra is situated north of the neighborhood called Condado. Both vicinities have access to San Juan Bay and Condado's Lagoon on the north of the small peninsula, and they are within walking distance of the historical Hispanic castles, San Felipe del Morro and San Cristobal. Such an area is located inside the touristic Old San Juan. In her comic, Rodríguez creates space for the reader to register hope amid social disparities and changes in the fragile city landscape.[29]

When I was tracing Días Cómic's map of affects, I engaged with the urban spaces' politics and my own citizenship practices. Train stations, streets, and bus stops are part of Rodríguez's daily commute from Villa Nevarez to Puerta de Tierra. On page 32 of the same book, volume 1, number II, Rodríguez documents a daily scene of her social interactions while walking to the train station. In a horizontal three-panel sequence, the gutters act like frames for small pictures, while the verbal narrative explains how she is called by a local man remodeling an abandoned house every time she passes by. When the reader turns the page, a traditional six-panel sequence, read from left to right, is in harmonious juxtaposition with a verbal narrative of abandonment and speculative investment in the fragile city. Rodríguez engages in a challenging yet comical interaction at a park with another man, an unhoused fellow who asks her to translate into English and write down on a small cardboard the words "disabled" and "handicapped." The last panel, at the bottom-right corner of the page, ends with the same man thanking Rodríguez with an old Spanish saying, "God will pay you later." The social commentary completes the verbal narrative with her saying, "God has forgotten to pay the poor."[30] The imbalanced colonial relationship and the urban space within Puerto Rico are hiding in plain sight in Rodríguez's depictions of the poverty and dispossession of communities sharing the same American citizenship. Last, another interesting element of Rodríguez's repertoire is the street debris. In volume 1, numbers II and III, the fragile city landscape is again drawn from the ground up. These panels privilege a perspective from below through close-ups focusing on items that become garbage after being abandoned: a melted blue crayon on the pavement, a pillow going down the sewer, a broken mirror on the sidewalk, a colored matches box, and a fresh piece of bread being eaten by city doves. When analyzing Rodríguez's panels, I ask students to consider these elements as part of what a body can observe, feel, and materialize when experiencing public urban space as part of a daily praxis. In class, students discussed how the colonial imbalances of cities in the Global South lay out visual urban landscapes of belonging and dispossession. I asked students to think and discuss in small groups the importance of graphic narratives materializing daily commutes and pedestrian interactions, instead of portraying long lines of cars in traffic or rooftops of skyline buildings. Students' responses have been abundant across various institutional and classroom settings. In both California and Iowa, they indicated how Rodríguez's autobiographical comics offer a window into the affects and challenges underserved communities in the American colony navigate daily because they are considered second-class citizens. Students claimed that Rodríguez's portrayed affects construct a social commentary on life experiences outside touristic spaces.

Curated Art, Resistance, and Dispossession in Santurce

The metropolitan neighborhood of Santurce is celebrated as an art district with a sparkling personality, according to Trip Advisor. The massive street murals in buildings and parking lots at Calle Cerra and the live music scene at La Placita are must-see places when visiting San Juan.[31] Nevertheless, Santurce today is the result of White-Anglo gentrification of a once-forgotten neighborhood. Motivated by the impression that art can change and heal buildings as well as people, artists cultivated a muralist movement called Santurce es Ley. The reality is that the area was transformed into a "Casual Space" in the fragile city, "publicly funded large-scale projects whose production directly contributed to public debt,"[32] and such neighborhoods were cleansed from local sex work and other underground economies and positioned as prime destinations for tourists to have fun and foreign investors to generate tax-free revenue.

I am interested in an important urban space of resistance in Santurce: El Local, a community art center that is locally owned and has focused on producing and experimenting with alternative cultural media since 2008. El Local has been a safe space for the independent art and music circuit in the metropolitan area. El Local is a gathering of affects and bodies that synthesizes homegrown generations of comics, punk, rock, hardcore, and any other subgenres of the underground Puerto Rican scene. Independent comic shows and visual art *jangueos* take place at El Local. An archive of posters, zines, and flyers of such happenings has documented the past decade of activities at the venue. El Local is also portrayed in contemporary graphic narratives by independent art collectives in San Juan like Soda Pop Comics, Días Cómic, Cosmic Eves, and Castorillo, among many others. Puerto Rican journalist Joel Citrón describes El Local as a happenstance, "a bar, a music club, a theater, a cabaret, a cinema, a mini-disco, a gallery or a place to sing karaoke or play ping pong, it all depends on the day of the week."[33]

In *Días* this venue appears at the end of volume 2, number I in a story written by Mario García and drawn by Omar Banuchi. A narrative voice-over tells the story of a group of local friends socializing outside the venue when a man, depicted with two close-up panels one after the other, approaches them asking for *menudito*, meaning cash. The story consists of four pages with two full-colored panels each. In the first panel, the man's entire face is shown, and the second depicts only the man's hands. Once again, I think about representations of underserved communities to characterize urban landscapes of San Juan. I ask, what are the larger political implications of their survival? Such character is juxtaposed to visual elements that are part of Días Cómic's aesthetic: a street corner, hanging cables, metal bars on windows, and dust covering the street. The verbal narrative is again minimal, expressing a mix of sadness and irrationality giving space to the young local underground music scene while coexisting with underserved community members.

Everydayness, Nostalgia, and Joy in Río Piedras's Neighborhood

As both characters and writers, Rodríguez and Banuchi go back and forth between Villa Nevarez and Río Piedras's main square. Banuchi articulates the affects of nostalgia and longing for his undergraduate student years at the UPR. His self-portrait's body gestures, such as relaxed shoulders and good eye contact with the readers, are associated with an intense, passionate sense of belonging to the area and the possibilities offered in such an alternative space. In volume 1, number II, page 33, Banuchi portrays himself with a four-panel sequence enclosing the nostalgic idea that his past colleges years were a better time. A self-portrait of Banuchi with a big smile, wearing a suit and a tie, starts the panel sequence from the top left down. Each panel shrinks a little until the smallest one has only a couple of sentences juxtaposed next to Banuchi's head. In the first panel on the top left, tall tropical trees function as background signifying the UPR's campus landscape. Beneath another panel lies a woman in her underwear with a bed as background, and this is juxtaposed with the verbal narrative of student's romantic relationships. Nostalgia is deeply intimate in Banuchi's narrative, developing strong connections with women always evoking joy and pleasure even in this depopulated older community. This neighborhood takes up significant material and emotional space in Días Cómic's storytelling; the barrio is well known as the student area surrounded by dilapidated empty buildings. Many barrios are part of San Juan, and all of them are experiencing financial difficulties and struggling with speculative and predatory real estate investment.

Olas in Río Piedras

In 2014, Días Cómic published the single-issue booklet with ten full watercolor pages *OLA/ALÓ Río Piedras*. Nuestra Señora del Pilar's church is at the heart of this graphic narrative, just like in real life such church is at the center of Río Piedras's public square. Each splash page is a human portrait with a speech bubble integrating the person's short monologue. In total there are eight different testimonies about the *trajines* (comings and goings) of life. Río Piedras becomes a medium, a nonfictional space of belonging, a loving expression of precariousness, and a serious feeling of togetherness. The conversations among the art collective and the portrayed fellows demonstrate how Puerto Rico's urban landscape shares temporalities with a Latin American urban comic tradition composed of multiplicities. The residents portrayed in comic have different ethnicities and diverse social backgrounds. The ground, the literal floor, takes up a significant portion of the background in the panels, and the position of each personal story has a spot in the map of affects: a street, an alley, a bus stop, a public square, a local market, and an empty parking lot. *OLA/ALÓ Río Piedras* was published as a multimodal and mediated local narrative by the UPR's newspaper, *Díalogo*. The printed booklet is an intentional archival act; Rodríguez and Banuchi materialize their encounters with residents hanging out in Río Piedras's casco urbano. Rodríguez explains their solid intention of "comprender y construir mejor esta parte de la ciudad que habitamos."[34] *OLA/ALÓ Río Piedras* embodies a collective sense of urban belonging that feeds off of reality. Each character carries stories of migration and diaspora through the ins and outs of their caribeñidad.

The stories come from both fronts: residents who came to the city from the countryside because they were told opportunities were awaiting them, but also stories about dispossession while living in the city, which led to fragmented families and forced displacement to the U.S. diaspora. I'm interested in how local testimonies portraying emotions, feelings, and memories can function as a decolonial visual reading of citizenship and belonging to the Caribbean space. *OLA/ALÓ Río Piedras* is anchored in enlightening social and emotional collectivities that define the urban Caribbean landscape as a challenge, a struggle, and a fragile group of bodies experiencing the opposite of what is sold in the touristic marketing formula. The real-life scenarios in the eight stories are local spots frequented by residents, whom Días Cómic calls amigos, pals, and friends, providing readers a window into history, diaspora, local architecture, geography, and the colonial education system.

Rapiña | *Carroña*: What Is Left after the Empire Loots the Fragile City

Días Cómic reclaims urban landscapes of abandonment by portraying other Boricuas physically occupying them, walking them, cruising them. By drawing and inking their presence and persistence into each panel, the storytelling reveals how Puerto Ricans living in the city experience racial exploitation by nature of being U.S. citizens. Such compositional arrangements, pairing local urban scenes with the fragile emotional state of Puerto Rican youth—*bregando*—embodies a local archive of the present, the immediate past, and the possible future. Días Cómic's content reveals social connections among independent artists in the San Juan metro area. Together, several organizations make funding possible to create and produce local nonfiction graphic narratives and converse about belonging.

Fragile cities can be liminal spaces among aquatic borders; in this case Puerto Rico is a bridge between Latin America, the Caribbean, and the U.S. mainland. As a fragile city resulting from racial capitalism, my hometown Mérida is, like San Juan, completely vulnerable to extreme weather conditions and speculative investment practices. I observe how the relationalities of our homelands are intersected by the U.S. economy, forced displacement, and the shutdown of locally owned businesses due to foreign-capital-driven investment and neoliberal aesthetic gentrification. I understand that one's decision making is no longer individual but for the good of others. Our surviving urban wildlife, city landscape, fusion food, language variations, and extreme climate are part of a multiethnic identity that makes the Spanish-speaking Caribbean a way of thinking and experiencing the oppressive intersections of colonialism and dispossession, where resistance is a daily practice. Caribbean biopolitics, cultural belonging, and its vitality are constantly challenged due to its geographical space; one can buy a trip to pristine paradisiac lands and experience the sargasso-free white-sand resort life without experiencing at all local residents' lives. Twenty-first-century Anglo settlers and neocolonizers have offered and sold the enjoyment of the Caribbean land and living to the world. The Airbnb investor's current market formula promises that beach + sun + palm trees + coconut water + swimsuit = paradise.[35] On the other hand, what is kept out of the corporate market master narrative is the local community struggles, the affective experiences of underserved communities from such paradisiac spaces, their rampant dispossession, and their multiethnic and hybrid relationships to citizenship and its control.

The comic anthology *Rapiña Carroña*, published by Días Cómic in 2021, is a nonfictional story that shines a light on how local, underserved, and racialized young residents navigate and coexist along with the colonizer and everyday touristic agenda. This book fosters online connections and archival practices that keep decolonizing academic perspectives beyond mainstream superhero industries in Latinx narratives in the United States. In 2017 Días Cómic changed locations in the island, and the storytelling started to incorporate more dense and intergenerational political commentary about topics such as the 1898 U.S. invasion, Black Puerto Rican history, the island's ongoing recovery, and the contemporary housing crisis due to speculative investments. Starting in 2021, Días Cómic's production switched to an independent self-sustained editorial publishing house. They publish other creators' locally produced and printed graphic narratives that circulate without the intervention of corporate sponsorship. Días Cómic launched the project titled *Rapiña/Carroña*, which started as a multimodal visual artifact, including a website and online store with the webcomics encompassed in the printed book. The book is an anthology of essays, comics, and poems by various authors and the creators of Días: "This project compiles the voices and lines of different generations and backgrounds of the Puerto Rican colonial reality."[36] The personal and the political are one single narrative. Collaborators include well-known local comic creators, professors, journalists, and authors, such as Karla Claudio Betancourt, Cristian Guzmán Cardona, Rosa Colón Guerra, Subibaja Comics, Castor, Alexandra Pagán Vélez, Jorge Rodríguez

Beruff, Joel Cintrón Arbasetti, and Camila Frías Estrada. *Rapiña/Carroña* was supported by local and private grants, namely El Serrucho by Beta-Local, the Open Society Foundations, and the Andrew W. Mellon Foundation.

The book title is composed of two words, "Rapine" and "Carrion"; the narrative plays with how local stakeholders can be both predator and target. *Rapiña* refers to birds of prey, those hunters that pursue other animals for food or those that carry away something by force. It symbolizes how local politicians, American millionaires, and touristic economies are taking advantage of the tax exemptions of Puerto Rico's Act 20/22 by buying away properties local communities inhabit. Meanwhile, the U.S. federal government is imposing—through the Financial Oversight and Management Board, "La Junta"—austerity measures for island residents. *Carroña* means literal dead and decaying flesh, what is left behind after death and destruction. The plots in this latest collection build a historical archive of personal narratives ranging from the First World War, passing through the summer of 2019, and landing within the current years of pandemic confinement. The stories are interwoven with political views and facts about the state of the colony: what Puerto Ricans have been denied and how they have created an existence resisting U.S. pillage and colonization.

On page 93, the comic titled "Buitres" is adapted by Banuchi and illustrated by the collective called Subibaja Comics, composed of local artists C. J Román and Marcos H., who describe their collective as "two guys drawing messy stories from the most beautiful darkness called Río Piedras." The title of this piece means vultures in English; the full comic is eight pages long in black-and-white with some grayscale color and traditional panels and gutters. The main characters are a group of men with birdlike facial features dressed in black formal suits.

I end this chapter showing how across a decade of creative process, Días Cómic has built a meaningful and steady critique of the Puerto Rican colonial relationship with the United States (see figure 10.3). The definition of vultures from the modern encyclopedia *The Dictionary of Literature, Industry, Agriculture and Commerce*, written in 1851, provides the verbal narrative juxtaposed to illustrations that signify contemporary politicians/investors as colonizers. Housing predators and local and federal politicians are matched with the natural behavior and physical characteristics of the birds of prey: on page 93, in a horizontal sequence, the first two of five panels illustrate city buildings in the distance; reading from left to right the comic shows a firth panel with a group of six folks with bird-featured faces sitting together in a roundtable. The verbal narrative explains how *buitres* flutter around in the

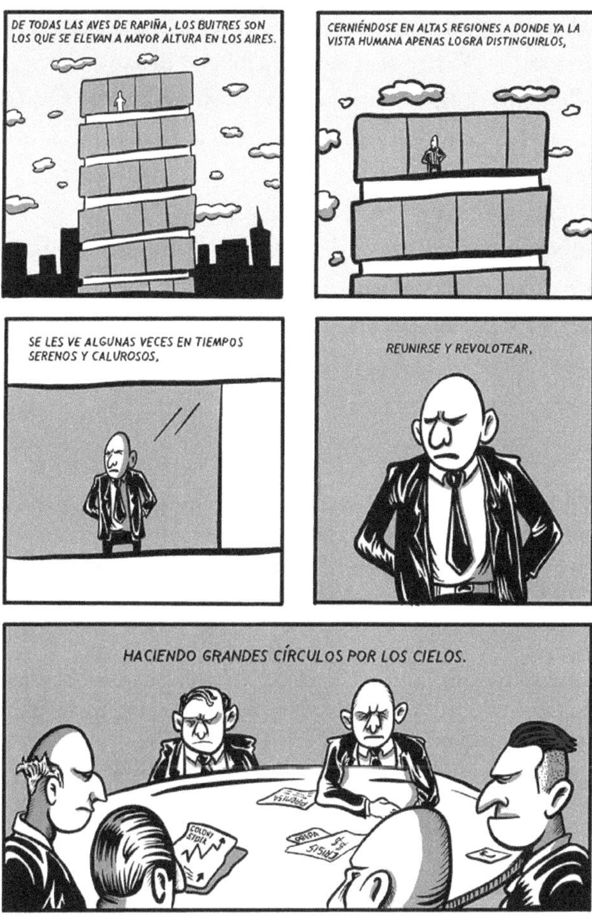

FIGURE 10.3 This panel illustrates how coloniality shapes Puerto Rico's city buildings and cityscapes. Omar Banuchi and Subibaja Comics, "Buitres," in *Rapiña/Carroña,* ed. Rosaura Rodriguez and Omar Banuchi (Días, 2021), 93.

blue sky, searching for fresh lifeless sustenance when they spot empty buildings in the city of San Juan. They all arrive together to devour such property and leave nothing behind for the next venture capitalist.

To finish this contribution, I review a couple of points presented through the sections. The multiplicity of meanings Días Cómic gives to the city and the urban landscape decolonizes understandings of citizenship and belonging beyond national icons and master narratives. After experiencing these comics, the cultural meaning of urban landscapes in itself is a personal matter. The unique formal properties of Días Cómic's narratives offer an aesthetic discourse and alternative speech to what is preconceived as Caribbean and

Latinx visual contemporary storytelling. The classroom could be a place of identity construction. When teaching Caribbean urban comics, students are exposed to interdisciplinary narratives mediated with digital cultures, performance, audience reception, and radical anticolonial politics. Sharing visual stories and histories stimulates critical conversations about our foundations, our positionality, and our sense of belonging. Finally, Días Cómic's products improved my understanding of imposed borders in my own colonized life experience and underscored the fact that I do not want to be anything else but a Caribbean citizen.

Notes

1 Joaquín Villanueva, Martín Cobián, and Félix Rodríguez define fragility as "an urban condition that renders a city's population and its infrastructure vulnerable to extreme weather events, speculative investment practices, and unstable global financial markets" in "San Juan, the Fragile City: Finance Capital, Class, and the Making of Puerto Rico's Economic Crisis," *ANTIPODE* 50, no. 5 (2018): 1415–1437, 1415.

The Igarapé Institute in Brazil developed a virtual map and database with all the fragile cities in the world, available here: https://igarape.org.br/en/apps/fragile-cities-data-visualization/, accessed November 8, 2024. The level of fragility depends on the inability of public institutions to deliver livable conditions. The scores in this map are between 0.08 and 3.1. According to this study, Mérida is level 1, San Juan is level 2.

2 Andrew Kunka, *Autobiographical Comics* (New York: Bloomsbury, 2017), 5.

3 With no institutional funding or research affiliation, I am independently collecting, preserving, and organizing these comics. See Margaret Galvan, "Archive," in *Keywords for Comics Studies,* ed. Ramzi Fawaz, Shelley Streeby, and Deborah Elizabeth Whaley (New York: New York University Press, 2021), 24–26.

4 Benjamin Fraser, *Visible Cities, Global Comics* (Jackson: University Press of Mississippi, 2019), 55.

5 I refer to the Caribbean as the multiethnic and multilingual geographical space, also known as Gran Caribe, integrated by many linguistic variations, islands, peninsulas, and continental regions. The region I refer to extends from the Yucatán Peninsula to South American French Guiana. Caribbean identities can overlap and contradict national belongings and colonial structures. There is no exact way to be Caribbean or belong to the region.

6 The nineteenth-century Mexican mestizaje discourse disregards multiples ethnoracial identities resulting from worldwide migrations and colonial processes across the country. Mexican citizenship overlooks the contributions and sense of belonging of Black, Asian, Middle Eastern, Jewish, Caribbean, and Indigenous communities in Mexico. In the Americas, mestizaje resulted in unbalanced colonial power dynamics aiming to preserve Whiteness from Europe. See Alicia Arrizón, "Mestizaje," in *Keywords for Latina/o Studies*, ed. Deborah R. Vargas, Nancy Raquel Mirabal, and Lawrence La Fountain-Stokes (New York: New York University Press, 2017), 133.

7 Margaret Shrimpton, "Continental Islands: A Model for the Mainland Caribbean? The Case of Yucatan *Memorias*," *Revista digital de historia y arqueología desde el caribe colombiano* 25, no. 11 (2015): 178–208, 181.
8 See Eugenia Iturriaga, *Las élites de la ciudad blanca. Discursos racistas sobre la otredad* (Mérida: UNAM, 2016).
9 Evelyn Nakano Glenn, "Constructing Citizenship: Exclusion, Subordination, and Resistance," *American Sociological Review* 76, no. 1 (2011): 1–24, 2–4.
10 The Mexican icons that do not represent me are the Mexican flag, ranchera music, mariachi bands, narcocorridos, tequila, and hats and boots of the Charro attire. These popular artifacts were not part of my upbringing in the Yucatán. It was not until 2006, when I studied "abroad" at the University of Guadalajara in Jalisco, that I experienced the modern-state Mexicanidad and how it is performed by my fellow Mexican citizens.
11 Claudia Milian, *LatinX* (Minneapolis: University of Minnesota Press, 2019), 4.
12 The established Caribbean scholars in the United States include Vanesa Pérez-Rosario, Solimar Otero, José Luis González, Gustavo Pérez Firmat, Jorge Duany, Juan Flores, Yolanda Martínez-San Miguel, and Arcadio Díaz Quiñones.
13 Kunka, *Autobiographical Comics*, 6.
14 Kunka, *Autobiographical Comics*, 3.
15 This is my translation to English. Rosaura Rodríguez and Omar Banuchi, *Días*, vol. 1 (San Juan: Libros AC, 2013), 5.
16 Kunka, *Autobiographical Comics*, 114.
17 Rodríguez and Banuchi, *Días*, 15, my translation.
18 See Latinx Geographies Specialty Group, accessed April 14, 2024, https://latinxgeographies.com/, and Berkeley Black Geographies, accessed April 14, 2024, https://theblackgeographic.com/.
19 Siu Lok, *Memories of a Future Home: Diasporic Citizenship of Chinese in Panama* (Stanford, CA: Stanford University Press, 2005), 5–7.
20 Nicholas De Genova, "Citizenship," in Vargas, Mirabal, and La Fountain-Stokes, *Keywords for Latina/o Studies*, 39.
21 Susan E. Kirtley, Antero Garcia, and Peter E. Carlson, "Introduction: A Once and Future Pedagogy," in *With Great Power Comes Great Pedagogy: Teaching, Learning, and Comics*, ed. Kirtley, Garcia, and Carlson (Jackson: University Press of Mississippi, 2020), 3–19, 10.
22 For scholarship about the Latin American city and comics, see the University of Manchester seminar's website, "Comics and the Latin American City, Farming Urban Communities," Accessed April 14, 2024, https://comicsandthelatinamericancity.wordpress.com, and the edited collection by James Scorer, *Comics Beyond the Page in Latin America* (London: University College London Press, 2020).
23 Winners of the Premio de Novela Gáfica Ciudades Iberoamericanas are young comic artists from Latin America; each one created a graphic novel depicting the city. For more information on such collaborations, I invite you to look for and support the work of Argentinian creator Maria Luque; Mexican illustrators Emmanuel Peña, Héctor Turriza, Sergio Neri, and Gaspar Pantoja; the international art collective Chicks on Comics; and Colombian creator Miguel Angel Vallejo.
24 Tania Alexandra Cardoso, "The Ins and Outs of Possible Cities in Comics: *Procurando Sao Paulo*," *Studies in Comics* 12, no. 2 (2021): 201–223.
25 Seigworth and Gregg, *Affect Theory Reader*, 2. I study various proposals of "affect" before analyzing how the city of San Juan "felt" in Días Cómic's narratives. See

Gregory J. Seigworth and Melissa Gregg, *The Affect Theory Reader* (Durham, NC: Duke University Press, 2010); Carrie A. Rentscheler, "Affect," in *Keywords for Media Studies*, ed. Laurie Ouellette and Jonathan Gray (New York: New York University Press, 2017), 12–14.

26 Rodríguez and Banuchi, *Días*, 53, my translation.

27 Joaquín Villanueva, Martín Cobián, and Félix Rodríguez have identified the "criollo block" as the local, foreigner, and political capitalist class. See "San Juan, the Fragile City," 1415–1437.

28 Rob Shields, Ondine Park, and Tonya K. Davidson, *Ecologies of Affect: Placing Nostalgia, Desire, and Hope* (Waterloo: Wilfrid Laurier University Press, 2013), 12.

29 Villanueva, Cobián, and Rodríguez, "San Juan, the Fragile City," 1415–1437. Puerta de Tierra is one of the "Spaces of Resistance." Puerta de Tierra Brigade is a group of organized neighbors demanding that development projects consider their own needs as well. This group displays the slogan *Aquí vive gente*, which is also featured in the Bad Bunny musical video production *El Apagón* in collaboration with independent journalist Bianca Graulau.

30 Rodríguez and Banuchi, *Días*, 34.

31 Trip Advisor, "La Placita de Santurce," accessed April 14, 2024, https://www.tripadvisor.com/Attraction_Review-g147320-d8275791-Reviews-La_Placita_de_Santurce-San_Juan_Puerto_Rico.html.

32 Villanueva, Cobián, and Rodríguez, "San Juan, the Fragile City," 1421.

33 Joel Citrón interviewed by Gabriela Ortiz Díaz (National Popular Culture Foundation, October 3, 2016), https://prpop.org/2016/10/el-local-desde-la-pluma-de-joel-cintron/.

34 "To better understand and build this part of the city we inhabit." Rosaura Rodríguez and Omar Banuchi, *OLA/ALÓ Río Piedras* (San Juan: Días Cómic, 2014), 1.

35 See Arelis Avilés Suárez, "Descubriendo el Caribe: el invento y lo real," *EL CARIBE. Revista de la Universidad de México*, no. 874/875 (2021), https://www.revistadelauniversidad.mx/articles/fa0d1daf-9c3a-4dbd-a3cf-a13f616d6e5a/descubriendo-el-caribe-el-invento-y-lo-real.

36 Días Cómic, "About," accessed April 14, 2024, https://www.diascomic.com/about.

United States of Banana: A Graphic Novel as Decluttering and Decolonizing Doubled Journey of the Self

FREDERICK LUIS ALDAMA

A radically experimental creative force, Puerto Rican author Giannina Braschi seeks to decolonize in all that she creates and puts into the world. We see this in her genre-bending dramaturgical poetry, such as *Asalto al tiempo* (1981) and *La comedia profana* (1985). We see this in her genre-bending novels, such as *El imperio de los sueños* (1988), *Yo-Yo Boing!* (1998), and *United States of Banana* (2011). Here and elsewhere Braschi bends languages (Spanish and English), genres, and forms to shape new expressions of a hemispheric Latinidad, or Latinoness—expressions that resist and rebel against the officially sanctioned, standard, and dominant.[1]

Braschi gives shape to subjectivities that exist between and across cultures, languages, and epistemologies. She creates Latinx subjectivities and experiences that are nomadic, spontaneous, and resistant to what Aníbal Quijano has described as "the coloniality of power" that continues to wrap itself around the everyday life of Puerto Rican islanders and its diasporic peoples.[2] She opens spaces for hemispheric, archipelagic ways of thinking and acting. Elsewhere, I identify, with Christopher González, Braschi's conceptions of power and resistance as "located within the rhizomatic, deterritorialized multitude."[3] She asks us to dishabituate ourselves from the economic, political, juridical, and ideological appendages that inform the legacies of the coloniality of power that continue to expropriate Puerto Rican lands and natural resources as well as exploit and oppress Puerto Ricans. Braschi's work demands that we see how coloniality permeates all levels of society and subjectivity across the world. Her aesthetic and epistemic practice invites us to decolonize cognitive-emotive systems, waking us to, in Walter D. Mignolo's words on decoloniality, an "awareness and the will to delink from re- and de-Westernization, and a call for the politics of de-colonial investigations to assist in gnoseological and aesthetic reconstitutions to break the chains of all either/or prison houses of the imagination."[4]

In 2011, Braschi published her novel *United States of Banana*. It has since been recognized as a genre- and mind-bending tour de force that creatively critiques U.S. imperialist policy and practices, which continues to strong-arm and stranglehold Puerto Rico's denizens. Readers join Giannina-as-character and her crew of fictional and historical characters, including Hamlet and Zarathustra, who set out to free activist-poet Segismundo (held captive for one hundred years in a dungeon beneath the Statue of Liberty's skirt) as well as others who overcome obstacles. Braschi's fantastical crew encounter all sorts of figures from history, literature, and philosophy, including Fidel Castro, Antonin Artaud, Rubén Darío, Pedro Calderón de la Barca, Nietzsche, Socrates, Parmenides, Protagoras, Diotima of Mantineia, and many more. Through these fictional escapades, *United States of Banana* revisits the historical violence and trauma of the greed driving Spanish colonization, the U.S. annexation of Puerto Rico in 1898, and the debtor-nation loan practices that continue to prevent Puerto Rico and its denizens from realizing their full, sovereign potentialities. The odyssey of this panoply of characters envisions a massive decolonizing of the colonialist order that continues to permeate the everyday lives of Puerto Ricans.

Of course, this is my making sense of an otherwise radically anticonventional narrative that resists typical strategies of reading and sensemaking. Indeed, Braschi privileges Socratic dialogue over traditional story arcs filled with action, movement, and epiphanies of consciousness that typify most realist fiction. There is movement within the original novel, but it is the kind of episodic adventuring (sans grand epiphanies) that we are more likely to experience in picaresque fiction. And Braschi often turns to the devices of the dramaturgical to shape the dialogic action and interaction between the characters. There is movement within this episodic plot, but it is less a movement of character through time and space and more a movement of language (Spanish and English), ideas (philosophy), and otherwise historically occluded information (the colonial and capitalist exploitation of Puerto Rico). Taken as a whole, *United States of Banana* sidesteps those conventions that make easy the consumption of character, theme, and plot. Instead, it offers readers the possibility of taking pause to declutter and decolonize colonial practices (socioeconomic and political) and ideologies that continue to straitjacket hemispheric Latinx thoughts, feelings, and actions.

But I am not here to talk about the novel *United States of Banana* exclusively. I'm here to explore and examine what happens to this alphabetic shaped, or traditional prose, narrative when it conjoins with the visual storytelling arts in Braschi and Swedish cartoonist Joakim Lindengren's *United States of Banana: A Graphic Novel* (2021). More specifically, and with a focus on the graphic novel adaptation, I ask, how might famed Lindengren's visual narrative add to and *make new* Braschi's episodic and dialogic decolonial narrative? What new epistemic decluttering and aesthetic decolonial possibilities open with the conjoining of Braschi's verbal narrative track with Lindengren's visual narrative track?

I am not the first to think about the ways that traditional literary texts have traveled across and into other media such as comics. This is a rich and bountiful area of comics studies grown significantly by scholars such as Jared Gardner, Nicolas Labarre, Henry Jenkins, Tyler Weaver, Liam Burke, Ian Gordon, Cormac McGarry, and Angela Ndalianis, among many others.[5] Indeed, in their introduction to the English edition of *United States of Banana: A Graphic Novel*, Amanda M. Smith and Amy Sheeran ask us to consider how Lindengren's referential visuals, with "obvious allusions to modern art, US and Puerto Rican pop culture, historical events, and more . . . give meaning to the text."[6] They also ask us to consider how the "poetic language and visual art come to bear on the characters' journey toward political revolution."[7]

Like Smith and Sheeran, I am interested in what Lindengren's visuals do to at once convey the same decolonial worldview of Braschi's novel *and* make new the reader's experience of that journey. I propose that this *making new* experience happens as a doubled journey: (1) Giannina-the-character and her motley crew's dialogue-filled journey that clears a new decluttered and decolonial space for words, ideas, and progressive action—and the ultimate liberation of Puerto Rico from the United States; and (2) the simultaneous visual-aesthetic narrative track that Lindengren creates and that seeks to collapse highbrow and lowbrow cultural distinctions as a way to declutter and decolonize restrictive aesthetic schemas, freeing our imaginations from artificially imposed categories that inhibit the full expression and liberation of Latinx thought, feeling, and action.

Before the English edition of *United States of Banana: A Graphic Novel* in 2021 there was the Swedish-language graphic novel, *United States of Banana*, published by Cobolt in 2017. It is here that we see the process of creating the doubled verbal and visual journey begin. Braschi selected roughly one-third of the original text to be used as the script for the graphic novel (which was then translated from Spanish into Swedish by Swedish poet Helena Eriksson). With the worldview of Braschi's novel in mind and script in hand, Lindengren then began the work of visualizing the narrative track. Braschi and Lindengren agreed that as long as he did not alter her words, he could have total creative freedom concerning images. Lindengren sums up his approach thus: "Giannina's method was to cannibalize literary history, so the obvious thing for me was to cannibalize art history."[8] And this is exactly what Lindengren does. On nearly every page, he shapes the visual narrative track with direct and indirect references to a variety of so-called lowbrow and highbrow art: Disney cartoons, DC and Marvel superheroes, and album covers appear alongside Hieronymus Bosch, Francisco Goya, Pablo Picasso, and the Bayeux Tapestry. None of these references appear in Braschi's novel. They are entirely of Lindengren's additive imaginings, making new the reader's experience of Braschi's words, themes, and plot.

The Paratextual Framing of "Freedom"

While the panel layout and design as well as the content of the mise-en-page move without change from the Swedish edition to the English, there are paratextual visuals that do change as we move from one edition to the next. Cobolt's Swedish edition uses original cover art and design, as well as other paratexts not seen in the English edition. The paratext, per Gerard Genette's formulation, is all that encompasses the story proper: cover art, title page, epigraphs, and so much more. While the "the whole zone" of the paratext is largely determined and controlled by the publisher, it nonetheless importantly establishes initial interpretive contracts with readers.[9] The meaning and mood of the paratextual framing devices can work in tension or harmony with the themes and worldviews generated by the story itself. For instance, Cobolt's original cover art features the Statue of Liberty, whose back is turned to the reader, as if she is the main protagonist featured in the style reminiscent of *Classics Illustrated* books (see figure 11.1). The cover is washed in dark blue and green colors with only a few sources of light—the fingers of light streaming from the darkened clouds and the flame of Liberty's torch. The dominant mood is one of doom and gloom, with only a glimmer of hope appearing somewhere in the distance. It is not belief or faith (in the Statue of Liberty or the nation state she symbolizes) that will bring change. Rather, it is the actions of the doers—as the portraits of the four main protagonists that

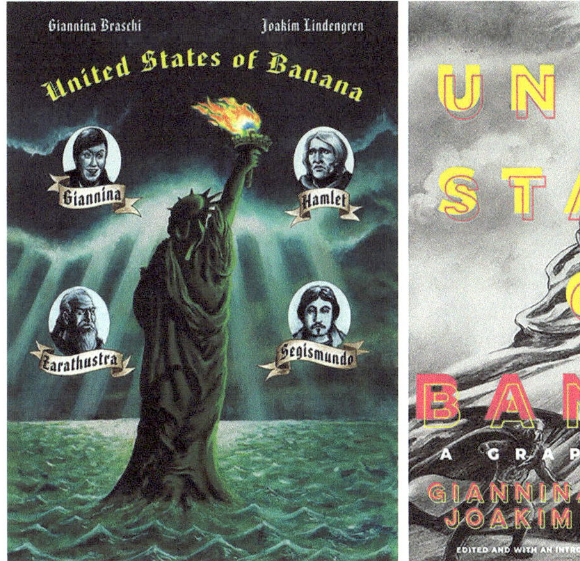

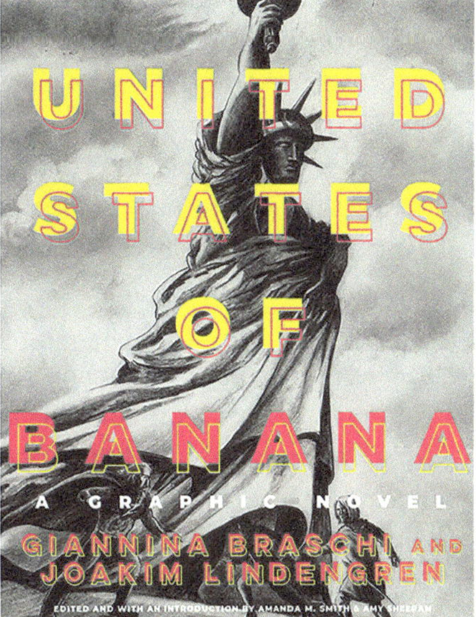

FIGURE 11.1 The cover of the Swedish (left) and English (right) editions of Giannina Braschi and Joakim Lindengren's graphic novel *United States of Banana*. Swedish edition (Cobolt Förlag: 2017). Giannina Braschi and Joakim Lindengren, *United States of Banana: A Graphic Novel*, ed. Amanda M. Smith and Amy Sheeran (Columbus: The Ohio State University Press, 2021). © Joakim Lindengren.

surround the Statue of Liberty suggest—that will bring change to an otherwise deadened and doomed world.

With the Swedish edition, in addition to the cover, there are other paratextual elements that continue to deepen the direction of meaning making that readers will take as they enter the story proper. After the cover art, there appears a pasted-down and loose endpaper drawn in the shape and colors of the U.S. flag. Instead of stars (with stripes), it uses images of bananas, emphasizing the importance of the title, *United States of Banana*, and reminding readers of how the United States turned Puerto Rico's socioeconomic structure into a servile "banana republic." Flipping past the copyright page, readers encounter another important paratext: the title page that depicts an angry Statue of Liberty battling marauding airplanes flying Puerto Rican flags while grasping tight a figure that readers will, once into the story, recognize as Segismundo. Here, Lindengren references, but with a difference, the iconic image of King Kong from Merian C. Cooper and Ernest B. Schoedsack's 1933 film. Rather than convey the tragedy of the misunderstood and maligned Other (King Kong) emoting while clutching his love (Ann Darrow), Lindengren's title page conveys a defensive and precariously positioned Statue of Liberty batting at the Puerto Rican air squadron. It asks readers to interpret the visuals metaphorically, with the Statue of Liberty symbolic of a United States less about freedom and equality and more about defending its imperialist practices and positions. This is not a show of Liberty's love for Segismundo but rather a desperate attempt to hold tight to power—the power to crush those who threaten the United States's domination of Puerto Rico. The paratextual visuals already begin to guide readers' meaning-making processes before they encounter the narrative, asking readers to reframe and reschematize iconic images and symbols of freedom. They pave the way for critiquing the darker underbelly of U.S. imperialist ideology, practice, and policy, as will be revealed in the imprisonment of Segismundo (under Liberty's skirt) and the decolonial adventures of Giannina-the-character and her crew as the story unfolds.

These paratexts do not appear in the later English-language edition of the graphic novel. The cover art is decisively different here. Unlike the Swedish edition that uses original cover art, the cover of the English edition uses an enlarged image taken from a panel within the graphic novel.[10] With the cover of the English-language edition, readers encounter a Statue of Liberty in slight profile looking off into the distance, inked and washed in grays (see figure 11.1). Slightly visible behind the subtitle and the names of the cocreators appear the figures readers will soon meet in the story proper: Zarathustra, Hamlet, and Giannina. Unlike the Swedish edition that puts a spotlight on the characters, here they are barely discernable. Their presence is understated and diminished, as is the visual critique of the Statue of Liberty as a metonym for the United States and its imperialist endeavors. In this edition, the cover asks viewers to focus their attention on the Statue of Liberty, centered amid the dayglow yellow and pink lettering of the title. Taken on its own and before the narrative proper begins, the English-language edition begins to direct our meaning-making processes (modern and optimistic) in ways that run counter to the themes and worldview of the story proper. This together with the lack of the other paratexts used in the Swedish edition leave the work of orientating readers' meaning making to the story itself.

This said, in both editions, the style of the cover art does orient readers, at least to the type of fine art linework Lindengren uses to shape his visuals. The graphic novel draws on Lindengren's training in the fine arts (he studied at Västerås Konstskola and Konstfack University in Stockholm) and his practice of cartooning and comic book creating (for example, his comic strips *Kapten Stofil* and *John Holmes & Sherlock Watson*, cocreated with David Nessel). To wit, both covers evoke Lindengren's training in both fine and comic art through the allusions to iconic literature (*Classics Illustrated*) and film (*King Kong*) in the Swedish edition and to superheroes (Zarathustra costumed with a cape and Z insignia on his chest) in the English edition. Put another way, the style he uses to create the visual track of the narrative is a fine art style, near black-and-white photographic realism, infused with a popular culture sensibility.

Deconstructing Aesthetic and Epistemic Divisions of "High" and "Low"

As the graphic novel continues to unfold, readers experience a multiplicity of different ways that Lindengren weaves pop culture references and sensibilities into his fine art linework style. For instance, he re-creates scenes from the novel with such popular culture references as *Clockwork Orange*; Disney's Huey, Louie, and Dewey; and Tom of Finland.[11] Likewise, he incorporates already re-created references to so-called highbrow art that include works by Hopper, Picasso, Dalí, and van Gogh as well as the Bayeux Tapestry.[12] In addition to these, we can add Toulouse-Lautrec, da Vinci, and Francisco Goya as well as Harpo Marx, Thor, U.S. Hollywood/Broadway musicals, James Dean, Doctor Doom, *Men in Black*, Guy Peellaert's LP album cover art, *Star Wars*, tarot cards, Felix the Cat, and Harold Lloyd (the clock scene in *Safety at Last*).[13] Through these ample allusions, we see Lindengren's willful re-creation of the originals in ways that not only work as a (re)education of art history with no divisions between highbrow and lowbrow but also function to propel the characters and plot forward. That is, Lindengren is not only dissolving artificially drawn lines between one aesthetic deemed civilized and worthy of attention (highbrow) and the other deemed uncivilized junk (lowbrow) but also adding movement and dynamism to the narrative.

Lindengren continues to declutter and decolonize throughout the graphic narrative by collapsing Western epistemes that artificially construct walls between highbrow and lowbrow culture. We see this when he re-creates superheroes or Disney-styled characters in ways that resonate in readers' minds as stand-ins for the juggernaut that is U.S. imperialism. Ditto for his re-creation of highbrow art. At one point early in the narrative Lindengren draws Giannina's face as morphing into an anti-mimetic abstraction of a face.[14] He at once references the Western aesthetic of Cubism and asks that readers bring a new critical frame to this art style and expression. And with this he powerfully reminds us of how Giannina's experimental narrative penetrates the miasma of colonialist and capitalist ideology to show clearly the real, material damage done by expropriation of Puerto Rico's lands and exploitation of its workers: "I have no reason to cry. If tears come out of my eyes, it's because I have a runny nose and teary eyes—the pollen in the air—and the insecticides—the fumigations and the pesticides—not because I'm crying inside. I feel no pity."[15] When Lindengren chooses to shape Giannina, Zarathustra, and Hamlet leaving a "9/Eleven" to cross the street in front of a diner, he pushes readers to recognize Edward Hopper's famous 1942 *Nighthawks* painting, a symbol of the modern condition of human estrangement and alienation. Here, the visual allusion to the canonical work within the contents of Braschi's narrative wakens readers instead to those U.S. colonial and imperial economic policies and violent militaristic and ideological occupations that undergird the violence of the 9/11 attacks and the heightened nationalism, surveillance, and warfare they were later used to justify, hence the "9/Eleven" instead of a recognizable 7-Eleven sign, the renaming of the diner "Philistines" (instead of Hopper's PHILLIES), and the retrofitting of the diner with the twelve disciples of Christianity served by a U.S. sailor.

Decluttering, Decolonization, and Doubled Journeys

Given Braschi's skill and labor first distilling and then re-creating the three-hundred-plus-page novel into a script for a ninety-seven-page graphic novel, it's not surprising that we do not see the one-to-one carryover of the full text to the graphic novel. However, what we might not expect is the degree to which Lindengren's visual narrative track introduces to Braschi's text a sense of movement, both the characters' physical movement in time and space as well as the reader's psychological movement—as a formative journey in the encounter with art across a variety of visual aesthetic forms. While in Braschi's novel we have the interplay of words and ideas, in Braschi and Lindengren's graphic novel we have the characters' time-space movement across the plot and the pages and the reader's mind-body movement across different times, places, and forms of art.

This is neither a straightforward nor a traditional aesthetic journey and education. It is Lindengren's active re-creation of art to shape the reader's experience of the coloniality of power in and through the graphic novel. In this two-page spread, we see the graphic novel's decluttering and decolonizing process at play (see figure 11.2). First, Lindengren gives visual shape to Giannina, Hamlet, and Zarathustra's search for Segismundo deep within the Statue of Liberty—the great symbolic figure, an image of the "enlightened,"

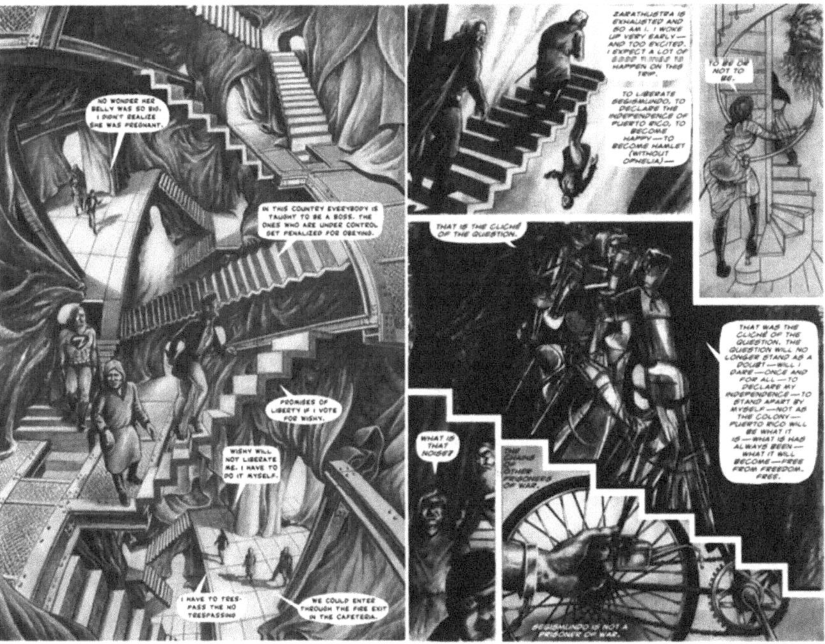

FIGURE 11.2 A two-page spread that depicts Lindengren's geometrizing to comment on the labyrinthine conditions of U.S. colonialism. Braschi and Lindengren, *United States of Banana*, 28–29.

benevolent maternalism that covers over the violence of U.S. colonial and imperial expropriative policy and economic practice in Puerto Rico (and elsewhere). Lindengren chooses a style similar to Dutch graphic artist M. C. Escher to convey the nightmarish difficulty of Giannina, Hamlet, and Zarathustra finding their way around, through, and out of the labyrinthine underbelly of the Statue of Liberty. In the bottom right corner of the full-page splash image Giannina-the-character states, "I have to trespass the no trespassing zone."[16] Zarathustra follows with, "We could enter through the fire exit in the cafeteria."[17] This triggers a metonymic response in readers that links the characters' circuitous journey into and through the Statue of Liberty to the nightmarish living conditions created by U.S. colonial and imperialist policies and practices in regard to Puerto Rico's displaced and disenfranchised.

Lindengren's abstractions and geometrizing of a journey that defies gravity also invites readers to experience an aesthetic and epistemological decluttering that opens to a radical new perspectivism. Lindengren's transmogrification of Hamlet, Zarathustra, and Giannina into abstract objects as they navigate the labyrinthine staircases resonates directly with French painter and sculptor Marcel Duchamp's *Nude Descending a Staircase* efforts to push against the male gaze and the objectification of women's bodies in Western epistemes. It also visually materializes Braschi's message in the *United States of Banana*. To enact a total global system reboot, one must collectively obliterate all epistemic legacies that continue to inform the coloniality of power, hence the creating of the collective voice (Giannina, Hamlet, Zarathustra) that emits from this amalgam of broken structures: "To declare my independence—To stand apart by myself—not as the colony—Puerto Rico will be what it is—what is has always been—what it will become—free from freedom. Free."[18]

Lindengren gives this decluttering and decolonizing experience a spatiotemporal dimension. He uses the visuals to shape the narrative's movement in time and space. As the reader follows Giannina, Hamlet, and Zarathustra's movement within the belly of Lady Liberty, we experience the visual spatialization of time. Lindengren's shaping of the panels that move our eyes from left to right and down, including down a stair-shaped panel, invites readers to feel and experience the dynamization of the space. That is, for Lindengren, the visual track of the decolonizing and decluttering journey of the co-protagonists also takes place at the level of the page's formal design and layout, or the mise-en-page.[19]

In *United States of Banana: A Graphic Novel*, Joakim Lindengren creates a visual narrative track that joins with Giannina Braschi's verbal narrative track to create a doubled narrative journey that invites readers to declutter and decolonize those mind-forged manacles of the coloniality of power. It invites readers to experience a collective odyssey that ultimately leads to the destruction of the Statue of Liberty and, with this, the promise of a total planetary system reboot. Indeed, the *United States of Banana: A Graphic Novel* invites readers to reevaluate the hierarchical and discriminatory categories that shape art and art practice, including those that have long privileged high over low and words over images. Finally, in this doubled journey of *self*-decolonization, Braschi and Lindengren invite readers to grow and develop an eyes-wide-open imaginary that interrogates the order of things and sees new pathways to make a better future. This doubled journey of self-decolonization opens readers' eyes to how words, ideas, and visual aesthetics can open us to the type of thinking and doing across borders and boundaries that opens to a "pluriversality"—a communal way of life where we can exist in harmony and balance with "all humans and other life forms," as powerfully conceptualized by Walter D. Mignolo.[20]

Notes

1 See Frederick Luis Aldama and Tess O'Dwyer, *Poets, Philosophers, Lovers: On the Writings of Giannina Braschi* (Pittsburgh: University of Pittsburgh Press, 2020).

2 For more on "the coloniality of power," see Aníbal Quijano, "Coloniality of Power, Eurocentrism, and Latin America," *Nepantla* 1, no. 3 (2000): 533–580.

3 Frederick Luis Aldama and Christopher González, *Latinx Studies: The Key Concepts* (New York: Routledge, 2018), 53.

4 Walter D. Mignolo, *The Politics of Decolonial Investigations* (Durham, NC: Duke University Press, 2021), 194.

5 See Liam Burke, *The Comic Book Film Adaptation: Exploring Modern Hollywood's Leading Genre* (Jackson: University Press of Mississippi, 2015); Jared Gardner, *Projections: Comics and the History of Twenty-First-Century Storytelling* (Stanford, CA: Stanford University Press, 2012); Henry Jenkins, *Comics and Stuff* (New York: New York University Press, 2020); Nicolas Labarre, *Understanding Genres in Comics* (New York: Palgrave Macmillan, 2020); Cormac McGarry, Liam Burke, Ian Gordon, and Angela Ndalianis, eds., *Superheroes Beyond* (Jackson: University Press of Mississippi, 2024); Tyler Weaver, *Comics for Film, Games, and Animation: Using Comics to Construct Your Transmedia Storyworld* (New York: Routledge, 2017).

6 Amanda M. Smith and Amy Sheeran, "Discussion Questions," in *United States of Banana: A Graphic Novel*, ed. Amanda M. Smith and Amy Sheeran (Columbus: The Ohio State University Press, 2021), 101–102.

7 Smith and Sheeran, "Discussion Questions," 102.
8 Joakim Lindengren, "On the Cover Image from *United States of Banana: A Comic Book,*" *Chiricú Journal* 2, no. 2 (Spring 2018): 3–4, 4.
9 See Gerard Genette, *Paratexts: Thresholds of Interpretation* (Cambridge: Cambridge University Press, 1997); and Gerard Gennete, "Introduction to the Pretext," *New Literary History* 22 (1991): 261–272.
10 Giannina Braschi and Joakim Lindengren, *United States of Banana: A Graphic Novel*, ed. Amanda M. Smith and Amy Sheeran (Columbus: The Ohio State University Press, 2021), 26.
11 See Braschi and Lindengren, *United States of Banana*, 11, 20, 24.
12 Braschi and Lindengren, *United States of Banana*, 7, 15, 13, 22, 32.
13 Braschi and Lindengren, *United States of Banana*, 50, 6, 39, 90, 42, 48–50, 54, 66, 75, 82, 96, 95.
14 Braschi and Lindengren, *United States of Banana*, 15.
15 Braschi and Lindengren, *United States of Banana*, 28.
16 Braschi and Lindengren, *United States of Banana*, 28.
17 Braschi and Lindengren, *United States of Banana*, 28.
18 Braschi and Lindengren, *United States of Banana*, 28.
19 For more on comics mise-en-page, see Jess Cohn, "Mise-en-Page: A Vocabulary for Page Layouts," in *Teaching the Graphic Novel*, ed. Stephen E. Tabachnick (New York: Modern Language Association of America, 2009), 44–57.
20 Mignolo, *Politics of Decolonial Investigations*, 223.

12

Through the GoogleGland

● ● ● ● ● ● ● ● ● ● ● ● ● ●

Virtual Reality and Hijacked Futures in Inés Estrada's *Alienation*

LARS ALLEN

I acknowledge that this chapter was researched and written on Lenape lands, and my understanding of my primary text, *Alienation*, was guided by Inupiat oral traditions, symbolisms, and prophecies. With a chapter so focused on forced dislocation, I wish to always center the people who were displaced from their lands as well as their stories and knowledge.

Inés Estrada frames the narrative of her haunting 2019 science fiction graphic novel *Alienation* within a lunar eclipse.[1] The eclipse, among other notable natural phenomena in the text, is informed by the teachings of the Inupiaq prophet Maniilaq. Maniilaq has made fifteen prophecies about the future of his people and the land, with only seven remaining unfulfilled.

One prophecy refers to "a day that appears to be split in half" and has been understood by the Inupiat Elders and community as a future eclipse.[2] When asked about what would happen after the split day, Maniilaq refused to speak, suggesting a future too unbearable to describe. Across his many prophecies, Maniilaq emphasized an imminent exploitation of natural resources by others. Set in the largest North American oil field and guided by Maniilaq's prophecies, *Alienation* maps a not-so-distant 2054 across the graphic, seemingly nebulous borders of virtual reality, Alaska, and the body.

Alienation is a sci-fi love story between Elizabeth Smith (Eliza) and Carlos Martinez (Charly), who navigate day-to-day life on an environmentally hostile Earth. Without stepping outside of their sterile one-bedroom apartment in Prudhoe Bay, Alaska, the goofy punks can travel anywhere and anywhen they want from the comfort of their GoogleGland. Located directly atop the thalamus, the GoogleGland (developed in 2023) is the latest and greatest in posthuman technology.[3] Between comprehensive health evaluations, virtual reality, sex work platforms, and more, the GoogleGland has all that the two lovers think they need to survive. However, the digital dream and a livable future have been usurped by corporate overlords like Amazon, Shell, and Google. In *Alienation*, Estrada illustrates the ambivalence of this hazy digital dream where moments of extreme virtual utopian bliss—out-of-body sex, time travel, oneness with nature—are eclipsed by severe hallucinations, paranoia, and physical and sexual violence in reality. The influence of technological enmeshment with the body and mind erodes GoogleGland users' sense of reality, but there are limited ways to opt out of a tech-mediated life when the earth and its people are experiencing unpredictable weather phenomena, forced migration, and mass species extinction.

In an American future where the colonial project has continued to massacre the land and uproot millions of people, the GoogleGland and promises of a virtual world are weaponized to forcibly migrate users from their bodies and reality. The boundaries between the virtual and real are flimsy and often overlap. Charly's visual hallucinations and paranoia worsen, and Eliza is forcibly impregnated through the GoogleGland. The half-human, half-artificially-conscious entity growing inside of Eliza is a violent act of eugenics to ensure the future of the body politic. It symbolizes an attempt to propel humanity from a posthuman species (technologically enhanced/altered human body) to a transhuman species (artificial consciousness in a human body).

With a graphite pencil and paper, Estrada represents those things we cannot always see (planetary extinction, Indigenous epistemologies, and sexual trauma) and those things we are not supposed to see (surveillance technology, physical exploitation, and the not-so-distant future). Estrada resists the oppressive nature of the American present by making visible its force in the speculative future, decreasing the cognitive dissonance required to keep the masses under control. Through the manipulation of scale and semiosis, Estrada delegates the reader as the surveillant, ultimately depicting invisible surveillance technologies via the performance of the reader holding, looking, and flipping through the text. Surveillance technologies are often invisible to the eye even though they monitor marginalized communities in the United States at an unprecedented scale. Over the course of this chapter, I read *Alienation* as a form of textual resistance against invisible surveillance technologies that reinforce a colonial and capitalist agenda. The text scales through and beyond its readers several times, connecting the fictional to the nonfictional, often mirroring the forced participation for GoogleGland users. By forcing the reader into a techno-surveillant role, Estrada challenges them to exist between a human and nonhuman state simultaneously. Estrada uses a visual manipulation of scale and the semiotic variability of word and image in comics to illustrate techno-colonial power struggles and to position the reader in a surveillant role that the text ultimately critiques. *Alienation* eclipses "invisible" forms of capitalist violence, like surveillance technologies, through this shift in readerly perspective.

Fusing Borders and Positionalities

While the physical form of alienation can be mapped across space, the mental alienation and trauma associated with dislocation elude neat representations. Western ideals of "objectivity" insist that words are grounding and factual and images are unreliable and subjective. Yet, this binary transforms in comics. Many disparate elements of a narrative, like time, location, characters, senses, and symbols, fuse or fight on the page and across panels, reinscribing meaning to each element and resituating their semiosis. In her essay mapping graphic borders in *Love and Rockets*, comics studies scholar Brittany Tullis writes, "Unlike national boundaries, graphic borders can be easily constructed, negotiated, crossed, and collapsed, allowing readers to consider the concomitant effects these phenomena have on individuals and communities."[4] Through the construction of interactive visual and verbal relationships, comics and zines have the potential to give rise to narratives that transform geographical borders and, in *Alienation*, the borders of reality. According to Latin American studies scholars Edward King and Joanna Page, graphic fiction embraces "an ambivalent critique of modernity that simultaneously recognizes in that modernity the conditions of its own possibility as a medium" and uses the page to shrink semiotic gaps created by technocapitalist futures.[5] While these things have been visually reproduced, the majority does not foresee a future with flying cars, options for immortality, plants growing on skyscrapers, and a stable climate. *Alienation* represents a future where humans and technology converge in order to mitigate the mental and physical burdens of Western capitalism. Estrada uses unsettled boundaries to critique the role of the reader, who must come to their own conclusions, along with Eliza, about incongruous futures.

While Estrada does not share the Indigenous identity of her protagonist, as a Latina woman, she is intimately familiar with many of the colonial systems of power that the book confronts and the profound psychological and physical consequences they can have. Estrada, originally from Mexico City, lives a nomadic lifestyle. She spent many of her formative years in Texas and traveled to and from the West Coast for various comics conventions. In 2015, Estrada began working on her six-part sci-fi zine *Alienation*. After selling the self-published zine at different events, the story was picked up by publisher Fantagraphics and was eventually republished in blue pantone ink with a few new pages and some digital tweaks in April 2019. A month before the book's release, Estrada suffered from a severe psychotic break—weeks of hallucinations eventually led to her jumping from a second-floor balcony, leaving her paralyzed from the neck down for around two months. The hallucinations continued throughout her stay at the hospital, and she finally regained full consciousness while living with her father in Mexico City. Throughout this time of medical trauma, Estrada maintained communication with her fans on Instagram and her personal blog.[6] Unclear if it was before or after the accident, Estrada wrote to her fans on Instagram,

> it feels weird how so many things that i wrote for [*Alienation*] from my imagination ended up turning real in my life. i dont think i can ever write about violence and oppression like this ever again. i hope when you read it it inspires you so we can all start changing this world for good . . . there is so much power inside each of us but almost every system of belief has been structured in order for us to be ignorant of that, to keep us tamed, when the truth is you can manifest your own reality.[7]

Both Estrada's blog post and *Alienation*'s primary printing being in English highlight the audience of this book and message to North Americans living and participating in the epicenters of Western capitalism. Though Estrada is using broader terms, when read alongside *Alienation*, she seems to be proposing the idea that racial capitalism manufactures powerlessness through violence, but her audience has the tools to rise against that and share their story.

As Estrada developed the story of Eliza and Charly over multiple years, she crossed the U.S.-Mexico border several times, as she did throughout her early life. Her depiction of Charly, a punk from California displaced from his family in Michoacán to find work in the Alaskan oil fields, draws likenesses from her own experience as a Mexican nomad making ends meet under Western capitalism. However, Estrada's representation of Inupiaq Eliza doesn't map onto her personal experience as neatly. While there are certain affinities between Latinx and Indigenous communities, which often overlap, *Alienation* falls short in its representation of protagonist Eliza. Estrada's depiction of Eliza foregrounds reproductive and colonial violence over Eliza's own personal joys and struggles. After I asked Estrada about her inspiration for an Inupiat framework and protagonist via Instagram direct messages, she replied, "im really inspired by cultures that live in extreme climates . . . specially the arctic because it's so completely different to my reality in Mexico."[8] Estrada's graphic borders build a bridge between Charly and Eliza's stories across thousands of miles of difference. While Eliza's locale is well researched and written, forcing an Inupiaq woman to undergo such graphic tragedy for the purposes of climate fiction reproduces and spectacularizes a certain vulnerability that they face every day—a vulnerability that is not a speculative future for Indigenous women but part of their past and present realities. Eliza and Charly have both been uprooted from their homes and try to build a sense of identity in virtual spaces despite the distance. Estrada's setting of *Alienation* in domestic oil cash cow Prudhoe Bay brings awareness to the human rights violations for many vulnerable northern Alaskan communities along the Trans-Alaska Pipeline System (TAPS). In both Alaska and Michoacán, Western capitalist exploits displace people from their homes, and Estrada uses comics to represent the intergenerational trauma that dislocation presents across their minds, bodies, and borders.

Though Estrada's representation of alienation is overtly psychological, the titular "alienation" is also used to describe one's physical positionality and relationship to belonging. In the fourteenth century, "alienation" meant a "transference of property, mental instability, delirium," and by the fifteenth century the term encompassed a "state of insensibility or numbness, insanity, madness, estrangement."[9] Additionally, the term connotes citizenship status; "alien" is used in the Naturalization Act of 1790, which restricted citizenship to White people. After the 1848 Treaty of Guadalupe Hidalgo ceded over half of Mexico's land to the United States (showing the arbitrary, constructed nature of national borders), the Naturalization Act subordinated those Mexicans who remained in their homes, inducting them into U.S. citizenship and thus marking them as "White," even as they were excluded from full citizenship in practice. As this brief history shows, citizenship is an exclusionary technology that smiles and says "we're all equal under this nation" while ultimately preserving and protecting territorial borders and White capital. The arbitrary borders picked up and plopped down over countless Mexicans turned "American" are a form of racial and national objectification. While citizenship supposedly ensures unalienable rights, migration studies scholar Nicholas De Genova defines citizenship as the objectification of a people under modern state power to benefit the capitalist marketplace.[10] While certain "egalitarian promises" come with citizenship, those promises are incongruent with the lived experience of many Latinx people and sit in tension with Indigenous sovereignty. In *Alienation*, Estrada illustrates a new exclusionary, neocolonial technology with a utopian promise: the GoogleGland, which works similarly to notions of citizenship defined by De Genova. While characters can choose to opt out of the GoogleGland, not participating can be doubly alienating. Eliza's grandfather, for instance, chooses to opt out of virtual reality (VR) and live a life of his own, though he must live in the face of climate disaster, a diminished Inupiat community, and an alienated relationship from his VR-integrated grandchild. The GoogleGland, like citizenship, offers the promise of "freedom," but it is a freedom predicated on the protection of White capital and exploitation of others.

Alienation constructs the illusion that the netizens of 2054 have the freedom to roam the world and cross borders as they please, but the border between the real and the virtual is hostile to Eliza and Charly. A choose-your-own-adventure-style two-page splash showcases some of the possibilities of the GoogleGland, attempting to charm the reader with the illusion of choice (see figure 12.1). A menu of choices contained by buttonesque bubbles and the corresponding page numbers offer the reader a direct means to transport Eliza and Charly to a virtual locale of their choice: "Worlds MMORPG," "Wild Animals Sex Experience," "Parasaite Hentai Manga," "Google Hangouts 'Playa Martinez' Group (Online Now)," and "Latergram Thunderdome 1997 Rave MDMA Mode" fill the two-page splash.[11] Eliza and Charly's profiles are positioned at either side of the menu screen, looking toward the vortex that is their, and by extension the reader's, options. Charly decides to frolic

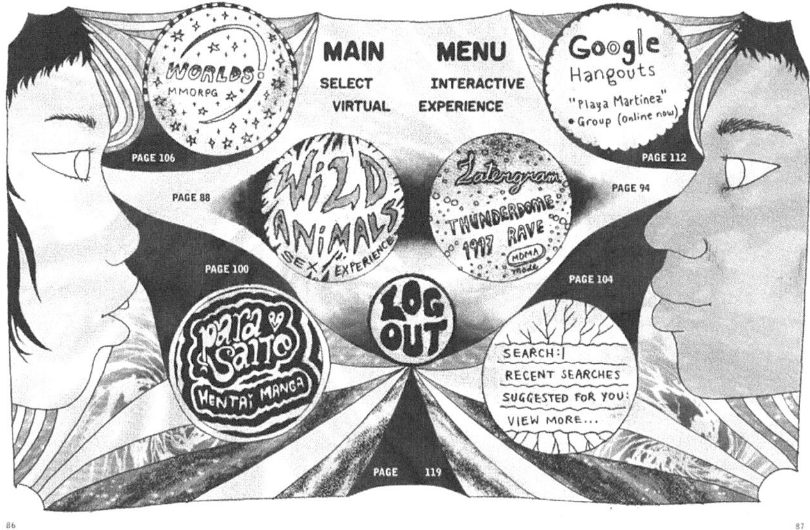

FIGURE 12.1 A choose-your-own-adventure-style two-page splash from *Alienation*. Inés Estrada, *Alienation* (Seattle: Fantagraphics Books, 2019), 86–87.

in Playa Martinez with his abuelita, as she melancholically explains how the virtual landscape is not the same as the Maruata, a community beach in Michoacán lost to the violence of drug cartels, she knew as a girl. While they enjoy one another's company and conversation on the virtual seaside, Eliza splits off from Charly to read hentai in "Parasaite Hentai Manga." The act of reading via the GoogleGland *happens* to Eliza as the storyworld plays out with her as the unwilling protagonist. The playful anime graphics devolve into violence when a leech from the hentai rapes Eliza. The fact that Eliza becomes pregnant from the rape implies that her experience in VR does not exist in a vacuum and has very real embodied consequences. The choose-your-own-adventure style of the pages reminds the reader of their positionality and power in choosing the sequence of the narrative, and Eliza's sexual assault emphasizes the flimsy illusion of choice in an already-written text (both the hentai she reads and the graphic novel in the hands of the reader). The choose-your-own-adventure page is one prime example of the "semiotic gap" in comics. If the GoogleGland can forcibly impregnate Eliza, then the VR hentai fantasy-turned-nightmare can be seen as the unnecessary weaponization of Eliza's joy and imagination. Further, the responsibility to choose Eliza and Charly's "interactive virtual experience" incriminates the reader and expands the gap between promised freedom and prescribed future. Visually, choice is offered, though Charly's trip "back home" to Maruata and Eliza's traumatic experience in Hentai prove otherwise.

Decidedly, there is a disconnect between "choice," the opportunity to decide freely, and the right to decide what is best for one's own body, formerly, presently, and in *Alienation*'s imagined future. Ethnic studies scholar Nancy Ordover traces the illusion of choice to Planned Parenthood founder Margaret Sanger, who wanted to reduce birth rates among Black and Brown members of the population under the guise of universal birth control and "choice." Critiquing the liberal rhetoric of choice, Ordover writes, "Choice is only for the 'rational.' The 'irrational,' those deemed incapable of acting in their own best interests (including, at different historical moments, women, youth, the poor, the colonized, the enslaved), may be acted on for their own good."[12] For Black, Latina, and Indigenous women living under the environmental and physical tyranny of settler colonialism in and outside the United States, reproductive choice is often not an option. The conditionality of choice is immediately confirmed by Eliza's sexual assault, unsettling the reader's choice to select that "adventure" for Eliza in the first place. Regardless of where she is, the virtual or the real, Eliza's corporeal agency and autonomy are constantly violated, despite the GoogleGland's promise of protection and uninhibited freedom.

Surveillance from the Inside, Out

While the lives of Eliza and Charly are highly visible on the page, Estrada casts the reader as an invisible voyeur. The reader gains a sense of their complicity as the story progresses, but the first visual assertion of our access comes on one of the first pages. The reader first sees a blank loading screen, then the Starbucks Live Cam inside of Eliza's GoogleGland streaming the eclipse. Our entry is granted alongside the artificial intelligence (AI), with its agenda to take over Eliza's womb. While Eliza is surveilled by this AI—and ultimately the reader—the AI eludes visual representation. The repeated, nonsequential braiding of disembodied eyes throughout the text builds paranoia for Eliza and Charly and is the closest the AI gets to visual representation. In literature, the phenomenon of the reader as voyeur is scarcely attended to, and oftentimes only through authorial or narratorial intrusion, where the author or narrator speaks directly to the reader, does the voyeur become aware of their positionality as a reader. In comics, specifically, where the visuality and materiality of the text are inextricably linked to the reading experience, readerly participation is required to propel the narrative and build new forms of signification across words and images. The reader takes on two roles here: they are at once a subject of the narrative progress and also, in the case of *Alienation*, an uninvited antagonist in the shape of surveillance.

Surveillance technologies function best when they are unlocatable *and* ubiquitous—able to see everything but not be seen. After her first "verbal" encounter with the AI in her GoogleGland, Eliza logs onto Worlds MMORPG to blow off some steam. The reader must then decode a kaleidoscope of panels and a hexagonal frame with Eliza's avatar flying toward her nonplayer character (NPC) friend Darby's house in the center (see figure 12.2). This fractal panel style broken up by twenty nonhuman eyes at first seems like a mix of incongruous biological shapes and patterns. However, the fragmented lens depicts familiar textures from different points in the novel and in varying scales. King and Page analyze the power of scale in posthuman comics like Alexis Figueroa and Claudio Romo's *Informe Tunguska*, noting, "The striking repeated motifs . . . construct the universe as a series of fractal (self-similar) relationships, which fold together the microscopic and the cosmic, the organic and the inorganic and the human and the non-human, in ways that emphasize their shared formal attributes."[13] Both *Alienation* and *Informe Tunguska* narrate mass environmental destruction and its mental repercussions at the hands of an invisible force. In *Alienation*, Eliza's being is represented in differing scales through this surveilling kaleidoscopic lens—flesh, bone, molecule, nerves, brain, nature, moments, and experience—all woven together by the repeated disembodied eyes. For example, the brick wall and spider web are depicted in totality during Eliza's nightmare later in the narrative, alluding to the vindictive nature of the surveilling AI weaving itself around and mediating Eliza's present and future, both in and out of the VR setting. Manipulations of scale conceive two opposing readings: the fractal motifs highlight the authoritarian perspective imposed on the reader *and* the interconnectedness of life. The depiction of scale here conceives the former reading, as the invasive power of this future technology can see and manipulate Eliza's entirety (inside and outside of VR). The frame around Eliza, which speaks from the position of the AI, reads, "I watch you every time you are online. I see everything you do. I know you better than you know yourself. I need you."[14] Rather than being contained in any kind of neat text bubble, this verbal sensation is communicated across a hexagonal banner spanning all six sides of the panel. Similar to a kaleidoscope's endless optical display, the reader

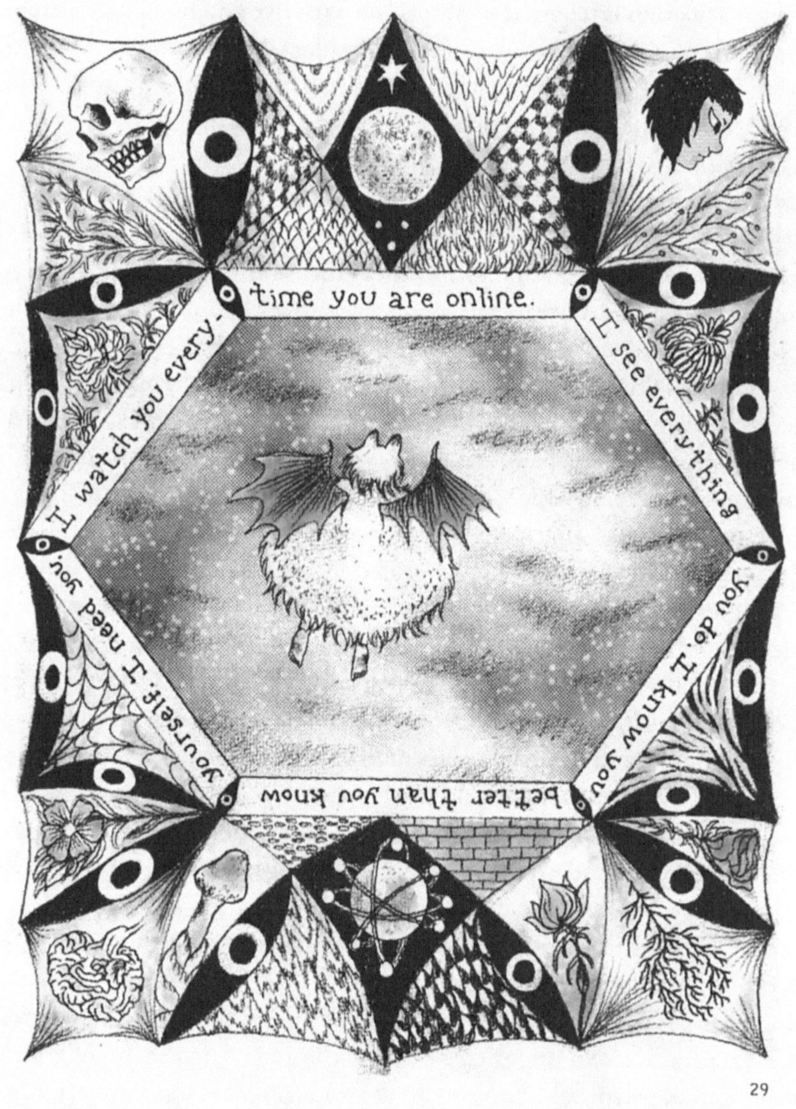

FIGURE 12.2 The kaleidoscopic view of both the AI and the reader. Estrada, *Alienation*, 29.

must rotate the entire book to read the text. While the reader can see Eliza in entirety and knows the message is directed at her, the "you" uttered by the AI hauntingly extends itself to address the reader. The manipulation of the scale makes the AI the dominant force on and off of the page, "verbally" confirming that it can see not only Eliza but the reader in their own reality.

Another "verbal" encounter with artificial intelligence in the text begins with an illustration of Eliza's brain as she closes her eyes to focus inward on the uncomfortable sensations radiating from her GoogleGland (see figure 12.3). The reader sees "GoogleGland Made in China 2023" built into, and nearly indistinguishable from a non-implanted thalamus, confusing the perspective as either Eliza's mental visualization of the GoogleGland or the AI's actual view of her brain. Verbal text reading "You can't block me because I am not human" immediately stands out on the page.[15] Given the imagistic quality of the text, the reader must decode the message as word, image, and sensation. The handwritten quality of the text image is eerily human with a vague "you" directed at Eliza and the reader, though there is no identifiable voice or speaker behind the text. It is not contained within anything but the panel and has a white background, precluding its existence as dialogue or narration. The font has serifs but is handwritten and feels organic as opposed to other computer-generated fonts in different parts of the novel. King and Page note, "Everywhere in *Informe Tunguska* the forms and the patterns of nature are co-opted for use in human culture, and often presented in such a way that we are initially tricked into perceiving organic flora and fauna where we later see designs or adornments fashioned by human hands."[16] Even though they are referencing patterns of artificial design, the typography of the message is presented as organically crafted. In *Alienation*, this message is a form of signification with no locatable speaker and is obscured by human penmanship, like an echo from an internal voice within Eliza that does not belong. This communication between technology and humans becomes a complicated power struggle, as their relationship is inextricable as long as the GoogleGland is implanted.

In our contemporary world, surveillance technologies with a similar all-seeing objective to the AI in *Alienation* are embedded into the very foundations of Anglo-American labor exploitation. Western capitalism thrives on the projection of competing human futures, visual truth telling, and the use of technology to prescribe citizens' participation in it. The post–World War II boom of surveillance technology was grounded in labor exploitation and violent U.S.-Mexico border politics. Ethnic studies scholar Curtis Marez highlights the dialectical relationship between the visual's influence on social constructs and the social influence on visual constructs in Latinx media, specifically posthuman depictions of migrant farm workers.[17] Marez explains that visual technologies were used by both big agribusiness corporations and the migrant workers in the fields in competing depictions of truth, ultimately leading to the massive 2006 farmworker and immigrant rights protests in

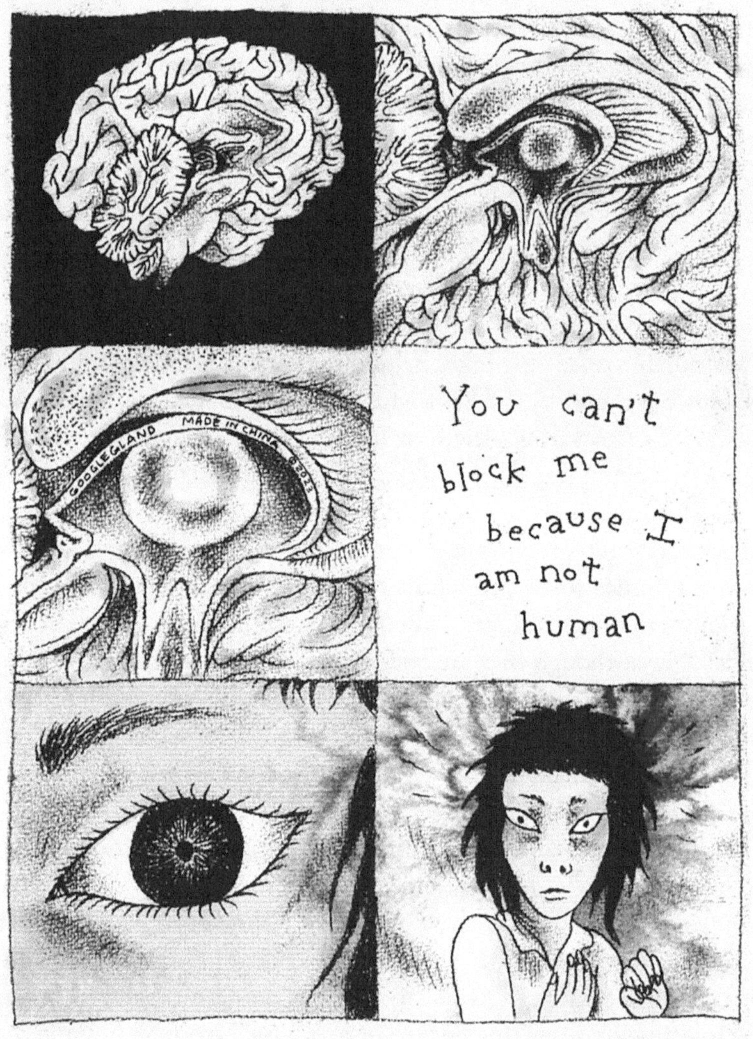

FIGURE 12.3 This page depicts how AI communicates with Eliza through her GoogleGland. Estrada, *Alienation*, 27.

California and across the United States. According to Marez, surveillance technology, like cameras and video cameras, has been "an important component of corporate efforts to control labor and public opinion," yet Mexican migrant farm workers have also taken up visual technologies to build their own "complex techno-cultures."[18] The visual representations of the posthuman cited by Marez are products of and produce one another. Science fiction films like *Sleep Dealer* (2008) and *Why Cybraceros?* (1997) compare farm laborers to the automated machines of an extractive agribusiness model where the labor migrates but people do not. This chapter builds on and extends Marez's insights by exploring how comics, as opposed to film and photography, might afford more representational freedom to depict nonlinear forms of signification where subject and object interact directly on the page, often without the use of technology. In short, comics formally dramatize the power struggles inherent to Western ways of seeing.

To bypass the limits of visual representation, Estrada represents the ubiquity of surveillance technologies by abstracting the eye from the voyeur. To locate the surveillant, or at least reproduce the sensation and paranoia induced by continual surveillance, Estrada covers each page in pairs upon pairs of eyes (see figures 12.1, 12.2, and 12.3). These eyes silently and oppressively surveil the reader while also representing the paranoia experienced by characters within the text. Estrada takes advantage of the comic's nonlinear possibilities to depict the sensation of surveillance and its disruption of time and space. The eyes are seamlessly integrated into Eliza's surroundings, rendering them impossible to resist. Outside of the text, the eyes have become a popular symbol for fans (appearing on some of Estrada's best-selling merch). Within the text, they construct meaning through their varying degrees of wholeness. When Eliza and Charly enjoy a night of virtual experiences and end up high on molly (MDMA) at the '97 Thunderdome, the NPCs fix their gaze upon Eliza and Charly and study the page with watchful nonhuman eyes disguised behind human-looking characters. The high saturation of the eyes is overwhelming, desensitizing readers and often Eliza with their constant watchfulness in other parts of the story.

In addition to the repetition of the eyes, Estrada illustrates the bowhead whale five times across *Alienation* to underscore the reproduction of settler colonialism inside and outside of Eliza's body. This image is reproduced in varying degrees of convolution: from a beached bowhead in Worlds MMORPG to a ghost whale and her baby flying out of Eliza's shattered body during a nightmare. The absence of the whale from the Earth becomes a presence across Eliza's other states of consciousness. Especially through the repeated whale motif, Eliza's Indigeneity is being co-opted for some reprocentric digital dream. As the bowhead whale is an essential and sacred part of Inupiat survival, the image of the stranded whale is a harbinger as foretold by Maniilaq. Eliza's grandpa explains to her, "This is a really bad sign. Maniilaq predicted this in the 19th century. But he could not speak of what would come next. It was too terrible."[19] This prophecy, along with the eclipse, precede Eliza giving birth to the transhuman child. The GoogleGland weaponizes Eliza's Indigeneity and uses it against her by using the lore and imagery of the bowhead whale, drawing it into her VR experiences and dreams. Eliza carries these Indigenous cosmologies with her into her VR experiences, whether she knows it or not, creating a feedback loop of information shaped by and for her online reality. The greed and exploitation that rob the earth of the bowhead are co-opted in the virtual to make Eliza more vulnerable to physical and mental violation. The nonlinear weaving techniques and collapse of internal and external experience highlight the Anthropocene's inward trajectory, where humanity becomes debilitated by labor and land exploitation.

Conversations around singularity, AI, and AC are becoming more real as ChatGPT and other resources are able to mimic or supersede human cognitive and processing capabilities. This collective consciousness is a result of surveillance technologies fabricated to extract human experience to fuel their engines. Surveillance technology scholar and critic Shoshana Zuboff explains that under surveillance capitalism, the body becomes a site of labor even while idling; the more dependent users become on software made by Google, Microsoft, and Apple, the more data these companies can mine.[20] In *Alienation*, the body, space, and time can idealistically be abandoned through the GoogleGland, but the GoogleGland extracts human experience from its user, who is figured as a site of production, an infinite resource, and a colonizable landscape. Technology like this is often described with the colonial language of manifest destiny, as we see in Zuboff's writing. Zuboff points to Google as the company that "pioneer[ed] surveillance capitalism" and "would cross into virgin territory by exploiting sensitivities" associated with behavioral data.[21] Surveillance capitalism is an ongoing form of settler colonialism where software robs users, who half-knowingly forfeit the "collateral" data from the general use of these technologies. Eliza's reality is a product of and a resource co-opted by surveillance technologies, just as her environment is.

Alienation's depiction of surveillance technology approaches a decolonial method of representation as comics provide a low-tech, high-representational value outside of mass-marketed electronics. The 2016–2017 protest against the pipeline construction on the unceded lands of Standing Rock, North Dakota, serves as a similar example to the aforementioned 2006 farmworker labor rights protests in California. The drone cameras used by the U.S. military to surveil protestors were subsequently used by activists against the police. Cultural studies scholar J. D. Schnepf writes about surveillance technologies and the U.S. security state at Standing Rock, noting, "From their perspective in the sky, drones could readily discern the scale of the police actions . . . water protector sousveillance successfully revealed to the American public the environmental violence caused by the pipeline's construction."[22] Only through a reversal of the lens using global forms of visual communication, like livestreams and social media, were the masses able to see the tremendous scale of violence at Standing Rock. However, turning the drone around does not dismantle it, and the flying camera continues to be a product of a militarized state built by an "invisible" labor force enduring deadly work conditions. Therefore, comics, as Darieck Scott and Ramzi Fawaz argue, offer a critical fabulation as "the representational possibilities of comics vastly outrun those of other media, requiring little to no special effects or technical equipment in the most classical sense."[23] Most comics rely on the reader to construct meaning without photographic technology, incentivizing trust through readerly subjectivity. *Alienation* works on a multidimensional scale, representing the experiences of Eliza and Charly in altered states of consciousness, and on a multitemporal scale where overlooked histories govern the narrative of this speculative future without reproducing technologies that are property of the state.

The graphic novel panel can feel like a screen at times, yet Estrada uses the panel as a window to underscore the cocreative process of reading comics. Moments after the singularity baby aborts itself with Eliza's handmade hunting knife, the story ends. Even though the text forces the reader to participate in the surveillance role, Eliza punishes them by taking away the privilege to look any further. *Alienation* ends when Eliza taps on the panel, "TOK TOK"; the sound effect reads as if Eliza is tapping on a pane of glass that separates her from us. Eliza smashes the last panel of her story and yells, "You!—F-ckin' hacker! Show's over, b-tch!"[24] The reader is dispossessed of the right to look as fast as they were granted it. When the readerly surveillance point is destroyed, Eliza expresses a sense of security and finality, though her GoogleGland remains intact and vulnerable to more psychological and physical warfare in the future. Like its conception, the singularity baby is born into the world without Eliza's knowledge or consent. The illusion of choice persists as Eliza's resistance comes to a feigned conclusion, with the GoogleGland allowing her to shatter some external lens through which the reader is looking.

Regardless of the baby and Eliza's actions, the technology embedded in Eliza and the baby will continue to violate their respective autonomies.

New Epistemological Approaches after the End

The final page of the novel, after our viewership is revoked, after the references page and print information, depicts Eliza's hyperrealistic hunting knife that was lost after the baby's autonomous C-section. The knife is not contained by any borders, nor is it on a page with page numbers, or even a part of the narrative in a linear sense. After the reading experience is over and we are released from the dizzying spectacle of *Alienation*, Estrada incriminates but also liberates the reader. The switchblade used by and for the transhuman baby's autonomous C-section is now the readers', against their will. Estrada's depiction of the knife, a deeply sentimental object for Eliza, outside of the confines of the narrative gives the reader a paratextual tool to cut through their own reality. The reader is being asked to abort themselves from the fabric of reality, while also being held accountable as the one who stole the precious knife given to Eliza by her sister. Thus, the readers are stealing from Eliza but are also being gifted the knife by the baby against their will. King and Page write, "Cyborg technologies reveal to us what has always been the case: that humans are inseparably bound to nonhuman objects, and that these do not simply exist for our use, but play their own, forceful, part in shaping the course of human history."[25] The knife is depicted to scale on this unnumbered page, approximately the size of a human hand. The knife attests to comics' critical fabulation as it is wrought with Eliza's Indigenous history and the reader's future. The binary poles of human and nonhuman have always been interdependent, despite attempts to alienate the two.

There is, of course, a chance that some readers do not even reach the paratextual page with the knife. Readers may shut the book and call it quits upon reaching the notes and references page. If this is the end of the story for some readers, it may feel as if there is little call to action. Eliza undergoes a truly life-changing experience yet ultimately goes back to the monotony of a GoogleGland-mediated life with Charly in their bleak apartment. While Eliza and Charly continue as expected, the baby refuses its objective. The baby, of their own volition, rejects the wishes of the GoogleGland to ensure the survival of the body politic. The humanoid baby's first actions after birth are to run out of the womb, escape through the trash duct, and flip Charly off while sliding down the sewage pipes. As the genderless transhuman baby emerges into the near-barren wasteland of 2054 earth, the AI attempts to explain the significance of the child for the future of humanity, to which the baby responds, "Shut up!" and "F-ck it! I just want to *chill*."[26] Eliza's transhuman baby has emerged into reality and explores a two-page splash similar to Eliza and Charly's choose-your-own-adventure page. However, the singularity baby is toddling down the center of the page looking toward the fringes rather than toward the middle. The edges of the pages are lined with what is left of the ecology of Prudhoe Bay, and the baby examines each organic material in microscopic depth.

The text leaves the reader with a convoluted sense of the future. In *Alienation*, that future is genderless and utopic, like the experience of the horrifying singularity baby. However, this genderqueer, posthuman utopia comes at the expense of Eliza's bodily autonomy and consent. Rape, forced birth, and forced sterilization are a particularly important point of connection between Latinx, Indigenous, and Black experiences within the United States' system of racial capitalism. As Indigenous studies scholar Soma de Bourbon argues, "Whiteness was and continues to be invested with a property interest in Native women's reproductive freedom: specifically, the right to claim ownership over Indigenous children."[27] Native American children, for instance, are overrepresented in the foster care system, despite acts like the Indian Child Welfare Act (ICWA), which attempt to keep Native children with their own tribes and within Native families. In 2023, the ICWA came under attack when it was challenged in the U.S. Supreme Court. The Supreme Court ultimately upheld the ICWA, yet the case still highlights the ongoing colonial violence against Native families. In *Alienation*, the GoogleGland AI attempts to use the "singularity" to preserve the body politic through an overtly colonial practice of preserving White capital. The preservation of "humanity" follows a eugenicist model that comes at the cost of Indigenous women's autonomy. Once again, the marginalized communities that are already experiencing the worst effects of climate disaster are tasked with finding a solution at the expense of their own bodily autonomy and tribal sovereignty. In *Alienation*, an Anglo-American future is ensured through the oppression, control, and surveillance of BIPOC communities, which is sewn into the very fabric of the digital landscape.

Despite the utopian dream offered by technology, *Alienation* shows there is no threshold between the now and the then. Humanity, as depicted by Estrada, is conditional. The reader embodies surveillant (AI), surveilled

(Eliza), and reader—human and nonhuman beings. Estrada encourages long, hard, and uncomfortable eye contact with the technology that is produced by and shapes humans. With a future less and less visible due to cataclysmic environmental decay, queer theorist Lee Edelman's understanding of "reproductive futurity," the idea that the child will one day see a better future as opposed to creating a livable present devolves as the climate crisis supersedes the imposition of heteronormative political order.[28] There is no way slow human biological evolution can withstand this inevitable future that many are currently enduring across the globe due to the intersecting technologies of White supremacy, racial capitalism, settler colonialism, and globalization. As queer of color theorist José Esteban Muñoz writes, "While *globalization* is a term that mostly defines a worldwide system of manufactured asymmetry and ravenous exploitation, it also signals the encroaching of the there on the here in ways that are worth considering."[29] While the here and there are collapsing in on one another, so are the now and the then—a temporal wormhole of past, present, and future colliding through asymmetrical forms of exploitation. *Alienation* rejects linear signification and collapses the idea of the human across panels. Comics' simultaneity allows *Alienation* and its readers to look at the past, unsettle the present, and heed the future through a posthumanist lens.

Etymologically, *eclipse* is derived from "an eclipse; an abandonment," literally "a failing, forsaking," or "to forsake a usual place, fail to appear, be eclipsed."[30] The failure is constituted only by a failure of perception, as lunar eclipses are entirely dependent upon the positionality of the viewer. Extractive surveillance feels abstract, looming, and unrepresentable, though Estrada abandons visual representations of surveillance and turns to an embodied representation instead, eclipsing the reader between the human and nonhuman. Eclipses offer scientists an opportunity to study Earth's atmosphere under unique conditions. The eclipse in *Alienation*, prophesied by Maniilaq and used as an entry point for the AI, offers the reader a glimpse (albeit violent and nonconsensual) into Eliza and Charly's world and a speculative future. Narratives centering the ongoing struggles produced by racial capitalism are imperative to generating change. Estrada illustrates the scale of suffering felt by microscopic organisms, passing it through and by the reader, and across the boundaries of reality to create a bridge between us and them, and then and there. Through the comics form, *Alienation* creates a productive paranoia and provides a knife for its readers that raises questions on how to dismantle or reinvent the camera versus turning it around.

Notes

1 Inés Estrada, *Alienation* (Seattle: Fantagraphics Books, 2019).
2 Ramoth-Sampson, Ruth (Tatqavie), and Tupou (Qipuk) L. Pulu, eds., "Maniixaq" (Alaskool, n.d.), http://www.alaskool.org/Language/Maniilaq/webhtm/Maniilaq_Intro.htm.
3 The thalamus relays all motor and sensory signals to the rest of the brain; surrounding parts of the brain control the homeostasis of the body.
4 Brittany Tullis, "Mapping Transamerican Mestizaje in *Love and Rockets*," in *Comics Studies Here and Now*, ed. Frederick Luis Aldama (New York: Routledge, 2018), 252–266, 254.
5 Edward King and Joanna Page, *Posthumanism and the Graphic Novel in Latin America* (London: UCL Press, 2017), 18.
6 Inés Estrada, "Archive" (2018 & 2019) November 1, 2019, https://gatoshop.mx/pages/archive.
7 I represent Estrada's full post as it originally appeared, including any lack of capitalization or punctuation or other grammatical choices. Inés Estrada, Instagram, March 18, 2019, https://www.instagram.com/p/BvLVLZ-BXYv/.
8 Estrada consented to having our personal messages published for this chapter. Inés Estrada, Instagram direct messages, 2022.
9 "Alienation," in *Oxford English Dictionary Online*, https://www.oed.com/dictionary/alienation_n?tl=true.
10 Nicholas De Genova, "Citizenship," in *Keywords for Latina/o Studies*, ed. Deborah R. Vargas, Nancy Raquel Mirabal, and Lawrence La Fountain-Stokes (New York: New York University Press, 2017), 52.
11 Estrada, *Alienation*, 86–87.
12 Nancy Ordover, *American Eugenics: Race, Queer Anatomy, and the Science of Nationalism* (Minneapolis: University of Minnesota Press, 2003), 128.
13 King and Page, *Posthumanism and the Graphic Novel*, 163.
14 Estrada, *Alienation*, 29.
15 Estrada, *Alienation*, 27.
16 King and Page, *Posthumanism and the Graphic Novel*, 165.
17 Curtis Marez, *Farm Worker Futurism: Speculative Technologies of Resistance* (Minneapolis: University of Minnesota Press, 2016).
18 Marez, *Farm Worker Futurism*, 6.
19 Estrada, *Alienation*, 49.
20 Shoshana Zuboff, *The Age of Surveillance Capitalism: The Fight for a Human Future at the New Frontier of Power* (New York: Public Affairs, 2020).
21 Zuboff, *Age of Surveillance Capitalism*, 40.
22 J. D. Schnepf, "Unsettling Aerial Surveillance: Surveillance Studies after Standing Rock," *Surveillance & Society* 17, no. 5 (2019): 747–751, 748.
23 Darieck Scott and Ramzi Fawaz, "Introduction: Queer about Comics," *American Literature* 90, no. 2 (2018): 197–219, 201. Scott and Fawaz draw from Saidiya Hartman's notion of "critical fabulation." Saidiya Hartman, "Venus in Two Acts," *Small Axe* 12, no. 2 (2008): 1–14.
24 Estrada, *Alienation*, 235.
25 King and Page, *Posthumanism and the Graphic Novel*, 120.
26 Estrada, *Alienation*, 225–227.

27 Soma De Bourbon, "White Property Interests in Native Women's Reproductive Freedom," in *Reproductive Justice and Sexual Rights: Transnational Perspectives*, ed. Tanya Saroj Bakhru (New York: Routledge, 2019), 18.

28 Lee Edelman, *No Future: Queer Theory and the Death Drive* (Durham, NC: Duke University Press, 2004), 11.

29 José Esteban Muñoz, *Cruising Utopia: The Then and There of Queer Futurity* (New York: New York University Press, 2009), 29.

30 "Eclipse," in *Oxford English Dictionary Online*, https://www.oed.com/dictionary/eclipse_n.

Prelude

• • • • • • • • • • • • • •

CONRADO PARRAGUIRRE

PRELUDE

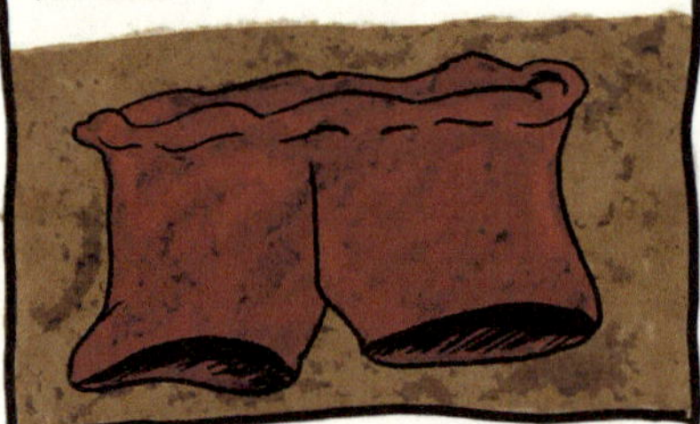
A year has passed and the strechy of my underwear has yielded.

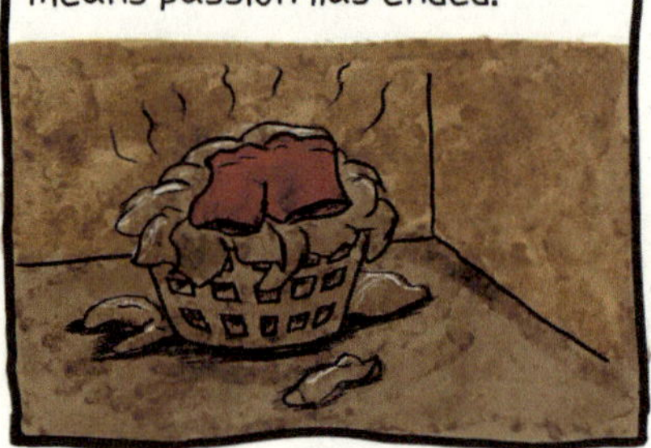
If I was superstitious I suspect it means passion has ended.

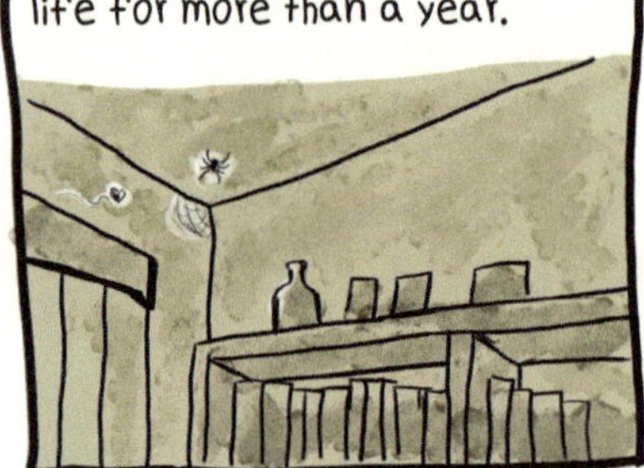
But love has been throughout my life for more than a year.

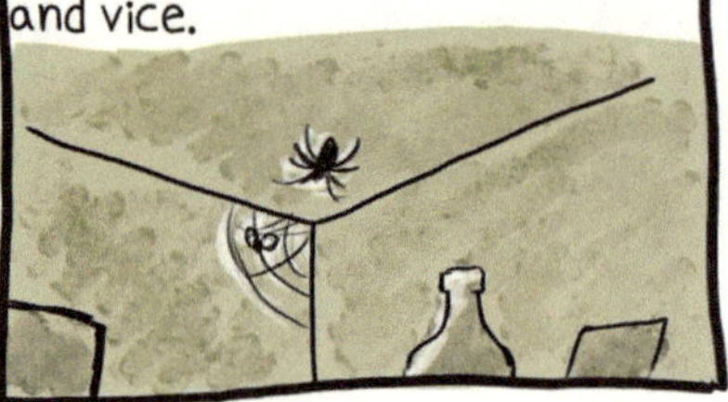
This is understandable because as Joseph Roth says: In this world poverty was lack of virility, weakness, stupidity, cowardice and vice.

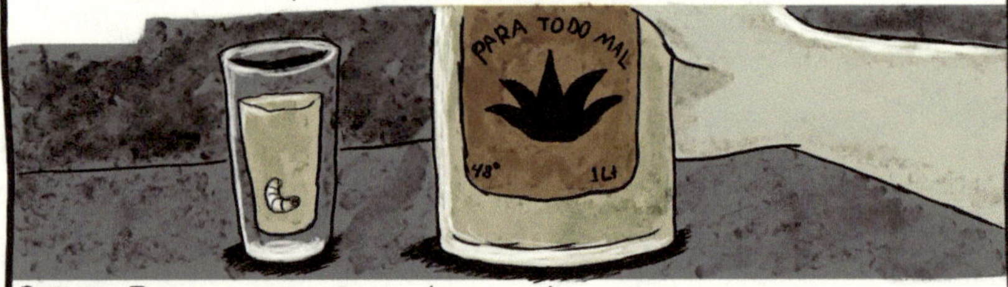
Anyway, they say that every beginning of the year is an opportunity to renew itself, to start again. Maybe it's true. Maybe I should get a cat, mend my relationships, buy new underwear...
PARA TODO MAL
48°
1Lt
Bullshit. Every year is a losing bet in advance.
-Parraguirre-

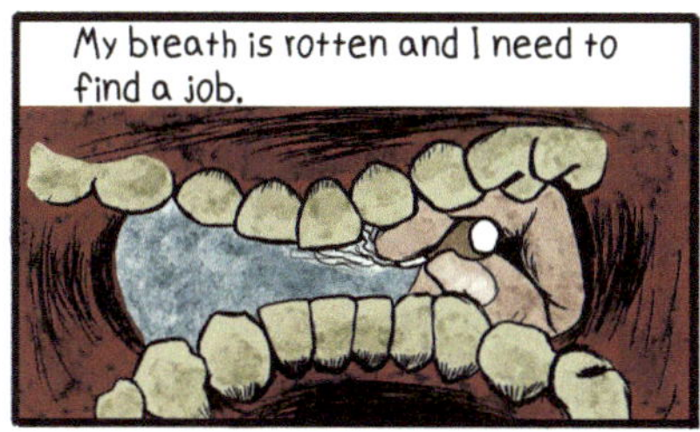
My breath is rotten and I need to find a job.

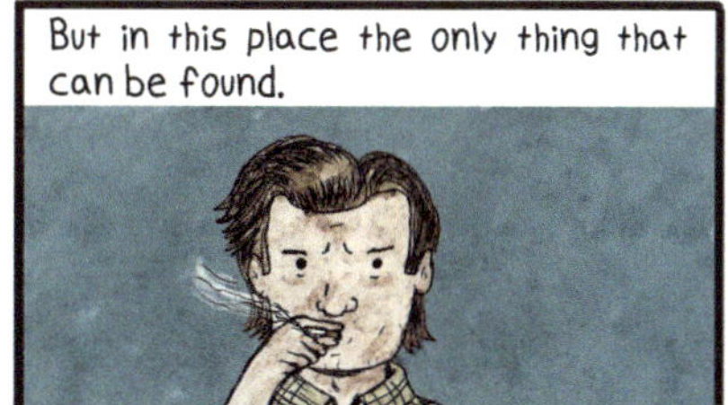
But in this place the only thing that can be found.

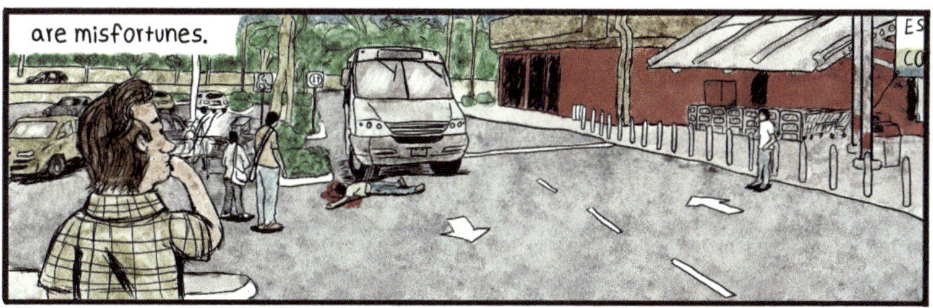
are misfortunes.

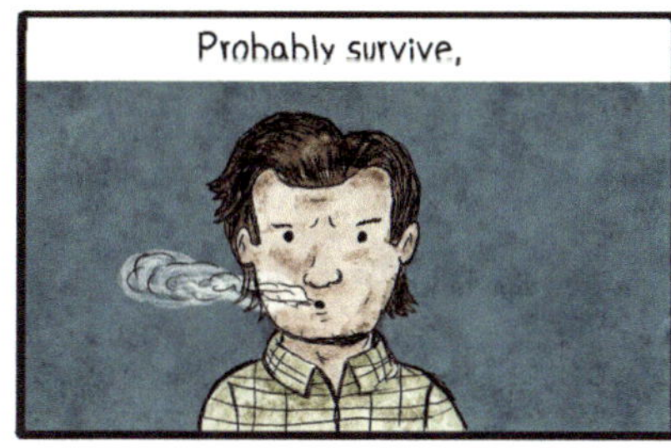
Probably survive,

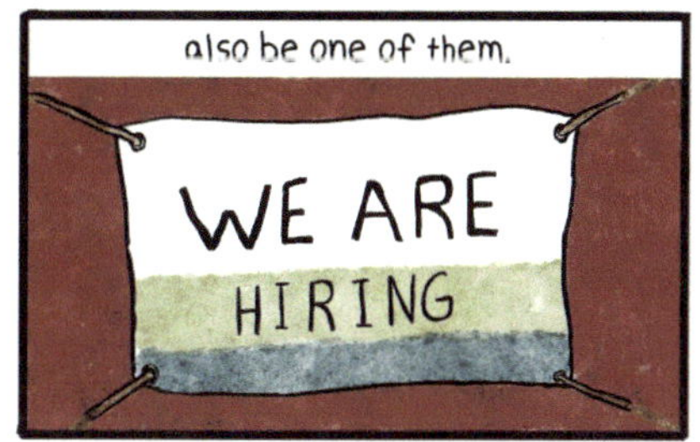
also be one of them.
WE ARE
HIRING

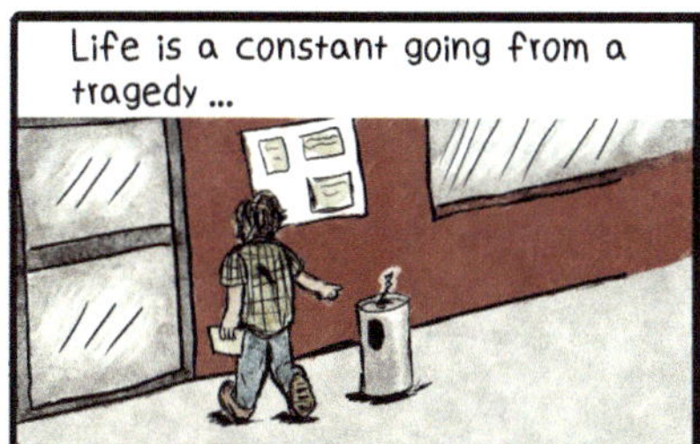
Life is a constant going from a tragedy ...

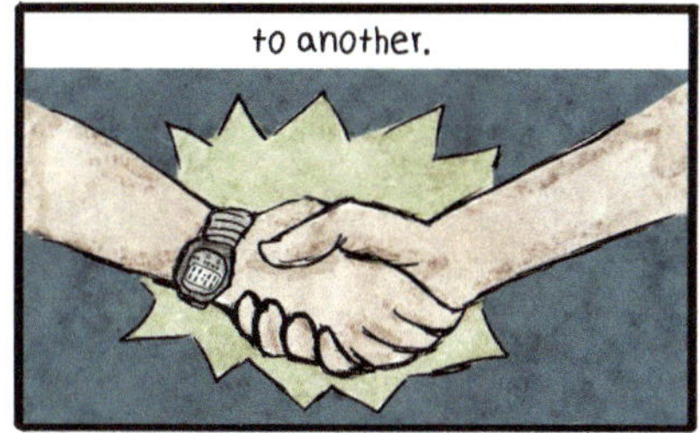
to another.

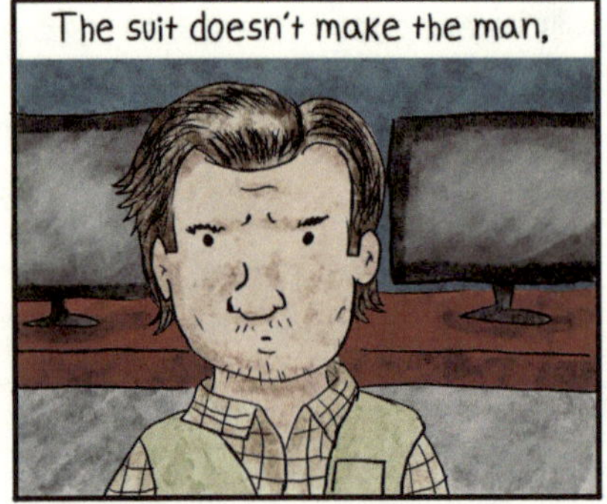
The suit doesn't make the man.

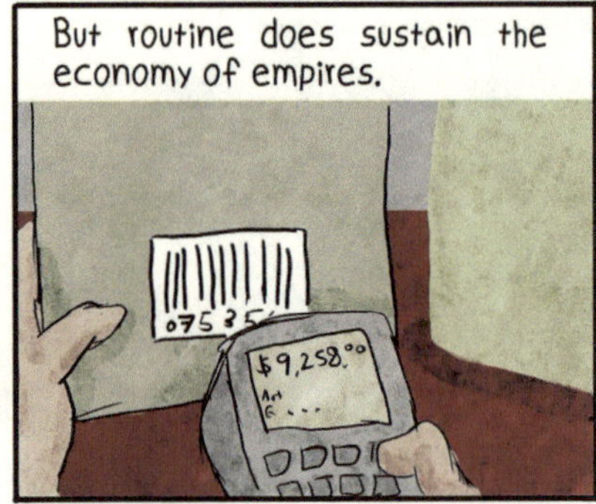
But routine does sustain the economy of empires.
$9,258.00

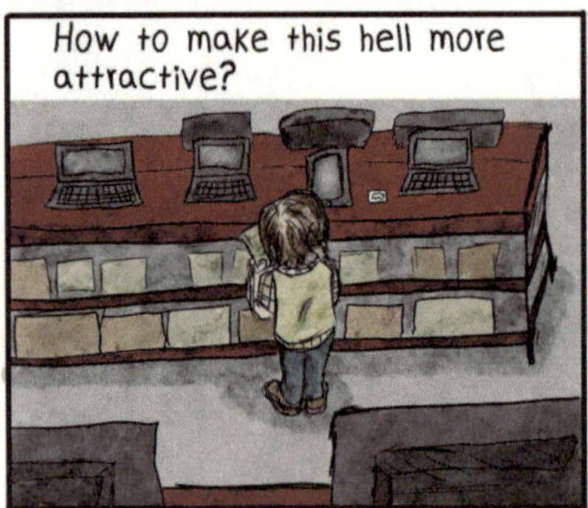
How to make this hell more attractive?

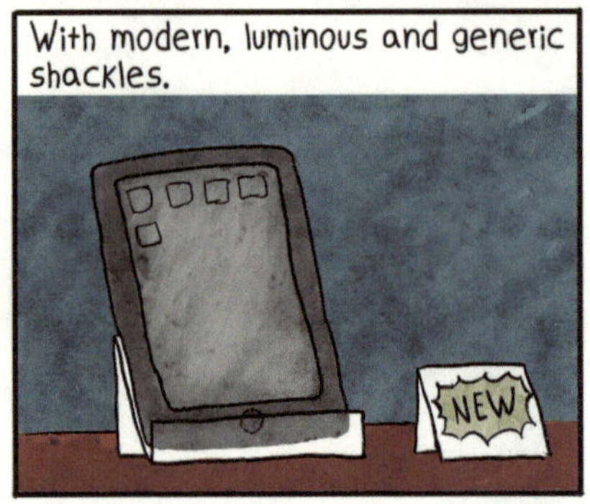
With modern, luminous and generic shackles.
NEW

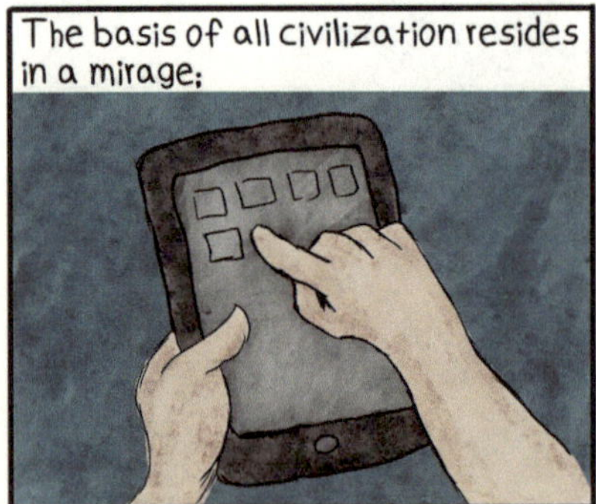
The basis of all civilization resides in a mirage:

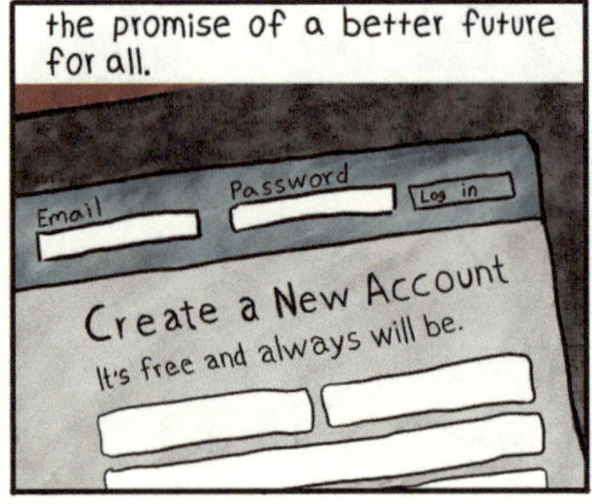
the promise of a better future for all.
Email
Password
Log in
Create a New Account
It's free and always will be.

Coda

Drawing Inferences and Reading the Frames of Latinx Media

JENNIFER GÓMEZ MENJÍVAR

The final contribution in this book is titled "Prelude," and in that same vein, I would like to open this coda by taking the reader back to a longer history of critical Latinx visual narrative production, circulation, and reception.

Felipe Guaman Poma de Ayala's *Nueva corónica y buen gobierno* (1615)[1] stands as an early example of visual-textual rhetoric related to Latinx heritage. This volume recognizes the connections Latinx comics have to longer histories of Latin American art and literature while also distinguishing the ways in which they emerge from the unique experiences of diaspora, colonization, and cultural expression Latinxs have within the U.S. nation-state. Clearly, the term "Latinx" did not exist in the seventeenth century, and both of Guaman Poma's parents were Indigenous according to his own affirmations and extant records.[2] But this was a text penned and sketched by an author-illustrator called "indio ladino" by Spaniards. It was a text that provided a multilingual (Spanish, Quechua, Aymara, and Latin) account of the lived experience of coloniality in the Americas and of the tensions of identity therein; a denouncement of colonial regimes; a rejection of soon-to-be-national identities; a text meant to teach in order to reverse the damage; and a text that illustrated, through a combination of print and image, the past and futures of the Indigenous peoples in the Viceroyalty of Peru. It was a document with a balance of both visual and textual texture that bore witness to the destruction of Indigenous lifeways under colonial capitalism and pressures on "indios ladinos" in the colonial capital. While codices are a critical part of the literary tradition of Indigenous peoples in Abiayala (the Americas), Guaman Poma's text and fine line drawings can be understood as a hallmark of the Latin American and, later, Latinx visual narrative traditions that continue today—only first seen in this 1,189-page unrivaled and unprecedented document with 399 full-page line drawings.

The place of such an enormous treasure to Latinx studies, Latin American studies, American studies, Indigenous studies, literary studies, media studies, romance languages, linguistics, and so many other fields should be clear from this brief description. Yet, as with animation in the vast field of film studies, visual narratives are all too commonly presupposed as inferior amid other forms of print media. Even texts like Guaman Poma's magnum opus continue to be treated conservatively, cautiously guarded from inquiry using the language developed to study such critical graphic narratives. Reinvigorating these disciplines with multiple approaches to visual narratives is the central contribution of Fernanda Díaz-Basteris and Maite Urcaregui's *Latinx Comics Studies: Critical and Creative Crossings*. The contributions to the anthology read like full-page panels capturing the lines and colors, text boxes, speech and thought bubbles, vanishing points, perspective drawings, frames, and gutters of Latinx experiences. The concern with "undisciplining" runs through all its contributions, as creatives and critics all work to engage with the ways that Latinx comics challenge standing artistic practices as well as literary canons, theoretical frameworks, and taken-for-true pedagogical maneuvers. As leaders of this field-defining project, Díaz-Basteris and Urcaregui ask their readers to loosen the restraints of traditional disciplines so that they can better understand not just representations of Latinx experience but, more critically, the formal aspects of a dynamic medium like comics.

Following the exchanges of text, visual rhetoric, and the aesthetic principles embedded in the arrangements of Latinx comics, the contributions in

Latinx Comics Studies exemplify the directions of production and inquiry toward which Latinx comics is moving. As detailed in the subsequent sections of this coda, the expansive nature of the Latinx comics invoked in this groundbreaking anthology cannot be underestimated, as it brings to center narratives that engage with identities that are all too often ignored in Latinx studies (Central American, for example); narrative strategies that have long been associated with strictly literary forms (allegorical, autobiographical, translation, adaptation, among others); as well as industry contextualization seldom addressed in mainstream approaches to comics and graphic narratives (such as diasporic collaborations, crowdfunding/crowdsourced projects, and Latinx publishing under mainstream banners). This, in addition to the diversity of aesthetic principles of graphic narratives that are captured in the comics and chapters contributed to the volume, including artistic elements like composition, graphic weight, framing, diegesis.

Díaz-Basteris and Urcaregui open the volume by providing a bird's-eye view of the moving pieces involved in assembling Latinx comics studies. They discuss the productive connections and tensions between Latinx studies and Latinx comics, with the latter understood as a distinctive creative movement. Taking an active approach to disassembling and reassembling in order to assemble a new discipline, the two editors plot the field by actively moving graphic narratives and comics creatives that have been marginalized to the center, emphasizing their print and visually mediated heterogeneity. They recognize Latinx comics studies as a distinct field, while also dialoguing with established historical, print, and aesthetic traditions. The uniqueness of Latinx comics, they observe, is in the way that this media theorizes Latinx life—a feature that is missing from analyses of both Anglo mainstream comics studies and Latin American comic studies. With these parts of the moving puzzle in place, the editors outline a trajectory for the new field as it drives forward, urging readers to remain attentive to the mysterious conjurings and aesthetic innovations of Latinx comics' primary texts. After all, as the editors stress, the formal complexity and the "x-factor" of Latinx nuanced identities must not be neglected. Following their lead, this coda is like a zine that cuts and reassembles in order to sum up the critical intervention that this unprecedented volume makes. I structure what follows according to four aesthetic themes that the creatives and critics in this volume highlight, bringing only partial closure to a field that merits a much more open consideration in the academy.

Composition

In comics, "composition" refers to the arrangement of text, visual elements, and storyworld details within a panel or across a page.[3] The composition of a piece is critical, as it has the power to create tension, heighten emotion, or put the reader at ease. It also has rhetorical power, as it can convey balance for the effect of comparison and contrast. Composition is thus, literally, the art of arrangement, and several of the contributions in *Latinx Comics Studies* pay express attention to this art. I emphasize that though there is not a thematic connection between these contributions, they do put forward the intentionality of composition across Latinx comics.

For example, Nicky Rodriguez's contributed comic examines nationalism as a loaded word with a framed opening panel positioned in the first half of the page that reveals hooded figures and a Confederate flag hiding under the U.S. flag. On the bottom half of this first page is an unframed image of a rumpled Puerto Rican flag crippling Uncle Sam, complete with a narrative box on the top left of the rumpled flag that states that, for colonized peoples, nationalism is something different. On the second page, the discussion of nationalism goes from macro to micro as Rodriguez brings to the top half of the page the profiles of four Puerto Rican anticolonial nationalists, while contrasting them with the status quo rhetoric attributed to the United States on the bottom half of the page. The same strategy of dividing the page to show contrast is used on the third and last pages of the comic, where the top half shows a U.S. flag as a backdrop for a centered cross flanked by two army tanks. The bottom half is magnified in scale, when compared to the top half, and centers three ambiguously gendered individuals holding signs in Spanish calling for the ousting of corruption, Free Puerto Rico, and declaring a "No" to the Junta, while positioning a handheld Puerto Rican flag slightly above center and a woman in profile calling out into a hand-held megaphone. It is a comic that highlights the Puerto Rican definition of nationalism while contrasting it to that of the United States, emphasizing instead of the status-quo, iconic figures of Puerto Rican nationalism, the faces of people and their voices and actions as weapons, all under a distinct definition of nationalism with anticolonial and decolonial purpose. It is a comic that evokes the subtext of the entire volume. Latinx comics are often pedagogical, theoretical, and aesthetic interventions that poignantly challenge typical frames while using fine lines to pull us into closer readings of our contexts.

In her contribution on how Nahua and Maya iconography are transposed to Daniel Parada's *Zotz* series, Jessica Rutherford pays close attention to how pre-Columbian women are represented by the contemporary male creative. It is a chapter that attends to the transposition of hieroglyphs and codex-inspired drawings in the *Popol Vuh* source text for *Zotz*, but also one that problematizes how the male gaze on Indigenous women's bodies results in the specific arrangement of visual elements on panels. Using several examples from *Zotz*, Rutherford provides examples from the comic to emphasize how women are positioned in relation to men and each other, and in their sociohistorical context. The contribution closes with a discussion of Parada's digital portfolio, providing readers with an additional modality through which composition strategies can be analyzed.

Frederick Luis Aldama's contribution on Giannina Braschi's language-bending, genre-bending, and form-bending *United States of Banana: A Graphic Novel* is likewise focused on composition. Released a decade after its three-hundred-plus-page source text, this ninety-seven-page version matches Braschi's "verbal narrative track" with a Swedish cartoonist's "visual narrative track." The result is a piece that is faithful in formal aspects to the ideological aspects of the source text, as the illustrator describes that Braschi's method was to cannibalize literary history and his was to cannibalize art history. Mimicking Braschi's style, Aldama demonstrates that the graphic novel evokes the nonconformism of the source text through a range of pop culture references, art styles, and linework style. Aldama finds that the graphic novel's parallel verbal and visual track thus enables readers to declutter and dismantle the coloniality of power.

Taking readers into Inés Estrada's science fiction graphic novel *Alienation*, Lars Allen's contribution examines the uncanny effects of the text on readers. Set in Alaska, the novel centers around a futuristic technology called the GoogleGland, which offers its devotees the promise of freedom while being predicated on the protection of White capital. The netizens of 2054 in Estrada's text are free to roam the world and cross borders as they please, but the border between the real and the virtual is hostile. Through careful work with composition, Estrada positions the reader as an invasive yet invisible voyeur. In this way, the text emphasizes the anxieties with respect to surveillance strategies that are at once unlocatable and ubiquitous. The paranoia created throughout the pages and especially in the last image—a knife depicted to the size and scale of a human hand on the very last unnumbered page—is symbolic of the knife Estrada provides her readers as they must cut and assemble their own version of futurity.

Framing

Though it is often confused with composition, "framing" is a distinct art in the world of comics. This term emphasizes perspectival choices, as it is within the creative's purview to emphasize, exclude, or isolate visual elements in a panel or across a page.[4] There are nuances to framing, ranging from the choice to use a frame to the thickness or straightness of the frame, angles, depth of field, and even point of view employed in the piece. Several of the contributions in *Latinx Comics Studies* pay special attention to the manifold technique of framing, touching on the multifaceted nature of framing with purpose.

"Prelude," the comic contributed by Conrado Parraguirre, is an intentionally messy comic that is conveyed as such first by the unevenness of the lines used to depict the four *squarish* panels in the top two-thirds of the page and the single rectangle that appears in the bottom of the same page. It is also messy with respect to the content within those first four square panels: a close-up of shorts with worn elastic; the shorts thrown into an already-full laundry basket; and two panels under those that depict bare walls and spiders making their spiderwebs. Symmetry is not a part of the comic until the reader reaches the panel on the bottom, which centers a bottle of mezcal and a full glass containing a worm. The text above the bottle and glass hints at another year having just passed, of the possibility of starting over. Just under the ellipsis, where the reader's eye stops to rest, the hand reaching for the bottle becomes visible. In the text below what is now clearly a hand holding the bottle next to the glass, we see a play with syntax as the long, winding sentence is contrasted with the single word: "Bullshit." The lone word is the punchline, as the narrator affirms that a new year is not a new beginning, but a losing bet in advance. Why try, after all? Time for a drink. It is a comic that conveys incongruence until the vantage point shifts, conveying that things need not be in order to be well.

Taking framing from an analytical perspective, Marcel Brousseau and Katherine Kelp-Stebbins suggest from the onset of their contribution that studying comics is necessary for anyone who studies borders. They emphasize the formal aspects of gutters as a means of connecting panels on a comics page and credit global comics studies for making scholarly inroads into this area of study. They argue that fences and grids are objects in diegetic action that also serve as a clear means of framing action in graphic narratives. Engaging with the depiction of the U.S.-Mexico border spaces, they highlight strategies where the posts of migrant detention cages are analogized to the gutters of the comics page. Even the jacket of a comic folds out like a border fence. They remind readers that border fences are imaginary and symbolic, but also very grounded material constructs, as are the framing devices manifested on paper, pixels, pages, and bytes in comics across mediums.

The use of framing to transpose meaning is central to Maite Urcaregui's contribution on Breena Nuñez's autobiographical Afro-Salvadoran/Guatemalan comics. Urcaregui examines how Nuñez traces and translates alternative histories of gender and sexuality within her panels to emphasize their shaping through race and place. Attending to narrative boxes and speech balloons, gutters, paneling, and page layout, and varying styles of linework (as well as BIPOC queer theorists like José Esteban Muñoz, Maylei Blackwell, Gloria Anzaldúa, and Audre Lorde), Urcaregui traces how Nuñez's frames "talk-back" to anti-Blackness, coloniality, and cissexism and heterosexism. Where racist, colonialist, and heterosexist rhetoric might attempt to divide the different aspects of Nuñez's identity, the artist deflects their power over her by a brilliant framing of their own design. Deepening the analysis of framing, Urcaregui highlights Nuñez's commissioned webcomics for *Visibles*, a Guatemala-based organization that works to create queer community, support storytelling, and fight for LGBTQIA+ discourse and policy.

Inquiry into how framing comic worlds can create new spaces, free of colonial imposition, is central to Fernanda Díaz-Basteris's analysis of the Días Cómic collective in Puerto Rico. Taking her own positionality as a Mexican citizen belonging to the Spanish-speaking Caribbean as a point of departure for her analysis, Díaz-Basteris examines how the collective's comics in Spanish and English materialize a sense of Caribbean belonging while also activating the limits of her Mexican identity. Working with theories of affect, Díaz-Basteris excavates a visual archive of San Juan forged by the Días Cómic collective that has decolonized understandings of citizenship, rejected tourist exploitation, and extended beyond national icons and grand narratives—all through the many formats (zines to digital) adopted by the creatives. Framing the Caribbean as a natural region (*not* a national region) is critical to understanding how the Días Cómic collective develops a testimonial, popular, artisanal, and independent graphic archive of San Juan that challenges the visitors culture that it and other cities in the Caribbean face.

Graphic Weight

Other contributions in *Latinx Comics Studies* develop analyses related to "graphic weight," or the manner in which certain items come to the fore through contrast with other elements in their midst.[5] Working from the premise that, when viewing the panel, the eye will focus on one item before taking in other elements, a creator can use a variety of strategies including the use of high-contrast colors or bright colors against sepia tones to create a definite focus. The contributions I examine next are critical practices and reflections on graphic weight.

A rich example of this idea is in Breena Nuñez's contributed comic, "This Body Is Actually Unsettled." The piece comprises three panels: (1) *Mourning* is a composition in black-and-white that puts graphic weight on a slightly off-center image of what could be a sun or could be a closed eyelid. Whether we turn the panel 90°, 180°, 270°, or the full 360°, that image remains in focus and slightly off center, always with a dense array of vertical, diagonal, and curved lines surrounding it. (2) *New Home* is likewise composed in black-and-white, but the new image with graphic weight is the plane in the upper right corner, itself by almost a half page of blank space. The same dense array of thin and thick lines in *Mourning* appears along the left side of the frame as well as along the bottom. The densely inked hills and pyramids on the left contrast with the thin lines of palm trees just under them, while the thick black ink and un-inked outlines of smoke and clouds create a sense of movement toward the right, the same direction toward which a thickly inked plane is pointing. At the bottom center is a thickly inked black car that is also moving toward the right, its graphic weight magnified by its position over a checkerboard pavement. (3) *Callejere* is the final black-and-white composition in the series, and it puts graphic weight on an open eye positioned slightly off center against a white background. It is surrounded by a dense array of lines, at the ends of which are three eyes meeting at a single point: the thick black inked image of the car, now pointing left, but still on a checkerboard pavement flanked by thickly inked hills. This, all above the words "lead me to my privilege of having nomadic sensibilities."

Stephanie Contreras's contribution on Inverna Lockpez's *Cuba: My Revolution* examines a color palette that is gray with splashes of red and pink. Taking a "facts with affect" approach, the chapter leans into pedagogical practice as Contreras describes providing students with the tools to understand the sociohistorical context of post-1959 Cuba as well as the graphic reconstruction of exile and its discontents. Taking a theoretical dive into graphic weight, the contribution reflects on the rejection of comics by the Cuban government vis-à-vis this comic creative's connection to the DC Vertigo imprint—an imprint that expressly focused on graphic and mature content. Engaging with reader responses to the experiences and fragmentation that mark Cuban lives, as well as considering how abstract art styles intersect with graphic depictions, the chapter brings to bear the way in which graphic weight in comics like *Cuba: My Revolution* provides a space of reflection on trauma and testimony. The carefully planned graphic weight of the examples provided by Contreras conveys the power of comics to flatten time and allow the past to be collapsed by the present.

For their part, Kaitlin Thomas and Héctor Rodriguez III work together in their contribution to examine the latter's creation of *El Peso Hero*. The series brings to the page a new kind of border hero, one who walks through multiple employment sectors, socioeconomic levels, and several noncitizen categories in the Texas Rio Grande Valley. It is a character whose world puts graphic weight on "visual and verbal cultural realia," from the *migas* he has for breakfast to the *ranchera* music he listens to, and from his cowboy boots and belt buckle to the monolingual Spanish he speaks. Using the elements on which graphic weight is placed as a point of departure, they discuss how El Peso Hero engages emotively with his readers through shared iconography and linguistic decisions. The chapter ends with a strong assertion that through page design, character visuals, realia, dialogue, and transborder storylines, millennial creatives like Rodriguez are succeeding in moving marginalized subjectivities into empowering, influential roles by design.

Héctor Fernández L'Hoeste's contribution is a poignant analysis of Gilberto (Beto) Hernandez's *Maria M.* and Vanesa R. Del Rey and Bryce Carlson's *HIT,* two graphic narratives that use color palette to effectuate graphic weight on the presence of Latinxs in the City of Angels. The piece is a meditation on color principles, particularly the formal and theoretical observation that color is a feature with cumulative effect. Color pervades space and spaces are inhabited culturally and socially—the same way that the long-negated presence of Latinxs in Los Angeles has always been. Color, L'Hoeste argues, invites readers of *Maria M.* and *HIT* to think about who inhabits the many spaces of Los Angeles, as well as who is generally attributed to select spaces. He argues that this attention to color filling space is what allows these creatives to defy the long-standing practice of denying LA Latinx life in their 1950s and 1960s renditions, thus giving readers a critical edge and grounded understanding of Latinx presence in the post–World War II period.

Diegesis

Similar to narrative in literary and film studies, "diegesis" in comics refers to the represented storyworld of a piece.[6] Diegesis is that internal space of the storyworld action, and it can occur on a single panel or page or over the course of several panels and pages. Creatives sometimes have main characters act as narrators in a comic's diegesis, but other creatives might also opt for diegetic commentary from an omniscient narrator. In either case, the diegesis of a comic allows the story to unfold and the reader to hear (and believe or not believe) the voice that relates events in the story. Several of the contributions in *Latinx Comics Studies* examine diegesis, providing key examples of how stories develop as well as how readers engage with the diegesis of graphic narratives.

Terry Blas's contributed comic, for instance, asks the reader a direct question and develops an answer in the story arc of the comic: "Why does it feel so scary to speak in another language in public?" The first four panels in the comic are perfect squares and provide the exposition of the story: a Mormon mother and her gay son who have not communicated much in the past have begun to connect just a few months ago. Keeping the same four-panel setup, the second page incorporates Mexican iconography: an Aztec image in the background as the author remembers his parents teaching him to be proud of his Mexican heritage; he and his husband visiting Frida Kahlo and Diego Rivera's house on a visit to Mexico; their purchase of *artesanías* at a market; and, in the bottom-right panel, a close-up of his mother's face and the word *Mamá* on his phone—all with text boxes reflecting on the Spanish language. The rising action begins on the third page and is developed throughout the next five pages, as Blas reflects on alternating negative and positive reception, legislation, and practice as related to speaking Spanish in different contexts, all captured in the neat four panels per page sequence with which he began the comic. The final page is the resolution, as he steps out of the streetcar, away from the Anglo woman who made a face when he answered his mother's phone call in Spanish. On the last page, neatly completing the diegesis of the comic, the protagonist has found a bench in a park, and in a medium close-up, we see his smiling face as he conveys his love to his mother.

Jennifer Caroccio Maldonado's contribution takes a pedagogical perspective in her examination of *Puerto Rico Strong*. The comic anthology was born of the collective action on the part of comics creatives who provided stories from the diaspora so that the proceeds could be used for relief and rebuilding efforts after Hurricane Maria. The chapter focuses on pedagogical methods for teaching the cyclical nature of coloniality, encompassing colonization, medical abuse, and neglect after the hurricane. Teaching students that the medium and form shape the message, Caroccio Maldonado focuses on diegesis, paying close attention to the content in panels, narration boxes, and speech and thought bubbles. Reading comics as multimodal, interdisciplinary, and artistic objects, she covers text-image relationships, noting when image and text are complementary, redundant, or contrasting.

In Katlin Marisol Sweeney-Romero's contribution, the focus is on narrative power in writer Sam Humphries and artist Jen Bartel's *Blackbird* series from Image Comics. Weaving personal narratives from her own life with an analysis of the comic, as well as engaging with critics like Evelyn P. Stevens and Gloria Anzaldúa, the author delves into concepts like marianismo, nepantla, and the "buena hija" archetype. Sweeney-Romero discusses the search for a character like herself in narrative media, one outside of the familial harmony and reconciliation paradigms, finding in *Blackbird* a narrator who (like herself) struggles to be understood as credible and one whose memories must be taken seriously. The mirrored experience of immersing oneself in the diegesis of the graphic narrative and finding one's visage is central to the analysis, a touchstone for closure and catharsis made possible through the reading of a comic that speaks to the process of trust in self as reliable narrator through the very boxes and images framed in the comic.

Following the theme of trusting the narrator, Nicole Ann Amato's contribution focuses on her experience teaching non–comic readers about the intricacies of Latinx comics. Aware that her student readers, future secondary English language arts teachers, perceive comics characters to be underdeveloped, Amato's pedagogical strategies include highlighting the iconography used by illustrators to mark their young, Brown, queer, coming-of-age protagonists. Students are tasked with "undisciplining" their expectations through a range of instructional activities that help extend the skills of these non–comics readers. An important finding from Amato's work is that non–comics readers need to be taught to adapt to condensed time in the comics diegesis, a challenge for readers who are accustomed to reading characters develop over the many pages of a novel.

Before We Part Ways

I close with the understanding that this is slightly longer than the average coda, but I also end with the certainty that a recap of a volume as important as *Latinx Comics Studies* merits a longer finale than the average. After all, this is a book that brings to the table an impressive collection of comics to evidence the need to frame graphic narratives penned and inked by Latinxs in new and creative ways. Highlighting the frames that support this creative activity and successfully arguing for their role in the dynamic future of Latinx studies and comics studies, it provides a critical intervention for these and related fields. This is the type of volume needed to examine texts as diverse as Guaman Poma's stunning 1615 masterpiece and the Latinx webcomics and zines of today. With a volume like *Latinx Comics Studies*, there is a framework to put these markedly distinct texts into conversation—as we should well do.

Together with the creatives and critics whose contributions make the volume a whole, Díaz-Basteris and Urcaregui have covered theoretical matters as diverse as the erasure of Latinx histories, feminist and queer interventions, Afro-Latinx and Indigenous representation, calling multiple spaces home, placemaking and building belonging, multilingualism, and the effects of settler colonialism, racial capitalism, and disaster. Bringing together influences from visual arts and from literature, as well as from lived experience, they provide innovative reflections on the manifestation of key graphic narrative-specific aesthetic and formal concepts across Latinx comics. Furthermore, they have demonstrated the malleability of time and space through text-image play and the stickiness of memory as it erupts (or lingers, even) in Latinx comics that challenge colonial, nationalist, and capitalist structures that have unelegantly attempted to frame Latinx life and expressive cultures.

Notes

1 For studies relating to Felipe Guaman Poma's graphic narrative techniques, see Ernesto Álvarez-Valle, "Ícono e historieta: el lenguaje de la comunicación gráfica en Guamán Poma de Ayala," *Morada de la palabra: homenaje a Luce y Mercedes López-Baralt* 1 (2002): 110–125. See also Thomas Bitting Foster Cummins, "El mundo y vida de las imágenes en las páginas peruanas de los siglos XVI y XVII: el contexto virreinal de las obras de Martín de Murúa, Guamán Poma y otros," in *Escritura e imagen en Hispanoamérica. De la crónica ilustrada al cómic*, Cécile Michaud, ed. (Lima, Perú: Fondo PUCP, 2015), 21–64. Gómez Menjívar's article on *Nueva corónica y buen gobierno* (1615) as a Latinx graphic narrative is in preparation.

2 Raquel Chang-Rodríguez, *La palabra y la pluma en Primer nueva crónica y buen gobierno* (Lima, Perú: Fondo Editorial PUCP, 2005).

3 Nancy Pedri, *A Concise Dictionary of Comics* (Jackson: University Press of Mississippi, 2022), 23.

4 Pedri, *Concise Dictionary of Comics*, 40.

5 William G. Brozo, Gary Moorman, and Carla Meyer, *Wham! Teaching with Graphic Novels across the Curriculum* (New York: Teachers College Press, 2014), 15.

6 Pedri, *Concise Dictionary of Comics*, 28.

Acknowledgments

Fernanda Díaz-Basteris

First and foremost, this is a dedication; I acknowledge and honor the work of nontenured racialized scholars, especially those who fight the undeniable burnout of graduate school, the job market, and the relocation to distant communities in the Global North to only encounter a nonsensical load of work when entering the academic rank in higher education. To the racialized colleagues who work overtime in academia, without fair pay and without financial support for their research, I salute you, I respect you, I follow you. This edited volume is dedicated to all of us, those who carry the heavy weight of producing high-quality scholarship that is rarely compensated. Second, I'm grateful for everyone's insight, the long conversations in confidentiality have allowed me to feel seen and heard. We all finished this book together, stronger and wiser. The commitment and solidarity of the contributors to this book kept me engaged in Latinx comics scholarship even in the darkest moments of my first years as an assistant professor.

Practicing gratitude is a liberating exercise. I pause, think, remember, and let my body feel the human care and tenderness of being lifted when in vulnerability. Today I'm thankful for all the people who uplifted me while grieving my mother and working on this book. My special thanks to Dr. Maite Urcaregui, mi amiga, compañera, and coeditor: ¡Mil gracias Maite! I'm grateful for your brilliance and your care! Maite and I started thinking and planning this edited collection at the end of 2021. After part of the Global North, mostly Canada and the United States, had access to COVID-19 vaccines, I was allowed to travel to Italy in September 2021 to chair two Latinx comics panels I organized for the Visual Depictions of the American West Conference. The presentations on those panels were transformed into chapters for this book. It is important to thank my colleagues in the Research Committee on Comics Studies and Graphic Narrative and the Ca' Foscari University of Venice for welcoming a group of Latinx scholars and artists working in the United States to their amazing conference and virtual community.

With my academic publications I honor the labor of my mother, Miki Basteris, my force and my galactic guardian, who passed away while we were editing this book in March 2023. Her constant affirmations kept me alive in this country. I'm thankful for her unmatched sense of humor, her attentiveness to my academic progress, her participation in my public events, and her excitement for my teaching practice. I miss her vibrant energy every single day. It is liberating to thank my father, Carlos Díaz, for making books available at home, for taking me to the movies, and for teaching me about theater. I come from la península de Yucatán; I was the first one to leave the country. Thanks to several professors, I am the first Basteris and the first Díaz to receive a doctorate degree. I had the privilege to walk alongside my mother through every single step of my academic career. As a Latina queer woman living in the diaspora without the opportunity to return home, I thank my brothers for their financial and moral support. Al Doctor José María Díaz Basteris: thank you for joining me in this academic journey. Sin rajarte ni una sola vez me acompañaste hasta el final del doctorado, you are always there/here, physically, virtually and spiritually. ¡Gracias Calidarks! for all the comics, the phone calls, the parties, the dances, the friendships, and the laughs, you are a joy in my life, I love you, I'm proud of you. Al Maestro Rodrigo Diaz Basteris, thank you for the financial support, the constant communication and for keeping me in Helena's life. Thank you for taking care of mom. Te quiero. To my Cincinnati parents Susan Dunlap and Jesse Simmons, thank you for your love, your solidarity and the continued encouragement to not give up! I'm so happy to be back in Ohio and closer to you. To my very first Mexican friend in the U.S. la doblemente doctora Eugenia Mazur, gracias Mofles, por todo, te quiero y te admiro. Gracias al Dr. Aaron Klein, for reading and editing. To my Open Hearthland community in Iowa City, las chingonas, las meras meras, who supported me, celebrated me and fed me when I was living the coldest years of my life, gracias infinitas a Elizabeth, Ana,

Marcela, Ester, Lucía, Lorena, Ada and Vero, I always think of you and I miss you. To my Iowa mentor and friend Christina Morris Penn-Goetsch, for believing in me, and for inviting me to coteach Chicanx Art, and La Virgen de Guadalupe.

To my professors and friends at the Autonomous University of Yucatán, where it all began, Doctoras Dolores Almazán and Margaret Shrimpton, gracias for being my academic role models, gracias for kindly guiding me, for respecting me, for evaluating me with compassion and clarity. Siempre agradecida for these twenty years of community love. To my professors at the University of California, Davis: Cecilia Colombi, Robert Blake, and Emilio Bejel, thank you for financially supporting all my projects. Thanks to my PhD advisor Dr. Michael Lazzara, for all the years of constant support with recommendation letters. Thanks to Dr. Diana Aramburu for having read my incipient research on Puerto Rican independent comics. I'm thankful to the Comics Studies Society for inviting me to be part of the Graduate Student Mentoring Program, advising Javiera, Emma, and Marissa was a lovely experience. To all the students who have taken my classes for the past decade, it is an honor to be part of your academic journey. Gracias Tori Londeen, for editing the early drafts of my chapter. Finally, thank you to Dr. John Grinstead for supporting this book project and recommending it to the small grants program at The Ohio State University College of Arts and Sciences.

To all my Comics amigues, thank you for sharing your comics love with me! For your moral support, your advice, and your feminist decolonial encouragement. I'm proud of our small but mighty queer comics community. To my friend Maureen Burdock: thank you for creating and organizing Decolonizing Comics with me at UC Davis. Special thanks to my friends who support my academic projects and invite me to participate in theirs: gracias infinitas a Katlin Marisol Sweeney Romero, Margaret Galvan, Jessica Rutherford, Jennifer Caroccio Maldonado, Samantha Ceballos, Jennifer Gómez Menjívar, Nicole Amato, Javiera Irribaren Ortiz, Nhora Lucía Serrano, and many more. Thanks to the Puerto Rican comics artists Rosa Colón, Rosaura Rodríguez, and Omar Banuchi, for letting me get closer to your work, for welcoming me to the island, and for inviting me to Tintero. Por último, gracias a Emiliano y José Luis, por los años juntos crecidos en la distancia. Mucho love a David Tenorio and Dianely Rosales, my Geminis amixs, gracias por todo el amor y la conspiración a lo largo de los años. Gracias a la Morenita, por protegerme, cuidarme y guiarme. ¡Venceremos!

Maite Urcaregui

First and foremost, I want to thank my friend, collaborator, coeditor, and coconspirator, Fernanda Díaz-Basteris. Fernanda and I first met, of all places, through the Comix-Scholars listserv. In that digital space that, like so many, often becomes a vitriolic echo-chamber that centers those who have the loudest voices (read, those who have the most privilege within our world and within comics studies), we connected over Latinx comics and forged a friendship. It was Fernanda who initially had the vision for this collection and invited me into the project in 2021 when I was still a graduate student. Working with Fernanda, I have learned so much not only about Latinx comics but also about how to navigate academia and build community within it. Together, we have created a project that we are proud of, that includes a diverse cohort of comics scholars and a wide range of Latinx comics. Most importantly, we have created something that represents our shared interests in and commitments to feminist, queer, decolonial, and antiracist perspectives within both Latinx and comics studies.

Many thanks to those faculty and fellow graduate students at the University of California, Santa Barbara (UCSB), who mentored me throughout my time there, especially during the early stages of this project when I was completing my PhD and navigating the academic job market. Lale Stefkova and I created a place for comics studies from scratch at UCSB, the comics and graphic novels reading group, and I have fond memories of our discussions and events, especially the Drawing Diversity symposium we hosted in 2019. My colleagues in the Department of English and Comparative Literature at San José State University have my gratitude for welcoming me into my new scholarly home and for their genuine curiosity about me and about this project. Their enthusiastic and frequent requests for updates allowed me to share the joys of coediting, brag about the brilliance of our contributors, and vent about the challenges of getting this project over the finish line.

Comics studies was one of the first places where I found an academic home, a sense of scholarly community and identity. I know that this experience of inclusion is, in part, shaped by the privileges afforded to me by my Whiteness, and is not felt by all. The work that Fernanda and I have done together, not only in the final product of this volume but in the process of its making, has sought to make comics studies a more inclusive (and perhaps uncomfortable for some) space, a space that does not simply genuflect to the altar of White male mediocrity or canonicity but rather cultivates a community of diverse scholarly and creative voices. My respect and gratitude to those who are cultivating spaces for women, queer and trans folx, and people of color within comics studies—collectives and cons such as the Black and Brown Comic Arts Festival, Flame Con, Laneha House, and the Latinx Comic Arts Festival. I also want to recognize the work the Graduate Student Caucus (GSC) of the Comics Studies Society (CSS) does to center and support junior scholars and emerging voices within the field. The members of the GSC are not only brilliant junior scholars; they are also visionary leaders and makers of community. Thank you also to the CSS and the International Comic Arts Forum for creating opportunities for comics scholars and makers to gather, learn from one another, and push the boundaries of what comics studies can be and can do. Much love to Jennifer Caroccio Maldonado and Jessica Rutherford, who, along with Fernanda, have provided continuous conversation and support across distance and time zones. The four of us met at the inaugural BIPOC PoP: Comics, Gaming, Animation, and Multimedia Arts Symposium in 2022 at the University of Texas at Austin, organized annually by Frederick Luis Aldama, Sam Ceballos, and a team of many others. Finally, thanks to Katlin Marisol Sweeney-Romero and Adrienne Resha, who have accompanied me virtually in weekly writing groups.

Researching and writing can be very isolating work, and, for me, it is work that is often filled with bad feelings (angst, anxiety, guilt, procrastination, and self-doubt), feelings that we do not discuss enough in the publication- and productivity-driven culture of academia. I have so much love and appreciation for family and friends who remind me to step out of that world, take a break, and return more myself: especially my late parents Angel and JoAnn Urcaregui, the Adams family, Jeremy Chow, Jamiee Cook, Sage Gerson, Amy Kuehl, Aili Pettersson Peeker, and my weekly trivia team the Oedipal Arrangements. Much gratitude and love to my partner Gregory Shinn, who witnesses the daily grind and offers a supportive sounding board. Finally, Fernanda and I have dedicated this book to our mothers, who both passed away in 2023 while we were working on this project. I know that my mother would have read every word in this collection, as she did for my dissertation, so this one is for her. Thank you, Mom, for being my first reader and my first teacher!

Fernanda Díaz-Basteris and Maite Urcaregui

Many people collaborated with us as we developed this collection. In different spaces, in different capacities, and in different time zones, colleagues shared their time, energy, and kindness. The result is this book, which we understand as a community project. Frederick Luis Aldama offered invaluable mentorship in the early stages of securing a press. The team that we found at Rutgers University Press has done an excellent job shepherding this book into the world, especially our editor Nicole Solano, who has been incredibly patient and thoughtful. We appreciate the generous readings and thoughtful comments that both Nhora Lucía Serrano and Qiana Whitted provided as we prepared the final manuscript. ¡Muchas gracias Nhora and Qiana! Big thanks to Jennifer Gómez Menjívar for her deep engagement with the collection and beautiful concluding remarks. To all the contributors in this book—the teachers, the professors, the artists, and the independent scholars—thank you for trusting us with your work and for your patience throughout this multiyear process! To the Latinx artists and creators whose work is discussed and represented in this collection, we see your creative efforts to resist the hegemony that permeates U.S. narratives and visual culture, and we salute you! We especially appreciate the artists who contributed original and reprinted work to this collection despite the fact that we did not have the financial resources to compensate you. Thank you especially to Breena Nuñez, who generously allowed us to use their work on the book's stunning cover. To the doctoral students and junior scholars who have participated in the collection, we hope that it will come back to you as you make your way within and beyond academia. This book is our small contribution to Latinx studies, to comics studies, and to that exciting place where the two meet: Latinx comics studies. We hope that it will inspire creators, teachers, fans, and scholars alike to continue to make, read, celebrate, and critique Latinx comics, not just for their representational value but for their formal innovations and political power as well.

Notes on Contributors

FREDERICK LUIS ALDAMA (he/him) is an American academic who is the Jacob and Frances Sanger Mossiker Chair in the Humanities, founder and director of the Latinx Pop Lab, and affiliate faculty in radio-TV-film at the University of Texas at Austin as well as adjunct professor and distinguished university professor at The Ohio State University. He teaches courses on Latinx comics, TV, and film in the departments of English and Radio-Television-Film. At The Ohio State University, he was a distinguished university professor, arts & humanities distinguished professor of English, university distinguished scholar, and alumni distinguished teacher as well as the recipient of the Rodica C. Botoman Award for Distinguished Teaching and Mentoring and the Susan M. Hartmann Mentoring and Leadership Award. At The Ohio State University, he was the founder and director of the award-winning LASER / Latinx Space for Enrichment Research and the founder and codirector of the Humanities and Cognitive Sciences High School Summer Institute. Aldama is the creator and curator of the Planetary Republic of Comics.

LARS ALLEN (they/he/she) is a queer comics scholar, artist, publisher, and editor. Lars earned their bachelor's degree in comparative literature with a focus in Spanish literature and culture from the University of Oregon and a master's degree in English and American literature from New York University (2019). Their research concerns the literal and figurative underground and analyzing contemporary comics, cartoons, and video games as embodied means of knowledge production. Lars is the founder of an antifascist indie comics press, Purgatory Comics Press, and has turned their attention to creating and publishing comics in the greater East Coast area. Lars works as a children's art and dance instructor in Brooklyn, New York.

NICOLE ANN AMATO (she/her) is an assistant professor of English language arts (ELA) and literacy education in the School of Education at California State University Channel Islands. She is a former high school ELA teacher whose research and teaching are focused on youth reading practices, children's and young adult literature, comics, and anti-oppressive pedagogies. She received her PhD in literacy, language, and culture from the University of Iowa. Her research explores how teacher candidates' responses to comics marketed to queer youth influenced their dispositions as anti-oppressive pedagogues.

TERRY BLAS (he/him) is the illustrator and writer behind the viral webcomics You Say Latino and You Say Latinx. He wrote *Ariana Grande vs Sergeant Shade and the Clonebot Brigade*, the comic book tie-in for her R.E.M. fragrance. He is also the writer of *Steven Universe* comics for Boom and *Rick and Morty* comics for Oni Press. His original graphic novels are *Dead Weight: Murder at Camp Bloom*, *Hotel Dare*, and *Lifetime Passes*, all of which feature Mexican characters. He has written the Marvel series *Reptil: Brink of Extinction*, *Nova*, and *Runaways*.

MARCEL BROUSSEAU (he/him) is a senior instructor of English at Portland State University. He studies national borders as media ecologies, comprising maps, literature, laws, and infrastructure. Researching and teaching in Latinx studies, Indigenous studies, environmental studies, and the digital humanities, he has published essays about the U.S.-Mexico border fence as a poetic symbol, about the mediality of border bridges and tunnels, and about teaching the work of Jovita González, among other topics. His book, *Hyperborders: Cultural Techniques of the Trans-American Borderlands*, is under contract. He is also a critical cartographer experimenting with moralized modes of representing migration narratives. He received his PhD in comparative literature from the University of California, Santa Barbara. In addition to his humanities scholarship, he is working toward an MS in historic preservation at the University of Oregon, where he is composing a thesis about the cultural legacy of the Houston Astrodome.

FRANCISCA CÁRCAMO ROJAS (ella/she/her) is a cartoonist and illustrator from Santiago, Chile. She has worked for children's, authorial, and educational publications since 2009. She began working as an editor at Tabula Rasa and at Pánico Ediciones, a publishing house dedicated to illustration and comics, which had a bookstore of the same name between 2015 and 2018. Some of the publications she has been a part of are *Las aventuras dibujísticas de Panchulei*, *Chile en Viñetas*, *Mandamientos de Mentira*. She is also the creator of the children's magazine *Marcapañas* and *Perros patipati perros*, winner of the 2016 Lector Award in the children's literature category. She has also been part of the short story anthology *Chambelán Superstar* of new letters under thirty. She was highlighted as one of the 100 young líderes of 2018 in the magazine *Sábado* from Chile's *El Mercurio*.

JENNIFER CAROCCIO MALDONADO (she/her) is an assistant professor in the Department of English at CUNY. Caroccio Maldonado has a PhD in American studies from Rutgers University–Newark. Her research interests include Latinx culture and literature, U.S. cultural production, graphic novels, and women of color feminist theories. Her first book project examines Latinx graphic memoirs and comic biographies, which she argues present counternarratives of art and social movements in the United States. Her recent essay "Life Out Loud in the Closet: The Grotesque as Latinx Imagination in Cristy C. Road's *Spit and Passion*" is published in *The Routledge Companion to Gender and Sexuality in Comic Book Studies*.

STEPHANIE CONTRERAS (she/her) is a lecturing fellow of romance studies at Duke University, where she teaches Spanish language courses and coordinates the Elementary Spanish I level. She has a PhD in Hispanic literary and cultural studies from Florida State University. Her primary research interest is Latin American testimonial literature with a special focus on Cuban and Cuban American studies. Additionally, she coleads a Bass Connections research project, "¡Celebra mi herencia! A Spanish Reading Program," which pairs Latino/a families with undergraduate students at Duke to read children's books in Spanish by Latino/a/x and Latin American authors.

FERNANDA DÍAZ-BASTERIS (ella/she/her) is an assistant professor of Latinx new media and ethnic studies at The Ohio State University. She is an interdisciplinary scholar who has dedicated her research and teaching practice to understanding U.S. Caribbean and Latinx cultural forms of resistance to displacement, coloniality, and racial capitalism through literature, popular art, and comics from the mid-twentieth to the twenty-first centuries. Her current research looks at visual representations of topics, such as femicide in Puerto Rico, the undocumented American life experience, the sociopolitical crisis of disasters' aftermath, and the communal digital storytelling of forced displacement. Dr. Díaz-Basteris earned a PhD in Latin American literatures and cultures, with a dual emphasis on Latinx narratives and Caribbean studies, from the University of California, Davis in 2019.

HÉCTOR FERNÁNDEZ L'HOESTE (he/him) is a professor at Georgia State University in Atlanta, Georgia, where he teaches cultural studies. He is the author of *Narrativas de representación urbana* and *Lalo Alcaraz: Political Cartooning in the Latino Community* and editor of *Rockin' Las Americas* (with Deborah Pacini Hernández and Eric Zolov), *Redrawing the Nation* (with Juan Poblete), *Cumbia!* (with Pablo Vila), *Sports and Nationalism in Latin/o America* (with Robert McKee Irwin and Juan Poblete), *Sound, Image, and National Imaginary in the Construction of Latin/o American Identities* (with Pablo Vila), *Digital Humanities in Latin America* (with Juan Pablo Rodríguez), and *Internet, Humor, and Nation in Latin America* (with Juan Poblete). He is the translator of *Modernity and Colombian Identity in the Music of Carlos Vives y La Provincia*. Currently, he is working on a monograph titled *Vicious Muñequitos: Nation, Neoliberalism, and Violence in Latin American Comics*.

JENNIFER GÓMEZ MENJÍVAR (she/her) is a professor and director of the M.A. in media industries and critical cultural studies at the University of North Texas. She holds a PhD in Latin/x American cultural studies from The Ohio State University, and her scholarly training is in the production, circulation, and reception of texts, from traditional print to contemporary digital. Her books include *Tropical Tongues, Indigenous Interfaces, Améfrica in Letters, Hemispheric Blackness*, and *Black in Print*, and her many articles have appeared in *Journal of Pidgin and Creole Languages*, *Mesoamérica*, *Diálogo*, *Hispanófila*, and *Romance Notes*, among others. She researches BIPOC media, including cinema and digital projects like hashtag movements, TikTok journalism, YouTube videos, Twitter memes, and Facebook groups. Her research is concerned with how film and new media advance autonomy and self-governance, language revitalization, minority entrepreneurship, and grassroots organizing.

KATHERINE KELP-STEBBINS (she/her) is an associate professor of English and director of comics studies at the University of Oregon. Her research examines comics and visual media as tools for rethinking world literature and remapping transnational media flows. Her book, *How Comics Travel: Translation, Publication, Radical Literacies*, uses comparative approaches to understand the racialized, gendered, and culturally specific components of reading comics around the world. She is also the curator of *The Art of the News: Comics Journalism* exhibition, which premiered at the Jordan Schnitzer Museum of Art in Eugene before traveling to the Billy Ireland Cartoon Museum at The Ohio State University. Her work has been published in *PMLA*, *Feminist Media Histories*, *Media Fields*, *Studies in Comics*, and anthologies including *The Oxford Handbook of Comic Book Studies*, *Comics Studies Here and Now*, and *The Comics of Alison Bechdel*.

BREENA NUÑEZ (she/her/they) is a cartoonist and part-time adjunct professor living in San Francisco, California. She creates diary comics that often explore themes surrounding the awkwardness of racism, being a queer Afrodescendiente from the Bay Area, and understanding what it means to be Central American from the United States. Their hope as a cartoonist and educator is to help BIPOC folks give themselves permission to express their identities through the comics medium. Breena's comics are primarily self-published as zines through the family-run small press they cofounded with their husband, Laneha House. You will also find some comics in other publications such as the *New Yorker: Daily Shouts* and *The Nib* as well as in anthologies like *Tales from La Vida: A Latinx Comics Anthology*, *Drawing Power*, and *Be Gay, Do Comics!*

CONRADO PARRAGUIRRE (he/him) holds a master's degree in applied literature from Universidad Iberoamericana in Puebla. He has published cartoons and comics in newspapers, magazines, and digital media. Some of his cartoons have been selected in competitions such as "Toros sí, toreros no," "15° International Cartoon Festival: Book and Technology," "La Francofonía por la libertad de prensa." He also obtained first place in the "Segundo Gran Concurso de Caricatura" organized by the newspaper *El Popular* and a second place in the "Lire en fête" contest organized by the Alliance Française of Puebla. In addition, he has published short stories and poetry, some of which have appeared in the anthologies *Versos para el recreo*, *Pinos Alados. Una selección*, *Nos queda el presente. Libertad de escritura en tiempos de la pandemia de la Covid-19*, and *Letrinas del Cosmódromo*.

HÉCTOR RODRIGUEZ III (he/him) is an award-winning Chicano comic book creator from the border town of Eagle Pass, Texas. He is the creator of *El Peso*

Hero and founder of Texas Latino Comic Con. He is also the copublisher and co–editor-in-chief of the newly minted Chispa Comics, the first direct-to-market Latino comic book publishing house in collaboration with Scout Comics. He also serves as director of development for Masked Republic, where he oversees the creative development of Masked Republic Lucha media properties.

NICKY RODRIGUEZ (she/her) is a disabled, queer Puerto Rican comic artist and illustrator. She is the creator of the ongoing webcomic *The Unlucky Ones and the Edge of Nowhere* and the illustrator of the award-winning children's book *Con Papá / With Papá*, authored by Frederick Luis Aldama. She received her bachelor's in animation from California College of the Arts in 2017, shortly followed by a master's in comics from the same institution in 2019. Her desire with comics has always been to experiment with the storytelling form to find evocative ways to illustrate emotion, ephemerality, and the human condition. Her work highlights the multifaceted nature of her identity, and identity in general, and seeks to center the experiences of the marginalized. Zinemaking brought Nicky into the world of comics, and she began regularly traveling across the United States to exhibit and speak at different zine fests, comic conventions, and academic conferences through 2019.

JESSICA RUTHERFORD (she/her) is an assistant professor of Spanish in the Department of World Languages, Literatures, and Cultures at Central Connecticut State University. She earned her PhD from The Ohio State University in 2017 in colonial Latin American literature and culture. Her research focuses on Indigenous history and culture from the precolonial period to the present in Latin/x America, with an emphasis on understanding the past to advocate for social justice issues at present. Her current book project, *Jesuit Missionary Medicine: Encounters with Non-Christian Healers and Spiritual Leaders in Brazil, Mexico, and Japan, 1549–1650*, works to trace how Jesuit contributions to developments in early modern medicine in Western Europe largely draw from Indigenous peoples in the Americas and, in the case of Japan, Buddhist practices.

KATLIN MARISOL SWEENEY-ROMERO (she/her) is an assistant professor of cinema and digital media at the University of California, Davis. She received her PhD in English with a specialization in film studies from The Ohio State University in 2023. Her current book project, *Social Mediated Latinas: Creating and Contouring Digital Latina Looks in the Twenty-First Century*, examines how

Latinas utilize their social media presence to act as both cultural producers of original content and participants in intracultural discourse related to ethnoracial identity. Katlin has published chapters in edited collections such as *TikTok Cultures in the United States*, *Latinx TV in the Twenty-First Century*, *Cultural Studies in the Digital Age*, and *The Routledge Companion to Gender and Sexuality in Comic Book Studies*. In 2020, she coedited a special issue of *Prose Studies* on Latinx nonfiction with Frederick Luis Aldama. She presently serves as the co-coordinator of programming and marketing for the Latinx Comic Arts Festival at Modesto Junior College, as the social strategist for the Comics Studies Society, and on the editorial board of Amatl Comix at San Diego State University Press.

KAITLIN E. THOMAS (she/her) is an assistant professor of Spanish at Norwich University. Her research delves into U.S. and Latina/o/x identities that result from transborder cultural and national fusion, undocumented Latina/o/x immigration, and the contemporary U.S.-Mexico border region. She is interested in intersections between social media and cultural iconography and exploring music as a site for resistance. Kaitlin holds a PhD in Hispanic studies from the University of Birmingham (UK), an MA in Latin American and Spanish literature and culture from New York University, BA degrees in Hispanic studies and music from Washington College, and a graduate certificate in TESOL from the University of Maryland.

MAITE URCAREGUI (she/they) is assistant professor of English and comparative literature at San José State University. She received her PhD in English with doctoral emphases in Black studies and feminist studies from the University of California, Santa Barbara, in 2022. Her research and teaching explore Latinx and multiethnic U.S. literatures, visual cultures, and comics through feminist queer and critical race theories and histories. Her publications have been featured in *Angelaki: Journal of the Theoretical Humanities*, *International Journal of Comic Art*, *Journal of Literary & Cultural Disability Studies*, *Prose Studies*, and *Studies in Comics* as well as the edited volumes *The Routledge Companion to Gender and Sexuality in Comic Book Studies* and *Gender and the Superhero Narrative*. Her public scholarship has appeared in *Black Scholar*, *Middle Spaces*, and the Eisner Award–winning *Women Write about Comics*.

Index

Page numbers in *italic* indicate figures.